STRATEGIC ASIA 2019

STRATEGIC ASIA 2019

CHINA'S EXPANDING STRATEGIC AMBITIONS

Edited by

Ashley J. Tellis, Alison Szalwinski, and Michael Wills

With contributions from

David Brewster, Michael S. Chase, Ja Ian Chong,
Samantha Custer, Rush Doshi, Andrew S. Erickson,
François Godement, Patricia M. Kim, Ashley J. Tellis,
Michael J. Tierney, Elizabeth Wishnick, and Joel Wuthnow

 THE NATIONAL BUREAU *of* ASIAN RESEARCH
Seattle and Washington, D.C.

THE NATIONAL BUREAU *of* ASIAN RESEARCH

Published in the United States of America by
The National Bureau of Asian Research, Seattle, WA, and Washington, D.C.
www.nbr.org

ISBN (print): 978-1-939131-57-7
ISBN (electronic): 978-1-939131-58-4

Cover images

Front: Lion statue at the Forbidden City, Beijing © baona/iStock

Back (left to right): Top view aerial view of deepwater port with cargo ship and container © apiguide/Shutterstock; Chinese soldiers in change of guard marching in Tiananmen Square © ChadwickWrites/Shutterstock; Electrical engineer © xijian/iStock; Night on Beijing's central business district buildings skyline, China cityscape © ispyfriend/iStock

Design and publishing services by The National Bureau of Asian Research.

Cover design by Stefanie Choi.

Publisher's Cataloging-In-Publication Data
(Prepared by The Donohue Group, Inc.)

Names: Tellis, Ashley J., editor. | Szalwinski, Alison, editor. | Wills, Michael, 1970- editor. | Brewster, David (David Halstead), contributor. | National Bureau of Asian Research (U.S.), publisher, sponsoring body.

Title: China's expanding strategic ambitions / edited by Ashley J. Tellis, Alison Szalwinski, and Michael Wills ; with contributions from David Brewster [and 11 others].

Other Titles: Strategic Asia ; 2019.

Description: Seattle ; Washington, D.C. : The National Bureau of Asian Research, [2019] | Includes bibliographical references and index.

Identifiers: ISBN 9781939131577 (print) | ISBN 9781939131584 (electronic)

Subjects: LCSH: Strategic culture--China. | China--Strategic aspects. | China--Military policy. | China--Economic policy. | United States--Strategic aspects.

Classification: LCC JZ1734 .C45 2019 (print) | LCC JZ1734 (ebook) | DDC 327.515--dc23

Printed in the United States.

The paper used in this publication meets the minimum requirement of the American National Standard for Information Sciences—Permanence of Paper for Printed Library Materials, ANSI Z39.48-1992.

Contents

Preface

Richard J. Ellings

On one subject there is consensus in Washington across the executive and legislative branches and two major political parties. Broad engagement with China has failed to produce the political reform upon which decades of U.S. engagement policy was based. Indeed, rather than democratize, the resilient Chinese Communist Party (CCP) has tightened its authoritarian grip, turned more repressive and nationalistic, and reached abroad to extend its values and influence, even to the United States itself.[1] And China is powerful. Under CCP rule, China has amassed sufficient economic and military wherewithal to expand its territorial grip and test U.S. international leadership and elements of the post–World War II order. Politicians in Washington may quibble about this or that dimension of the challenges presented by China, how to prioritize these dimensions relative to other concerns, and therefore what U.S. policy responses are required, but they do not argue along party lines with the notion that China presents the major strategic and economic threat to the United States. In the words of Secretary of State Mike Pompeo, "Over the 5-, 10-, 25-year time horizon, just by simple demographics and wealth, as well as by the internal system in that country, China presents the greatest challenge that the United States will face in the medium to long term."[2]

Japan, India, Australia, and other neighbors of China are reaching comparable strategic conclusions. Separately and together, Japan and India

---

[1] See Larry Diamond and Orville Schell, "Chinese Influence and American Interests: Promoting Constructive Vigilance," Hoover Institution, Report, November 29, 2018; Robert Sutter, "The 115th Congress Aligns with the Trump Administration in Targeting China," Pacific Forum, PacNet, no. 62, August 30, 2018, https://www.pacforum.org/analysis/pacnet-62-115th-congress-aligns-trump-administration-targeting-china; and David Shambaugh, "The New American Bipartisan Consensus on China Policy," China-US Focus, September 21, 2018.

[2] Mike Pompeo, "Secretary of State Pompeo on the UN and Israel, Russia and the PRC," interview by Hugh Hewitt, December 10, 2018, http://www.hughhewitt.com/secretary-of-state-pompeo-on-the-u-n-and-israel-russia-and-the-prc.

have been adjusting for more than a decade to the gathering threat they perceive from China. Some of the European countries appear increasingly to be in agreement. Russia, on the other hand, has opted to bandwagon with China, greatly complicating the challenge to the democracies.[3]

The private sector is in a quandary. Many U.S., Asian, and European firms still make money in China and are deeply committed there. At the same time, they are cautious, with most having learned harsh lessons over several decades.[4] Firms have confronted a toughening business environment in China in recent years, one that continues to be managed by a powerful industrial policy driven to achieve urgent national goals. Made in China 2025 is the most notorious policy, but underlying it are extensive plans and processes likely embedded irrevocably in the party-state. Given its record of talking liberal reform and doing just the opposite, any CCP pronouncements that renounce a planning goal ought to be weighed against the evidence we have of the interests and habits of the party. The business environment continues to be fraught with intellectual property (IP) theft and pressure to transfer IP, the requirement to store and process data in China, an opaque and biased regulatory environment favoring local companies, special subsidies to advantage Chinese firms, a judicial system that is politicized and provides inadequate and uneven legal remedies, CCP structures woven into foreign company staffs, powerful and favored "national champion" Chinese companies that are frequently state-owned enterprises (SOEs) or that have cozy relationships with SOEs and CCP leaders, and so on.[5] If that were not enough, U.S. and other companies continue to find their operations outside China targeted for IP theft and other predatory practices. Moreover, international firms now find themselves with assets, suppliers, and markets caught in the crossfire resulting from China's power and ambitions, which have ignited a geopolitical struggle between the world's two superpowers. That specialists have argued over the past quarter century

---

[3] See Richard J. Ellings and Robert Sutter, eds., *Axis of Authoritarians: Implications of China-Russia Cooperation* (Seattle: National Bureau of Asian Research [NBR], 2018), especially chap. 1 and 6.

[4] Injured or destroyed U.S. companies number in the thousands. See Commission on the Theft of American Intellectual Property, *The IP Commission Report* (Seattle: NBR, 2013); Commission on the Theft of American Intellectual Property, "Update to the IP Commission Report," 2017; Brian Spegele and Kate O'Keefe, "Boeing Backs Out of Global IP Satellite Order Financed by China," *Wall Street Journal*, December 6, 2018, https://www.wsj.com/articles/boeing-backs-out-of-global-ip-satellite-project-financed-by-china-1544142484; and James T. Areddy, "American Entrepreneurs Who Flocked to China Are Heading Home, Disillusioned," *Wall Street Journal*, December 7, 2018, https://www.wsj.com/articles/american-entrepreneurs-who-flocked-to-china-are-heading-home-disillusioned-1544197068.

[5] See "How China's Economic Aggression Threatens the Technologies and Intellectual Property of the United States and the World," White House Office of Trade and Manufacturing Policy, June 2018; "2018 Special 301 Report," Office of the U.S. Trade Representative, April 2018; and Commission on the Theft of American Intellectual Property, "Update to the IP Commission Report."

that this struggle was highly probable if China continued to grow quickly and remain authoritarian is no consolation to the companies that sped down the highway to the country without constructing off-ramps.[6]

The Trump administration's strategy of using tariffs to respond to the economic dimensions of the China challenge is controversial, but there is bipartisan support for its national security and defense strategies, which prioritize China. In particular, there is bipartisan support for expanding national security powers to limit Chinese purchases of U.S. products and investment in American companies; for combatting IP theft, dumping, and other unlawful and unfair economic actions; and for increasing the defense budget to address readiness problems, the rebalance, and other issues.[7]

Still, important questions remain, and hence this volume. The questions that the American people and their elected leaders, together with their counterparts around the world, need answered are fundamental. What precisely is China aiming to accomplish internationally? What is it doing to achieve those aims? What does the country's recent record suggest about its likely future international impact, not just its intended impact? How long can the United States expect strategic competition with China? Where are the key points of conflict that derive from Chinese aims?

As leaders in Congress and the administration absorb more deeply what China means for the United States and the world, additional policy issues arise. Policies can serve one or both of two basic purposes. The first set addresses the structural contest, in this case policies that would seek to reverse the negative trend in the balance of power so that the democracies expand their power versus China and Russia. For example, is there a reduced level of U.S. economic integration with China that is optimal to reduce vulnerabilities to predatory industrial policies? How, in fact, should the United States disaggregate China's predatory policies and threats to the

---

[6] See, for example, Edward A. Olson and Richard J. Ellings, "Asia's Challenge to American Strategy," *NBR Analysis*, June 1992, 10, 12; Richard Bernstein and Ross H. Munro, *The Coming Conflict with China* (New York: Alfred A. Knopf, 1997); Aaron Friedberg, "The Struggle for Mastery in Asia," *Commentary Magazine*, November 2000; and Aaron L. Friedberg, *A Contest for Supremacy: China, America, and the Struggle for Mastery in Asia* (New York: W.W. Norton, 2011). See also Aaron Friedberg's introduction to the first volume in the *Strategic Asia* series, *Strategic Asia 2001–02: Power and Purpose*, which provides both historical analysis and a forward-looking assessment of China's development. The Strategic Asia Program was founded in 2000 and has been led over the past fifteen years by Ashley Tellis. Under his direction, the program has assiduously tracked the rise of China and the implications for both the region and the United States.

[7] See the White House, *National Security Strategy of the United States of America* (Washington, D.C., December 2017), 1–4, https://www.whitehouse.gov/wp-content/uploads/2017/12/NSS-Final-12-18-2017-0905.pdf; Mike Pence (remarks at the Hudson Institute, New York, October 4, 2018), https://www.hudson.org/events/1610-vice-president-mike-pence-s-remarks-on-the-administration-s-policy-towards-china102018; and U.S. Department of Defense, "Summary of the 2018 National Defense Strategy of the United States of America: Sharpening the American Military's Competitive Edge," January 2018, 8, https://dod.defense.gov/Portals/1/Documents/pubs/2018-National-Defense-Strategy-Summary.pdf.

U.S. defense industrial base, and what policy tools ought to be employed to defend against them? We might refer to this approach as complex disengagement in view of the current extraordinary interdependence between the two countries. Given China's race to build military power, what should defense investment priorities be, and how urgent are the development of new systems and new force deployments to defend against and defeat the best of China's systems? On the multilateral level, how should defensive economic policies such as investment, export, and supply chain controls be coordinated with overseas partners? What enhanced level of economic engagement with allies and friends would boost growth and productivity rates among them to match or beat Chinese growth? Essential to winning the contest of capabilities, how can alliances be strengthened?

The second set consists of policies that are intentionally coercive and aim to change China's behavior. Most often these policies include both structural contest and behavioral aims. For example, might tightening export and investment controls and otherwise seriously cutting off access to the U.S. market slow China's economic growth and pressure the country to reform? Could the introduction of a scoring system—FICO-like—that rated companies and entities in line with their free market and legal behavior induce international firms to choose business partners accordingly and Chinese entities and their party-state sponsors to conform better to international standards? Is a version of the Trans-Pacific Partnership valuable in part to enhance U.S. credibility among friends and allies, with membership for China reserved for when it qualifies to entice it to change? What defense investments and deployments would be most effective in enhancing deterrence against China? What is required unilaterally and with NATO to fully deter Russia in Europe for the purpose of eliminating the major strategic advantage of China's growing alignment with Russia, that of dividing U.S. forces and attention geographically?[8] Might new or enlarged alliances be useful to deter additional Chinese territorial ambitions? To bring it down to a budgetary question, how much more do the United States' allies and friends need to invest in defense to sustain stable balances of power in Asia and Europe to avoid a repeat of the first half of the twentieth century—and this time with the specter of the consequences of nuclear proliferation? Policy planners must keep in mind that a favorable balance of power provides the basis for successful diplomacy of influence.

Finally, who besides the United States is up to the task of international leadership? The struggle over power and influence requires a leader, not merely "kumbaya" among the democracies. Put directly, with what

---

[8] Richard Ellings, "The Strategic Context of China-Russia Relations," in Ellings and Sutter, *Axis of Authoritarians*, 36–37.

democratic nation, if any, will those who wish to resist China's influence join forces and commit their fate? The answer to this question, at least, is easy. As Ashley Tellis observes in his chapter, the world is again becoming bipolar in structure. Only the United States has the potential, the ingredients of leadership—the power, geopolitical position, and authority—to organize the coalition of democracies to achieve a stable balance of power, to sustain a viable and fair world economy, and to defend the values of an open and free world, including rule of law and sovereign, representative government.

China is projected to overtake the United States in total economic output between now and 2030.[9] Its industrial output already exceeds that of the United States by over 50%.[10] China's growth rates appear to continue to exceed those of the democracies, adding urgency to the challenge of its expanding strategic ambitions and to the policy issues noted above. Faith in the undeniable advantages of the democracies is no substitute for action. With this in mind, the studies in this volume make a critical contribution to the development and implementation of national and global strategies.

Acknowledgments

Ashley Tellis has been research director of the Strategic Asia Program since 2004, and his guidance has been integral to the program's intellectual growth and continuing success. Because of his leadership, the program is accumulating the authoritative record and assessments of the world's major strategic developments in the first decades of the 21st century. We are immensely grateful for his ongoing commitment. Special thanks are likewise due to co-editors Alison Szalwinski and Michael Wills for their substantial effort on this year's volume. Also deserving thanks are Roy Kamphausen and Dan Aum in NBR's Washington, D.C., office for their tireless work to coordinate and expand policy outreach activities for the Strategic Asia Program.

Last, and perhaps most importantly, all of NBR's projects are a direct result of the dedication and professionalism of the wider staff and associates who work here. Nowhere is this more clearly exemplified than in this important volume of *Strategic Asia*, the eighteenth in the annual series. The volume's success would not be possible without the joint effort of both NBR's Seattle and Washington, D.C., offices and the contributions of its entire staff. In particular, the publications team, led by Joshua Ziemkowski and assisted by Jessica Keough, Alexandria Baker, and Dylan Plung, was

---

[9] Simon Kennedy, "China Will Overtake the U.S. in Less Than 15 Years, HSBC Says," Bloomberg, September 25, 2018.

[10] World Bank, World Integrated Trade Solution database, https://wits.worldbank.org.

responsible for the technical editing, layout, and proofreading. Moreover, several exceptional members of NBR's Political and Security Affairs group—Melanie Berry, Ned Collins-Chase, Alicia Fawcett, Mary Hamilton, Hao Tian, Seo Jung Kim, Melissa Newcomb, and Brian O'Keefe—provided research and logistical support.

Of course, this acknowledgment section would be incomplete without mentioning the incredible skill and dedication of the scholars who put in the hours of research and writing to craft their chapters. We appreciate the set of challenges inherent in producing this high caliber of scholarship under such strictly enforced time limits. This year's authors, in producing nuanced assessments of China's strategic ambitions relevant to policymakers, academics, and business leaders alike, have joined the ranks of over 150 scholars who have dedicated their time and energy to making *Strategic Asia* the valuable resource that it is. I am profoundly grateful for their tremendous contributions, as well as for the expert guidance of several anonymous peer-reviewers.

Organizing and producing this work has not been a simple task. The urgent challenges that China poses—to the international economic and political order, to the United States and its allies, and to regional and global security—are broad, complex, and multifaceted. Honest and forward-looking analysis of these circumstances must likewise be broad, complex, and multifaceted in scope. Hence this volume of *Strategic Asia*.

Richard J. Ellings
President
The National Bureau of Asian Research

STRATEGIC ASIA 2019

EXECUTIVE SUMMARY

This chapter analyzes the progression of China's efforts to expand its global reach in ways that will challenge U.S. primacy.

MAIN ARGUMENT

China has undergone a dramatic transformation in recent decades. Its growing national power will enable the country to eventually challenge the unipolar status enjoyed by the U.S. since the end of the Cold War. This change has occurred over three distinct phases. The first, beginning with Deng Xiaoping's consolidation of power in 1978 and lasting until the end of the Cold War in 1991, laid the foundation for China's economic modernization. From 1991 to 2008, the country built on this progress through a series of muscular state-controlled reforms that led to its entry into the WTO. The third phase, beginning with the 2008 financial crisis and continuing to the present day, has confirmed China's drive to establish itself as a global power and become a peer of the U.S.

POLICY IMPLICATIONS

- Beijing possesses a clear vision and deliberate strategy for recovering the centrality that it once enjoyed in Asia, and these efforts have put it on track to become a peer competitor of the U.S.

- The principal task of U.S. grand strategy going forward must be to prevent China from displacing the U.S. as the primary security provider in Asia and supplanting it as the most important global power.

- A sensible U.S. strategy toward this end will emphasize penalizing China's exploitative economic practices while protecting globalization, strengthening U.S. alliances by reducing trade conflicts with allies, and sustaining military modernization to emphasize effective power projection.

Pursuing Global Reach: China's Not So Long March toward Preeminence

Ashley J. Tellis

Forty years after Deng Xiaoping launched his epochal reforms in 1978, the results are as remarkable as they are obvious: China is now the great power that Mao Zedong could only have dreamt about. Within the space of a few decades, China has transformed itself from a predominantly agricultural economy into a manufacturing powerhouse, whose southern provinces were once described by the *Economist* as "the contemporary equivalent of 19th century Manchester—a workshop of the world."[1] This success in manufacturing has been complemented by impressive achievements in agriculture: having rid itself of communal farms thanks to Deng's reforms, China today is one of the world's largest producers of cereals, meat, and vegetables, demonstrating remarkable productivity growth that has enabled it to feed 22% of the world's population with merely 7% of the arable land.[2]

China's capacity for innovation too has impressively kept pace with its other accomplishments. From starting out as a reproducer of technology developed elsewhere, China today can hold its own where developing advanced technologies indigenously is concerned: its scientific publications,

Ashley J. Tellis is the Tata Chair for Strategic Affairs and a Senior Fellow at the Carnegie Endowment for International Peace. He is also Research Director of the Strategic Asia Program at the National Bureau of Asian Research. He can be reached at <atellis@ceip.org>.

[1] "The Pearl River Delta: A New Workshop of the World," *Economist*, October 10, 2002.

[2] Colin A. Carter, "China's Agriculture: Achievements and Challenges," University of California, Giannini Foundation of Agricultural Economics, ARE Update, May/June 2011, 5–7, https://s.giannini.ucop.edu/uploads/giannini_public/42/47/42478f51-6d6a-4575-8dae-d88e2dcf174f/v14n5_2.pdf.

patenting activity, and R&D expenditures, when examined comparatively, suggest that China is well positioned to make the transition from an industrial- to a knowledge-based economy in the future.[3]

And perhaps in the most startling shift, China has now increasingly become a major global financier, especially for infrastructure. Although the country has achieved this status due to concerted state policy that exploits its national achievements of being the world's biggest saver and the repository of the largest foreign currency reserves, it is nonetheless remarkable that China today routinely exports more capital (even if mainly to overseas Chinese firms) than it imports annually. As one recent report succinctly summarized this metamorphosis, "China has become the world's largest development bank....[T]he China Development Bank and the Export-Import Bank of China now provide as much financing to developing countries as the World Bank does."[4]

These examples illustrate but do not exhaust the extent of the transformation that China has undergone in recent decades, a change that is often summarily conveyed by China's dramatic double-digit growth rates during most of the reform era. To be sure, each of the major sectors of the Chinese economy still has its weaknesses—often conspicuous—but even these shortcomings, singularly or collectively, do not undermine the fact that China's economic growth and the structural alterations that it has stimulated have been nothing short of breathtaking. These shifts have enabled China to expand its economic, political, and strategic reach in ways that were not foreseen 40 years ago.

Yet it is this very success that China, its neighbors, and the United States must now reckon with. This task is inescapable because China's economic renovation has not remained confined to the commercial dimension alone. Rather, like all great powers before it, China is utilizing the fruits of its expanding economic strength to alter the character of the global political system itself, with particular consequences for the distinctive unipolar status enjoyed by the United States since the end of the Cold War. While the possibility of systemic change is serious—and therefore must be considered carefully by Washington—it is likely that the fullest manifestations of this transformation are still many years, possibly even decades, away. The building blocks that presage such change, however, are steadily falling in place contemporaneously, sometimes being erected consciously by deliberate

---

[3] *Evolution of China's Innovation Performance, 2000–2013* (Luxemburg: European Commission, 2015), https://ec.europa.eu/research/innovation-union/pdf/evolution_of_china_innovation_performance.pdf.

[4] Kevin P. Gallagher, "Opinion: China's Role as the World's Development Bank Cannot Be Ignored," National Public Radio, October 11, 2018, https://www.npr.org/2018/10/11/646421776/opinion-chinas-role-as-the-world-s-development-bank-cannot-be-ignored.

Chinese strategy while at other times emerging inadvertently because of China's growing material capabilities.[5]

This volume in the *Strategic Asia* series, *China's Expanding Strategic Ambitions*, assesses several dimensions of Chinese activity that are contributing toward the transformation of the international system. Through a combination of regional and functional studies encompassing different aspects of Chinese interests, the book as a whole documents the current state of China's evolution as a great power. Each chapter carefully examines China's motivations as well as its activities in the area in question to provide a forward-looking assessment of how the country has begun to shape its wider environment in ways that were unimaginable even a few years ago.

When Beijing irrevocably moved away from its revolutionary past—at the 3rd Plenary Session of the 11th Central Committee of the Chinese Communist Party (CCP) in December 1978—it appeared as if the then stated ambition to "make China a modern, powerful socialist country before the end of the century"[6] was yet another vision that could have been waylaid by the vagaries of domestic and international politics, just as easily as Mao's own vision of building a revitalized Chinese state had been up to that point. But China's fortunes held robustly partly because of favorable international developments, varying U.S. preoccupations, helpful features of U.S. state-society relations, and Beijing's own deliberate behavior, all of which combined in diverse ways at different points in time to aid China's rise as a genuine great power. The process of coming to terms with this new reality has been hesitant and confused in the United States, partly because China's own strategic evolution has been gradual and sometimes difficult to discern, except in retrospect. But looking backward, there have been three distinct phases: consolidating within while seeking peace without (1978–91), accelerating global integration while preparing for new great-power threats (1991–2008), and claiming trusteeship of globalization while asserting international leadership (2008–present).

1978–91: Consolidating Within While Seeking Peace Without

The first phase, which began with Deng's consolidation of power in December 1978 and lasted until the end of the Cold War in December 1991, laid the foundation for China's resurgence as a global power. For most of this

---

[5] For a useful overview of the question of what replaces unipolarity, see Laris Gaiser and Igor Kovač, "From Bipolarity to Bipolarity: International Relations Repeating Again," *Journal of Global Policy and Governance* 1, no. 1 (2012): 49–63.

[6] Cited in Peter Nolan, *China's Rise, Russia's Fall: Politics, Economics and Planning in the Transition from Stalinism* (London: Macmillan, 1995), 162.

period, Chinese grand strategy, overseen personally by Deng, was oriented toward overcoming the cataclysms of the Maoist era in order to secure the acquisition of "comprehensive national power."[7] This effort embodied a rejection of Mao's excesses—in particular, his violent and convulsive domestic politics, his destructive collectivization of the economy, and his attempted subversion of the international order by supporting armed revolutions worldwide.

However dramatic Deng's shift away from this traditional Maoist agenda may have been, it was not intended to renounce Mao's fundamental bequests to China: the creation of a unified state from the detritus of both the Qing Dynasty and the Nationalist regime that preceded the Communist Revolution; the primacy of the CCP as the sole ruling entity in the nation; and the recovery of China's centrality to international politics by carefully exploiting the opportunities and contradictions inherent in the existing international system.[8]

In order to realize Mao's core ambitions, Deng's internal reforms traded Mao's obsession with equality to focus consciously on rebuilding Chinese power through the "four modernizations" intended to transform China's agriculture, industry, science and technology, and the military in that order.[9] The importance of concentrating on agriculture first was self-evident because it was the source of employment for the majority of the Chinese population. Mao's collectivization program had yielded a dreadful record in terms of productivity, and hence agricultural reform was critical in order to spur income growth that would spread to the larger economy. Increasing agricultural productivity was also vital to enable surplus labor to move out of subsistence farming and be eventually absorbed by the industrial sector, which was similarly slated for modernization through organizational and price reforms.

Deng's revolutionary initiatives consisted of replacing Mao's agricultural communes with household-based private production, coupled with modest reforms of state-owned industries, which were, among other things, now permitted to produce goods for private markets over and above what was owed to the state. These reforms, supplemented by the introduction of private businesses for the first time in Communist China, were indeed pathbreaking. When linked to the preliminary opening of the country to

---

[7] For an overview, see Ashley J. Tellis, "China's Grand Strategy: The Quest for Comprehensive National Power and Its Consequences," in *The Rise of China*, ed. Gary J. Schmitt (New York: Encounter Books, 2009), 25–51, 159–60.

[8] Jian Chen, *Mao's China and the Cold War* (Chapel Hill: University of North Carolina Press, 2001), 1–15.

[9] The origins and evolution of this program up to Deng Xiaoping are usefully reviewed in Lai Sing Lam, *The International Environment and China's Twin Models of Development* (Oxford: Peter Lang, 2007), 1–130.

foreign trade—primarily through the creation of special economic zones in the coastal areas—the door was opened for the industrial and technological modernization that would change the face of China's economy forever.[10]

In retrospect, these early reforms seem quaintly conservative, but against the backdrop of the Maoist inheritance, they were revolutionary. Although they mainly involved initial efforts at introducing China to the market rather than comprehensive economic liberalization—for example, land, capital, important state-owned enterprises (SOEs), and key natural resources were still controlled by the CCP—the changes proved sufficient to shift China's economic growth upward for the first time since the establishment of the People's Republic. By so doing, China began the process of lifting millions of people out of poverty and creating the foundation for further reforms.

Despite the benefits of increased growth, Deng's reforms created two unsettling outcomes. The economic dislocations caused by the shift to a partial market system created new forms of corruption and incited inflation of a kind that was unfamiliar in the previously planned economy. Among the newly wealthy in the urban areas, economic liberation also provoked aspirations for some political freedom. Managing these challenges in the face of a conservative backlash would tax Deng's political acumen, but his task was eased by the changes in the international environment that had occurred since the normalization of U.S.-China relations in 1979.

During the early phase of Deng's reforms, the Soviet Union remained the biggest national security threat. The U.S. rapprochement with China, however, which began with President Richard Nixon's historic visit to Beijing in 1972, permitted China for the first time to tacitly ally with the United States to keep its northern rival in check. During Deng's 1979 visit to the United States, a few weeks after U.S.-China relations were formally restored, the Chinese leader urged Washington to consider greater cooperation in dealing with the Soviet danger, including reducing the prohibitions that limited China's access to arms and advanced technologies from the United States.[11]

The later intensification of the Cold War with the Soviet Union, during President Ronald Reagan's term in office in the United States, aided China further: it reduced the pressure on China's landward border as U.S.-Soviet competition focused once again on Europe and increasingly the Third World; it led to modest adjustments in U.S. arms export policies that enabled China for the first time to acquire U.S. weapon systems or components; it increased the crushing burdens on the Soviet economy at exactly the time when its productive foundations were in growing disrepair; and, finally, it created a

---

[10] Jan S. Prybyla, "China's Economic Experiment: From Mao to Market," *Problems of Communism*, January 1986, 21–38.

[11] Jonathan Steele, "America Puts the Flag Out for Deng," *Guardian*, January 30, 1979.

favorable environment for Beijing because the resurgence of the United States under Reagan and the restructuring of the U.S.-Japan alliance also increased the strategic pressure on the Soviet Union along its eastern periphery.

Deng's own approach to foreign policy aided the goals of Chinese economic modernization immensely. By following a sober approach that would later be summarized as the "24-character strategy"—"Observe calmly; secure our position; cope with affairs calmly; hide our capacities and bide our time; be good at maintaining a low profile; and never claim leadership"—Deng consciously sought to create the political space that would allow China to pursue its internal economic modernization without the distraction of external entanglements, to the degree possible.[12] This did not imply China's withdrawal from the world. Far from it. China jealously guarded its prerogatives at all times and did not hesitate to use force when it was perceived to be necessary. On this score, Deng held fast to the traditional Chinese preference for using demonstrative force to protect its national interests, a policy that often took the form of a "first strike in the last resort."[13]

Thus, for example, Deng would personally oversee—early in the reform period—the punitive war with Vietnam in 1979. And again under his leadership, China came close to a border confrontation with India in 1987. But these were generally exceptions: the former was intended to punish a Soviet proxy that had grown too ambitious and threatening in Chinese eyes, whereas the latter was intended to signal China's willingness to protect its claims along a disputed border. Both episodes were important, however, because they indicated the limits of Chinese restraint, even when economic restructuring was otherwise the main priority. The war with Vietnam suggested that China would not hesitate to use preemptive force whenever necessary to punish troublesome local challengers, thereby underscoring its vision of what constitutes good hierarchical order in Asia.[14] The border crisis with India, in addition, highlighted that Beijing remained resolutely committed to completing its agenda of "national reunification" involving unsettled borders, even as it pursued the difficult tasks of restructuring the domestic economy.[15] In other words, reintegrating those territories that China viewed as lost over

---

[12] The rough translation of Deng's aphorism is taken from Bradley A. Thayer and John M. Friend, "The China Threat and What the U.S. Should Do about It," Strategy Bridge, August 1, 2017, https://thestrategybridge.org/the-bridge/2017/8/1/the-china-threat-what-the-us-should-do-about-it.

[13] For a useful discussion, see Mark Burles and Abram N. Shulsky, Patterns in China's Use of Force: Evidence from History and Doctrinal Writings (Santa Monica: RAND Corporation, 2000).

[14] For a useful overview, see King C. Chen, China's War with Vietnam, 1979: Issues, Decisions, and Implications (Stanford: Hoover Institution Press, 1987).

[15] V. Natarajan, "The Sumdorong Chu Incident," October 12, 2006, https://www.bharat-rakshak.com/ARMY/history/siachen/286-Sumdorong-Incident.html.

time, including during the "century of national humiliation," remained a political priority, although Deng's policies naturally pursued "peaceful" solutions whenever possible.[16]

While the incidents involving Vietnam and India suggest that China did not renounce the threat or the use of demonstrative force when necessary, the persistence of Beijing's justificatory locution in both cases—"to teach a lesson"—highlighted the critical assumption in Chinese geopolitics, namely, that respect for China's centrality in Asia was necessary for peace.[17] Under Deng, however, China preferred that its neighbors reach this conclusion independently without having it forced on them. Hence, the country was careful throughout this first phase of its strategic resurgence to avoid making excessively assertive international behavior the central feature of its grand strategy. Deng recognized all too clearly that although China enjoyed many of the formal prerogatives of great-power status during this time, it lacked the material capabilities that invariably distinguish true great powers from the pretenders. Rebuilding the foundations that remained weak throughout the Maoist era was thus the fundamental priority, and China needed a period of relative peace both within and outside its frontiers to achieve this aim.

Consequently, Deng was adamant that China not only must "hide" its power and "bide" its time so as not to unnerve its neighbors while building up national power, but it also must refuse to "claim leadership" in any way that would force it to make hard choices that could alienate bystanders and competitors. Instead, China was to look predominantly within, patiently building its strength until its material capabilities changed so fundamentally that a transformed international status became inevitable. Because a pacific external environment was essential for achieving this outcome, force had to be used only when necessary, and even then economically, in order to advance the fundamental aim of the authoritarian party-state: holding on to power while successfully completing China's resurgence. Consistent with this calculus, Deng did not shy away from using force against his own people at Tiananmen Square in 1989. Faced with thousands of young Chinese protesting corruption and yearning for greater political freedoms, he ordered the People's Liberation Army (PLA) to violently suppress the uprising.[18]

That this event occurred barely a decade after Deng's economic reforms had begun confirmed that he remained true to the core of the

---

[16] See the discussion in Peng Guangqian, "Deng Xiaoping's Strategic Thought," in *Chinese Views of Future Warfare*, ed. Michael Pillsbury (Honolulu: University Press of the Pacific, 2002). Consistent with this approach, China, for example, successfully pressed Portugal to return Macau in 1999.

[17] Aaron L. Friedberg, "The Sources of Chinese Conduct: Explaining Beijing's Assertiveness," *Washington Quarterly* 37, no. 4 (2015): 133–50.

[18] For details, see Timothy Brook, *Quelling the People* (Stanford: Stanford University Press, 1999).

Maoist project: China would overcome its perennial struggle against chaos only through maintaining an authoritarian hierarchical order at home.[19] While an "embedded" economic liberalization was now necessary to buttress the foundations of this hierarchy, it could never be permitted to extend into anything that implied the genuine consent of the governed—which would only be an invitation to the return of anarchy.

This vision of hierarchy as necessary for domestic peace, which incidentally is deeply rooted in a prerevolutionary Chinese political tradition, also nourished the traditional Chinese conception of what constituted good political order internationally: namely, the analogical recreation of a hierarchical system with China at the apex (or at the core).[20] This version of *Pax Sinica*, harkening back to the regional order associated with imperial China in Asia, was beyond the reach of Deng's China in the first phase of the reform period. However much Deng appeared to reject this goal by his insistence that China must "never claim leadership," events both during Deng's tenure and thereafter would confirm that such abdication was only temporary and instrumental. The demand for respect accorded to China's standing, centrality, and power by others was fundamentally nonnegotiable, and as China increased in capabilities in the decades after Deng, the notion of China as the arbiter of good order in international politics would prove hard to eradicate from its strategic consciousness.[21]

In any event, the catalyzing event at Tiananmen Square would take Chinese leaders in two different but complementary directions. On the one hand, they invested heavily in enhancing their internal security capabilities to free up the PLA from having to prosecute that role.[22] On the other hand, they reaffirmed the rejection of genuine liberalization within China in favor of promoting a new social contract whereby public acquiescence to the CCP's lock on power would derive increasingly from the dissemination

---

[19] This theme has been explored systematically in Michael Swaine and Ashley J. Tellis, *Interpreting China's Grand Strategy: Past, Present and Future* (Santa Monica: RAND Corporation, 2000), 9–20; and more recently in Sulmaan Wasif Khan, *Haunted by Chaos: China's Grand Strategy from Mao Zedong to Xi Jinping* (Cambridge: Harvard University Press, 2018).

[20] Yongjin Zhang, "System, Empire and State in Chinese International Relations," *Review of International Studies* 27, no. 5 (2001): 43–63. See also the penetrating analysis in Christopher A. Ford, *The Mind of Empire: China's History and Modern Foreign Relations* (Louisville: University Press of Kentucky, 2010).

[21] Yang Jiechi, China's then foreign minister, underscored this expectation brutally when during an angry 2010 encounter with his ASEAN counterparts in Hanoi he declared, "China is a big country and you are small countries and that is a fact"—implying that power, more than rectitude, constituted the simple measure by which right was to be judged. Tom Mitchell, "China Struggles to Win Friends over South China Sea," *Financial Times*, July 13, 2016.

[22] Murray Scot Tanner, "The Institutional Lessons of Disaster: Reorganizing the People's Armed Police after Tiananmen," in *The People's Liberation Army as Organization*, ed. James Mulvenon (Santa Monica: RAND Corporation, 2002), 587–635.

of economic prosperity and a modicum of expanded personal—but not necessarily political—freedoms.[23]

The United States was a helpful accomplice during this first phase of China's return to center stage: its active deterrence of Soviet power created the conducive regional environment that permitted Deng to focus on economic transformation rather than military modernization as a first priority. Washington watched the progress of the "four modernizations" with great interest, convinced that U.S. objectives vis-à-vis the Soviet Union would be better supported by a more capable China.[24] The continuing ambivalence about China as a Communist state, however, prevented Washington from rushing in to ambitiously arm China or even assist vigorously with Deng's economic transformation, but modest initiatives too would nevertheless have outsize effects in time. Thus, for example, the early U.S.-China scientific exchanges had a beneficial impact on Beijing's technological advancement, including arguably in its nuclear weapons program.[25] The same was true on the commercial side as American business—a prominent actor in U.S. state-society relations at this time—constantly looked for better opportunities to penetrate the Chinese market. These would appear most consequentially in the next phase of China's evolution.

The massacre at Tiananmen Square, however, complicated relations in the interim. It provoked widespread revulsion among political elites in the United States and led to the suspension of the modest military technology cooperation with China that had begun earlier in the 1980s. Although the suspension of these military sales has survived to this day, the hiatus in U.S. economic and diplomatic intercourse with China was short-lived.[26] Hence, by the time the first phase of China's strategic reorientation ended with the conclusion of the Cold War, U.S.-China relations were poised for a great leap forward, with the dramatic consequences that have now come to challenge the United States.

---

[23] Tellis, "China's Grand Strategy," 30.

[24] For a detailed overview, see *China under the Four Modernizations: Selected Papers Submitted to the Joint Economic Committee, Congress of the United States* (Washington, D.C.: U.S. Government Printing Office, 1982).

[25] For a useful overview, see Zuoyue Wang, "U.S.-China Scientific Exchange: A Case Study of State-Sponsored Scientific Internationalism during the Cold War and Beyond," *Historical Studies in the Physical and Biological Sciences* 30, no. 1 (1999): 249–77. The impact of U.S.-China technical exchanges on China's nuclear weapons program is referred to, albeit controversially, in the *U.S. National Security and Military/Commercial Concerns with the People's Republic of China* (Washington, D.C.: U.S. Government Printing Office, 1999).

[26] See Robert L. Suettinger, *Beyond Tiananmen: The Politics of U.S.-China Relations 1989–2000* (Washington, D.C.: Brookings Institution, 2003), chs. 2–4.

1991–2008: Accelerating Global Integration While Preparing for New Great-Power Threats

The end of the Cold War transformed the international environment in dramatic ways, not least of all for China. The dissolution of the Soviet Union removed China's most immediate security threat, freeing it from the ancient historical nightmare of having to protect its longest and most vulnerable northern border. The elimination of this landward peril would permit China in time to once again shift its strategic gaze toward its maritime frontiers. The disappearance of the Soviet Union should thus have been enormously reassuring for Beijing—and it was, but for three other challenges.

First, the demise of the Soviet Union—a major pole in global politics—reminded the CCP of both the brittleness of authoritarian regimes and the perils of possessing a weak economy. Both dangers applied to China in distinctive ways, and the Chinese leadership spent the first few years after 1991 thinking seriously about what must be done to avoid a similar crisis from engulfing China.[27]

Second, the debacle at Tiananmen Square reminded Chinese leaders that the problems of legitimacy had not yet been resolved in any lasting fashion. Although economic reforms had increased prosperity, the corruption, social dislocation, and personal grievances that materialized in their wake had to be addressed or else the CCP's control on power in China itself would be jeopardized. Tiananmen, in fact, was a painful reminder that the disappearance of the Soviet Union did not imply the disappearance of threats to the Chinese state, merely their mutation in form and direction.[28]

Third, and perhaps most importantly, the collapse of the Soviet Union highlighted for China that the United States had indeed survived as the triumphant victor of the Cold War. Although Washington and Beijing had nurtured a rapprochement in the decade before the Soviet meltdown, the CCP leadership was always conscious of the fragility of this entente. In Chinese eyes, the United States was always a liberal imperial power—now it was an unrestrained one.[29] It had threatened China at various points historically, most recently by penalizing it through punitive sanctions after the Tiananmen Square massacre. With the Soviet Union now out of the way, China had to prepare to face the United States largely alone.

---

[27] David Shambaugh, *China's Communist Party: Atrophy and Adaptation* (Berkeley: University of California Press, 2008).

[28] Ibid.

[29] For an insightful analysis, see David Shambaugh, *Beautiful Imperialist: China Perceives America, 1972–1990* (Princeton: Princeton University Press, 1991).

Furthermore, Washington's zeal to expand the liberal international order, which appeared triumphantly uninhibited, given the U.S. victory in the Cold War, threatened to undermine Chinese interests in multiple ways. The expansion of institutions such as NATO would amplify the United States' military reach. The promulgation of new international doctrines such as the "responsibility to protect" would threaten China by undermining the traditional notion of sovereignty. And the adoption of "peaceful evolution" as the new goal of U.S.-China relations—meaning the desire to encourage China's transformation into a fully democratic state—would dangerously undercut the CCP's ambition to hold on to power in perpetuity.[30]

All told, then, the end of the Cold War brought China vital relief from the long-standing Soviet peril. But it also promised significant new dangers to China's authoritarian regime from both within and without at a time when its economic reforms were incomplete, its material deficiencies in national power were conspicuous, and its military forces were astoundingly obsolete—a fact that was driven home for Chinese leaders by the decisive U.S. victory over Iraq in 1991.[31]

China responded to this concatenation of challenges in multiple ways that would further enhance its national power. Recognizing that domestic discontent had to be addressed resolutely for the future benefit of the CCP, Chinese leaders attempted to resolve the problems of corruption and social dislocation through a combination of party reform, more stringent state supervision over society, and most significantly, a new emphasis on resurrecting nationalism at the state, societal, and ideological levels as a means of preserving social control.[32] Nationalism, in effect, now came to supplement the older emphasis on increasing material prosperity as a device for ensuring stable and permanent CCP rule.

As a complement to nationalism, expanded economic reform received renewed attention. After Deng undertook his famous "southern tour" in 1992 (after his formal retirement), the floodgates of economic reform burst open. As Barry Naughton summarized this period, "beginning in 1993, a series of muscular reform policies were adopted that departed in virtually all aspects

---

[30] Joseph Yu-shek Cheng, "China's Foreign Policy in the Mid-1990s," Centre for Asian Pacific Studies (CAPS), CAPS Working Paper Series, no. 28, 1995, http://commons.ln.edu.hk/cgi/viewcontent.cgi?article=1077&context=capswp.

[31] David Shambaugh, *Modernizing China's Military: Progress, Problems, and Prospects* (Berkeley: University of California Press, 2002), 69–74.

[32] Suisheng Zhao, "Chinese Nationalism and Pragmatic Foreign Policy Behavior," in *Chinese Foreign Policy*, ed. Suisheng Zhao (New York: M.E. Sharpe, 2004), 66–88.

from the reform policies that characterized the 1980s."[33] These reforms, in their essence, deepened the price liberalization and privatization that had begun earlier, enabled the corporatization of the SOEs to increase market responsiveness and profitability, introduced fiscal reforms that expanded central government revenues, rationalized the banking system by creating a central bank that oversaw all activities of commercial banks, and carefully expanded the foreign trade regime to enable increased FDI in support of export-oriented activities.[34] In time, these targeted trade reforms would serve as the mechanism for the transfer of advanced technology to China, while bequeathing both to the private entities involved and to the Chinese state large foreign-exchange earnings that could be put to other economic and political uses. This broadened, but still qualified, openness to foreign trade would set China on the path to becoming, within the decade that followed, the new manufacturing hub of the global economy.

That the post-1993 reforms represented a conscious effort to exploit globalization for rebuilding Chinese power is not in doubt. What is fascinating, however, is the extent to which the CCP still retained control over the market and directed even the newly privatizing activities within China toward the goal of strengthening state control and expanding national power. China was indeed recognizing the benefits of the market within and without, but it retained a fundamental suspicion about liberal notions of economic freedom.[35] Domestically, untrammeled economic liberalization could end up threatening CCP rule by compelling the state to let go of the critical resources it controlled and by empowering citizens who might demand political rights; internationally, expansive openness to the global economy could increase China's vulnerability by exposing it to external volatility and by preventing the state from pursuing its agenda for maximizing national power. Consequently, China's turn toward the market necessarily had to be circumscribed.

To the degree that markets increased wealth without subverting state control, they were to be encouraged because of the economic and political benefits they produced simultaneously.[36] Markets stimulated sharp increases in China's growth rates, which had the effect of enlarging both personal prosperity and national wealth. Expanding personal well-being was critical to maintaining social stability and securing the support of the masses for

---

[33] Barry Naughton, "A Political Economy of China's Economic Transition," in *China's Great Economic Transformation*, ed. Loren Brandt and Thomas G. Rawski (Cambridge: Cambridge University Press, 2008), 116.

[34] Ibid., 116–19.

[35] For details, see Teresa Wright, *Accepting Authoritarianism: State-Society Relations in China's Reform Era* (Stanford: Stanford University Press, 2010).

[36] Li Xing and Timothy M. Shaw, "The Political Economy of Chinese State Capitalism," *Journal of China and International Relations* 1, no. 1 (2013): 88–113.

durable CCP rule. Controlled external integration had other benefits as well. It made China's manufacturing firms, which invariably started out as joint ventures with foreign counterparts, into export powerhouses that rapidly secured huge international market shares because of their ability to exploit China's lower-skilled labor costs while maintaining superior quality. This expansion contributed to the dramatic enlargement of China's state revenues, which in turn was used to support SOEs and their modernization. Finally, by making foreign companies important stakeholders in China's economic rise—by providing them regulated access to Chinese markets—Beijing acquired important agents of influence in major countries around the world, including and especially in the United States, where the system of government is particularly susceptible to being swayed by special interests.[37]

Prior to China's 2001 accession to the World Trade Organization (WTO), for example, when China's admission to the U.S. market was dependent on an annual waiver that granted it normal trade relations, major U.S. corporations with large interests in China were invariably the strongest advocates of such exemptions. Through such a mechanism, which permitted Chinese goods entrée into the world's largest and wealthiest market, the United States became a de facto partner in assisting China's economic ascendency. Recognizing the importance of this reality, Chinese policymakers came to rely on deeper economic integration with the United States as the means for increasing their own wealth and power, while simultaneously counting on the private benefits enjoyed by U.S. business and others in China to influence Washington in regard to actions that would advance Beijing's interests.

These efforts paid off decisively in 2000, when the United States finally granted China permanent normal trade relations (which then enabled it to join the WTO in 2001). As a result, the floodgates of U.S. investment in China were finally opened as American corporations, freed from the uncertainty associated with yearly waivers, decisively joined their European and Japanese counterparts in moving manufacturing on a large scale to China—with all the consequences for increased Chinese wealth and power that are now familiar.[38]

Significantly however, China's responses to its immediate post–Cold War challenges—domestic discontent, economic fragility, and the prospect of new great-power rivalry—were not limited to the resurrection of nationalism and the acceleration of economic reform. They also extended more portentously to military modernization. At the end of the Cold War, the PLA was a bloated and antiquated force. The availability of new wealth, the persistent desire to complete national reunification, and the fear of new

---

[37] Aaron L. Friedberg, "Globalisation and Chinese Grand Strategy," *Survival* 60, no. 1 (2018): 7–40.

[38] David H. Autor, David Dorn, and Gordon H. Hanson, "The China Shock: Learning from Labor Market Adjustment to Large Changes in Trade," *Annual Review of Economics* 8, no. 1 (2016): 205–40.

external threats—primarily the United States with its ambitious liberal imperialism—all combined to stimulate a remarkable burst of military investments since 1991, with annual growth often in double digits.[39] This shift indicated that the lower prioritization of defense under Deng's four modernizations was finally over. The rush to acquire advanced combat systems from Russia, the increased allocation to domestic defense R&D, and the beginnings of the rejuvenation of the Chinese military as a whole implied that China was preparing to cope with emerging security threats, protect the gains associated with its ascendency, and defend its historic claims all at the same time.

Even as this transformation in China's military posture was steadily occurring in the early 1990s, the country attempted to preserve a tranquil regional environment so as to sustain its economic growth without serious crises. Accordingly, it began negotiating agreements over its disputed borders and ultimately concluded them with most but not all of its rivals in Asia: the land borders with India remained unresolved, and the maritime boundaries with Japan and various Southeast Asian states remained a source of irritation.[40] Yet even as China focused on eliminating its terrestrial boundary problems—and the agreements with Russia and the Central Asian states were significant in this connection—it began to reassert expansive maritime claims, especially in the East and South China Seas. It did so partly for economic reasons and sometimes in reaction to usurpatory actions by the smaller regional states.[41] These wrangles, however, soon provoked Chinese efforts at creating new facts on the ground. The earliest manifestation of this phenomenon involved new Chinese construction on Mischief Reef in 1994–95 despite protests by the Philippines. This development occurred against the backdrop of growing fears of Chinese power throughout Asia more generally.

Beijing, recognizing the dangers inherent in the consolidation of what it dubbed the "China threat theory," attempted to pacify international concerns by "expropriating the language of the Clinton administration"[42] to describe

---

[39] Richard A. Bitzinger, "China's Double-Digit Defense Growth," *Foreign Affairs*, March 19, 2015, https://www.foreignaffairs.com/articles/china/2015-03-19/chinas-double-digit-defense-growth.

[40] For a useful overview, see Bruce A. Elleman, Stephen Kotkin, and Clive Schofield, *Beijing's Power and China's Borders: Twenty Neighbors in Asia* (Armonk: M.E. Sharpe, 2013); and Eric Hyer, *The Pragmatic Dragon: China's Grand Strategy and Boundary Settlements* (Vancouver: University of British Columbia Press, 2015).

[41] For details, see the Hearing on China's Maritime Disputes in the East and South China Seas, U.S.-China Economic and Security Review Commission, Washington, D.C., April 4, 2013, https://www.uscc.gov/sites/default/files/transcripts/USCC%20Hearing%20Transcript%20-%20April%204%202013.pdf.

[42] Susan L. Shirk, *China: Fragile Superpower* (New York: Oxford University Press, 2007), 107, cited in Yong Deng, "China: The Post-Responsible Power," *Washington Quarterly* 37, no. 4 (2015): 117–32.

itself as a "responsible power."[43] Although it did not receive much attention at the time, the invocation of "responsibility" actually confirmed the demise of the earlier "hide and bide" approach articulated by Deng. When coupled with the new emphasis on Chinese naval modernization that had become increasingly obvious by the mid-1990s—design work on China's new ships, for example, had begun in the late 1980s, as had active planning for the acquisition of an aircraft carrier—the notion of China as a "responsible great power," as even reputed American scholars began describing it, conveyed a different disposition from that associated with the "hide and bide" outlook.[44]

The 1996 Taiwan Strait crisis, during which the United States deployed two aircraft carrier strike groups to waters near Taiwan in response to China's coercive missile tests, gave China's military modernization both a clear new direction and a heightened sense of urgency. The goal henceforth would be to modernize all China's military forces—from the strategic nuclear deterrent at one end to conventional forces at the other—to successfully quell Taiwan's *de jure* independence (or any other independence movements within China) quickly, while deterring any supporting foreign intervention.[45] This objective, in turn, would require Chinese military forces capable of rapidly defeating local challengers, be they internal secessionist movements or regional neighbors, while holding at bay any extraregional power, primarily the United States, from being able to come to their rescue. This new military direction was consolidated by the time Deng's successor, Jiang Zemin, stepped down from office as general secretary of the Central Committee of the CCP in late 2002.

If the 1996 crisis provided the Chinese military with a new opportunity to demonstrate its utility in resolving pressing national security problems, the Asian financial crisis of 1997 provided China with an opportunity to exemplify the positive dimension of responsibility in protecting the regional order. By aiding its distressed neighbors at a time when the United States was conspicuously absent, China was able to convey that being a trustworthy emerging power implied "attentiveness to international responsibilities, in addition to domestic self-strengthening reforms and defense of territorial integrity."[46] The year 1997 thus turned out to be a good one for China: Beijing took another giant stride toward completing its national reunification agenda by securing the transfer of Hong Kong from British jurisdiction while winning

---

[43] For an excellent overview, see Deng, "China: The Post-Responsible Power."

[44] Joseph S. Nye, "The Case for Deep Engagement," *Foreign Affairs*, July/August 1995, 90–102, cited in Deng, "China: The Post-Responsible Power."

[45] Ashley J. Tellis, "Uphill Challenges: China's Military Modernization and Asian Security," in *Strategic Asia 2012–13: China's Military Challenge*, ed. Ashley J. Tellis and Travis Tanner (Seattle: National Bureau of Asian Research [NBR], 2012), 3–26.

[46] Deng, "China: The Post-Responsible Power," 120.

plaudits from many Southeast Asian states for its helpful role in managing the Asian financial crisis.

Unfortunately for Beijing, the goodwill it had earned during the crisis progressively dissipated as the continued growth of Chinese economic and, increasingly, military power began to be felt throughout Asia and in Washington as well. Although U.S.-China relations stabilized after the EP-3 crisis early in the George W. Bush administration, the suspicion of China as a "strategic competitor" persisted in many quarters.[47] The Chinese economy was continually expanding in size and technological capacity; both the Chinese government and Chinese private firms continued to illicitly target U.S. advanced technology; and the Chinese economy, despite several bouts of liberalization over the years, still remained highly controlled by an authoritarian state that was determined to favor its own industries at the expense of its trading partners.[48] These features only deepened the anxieties about China's economic development, which had been slowly festering because of the meltdown of U.S. manufacturing in the aftermath of the country's accession to the WTO.

The fact that China's military modernization was also accelerating—and that it was fueled by China's trade gains arising from its intercourse with the United States and the larger liberal international economic order maintained by U.S. political, economic, and military resources—should have made it doubly problematic from Washington's point of view. When it became clear that the modernization of the PLA was increasingly focused on threatening U.S. allies in Asia, regulating foreign military activities in China's exclusive economic zone in illegitimate ways, and undermining U.S. military primacy in the western Pacific more generally, the specter of the China threat should have raised an alarm and provoked responsive balancing by the United States and others.[49] This reaction should in fact have solidified after the Bush administration came into office because China, setting up for itself the goal of quickly defeating internal and local challengers as well as their foreign allies, was moving swiftly in the direction of seeking to dominate the waters adjacent to its coastline (as well as the other commons affected by this objective). These activities, in turn, ought to have deepened regional anxieties about China's

---

[47] Thomas W. Lippman, "Bush Makes Clinton's China Policy an Issue," *Washington Post*, August 20, 1999.

[48] The pervasiveness of the Chinese targeting of U.S. technology, either through direct theft or the violation of intellectual property, is discussed in detail in Commission on the Theft of American Intellectual Property, *The IP Commission Report* (Seattle: NBR, 2013), http://www.ipcommission.org/report/ip_commission_report_052213.pdf; and Commission on the Theft of American Intellectual Property, "Update to the IP Commission Report," 2017, http://ipcommission.org/report/IP_Commission_Report_Update_2017.pdf.

[49] The failure to confront China on these and other issues has been discussed in Kurt M. Campbell and Ely Ratner, "The China Reckoning: How Beijing Defied American Expectations," *Foreign Affairs*, March/April 2018, 60–70.

military modernization, which ironically was nourished by the country's ever denser economic integration with both its Asian neighbors and the West more generally.

As usual, the Asian states were waiting on Washington to take the lead in crafting a responsible strategy of balancing China, as Bush had promised during his presidential campaign. But unluckily for the United States, his administration was waylaid by the dreadful events of September 11 and the global war on terrorism that followed (including the costly and protracted wars in Afghanistan and Iraq). Although initially disconcerted by Bush's view of China as a strategic competitor—a perception that was stiffened by the EP-3 crisis and China's other disturbing behaviors—Beijing quickly and craftily offered support for the global war on terrorism, using the campaign to target its own domestic dissidents as "terrorists" while ingratiating itself with Washington as a constructive partner.[50] U.S.-China relations thereafter became more congenial, at least on the surface. As the Bush administration's growing dismay with North Korea's Kim Jong-il and Taiwan's Chen Shui-bian deepened, the importance of working with China pushed any concerted effort at balancing deep into the background.

After Hu Jintao replaced Jiang Zemin as supreme leader in 2002, Beijing could begin to breathe easier. Having settled on a dual approach of cooperating with Washington on the one hand, while "bargaining, binding and buffering" it on the other, China began to respond to the fears of its growing power with greater aplomb.[51] Without the diffidence associated with the adoption of the previous label "responsible power," China began to plainly declare around 2003 that it had "core interests" that must be respected by all outside powers.[52]

Although the specification of these interests varied depending on the interlocutor, the white paper *China's Peaceful Development* issued much later (in 2011) definitively affirmed that China's core interests include state sovereignty (implying freedom from external interference in its internal affairs), national security (implying freedom from internal and external threats), territorial integrity (implying respect for China's spatial boundaries), national reunification (implying respect for China's prerogative to integrate the territories it claims even if they are currently controlled by others), China's political system established by the constitution and overall social stability (implying respect for its authoritarian party-state and whatever means it

---

[50] Michael D. Swaine, "China: Exploiting a Strategic Opening," in *Strategic Asia 2004–05: Confronting Terrorism in the Pursuit of Power*, ed. Ashley J. Tellis and Michael Wills (Seattle: NBR, 2004).

[51] Peter Hays Gries, "China Eyes the Hegemon," *Orbis* 49, no. 3 (2005): 407.

[52] For a useful overview, see Caitlin Campbell et al., "China's 'Core Interests' and the East China Sea," U.S.-China Economic and Security Review Commission, 2013.

chooses to ensure order), and basic safeguards for ensuring sustainable economic and social development (implying respect for all Chinese behaviors intended to promote the growth of its national power).[53]

The efforts to solicit respect for these desiderata were accompanied by a concerted campaign at articulating a new theory of "peaceful rise" (later replaced by the term "peaceful development").[54] This argument contended that China's ascendency—although real and potentially capable of causing dangerous structural disequilibrium in the international system—would be entirely peaceful because China will

> transcend the traditional ways for great powers to emerge, as well as the Cold War mentality that defined international relations along ideological lines. China will not follow the path of Germany leading up to World War I or those of Germany and Japan leading up to World War II, when these countries violently plundered resources and pursued hegemony. Neither will China follow the path of the great powers vying for global domination during the Cold War. Instead, China will transcend ideological differences to strive for peace, development, and cooperation with all countries of the world.[55]

Although the notion of peaceful rise was intended to reassure the international system about China's benign intentions, it eventually failed—as might have been expected—because both neighboring countries and the United States in particular were compelled to take their bearings not from the theory but from three other palpable realities.[56] First, the Chinese economy, though growing in material terms, had failed to produce either a cosmopolitan civic culture or a democratic political system that might have mitigated the rising nationalism within China. Second, China's political leaders, though presiding over the fastest-growing trading economy in the world, did not seem to moderate their external ambitions with regard to either revanchist territorialism or the desire to recreate a hierarchical order in Asia where Chinese preferences would be accorded primary deference. Third, China's military transformation, though initially advertised as little other than the long-overdue modernization of an antiquated force, appeared to be rapidly moving toward capabilities that would allow China to dominate the entirety of its periphery, severely restrict the military freedom of action of the United States in maritime Asia, and eventually decouple the United States from its Asian allies.

---

[53] Information Office of the State Council of the People's Republic of China (PRC), *China's Peaceful Development* (Beijing, September 2011), https://www.fmprc.gov.cn/mfa_eng/topics_665678/whitepaper_665742/t856325.shtml.

[54] Ashley J. Tellis, "China's Grand Strategy—A Kinder, Gentler Turn," *Strategic Comments* 10, no. 9 (2004).

[55] Zheng Bijian, "China's 'Peaceful Rise' to Great-Power Status," *Foreign Affairs*, September/October 2005.

[56] For an extended elaboration, see Ashley J. Tellis, *Balancing without Containment* (Washington, D.C.: Carnegie Endowment for International Peace, 2014), 1–25.

If there was any doubt that the doctrine of peaceful rise would not suffice to instill confidence in China's benign intentions, Hu Jintao's 2004 speech on the "new historic missions" of the PLA clearly signaled that the country's growing contemplation of international leadership would now entail a military role that was diametrically at odds with Deng's vision of a military called "to shoulder the sacred responsibility of consolidating national defense, resisting aggression, protecting the motherland, and protecting the peaceful labor of the people and to participate in national construction."[57] Ever since the end of the Cold War, China had steadily departed from its previous policy of maintaining a healthy distance from the international system, except when required by necessity. By 2003, it had completely changed course on this issue as well—actively joining every major international organization that mattered, comprehensively expanding and deepening its engagement with these institutions, and taking an active and leading role in these bodies.[58] This shift occurred partly to deflate the "China threat theory" by demonstrating good citizenship and partly to secure the material benefits that could sustain its ascendency as a global power.

Hu's speech on the new historic missions suggested that the PLA, while "retaining the core missions of defense of the CCP and national sovereignty," would now be preparing to address "a wide range of new contingencies compelled by Beijing's increasingly global set of engagements and entanglements."[59] This tasking implied that the PLA would henceforth be employed along a wider Chinese periphery: the missions relating to Taiwan and other border contingencies would thus become part of broader requirements "ranging from defense of sea lines of communication for energy security to international peacekeeping operations."[60] The struggle to bring Taiwan back under Chinese control would still remain a critical objective, as Michael Chase's chapter in this volume emphatically underscores. This emphasis on completing national reunification, which had been part of the traditional Chinese focus on what might previously have been viewed as "homeland defense," was now integrated into the larger objective of

---

[57] Jia Yong, Cao Zhi, and Li Xuanliang, "Advancing in Big Strides from a New Historical Starting Point—Record of Events on How the Party Central Committee and the Central Military Commission Promote Scientific Development in National Defense and Army Building," Xinhua, August 7, 2007, cited in James Mulvenon, "Chairman Hu and the PLA's 'New Historic Missions,'" Hoover Institution, China Leadership Monitor, no. 27, 2.

[58] Zhihai Xie, "The Rise of China and Its Growing Role in International Organizations," ICCS Journal of Modern Chinese Studies 4, no. 1 (2011): 85–96.

[59] Mulvenon, "Chairman Hu and the PLA's 'New Historic Missions,'" 9.

[60] Ibid.

"frontier defense."[61] The "frontier" in question is no longer a limited physical perimeter but an elastic periphery shaped by expanding strategic and economic interests.[62] As such, this more capacious conception only mirrors the transformation in China's larger international engagement that had been underway since the end of the Cold War.

In many ways, this reorientation could have been defended as an anticipatory response to then deputy secretary of state Robert Zoellick's 2005 appeal that China become "a responsible stakeholder" in the international system.[63] The country's new participation in international organizations and willingness to bear some of the costs of preserving the global order through military contributions arguably could function as Beijing's effort to give something in return for the benefits it received from the extant liberal international order built by U.S. power. That was exactly how many Chinese scholars and policymakers defended their country's newest turn early in the 21st century. Many constituencies in the United States, which either were fearful of provoking fresh crises with China or viewed its evolving activism as the understandable consequence of its growing power, accepted these explanations with equanimity. The Bush administration, for its part, was too consumed by the global war on terrorism to respond effectively to these emerging expressions of Chinese power. For the most part, it concentrated on indirect approaches, such as building up the power of China's neighbors or relying on diplomacy to induce good behavior.[64]

Given China's growing power at a time when the United States was increasingly dissipating its resources in the Middle East, it was unlikely that greater economic integration and diplomacy, alone or together, would persuade China to become a responsible stakeholder in a U.S.-led global order. This entreaty itself may have been misconceived because the fundamental questions were rather different. First, would China be content to remain something other than the manager of the global system once it had fully risen and perhaps displaced the United States at the apex of the global hierarchies of power and prestige? And, second, would China then behave as a liberal hegemonic power that remained committed to certain broadly

---

[61] Strategic Research Department, *The Science of Military Strategy* (Beijing: PLA Academy of Military Science Press, 2013), 106.

[62] You Ji, "The Indian Ocean: A Grand Sino-Indian Game of 'Go,'" in *India and China at Sea: Competition for Naval Dominance in the Indian Ocean*, ed. David Brewster (New Delhi: Oxford University Press, 2018), 90–110.

[63] Robert B. Zoellick, "Whither China? From Membership to Responsibility" (remarks to the National Committee on U.S.-China Relations, New York City, September 21, 2005), https://2001-2009.state.gov/s/d/former/zoellick/rem/53682.htm.

[64] For details, see Michael J. Green, *By More Than Providence: Grand Strategy and American Power in the Asia Pacific Since 1783* (New York: Columbia University Press, 2017), 482–517.

accepted rules of conduct, or would it subsist as an authoritarian overlord that continuously demanded both obedience and obeisance to its own interests? China's neighbors in Asia seemed to have made up their minds on these issues: as Zoellick himself summarized, "many countries hope China will pursue a 'peaceful rise,' but none will bet their future on it."[65]

By the time of the global financial crisis of 2008, therefore, China had arrived as a new great power in international politics. Its economy had grown continuously since the end of the Cold War thanks to its deepened integration with the global trading system, putting the country on course to overtake Japan as the world's second-largest economy within a year.[66] Chinese military capabilities also had expanded in unrecognizable ways. China was well on the way to acquiring the ability to dominate its periphery and project power into those maritime spaces wherein it had not operated before. Andrew Erickson's chapter on China's global maritime interests and investments in the "far seas" carefully delineates the different factors that have taken Beijing along this path and offers an assessment of its consequences and limitations. That China has embarked on such a course at all obviously conveys its growing confidence: reflected in Hu Jintao's articulation of the PLA's new historic missions, these developments confirm China's desire to take on expanded responsibilities beyond the mere defense of its homeland.

The record relating to this second phase of China's strategic evolution corroborates the proposition that the United States was an active collaborator in the country's rise. In many ways, this outcome was the natural consequence of Washington's enlargement of the liberal international economic order by integrating China in 2000 and beyond. This decision intensified a global division of labor that undoubtedly created significant welfare gains for U.S. citizens, but it also ended up expanding Chinese power and steadily making the country a powerful rival to the United States.[67] The U.S. role in assisting China's assimilation into the global economy was thus critical: it was driven partly by the peculiar character of U.S. state-society relations, which permitted various societal interests to champion China's integration because of the benefits accruing to them selectively.

But this choice was ultimately made by the U.S. government on fundamentally liberal expectations: that China's deeper connectivity with U.S. and global markets would transform Chinese society toward

---

[65] Green, *By More Than Providence*, 482–517.

[66] "China Economy Shows Strong Growth in 2009," BBC, January 21, 2010, http://news.bbc.co.uk/2/hi/8471613.stm.

[67] For an extended analysis of this predicament, see Ashley J. Tellis, "Power Shift: How the West Can Adapt and Thrive in an Asian Century," German Marshall Fund of the United States, January 22, 2010, http://www.gmfus.org/publications/power-shift-how-west-can-adapt-and-thrive-asian-century.

cosmopolitanism and stimulate the evolution of its political system toward democracy as the country grew in prosperity. Although exogenous factors such as the revolutions in transportation and information and communications technology played an enabling role, Washington's confidence in its liberal presumptions was critical, and this assurance only deepened because of the U.S. victory in the Cold War. It also permitted American elites to presume that unipolarity would survive for a long time to come, implying that even the comprehensive integration of a large country such as China, which was not an ally of the United States, would arguably have no transformative impact on the global balance of power. In retrospect, all these assumptions proved to be false. As China increased in economic strength throughout the post–Cold War period, it steadily expanded its international interests, military capabilities and reach, and demands for deference—at the United States' expense.[68]

2008–Present: Claiming Trusteeship of Globalization While Asserting International Leadership

Although it is now commonplace to assert that China had jettisoned its traditional policy of keeping a "low profile" in international politics with the rise to power of Xi Jinping, the preceding discussion indicates that the "hide and bide" approach had effectively ceased to exist after the end of the Cold War. This outcome is not surprising. Once China found itself facing the United States as the victorious survivor of the preceding bipolar era, its economic, military, and geopolitical trajectory inevitably took the country in a direction where greater investments in protecting its security regionally and expanding its influence globally were inevitable. The post–Cold War period until the 2008 global financial crisis, accordingly, witnessed the steady exhibition of rising Chinese power that made Deng's hide-and-bide policy curiously anachronistic. The financial crisis, however, would transform this progressive shift into a decisive rupture.

The crisis exposed the weakness of poorly regulated market capitalism in dramatic ways. Originating in the United States, it spread to the international economy, threatening to destroy the entire financial system, weaken the U.S. dollar as a reserve currency, and plunge the global economy into a lengthy recession that could precipitate various forms of collapse in

---

[68] Ashley J. Tellis, "Protecting American Hegemony," in Ashley J. Tellis and C. Raja Mohan, *The Strategic Rationale for Deeper U.S.-Indian Economic Ties* (Washington, D.C.: Carnegie Endowment for International Peace, 2015), 12–23.

major states.[69] Because China's integration into the global economy was highly state-controlled, even after its accession to the WTO in 2001, the Chinese economy was not as exposed to the crisis as its other major partners were.[70] This constrained integration now suddenly seemed like a virtue insofar as it allowed Chinese commentators to claim that the "Washington consensus," which advocated comprehensive internal and external openness, proved hollow in contrast to the "Beijing consensus," which advocated command politics, incremental reforms, export-led growth, state capitalism, and circumscribed external openness.[71]

That state controls over the Chinese economy undoubtedly played an important role in limiting the effects of the crisis on China cannot be doubted. But triumphalist Chinese claims were nonetheless spurious because China's advantages, which consisted of limited overseas investments (in 2008), huge foreign exchange reserves, and a closed capital account, would not have existed if all other states had chosen to emulate Beijing's economic strategy. In other words, China's immunities derived from its particular kind of international integration, which its Western partners deliberately or inadvertently tolerated. The payoffs accruing to China from this strategy were admittedly great. Its huge currency reserves were employed to fund a gigantic fiscal stimulus domestically. This action permitted China to neutralize the threat of a crisis-induced recession within the country but at the price of perpetuating the investment-heavy pattern of growth that had exacerbated global distortions ever since China entered the international economy. Financing investment-led growth also took China abroad in distinctive ways. Beijing's "other official flows," which denote resources committed to funding its commercial activities abroad, mostly infrastructure development, increased sharply from 2008 onward.[72] The importance of this growing development spending abroad is scrutinized in

---

[69] For a survey of the impact of the crisis on Asia in particular, see Ashley J. Tellis, "The Global Economic Crisis and U.S. Power," in *Strategic Asia 2009–10: Economic Meltdown and Geopolitical Stability*, ed. Ashley J. Tellis, Andrew Marble, and Travis Tanner (Seattle: NBR, 2009), 3–35.

[70] Pieter Bottelier, "China and the International Financial Crisis," in Tellis et al., *Strategic Asia 2009–10*, 71–104.

[71] For an example of this view, see Wei Pan, "Western System Versus Chinese System," University of Nottingham, China Policy Institute, Briefing Series, no. 61, July 2010. The original exponent of the virtues of the China consensus was Joshua Cooper Ramo, *The Beijing Consensus* (London: Foreign Policy Center, 2004). For useful analyses that set the notion of the superiority of the Beijing Consensus in context and insightfully critique it, see Joseph Fewsmith, "Debating 'the China Model,'" Hoover Institution, China Leadership Monitor, no. 35, Summer 2011; and Shaun Breslin, "The 'China Model' and the Global Crisis: From Friedrich List to a Chinese Mode of Governance?" *International Affairs* 86, no. 6 (2011): 1323–43.

[72] See Nyshka Chandran, "5 Charts That Show How China Is Spending Billions in Foreign Aid," CNBC, October 13, 2017, https://www.cnbc.com/2017/10/13/china-development-aid-how-and-where-beijing-is-spending-its-cash.html. This report draws heavily from the published work of Samantha Custer and Michael Tierney.

depth in Samantha Custer and Michael Tierney's chapter, which highlights both the evolution of China's activities and the interaction of the economic and geostrategic variables that drive them.

When viewed in retrospect, the global financial crisis clearly was the moment when Chinese leaders, perceiving that U.S. primacy was finally ebbing, saw the opportunity to strike out and claim leadership on the global stage. It is interesting that within a year of the onset of the crisis, Hu Jintao, the president at the time, would argue at the closed-door 11th Ambassadorial Conference in Beijing that "the prospect of global multipolarization has become clearer" and that in these circumstances, China must "actively advocate multilateralism [and] promote [the] democratization of international relations."[73] Even as he ritually reiterated Deng's admonition to "not take the lead," Hu subtly shifted tack to assert that China should focus on "actively getting something accomplished."[74] The new Chinese foreign policy, consequently, was called on to manifest "four strengths." As one analyst summarized, this policy meant that "China should attain greater influence in international politics, strengthen its competitiveness in the global economy, cultivate 'more affinity in its image' and become a 'more appealing force in morality.'"[75]

Xi's ascent to leadership took this shift in more radical directions. Unlike his two predecessors, Hu and Jiang Zemin, who were both content to represent the collective rule of the Central Committee of the CCP, Xi moved rapidly to consolidate his personal power, using a fierce anticorruption campaign to eliminate a variety of political challengers at the central and provincial levels. Presaging a return to the "great leader" tradition of Mao, Xi assumed extraordinary powers, eventually successfully ending the two-term presidential limit in 2018 and thus opening the door for his continuation in office indefinitely. By all accounts, he has successfully moved away from both the old norms of collective leadership and reliance on the traditional bureaucracies in favor of new reconfigured "central leading groups" that bypass the decision-making of the traditional ministries and are often led by Xi personally.[76]

Beyond these political machinations, however, Xi is driving an even more dramatic shift in China's strategic direction, which in effect involves

---

[73] Cited in Bonnie S. Glaser and Benjamin Dooley, "China's 11th Ambassadorial Conference Signals Continuity and Change in Foreign Policy," Jamestown Foundation, China Brief, November 4, 2009.

[74] Glaser and Benjamin Dooley, "China's 11th Ambassadorial Conference."

[75] Masayuki Masuda, "Why Has Chinese Foreign Policy Become More Assertive?" East Asia Forum, February 20, 2016.

[76] For a superb overview of the Xi era, see Elizabeth C. Economy, *The Third Revolution: Xi Jinping and the New Chinese State* (New York: Oxford University Press, 2018).

preparing for the return of bipolarity and the associated global strategic competition with the United States. These intentions were presaged by Xi when he appropriated Hu's bold proposal for "a new type of great-power relationship" with the United States.[77] By vigorously advocating such a "G-2 with Chinese characteristics," Xi clearly conveyed the fundamental shift in China's evaluation of its own power relative to the United States and other countries.[78] Beijing now viewed itself as Washington's peer in a relationship that imposed, among other things, symmetrical obligations on both parties.

This perception would in time drive other, more far-reaching implications. For example, Xi's May 2014 speech in Shanghai delivered at the Conference on Interaction and Confidence Building Measures in Asia articulated a new "Asian security concept," which, taking the form of a Chinese Monroe Doctrine, called on "the people of Asia to run the affairs of Asia, solve the problems of Asia and uphold the security of Asia."[79] This address, which insinuated the idea that U.S. alliances were obsolete inheritances of the Cold War and hence ought to be replaced by greater reliance on intra-Asian cooperation, represented a reformulation of an older idea that had been frequently proffered by the Soviet Union—namely, that the creation of an Asian collective security system was the best means for ensuring security governance. As Xi framed the argument this time around, "The people of Asia have the capability and wisdom to achieve peace and stability in the region through enhanced cooperation."[80] Yet however noble these sentiments are, they cannot disguise the fact that the arrangements Xi proposed are in effect aimed at replacing the prevailing security architecture in Asia—which relies on U.S. protection at its core—with new structures that would ultimately become beholden to China as the largest and most powerful resident in the region.

Two chapters in this volume illustrate this dynamic exquisitely. Patricia Kim's examination of Northeast Asia illuminates how Beijing's desire for regional acquiescence to its great-power ambitions shapes its political strategy toward the Korean Peninsula, Japan, and the East China Sea. At the same time, Beijing's economic strategy deepens neighboring countries' dependence

---

[77] For an insightful analysis, see Michael S. Chase, "China's Search for a 'New Type of Great Power Relationship,'" Jamestown Foundation, China Brief, September 7, 2012, 12–16.

[78] Jinghan Zeng and Shaun Breslin, "China's 'New Type of Great Power Relations': A G2 with Chinese Characteristics?" *International Affairs* 92, no. 4 (2016): 773–94.

[79] Xi Jinping, "New Asian Security Concept for New Progress in Security Cooperation" (remarks at the Fourth Summit of the Conference on Interaction and Confidence Building Measures in Asia, Shanghai, May 21, 2014), https://www.fmprc.gov.cn/mfa_eng/zxxx_662805/t1159951.shtml.

[80] Ibid. Although the United States' cold response to this address has resulted in these ideas not being reiterated in Xi's subsequent speeches, the fact that they were publicly articulated in the first place reveals deeply held Chinese views about the desired future evolution of Asia.

on China even as its expanding military capabilities intimidate them in ways that reinforce its regional primacy. A similar dynamic is apparent in China's relations with the Southeast Asian states, as Ja Ian Chong's chapter confirms. The density of China's economic ties with this region, its ability to influence local leadership preferences, and its significant military superiority over the smaller resident states are all aimed at limiting the utility of the United States as an external protector, thereby magnifying China's own power. When this dynamic is considered in tandem with Michael Chase's assessment of Taiwan, the Chinese objective of deepening the insulation of the Asian rimland from the United States through multiple instruments—the heart of Xi's Asian security concept—becomes unmistakably obvious.

China's ambition to position itself as a new global pole after the financial crisis clearly represents an evolution of the trends that were underway before the economic meltdown. These trends have progressed along three separate, but complementary, pathways.

First, in the final interment of Deng's hide-and-bide strategy, Xi exudes confidence that China can at last demonstrate its capacity for global leadership without hesitation or reservation. Although this assurance is inextricably linked to his own consolidation of power in Beijing, it is also shaped by China's external environment and in particular the advent of Donald Trump's ambiguous commitment to the United States' leadership in preserving the liberal international order. Trump's "America first" doctrine has created doubts worldwide about Washington's desire to uphold the global system that the United States has assiduously built and maintained since the end of World War II. The skepticism repeatedly expressed by Trump about the value of both liberalism and internationalism have created space for Xi to position China as the gallant defender of the established order.[81]

Xi's defense, however, is both selective and incomplete. It focuses on preserving only those elements of economic integration that have aided China's rise, which (often for justifiable reasons) provoke Trump's ire. Thus, Xi continually solicits open access to U.S. and international markets without offering to rectify the prevailing structural impediments to market access in China, unless compelled to.[82] This defense of "globalization" has been complemented by a rush to fill the gap left by Trump's exit from the Trans-Pacific Partnership (TPP), including by concluding the Regional Comprehensive Economic Partnership. The latter, an initiative originally

---

[81] For a useful survey of the problems leading up and consequent to hegemonic abdication, see Peter Marcus Kristensen, "After Abdication: America Debates the Future of Global Leadership," *Chinese Political Science Review* 2, no. 4 (2017): 550–66.

[82] See the apt judgment of Scott Kennedy, "In the U.S.-China Dinner Episode, Trump Wins by a Hair," Center for Strategic and International Studies, Commentary, December 3, 2018.

proposed by the Association of Southeast Asian Nations, which China has wholeheartedly embraced, is at best a shallow competitor to the TPP, but it could end up becoming the nucleus of a Chinese-dominated trading bloc in Asia.[83]

More problematically, Xi's defense has also taken the form of creating new international institutions that are intended to substitute, supplant, or subvert U.S. economic or financial power. Rush Doshi's chapter illuminates how China's effort to prepare for hegemonic competition with the United States (and other security rivalries with its Asian competitors) has pushed it in the direction of blunting U.S. financial power, while inveigling its regional partners into an economic embrace that, whatever its immediate benefits, would ultimately bequeath China with asymmetric leverage.

All this implies that Xi's defense of the global order emphatically does not extend to defending either real liberalism, which protects natural rights in the face of coercive power, or genuine internationalism, which seeks to tame inequalities of might by creating institutions of restraint. Instead, he seems focused on defending the international order only to the degree that it advances China's further ascendency, concentrating solely on those elements that are necessary to help China eventually replace the United States at the apex of the international order.

Achieving this goal cannot be realized by external activities alone. Even as Xi has become a self-serving advocate of "globalization," he has made "striving for achievement" his catch phrase to define China's ambitions both at home and abroad.[84] Far from lying low and eschewing leadership, Xi has challenged his people to focus on national rejuvenation to realize the "China dream"—a pregnant concept that fuses the struggle for success, the recovery of past glory, and the erasure of historic humiliation in order to prepare for China's return to centrality not just in Asia but globally.[85] In his excellent treatise on Chinese grand strategy, Ye Zicheng identifies "a close connection between the rejuvenation of the Chinese nation and China's becoming a world power." He explains that "if China does not become a world power, the rejuvenation of the Chinese nation will be incomplete. Only when it becomes a world power can we say that the total rejuvenation of the Chinese nation has been achieved."[86]

---

[83] Fan He and Panpan Yang, "China's Role in Asia's Free Trade Agreements," *Asia and the Pacific Policy Studies* 2, no. 2 (2015): 416–24.

[84] For a useful analysis, see Camilla T.N. Sørensen, "The Significance of Xi Jinping's 'Chinese Dream' for Chinese Foreign Policy: From 'Tao Guang Yang Hui' to 'Fen Fa You Wei,'" *Journal of China and International Relations* 3, no. 1 (2015): 53–73.

[85] Ibid.

[86] Ye Zicheng, *Inside China's Grand Strategy: The Perspective from the People's Republic* (Lexington: University Press of Kentucky, 2010), 72.

Toward this end, Xi has mobilized an unprecedented upsurge of nationalism in China, while simultaneously presiding over a stifling increase in state control. Both of these policies are ostensibly aimed at defeating various foreign and internal threats but in actuality are also oriented toward preserving the unchallenged primacy of the CCP, not to mention Xi's own personal power.[87] Even as Xi claims to draw on indigenous traditions of politics and governance, including supposedly Confucian ideas of virtue, he has begun to implement an Orwellian system of political control centered on the notion of "social credit." Every citizen is scored based on their personal behaviors, beliefs, and activities as recorded by diverse systems of state surveillance.[88]

While the campaign for national rejuvenation in support of the China dream is undoubtedly motivated by the desire to maximize power comprehensively, Beijing has realized that the application of power is most effective when there is a modicum of acceptance and consent. This awareness, accordingly, has driven China's diplomatic engagement to the peripheries of the globe. Far beyond Asia, China now has deep involvements in Europe, Africa, Oceania, and Latin America.[89] It has begun to heavily promote an awareness of Chinese history, culture, and language through its Confucius Institutes worldwide, which are likely to number over a thousand by 2020.[90] Simply put, China is actively involved in every significant international institution today, participating in their activities to protect and expand its interests.

More interestingly, it is beginning to supplement its long-standing criticisms of Western worldviews and norms by toying with the development of alternative ideational systems. From seeking the formulation of new "Chinese theories of international relations"[91] to reconsidering how foundational ideas drawn from the Chinese past—like the notion of *Tianxia* (the imperial mandate to rule "all under heaven")—might be updated to legitimize China's quest for renewed hierarchization in the

---

[87] Robert D. Blackwill and Kurt M. Campbell, "Xi Jinping on the Global Stage," Council on Foreign Relations, Special Report, no. 74, February 2016.

[88] Paul Rowan Brian, "The Chinese Social Monitoring System and Why Americans Should Take Note," *Public Discourse*, October 10, 2018, https://www.thepublicdiscourse.com/2018/10/43905.

[89] For an excellent survey, see David Shambaugh, *China Goes Global: The Partial Power* (New York: Oxford University Press, 2013).

[90] James F. Paradise, "China and International Harmony: The Role of Confucius Institutes in Bolstering Beijing's Soft Power," *Asian Survey* 49, no. 4 (2009): 647–69.

[91] For a discussion of the possibilities, see Song Xinning, "Building International Relations Theory with Chinese Characteristics," *Journal of Contemporary China* 10, no. 26 (2001): 61–74.

new century,[92] the Chinese state is encouraging its scholars to develop alternative conceptual foundations to the current liberal international order. As François Godement's chapter on China's dalliance with values reminds us, these efforts thus far have fallen woefully short. The search for a new *Weltanschauung* often degenerates into slogans, and the medium quickly becomes the message, with China's advertised values serving as little other than a gloss masking its interests.

Second, Xi's drive to prepare China for its future role as a peer of the United States is obviously not limited to merely internal regeneration, expanded international engagement, or ideational renovation. However necessary these dimensions are for systemic leadership, China's ability to acquire and sustain its role as an emerging superpower will depend greatly on its material capabilities. That the CCP is still fundamentally a Leninist entity, which draws deeply from Mao's reinterpretation of Marx, only makes the primacy of the material even more critical. Ever since he took office as the general secretary of the CCP in 2012, Xi understood the importance of bringing to completion the economic reform efforts he had inherited. While Deng's reform centered largely on liberalization, this emphasis was always constrained by the necessity of ensuring that economic freedom did not result in nurturing political threats to the Communist regime. This calculation has limited all Chinese reform efforts since, which have taken the form of allowing enough freedom to sustain economic growth while still leaving the state with considerable control over large SOEs, land, finance, and energy (among other sectors).

Under Hu, China's economic liberalization underwent a sharp retardation as the regime began to slow down privatization, reinvest heavily in SOEs, and increase controls over lucrative sectors such as real estate. Economic growth, which derived historically from increased efficiency as well as bigger injections of labor and capital, began to slow by the time Xi took office. From the meteoric double-digit growth rates of yesteryears, China's official growth rate has now weakened to around 6% annually. The quadripartite problems of rising debt, an aging population, capital controls, and the threat of a middle-income trap now hang heavily over China. But the solutions that might have alleviated these challenges—reducing state control in favor of market pricing and liberalizing the currency market—could produce volatility that will have untoward political consequences.[93]

For a while, it seemed as if Xi would pursue such economic reforms despite their risks. At the Third Plenum of the 18th Central Committee

---

[92] An excellent critique of this notion can be found in William A. Callahan, "Chinese Visions of World Order: Post-Hegemonic or a New Hegemony?" *International Studies Review* 10, no. 4 (2008): 749–61.

[93] George Magnus, *Red Flags: Why Xi's China Is in Jeopardy* (New Haven: Yale University Press, 2018).

in November 2013, the CCP signaled a commitment to "comprehensive deepening reforms" that involved "market forces" playing a "decisive" role in allocating resources.[94] The state was supposed to have reduced its role in controlling capital allocations, shifting the emphasis away from SOEs and reforming the labor market. These hopes were short-lived. Although some modest reforms such as piecemeal changes in China's one-child policy occurred, Xi shifted course and doubled down on the statist policies that had distinguished the later years of the Hu government. The commitment to market pricing still remains in principle, but this does not involve allowing clearing prices to be set through the activities of private agents (as prices in capitalist markets ordinarily are). Rather, it involves deliberate state interventions, such as targeted controls, subsidies, or other administrative measures to produce a given desired clearing price. Over and above such manipulation, however, Xi's policies heavily emphasize increasing bureaucratic and operational efficiencies, while rebalancing decision-making among the central and local levels of government in favor of the former. The heart of his economic "reforms," accordingly, far from limiting the role of the state, is driven entirely by the objective of making the government the nodal institution for the management of the entire economy.[95]

There is no better demonstration of this reality than Xi's signature projects: the Made in China 2025 and the Belt and Road Initiative. It has long been recognized in China that the prospects for sustained export-driven growth will weaken over time as the nation's labor costs increase and new competitors in Asia wean foreign investments away from China toward other lower-cost locations. The sensible long-term solution to this challenge would consist of enabling Chinese industry to move up the value chain by investing in expanding human capital at home, developing property rights to safeguard innovation, and increasing investments that will improve productivity gains.

Instead of focusing on the institutional elements that would enable this transformation to take place in an evolutionary way, Xi has invested heavily again in the state-directed Made in China 2025.[96] This initiative is aimed at enabling China to dominate global manufacturing in high technology

---

[94] "Communiqué of the Third Plenary Session of the 18th Central Committee of the Communist Party of China," January 15, 2014, http://www.china.org.cn/china/third_plenary_session/2014-01/15/content_31203056.htm.

[95] For an excellent review of these issues, see Evan Feigenbaum, "A Chinese Puzzle: Why Economic 'Reform' in Xi's China Has More Meanings than Market Liberalization," Paulson Institute, MacroPolo, February 26, 2018, https://macropolo.org/chinese-puzzle-economic-reform-xis-china-meanings-market-liberalization.

[96] A clear overview can be found in Jost Wübbeke et al., "Made in China 2025: The Making of a High-Tech Superpower and Consequences for Industrial Countries," Mercator Institute for China Studies, MERICS Papers on China, no. 2, December 2016.

through the use of massive government subsidies, the mobilization of SOEs in designated high-leverage technology sectors, and the licit and illicit acquisition of intellectual property from the West. "Making China great again" in this way bears the quintessential Xi imprint. The initiative may or may not succeed in transforming the country's developmental trajectory, but it is likely to enable China to acquire various critical technologies that will increase both the industrial and the military threats posed to its Western partners. Because of the mechanisms employed to shift the Chinese technological frontier outward, Made in China 2025 holds the promise of further weakening the global trading system: it would position the Chinese state as a predator in what was meant to be primarily an arena for the exchange of private goods across borders. In so doing, it will strengthen the momentum toward protectionism and trade wars, while locking China into deeper conflicts with the West and particularly the United States.[97]

If Made in China 2025 represents an egregious form of exploiting globalization, the Belt and Road Initiative exemplifies a similar exercise of statism. The efforts at reforming the Chinese economy before Xi were grounded on the recognition that China's growth strategy over the decades had made its economy "unstable, unbalanced, uncoordinated, and unsustainable"—as then premier Wen Jiabao finally conceded in 2007.[98] The reform effort since the end of the Jiang Zemin era, accordingly, aspired to "rebalance" the Chinese economy away from investment into consumption. This shift was necessary to correct the decades-old governmental obsession with suppressing private consumption in order to increase investment. While this approach produced high levels of growth initially, it became unsustainable after the state-controlled financial sector maintained the momentum largely through the spread of cheap money. The huge amount of excess capacity that had built up in the Chinese economy, especially in the construction, steel, and engineering industries, had to either find new ways of being employed productively or be written off as barren assets.

Xi's statist predilections took China away from concerted rebalancing toward an expanded and renewed emphasis on investment—but in a remarkable shift of direction focused outside China rather than inside it. The Belt and Road Initiative became Xi's miraculous solution to the challenge of further reform. It allowed China to supplement consumption at home by putting its excess capacity to work on creating infrastructure abroad, which in turn was financed by its foreign exchange reserves and its new

---

[97] U.S. Chamber of Commerce, *Made in China 2025: Global Ambitions Built on Local Protections* (Washington, D.C., 2017).

[98] International Monetary Fund, "IMF Survey: China's Difficult Rebalancing Act," September 12, 2007, https://www.imf.org/en/News/Articles/2015/09/28/04/53/socar0912a.

development banks. This grandiose effort, intended to link China westward across the Eurasian landmass to Europe through multiple routes, also includes a complementary maritime component that seeks to connect China through Southeast and South Asia to East Africa, through the Suez Canal to Southern Europe, and across the Pacific Ocean to Latin America.

If successful, China will have realized multiple ambitions simultaneously through the Belt and Road Initiative. It will have secured political influence by serving as a new source of infrastructure investment around the world, while also acquiring new facilities for military operations along the way. It will have employed China's fallow assets productively to correct or stabilize falling growth levels, even though in some cases these gains have come at the cost of enervating several recipient countries and subverting their domestic politics. It will have burnished Xi's credentials as a transformative leader who set China durably on the course to becoming a superpower with global reach by the one hundredth anniversary of the founding of the People's Republic in 1949. And to the degree that the initiative comes to enshrine a new way of stimulating development around the globe, it will have legitimized China's often corrosive foreign economic activities in both practical and normative terms.[99] Joel Wuthnow's chapter on the Belt and Road Initiative highlights its protean character, demonstrating how the initiative's political, economic, and geostrategic facets end up being mutually reinforcing but with no obvious certainty as to its ultimate success.

Third, and finally, Xi's emphasis on cementing China's claims to leadership and sustaining economic growth at stable levels has been complemented by a comprehensive military modernization program befitting an emerging superpower. The initial emphasis on eliminating obsolescence and the later transition to building a capability that can defeat local adversaries while staving off foreign intervention have now given way to a full-fledged transformation directed toward acquiring the most sophisticated military forces possible, instruments that would be capable of both securing regional dominance and sustaining a presence in different forms worldwide. As a result of these ambitions, all dimensions of China's military capability—including its strategic nuclear forces, conventional warfighting elements, and space, cyber, and electronic warfare components—are being comprehensively modernized. What is even more impressive is that these improvements are not always

---

[99] As Nadège Rolland phrased it succinctly, the Belt and Road Initiative has become "the organizing foreign policy concept of the Xi Jinping era." Far from being "just a series of engineering and construction plans…to complete a fragmented Eurasian transportation system," it represents "a thoroughly considered and ambitious vision for China as the rising regional leader." See Nadège Rolland, *China's Eurasian Century? Political and Strategic Implications of the Belt and Road Initiative* (Seattle: NBR, 2017), 1, 43.

evolutionary but often incorporate dramatic technological breakthroughs that in many cases are indigenous.[100]

While the induction of advanced technology often garners conspicuous public attention, the institutional changes promulgated by Xi are particularly noteworthy because they will make a profound difference to whether the future PLA remains merely apparently powerful or actually so. Consistent with Xi's larger efforts at centralizing authority, he has restructured the Central Military Commission (CMC) to eliminate key subordinate positions so that all critical military decision-making will remain vested in himself. Eliminating the various general departments, which were the repository of significant independent power, and absorbing them into the CMC, over which Xi has absolute control, now permits him to supervise change throughout the armed forces as whole. This effort to bring the warfighting instruments of the state under tighter control of the party has resulted in an increased emphasis on political work, which seeks to ensure ideological conformity with the CCP's aims and the party's "absolute leadership" over the armed forces.[101]

These transformations at the highest levels of command have been complemented by a remarkable rationalization within the military itself. For starters, the ground forces of the PLA now have their own headquarters, thus making the army a separate service along with the navy and the air force, which have also been elevated to formal parity with the land forces. The PLA's strategic assets, previously lodged in the army's Second Artillery Corps, have been separated into a new service: the PLA Rocket Force. And all the supporting components involved in China's cyber, space, and electronic warfare operations have also been melded in a new entity, the Strategic Support Force, which is equal in stature to its four new peers.

These changes at the service-level convey a recognition that China's interests in the future cannot be satisfied by an army-dominant military. Rather, they will need other combat services as well as military operations farther from the mainland as power-projection missions come to increase in importance. The indispensability of joint operations—meaning the synergistic employment of all warfighting arms—has resulted in an even more consequential change. Under Xi, the traditional seven military regions, which were geographic areas where specific components of the army, air

---

[100] Useful overviews of China's military modernization can be found in Richard D. Fisher, *China's Military Modernization: Building for Regional and Global Reach* (Stanford: Stanford University Press, 2010); Tellis and Tanner, *Strategic Asia 2012–13*; and Larry Wortzel, *The Dragon Extends Its Reach: Chinese Military Power Goes Global* (Washington, D.C.: Potomac, 2013).

[101] This and the following four paragraphs draw greatly from the excellent survey by Joel Wuthnow and Phillip C. Saunders, *Chinese Military Reforms in the Age of Xi Jinping: Drivers, Challenges, and Implications*, China Strategic Perspectives, no. 10 (Washington, D.C.: National Defense University Press, 2017).

force, and navy were lodged and operated (sometimes cooperatively but never cohesively), have been replaced by five new theater commands, each oriented against specific regional threats. These theater commands, each led by a single military officer who controls all the service components within his area of responsibility in wartime, function as the highest joint headquarters responsible for training and the development of operational plans in peacetime as well as the command and employment of all the available service components in the event of conflict. This joint system at the theater level reports to a new joint command-and-control structure at the CMC and, once mature, will allow China to maximize its combat power by fielding joint forces capable of conducting a wide variety of military operations.

While this conscious investment in jointness represents a clear desire to field effective combat capabilities across the warfighting spectrum, the lethality of the force ultimately depends on the military technology it possesses (assuming that personnel proficiency, combat logistics, and warfighting doctrine have all enjoyed the requisite attention along the way). China has invested significant resources in fostering improvements in all these areas, but the most remarkable and eye-catching transformations have occurred in the area of new military technology introduced into the force. To enable major investments in advanced combat systems across the board, China has deliberately reduced the size of its ground forces in order to free up resources for larger equipment acquisitions. It has also impressively increased the scale of its own domestic R&D efforts, especially those focused on developing cutting-edge (including disruptive) defense technologies. Equally significant, Xi's military reforms have focused on increasing the cross-fertilization between the civilian and defense industrial bases so as to permit innovations in one domain to be absorbed rapidly by the other.

The Sino-Russian relationship has proved to be of great value where modernizing China's military inventory is concerned. As Elizabeth Wishnick's chapter on Russia and the Arctic elucidates, Russia and China share an affiliation that has proved important to China in multiple ways: providing mutual solidarity in the larger competition with the United States, serving as an important source of energy for China, and serving as a fount of sophisticated military capabilities that fill the gap when China cannot produce certain systems indigenously. This analysis confirms that Russia now plays an expansive role in China's global strategy, and the significance of this alignment for dividing and weakening U.S. capacity and attention can hardly be overstated.[102]

---

[102] For an insightful and troubling discussion of the growing cooperation between China and Russia, see Richard J. Ellings, "The Strategic Context of China-Russia Relations," *Axis of Authoritarians: Implications of China-Russia Cooperation*, ed. Richard J. Ellings and Robert Sutter (Seattle: NBR, 2018), 3–48.

Despite the problems that have bedeviled Sino-Russian military cooperation in the past, both states have found it to be in their common interest to cooperate on a wide range of issues and increasingly converge in their opposition to the United States. However transient such cooperation may ultimately turn out to be, Russia's recent defense technology transfers to China have improved Beijing's military capabilities significantly, especially in the arenas of air and naval warfare and strategic air defense.

When the technological improvements across the Chinese military services are considered systematically, the least dramatic change seems to have occurred in the ground forces. This is not surprising because China no longer faces significant terrestrial threats to its security. Thus while improvements have occurred in the Chinese army, such as the enlargement of combat aviation and electronic warfare elements in the ground units, along with significant increases in mechanization, anti-air warfare systems, and special forces capability, these shifts generally have been more evolutionary than the changes occurring in the navy and air force have been.[103]

The technological transformation in the naval and air arms has been dramatic, given the emphasis China now places on extended military reach. The navy, for example, has experienced striking improvements in surface warfare and surface-based anti-air warfare capabilities.[104] The new naval combatants are large in size, have great magazine depth, have huge weapon engagement zones, and can operate at great distances from shore for considerable periods of time. China has begun to invest in large aircraft carriers as well and is developing new advanced conventional and nuclear-powered submarines, again mainly for the surface warfare role.

The Chinese air force is slowly transitioning toward fourth-generation combat aircraft as the mainstay of its future fighter force, while developing two different kinds of fifth-generation aircraft in an effort to keep up with the United States. More significantly, China's fighter force is investing heavily in extremely long-range air-to-air missiles in order to neutralize enemy fighters at standoff ranges as well as their combat support platforms, like aerial tankers and airborne warning and control aircraft, which operate deep in the rear. Continuing a long-standing tradition, China has also extensively modernized its national air defense systems, and it has continued to upgrade and enlarge its bomber force for long-range standoff attacks as well as its inventory of

---

[103] Ian E. Rinehart, "The Chinese Military: Overview and Issues for Congress," Congressional Research Service, CRS Report for Congress, R44196, March 24, 2016.

[104] A comprehensive summary of China's naval modernization can be found in Office of Naval Intelligence, *The PLA Navy: New Capabilities and Missions for the 21st Century* (Washington, D.C., 2015), https://fas.org/nuke/guide/china/plan-2015.pdf; and Ronald O'Rourke, "China Naval Modernization: Implications for U.S. Navy Capabilities—Background and Issues for Congress," Congressional Research Service, CRS Report for Congress, RL33153, August 1, 2018.

combat support aircraft such as reconnaissance, electronic warfare, and airborne early-warning and command-and-control platforms.[105]

It is impossible to do justice to the technological improvements occurring in the PLA Navy and Air Force in the space of a few paragraphs, except to emphasize that, as a result of the investments over the last two decades, these services—despite many extant weaknesses—are on the way to becoming highly formidable adversaries, even when compared with the sophisticated military capabilities of the United States. The PLA Navy today is already larger than its U.S. counterpart, and the PLA Air Force is steadily evolving toward a force strength where its late-generation combatants will one day match the U.S. Air Force in numbers. When the resourcefulness exhibited by the development and integration of disruptive Chinese technologies—such as anti-ship ballistic missiles, air-launched ballistic missiles, myriad counterspace weapons, and the highly accurate conventional ballistic and cruise missile inventory—are accounted for (along with the concepts of operation developed for their employment), there is little doubt that China is becoming a military peer of the United States, even exceeding the technological threats posed by Russia along many dimensions.[106]

The steady distention of China's operational reach is significant as well. For the longest time, the navy and air force rarely operated beyond the "first island chain" that encloses the seaward approaches to the Chinese mainland. Today, both the sea and air services have breached this eidetic barrier.[107] The navy can be found routinely operating as far west as the Indian Ocean, preparing and training for the day when it is likely to conduct missions directed at protecting its sea lines of communication west of the Strait of Malacca.[108] David Brewster's chapter on China's future as an Indian Ocean power documents the intersecting economic, political, and strategic interests that have propelled China to cast its gaze toward the Indian Ocean. This effort involves significant investments along the ocean's littorals as well as the deployment of naval contingents in its waters. For the moment, the latter activities are focused mostly on constabulary duties, noncombatant protection, operational familiarization, and training for long-distance open-ocean operations, but these missions will evolve further as China's

---

[105] For details, see China Aerospace Studies Institute, *PLA Aerospace Power: A Primer on Trends in China's Military Air, Space, and Missile Forces* (Montgomery: China Aerospace Studies Institute, 2017).

[106] Wortzel, *The Dragon Extends Its Reach*; and Fisher, *China's Military Modernization*.

[107] Mark R. Cozad and Nathan Beauchamp-Mustafaga, *People's Liberation Army Air Force Operations over Water* (Santa Monica: RAND Corporation, 2017).

[108] Jérôme Henry, *China's Military Deployments in the Gulf of Aden: Anti-Piracy and Beyond*, Asie.Visions, no. 89 (Paris: Institut français des relations internationales, 2016).

expeditionary capabilities increase and as it acquires more local support facilities around the Indian Ocean basin over time.

Athwart the coastline of China, its naval contingents now routinely operate east of Taiwan, often conducting patrols around Japan and in the Philippine Sea.[109] China's naval doctrine demands enduring sea control in the Yellow, East China, and South China Seas, and, toward that end, China is preparing to undertake intense sea-denial operations beyond the first island chain. Its strategic investments in the South China Sea—which involve the militarization of several reefs that have been reclaimed since late 2014—and its efforts to construct strategic installations in the small islands in Oceania are aimed at preventing the United States from enjoying the traditional military freedom of action it took for granted in these areas. If these dangers intensify, the threat to the U.S. Navy's ability to surge military power from outside the theater toward the Asian rimland will only be exacerbated.

The PLA Air Force, for its part, now aims to secure air superiority over the same areas where China seeks sea control and in support of this objective plans and trains for long-range strike missions as far away as Guam.[110] China's formidable shore-based missile forces can already enforce costly forms of sea denial about one thousand miles from its shoreline.[111] While China's capacity to easily project power will diminish beyond that circumference—a point carefully elaborated by Andrew Erickson's chapter—the fact that it can hold at risk the major-power centers (and military assets) in Japan, South Korea, Taiwan, and important parts of Southeast Asia enables China to exercise regional dominance of the kind that was beyond its reach even as recently as two decades ago. When China's cyber and space warfare capabilities are considered in addition, its military horizon extends to the farthest peripheries of the globe.

China's growing military influence does not derive merely from the enlargement of its coercive reach. Its impressive expansion of military diplomacy is just as telling. In 2017 alone, the Chinese military appears to have conducted 52 exercises with its foreign counterparts, with 78% of these exercises being held outside China. Among the PLA services, the navy engages in the most foreign exercises, with the army following. The spatial distribution of these activities is equally impressive. The navy and army have participated in exercises in East and Southeast Asia, the Indian Ocean (to include the

---

[109] David Lague, "Special Report: China's Navy Breaks Out to the High Seas," Reuters, November 26, 2013.

[110] Derek Grossman et al., *China's Long-Range Bomber Flights: Drivers and Implications* (Santa Monica: RAND Corporation, 2018).

[111] Stephen Biddle and Ivan Oelrich, "Future Warfare in the Western Pacific: Chinese Antiaccess/Area Denial, U.S. AirSea Battle, and Command of the Commons in East Asia," *International Security* 41, no. 1 (2016): 7–48.

Persian Gulf and the Red Sea), Africa, the Mediterranean, the Baltic Sea, and the northern Atlantic Ocean.[112] Even the Arctic has become an important recent priority for Beijing. Although China is not a littoral state as Russia is in the Arctic, Wishnick's analysis elaborates how China has claimed "near Arctic" status to defend its economic interests—the ability to use a shortened sea route to Europe—and advance its role as a global rule-maker—which, she succinctly notes, "is important for its great-power aspirations." This last consideration is fecund: it is already shaping the evolving patterns of PLA operations in ways suggesting that China will be able to maintain some sort of a global military presence by mid-century. China has already embarked on the acquisition of maritime facilities in the Persian Gulf, South Asia, and the Mediterranean Sea; it is exploring additional acquisitions to support a naval presence along the East and West African coasts and in time will acquire the capability to maintain a naval presence in the Western Hemisphere on a more or less permanent basis.[113]

On balance, the evidence suggests that China is well on its way to becoming a functional peer competitor of the United States along multiple political, economic, and strategic dimensions. These increases in capability, which have often come at the United States' expense, are the fruits of several decades of economic growth and derive greatly from Washington's many decisions over the years to support China's integration into the liberal international economic order. To be sure, China's growing strengths are still marked by several conspicuous shortcomings, and it is possible that its evolution toward superpower status could yet be arrested by some unanticipated developments either within or outside China. If such unpredictable contingencies are left aside for the moment, however, China will on current trends steadily evolve into a genuine rival of the United States over time. Admittedly, it will still be a precocious competitor: for example, as China's GDP continues to grow and perhaps even exceeds that of the United States, its per capita income will still lag considerably behind. But China will possess economic strength in sheer mass and, compared with all other countries in the international system, will enjoy comprehensive power most closely approximating that of the United States. Under Xi, China certainly is pursuing such parity, and if its aspirations are realized—as appears likely

---

[112] Open Source Enterprise, "People's Liberation Army Exercises with Foreign Armed Forces in 2017," CHW2018042312082076, April 24, 2018.

[113] Ashley J. Tellis, "Protecting American Primacy in the Indo-Pacific," testimony before the U.S. Senate Armed Services Committee, Washington, D.C., April 25, 2017.

today—the international system will progressively shift from its current unipolarity toward a new bipolarity.[114]

By the time Barack Obama took office as president in 2009—at about the same time that China was exhibiting new inclinations toward global leadership—the broader trend about China's ascendency was beginning to register in the United States. Unfortunately, the pressures of the global financial crisis combined with the realities of globalization to produce a fatalism in U.S. strategic thinking about how to cope with China's rise. The liberal inheritance of the United States only muddled Washington's response further, with Obama declaring on several occasions that "we welcome China's rise. We just want to make sure that that rise is done—that that rise occurs in a way that reinforces international norms and international rules and enhances security and peace, as opposed to it being a source of conflict either in the region or around the world."[115]

To guard against failure on this count, however, Obama responded concurrently by attempting a "rebalance" to Asia.[116] Although intended as a wide-ranging shift in attention and resources from the Middle East to the eastern Asian rimland, this initiative found its greatest traction only in the diplomatic (and to a lesser degree in the military) arena. U.S. engagement with East, Southeast, and South Asia deepened; U.S. military resources began to shift gradually toward Asia; and the Department of Defense embarked on a "third offset" program that focused on overcoming the recent Chinese military advantages that threatened to blunt U.S. power projection.

While this response was worthwhile and long overdue—it had the merit of consciously recognizing China's rise as a strategic competitor, even if it failed to admit so publicly—the larger question of how to deal with a China that was still exploiting globalization to mount economic and security threats to U.S. interests writ large was unresolved. Many in the United States believed that this problem was essentially insoluble and that the evolution of the international system would ensure that this conundrum persisted enduringly: if the international trading order were constricted to limit China's growth (assuming that such a policy could be successfully engineered to begin with), American welfare would be reduced significantly. Therefore, if the United States' prosperity was to be protected, China's superior growth

---

[114] Yan Xuetong, "Why a Bipolar World Is More Likely than a Unipolar or Multipolar One," *New Perspectives Quarterly* 32, no. 3 (2015): 52–56.

[115] "The President's News Conference with President Hu Jintao of China, January 19, 2011," in Barack Obama, *Public Papers of the Presidents of the United States*, 2011, Book 1 (Washington, D.C.: U.S. Government Printing Office, 2014), 36.

[116] Mark E. Manyin et al., "Pivot to the Pacific? The Obama Administration's 'Rebalancing' toward Asia," Congressional Research Service, CRS Report for Congress, R42448, March 28, 2012.

would have to be tolerated, despite the disadvantages it engendered for U.S. power. This dilemma brooked no easy solutions.

The election of Donald Trump, however, reflected the deep American disenchantment with this predicament, and his first two years in office have witnessed deliberate U.S. efforts to deal with this fundamental problem. Through a series of official documents, the administration began by clearly declaring that the era of great-power competition had indeed returned and that China, along with Russia, was in fact a strategic competitor of the United States.[117] After decades of obfuscations, such clarity is refreshing.

The Trump administration has followed up on this assessment by increasing the U.S. defense budget in order to revitalize the military after two decades of overstretch. The president's larger economic policies, however, will most likely not allow this initial spurt to be sustained. Furthermore, Trump's diplomatic engagement in Asia has been messy. He signed off on a bold Indo-Pacific strategy that aims to buttress the economic, political, and strategic dimensions of the U.S. presence in the wider Asian rimland, but this initiative risks being undermined by his affection for Xi, his rhetoric questioning the benefits of key U.S. alliances in Asia, and the trade frictions between the United States and its Asian allies. Even his most resolute action to date—confronting China's four-decade old exploitation of the liberal international economic order—may prove to be inadequate. Trump has concentrated his attention on correcting the U.S. trade deficit with China. However worthwhile that objective may be, it would be unfortunate if this fixation on trade balances came at the expense of rectifying deeper structural problems: the continuing impediments to U.S. (and international) business in China, China's coercive transfer of technology, its theft of intellectual property, its open-ended support to its SOEs in the global trading system, and its pernicious entrenched system of state capitalism.

Unless these problems are rectified, the threats posed to U.S. power and prosperity by China's participation in the global economy will persist. At this point, it is not clear whether the Trump administration has either a coherent or a comprehensive solution for addressing these perils. Beijing, in contrast, seems to have both a clear vision and a deliberate strategy for recovering the greatness and the centrality that it once enjoyed in Asian, if not global, politics. This does not imply that China has operated in accordance with some sort of a "master plan" for expanding its power in the post–Cold War era. But its efforts, both deliberate and opportunistic, have clearly been shaped by the overarching aim of achieving, in Xi's phraseology, "the great rejuvenation

---

[117] See, for example, White House, *National Security Strategy of the United States of America* (Washington, D.C., December 2017), 25f.; and U.S. Department of Defense, "Summary of the 2018 National Defense Strategy of the United States of America," 2018, 1f.

of the Chinese nation."[118] Thus far at least Beijing appears to be on track to achieving some meaningful facsimile of this ambitious undertaking.

Conclusion: The Need for a Sensible U.S. Strategy

China's startling successes over the past four decades have undoubtedly been due to its progressive integration into the liberal international order built and sustained by U.S. power since 1945. The United States aided China's rise by supporting the country's entry into, and participation within, this system even when it was abundantly clear that China was receiving asymmetric benefits from its involvement. To be sure, the United States had integrated the war-torn economies of Germany and Japan into the international order on comparable terms in an earlier generation, but those countries, which grew into democratic allies, did not allocate the superior gains from assimilation toward the production of military instruments intended to threaten the United States. China is fundamentally different on both counts: it is neither a democratic regime nor a U.S. ally. In fact, China is very much a competitor that seeks to eventually displace the United States as the principal security provider in Asia, while supplanting it globally as the most important power in the international system.[119]

These strategic ambitions represent a fundamental threat to American primacy, and, hence, countering them must be the principal task of U.S. grand strategy going forward. For at least two decades, U.S. policymakers had hoped that rising Chinese power could be tamed by even deeper integration into the liberal international order. The evidence thus far suggests that these expectations have not been realized, and for understandable reasons: why would an increasingly powerful China seek to subordinate its own interests to, as Henry Kissinger once succinctly put it, the demands of "membership in an international system designed in its absence on the basis of programs it did not participate in developing"?[120]

With Trump's election as president, the American polity has indicated—on a rare bipartisan basis—that the United States should not acquiesce to China's continued unfair enjoyment of higher relative gains from trade as it has done in the past. Rather, new policies that level the playing field should be pursued so that any benefits accruing to China

---

[118] Charlie Campbell, "Xi Jinping's Party Congress Speech Leaves No Doubts Over His Leadership Role," *Time*, October 18, 2017, http://time.com/4986999/xi-jinping-china-19th-congress-ccp.

[119] Tellis, "Power Shift"; and Robert D. Blackwill and Ashley J. Tellis, *Revising U.S. Grand Strategy Toward China* (New York: Council on Foreign Relations, 2015), https://www.cfr.org/report/revising-us-grand-strategy-toward-china.

[120] Henry A. Kissinger, "Avoiding a U.S.-China Cold War," *Washington Post*, January 14, 2011.

from its participation in the international economy arise solely from its comparative advantages instead of the structural impediments it has assiduously maintained.

Attacking these problems requires a scalpel, not a hammer. The solutions pursued must focus on China's exploitation of the current trading order and not degenerate into an assault on globalization writ large or even trade with China more narrowly, given that both have produced undeniable increases in U.S. welfare that should not be sacrificed. Attacking the economic threats to U.S. power and prosperity must, therefore, be first grounded on the recognition that there is a distinction between China and all other trade partners of the United States. The problems posed by China are different, both in scale and in quality, and, hence, merit focused remedies rather than a generalized war against trade itself or against all U.S. trading partners indiscriminately. Any effort to constrict globalization on ideological or nationalist grounds will damage the United States in both economic and strategic terms. There is no assurance that Washington, for all its power, will be able to either roll back international economic integration entirely or prevent other states from arriving at mutually convenient trading agreements that exclude the United States. Both outcomes would subvert the long-term viability of American primacy and should, therefore, be avoided.[121]

The optimal strategy for the United States in the economic realm, accordingly, consists of a combination of the following elements: a singular emphasis on pressing China to correct its structural impediments to trade (rather than just its trade deficits) by holding at risk if necessary its access to the U.S. and other markets; a greater forbearance with allied partners on bilateral trade disagreements in order to recruit their cooperation in defeating the bigger problem posed by China's trade violations; an accelerated effort to bind U.S. friends (within the Western Hemisphere, in Europe, and in Asia) through high-quality preferential trading agreements that bestow higher gains from trade to all participants, thereby enabling the United States and its partners to better cope with China as an economic and political competitor; and, finally, to seriously begin the tasks of economic reform at home without which all efforts at improving the trading system outside would fall short. The core objective of such a strategy consists of permitting the United States to gain the maximum possible benefits from globalization for itself and its friends, while simultaneously curtailing the asymmetric gains that China has enjoyed thus far because of Washington's

---

[121] For an extended elaboration of this argument, see Tellis, *Balancing Without Containment*.

resignation or inattention.[122] The Trump administration's efforts hitherto seem to be going in a different direction.

An economic strategy of the kind outlined above cannot succeed without the full support of U.S. allies and partners. To the degree that such a reformed approach aims at benefiting from international trade while limiting its abuse by China, the geopolitical dimension becomes a vital complement. The heart of the geopolitical component consists of deepening the solidarity between the United States and its allies with respect to taking on the challenges posed by China. Whether the threats are Beijing's quest for new technological standards that will disadvantage the United States and its partners, or China's efforts to promote ideational alternatives on issues ranging from development assistance to the freedom of the seas, or China's activities aimed at procuring controlled technologies from the developed world, Washington's ability to counter them will hinge greatly on the extent of cooperation between the United States and its friends and allies because globalization today limits the success of any unilateral U.S. action.[123]

Any policy that devalues U.S. alliances and partnerships by treating friends as akin to adversaries is deeply counterproductive for the larger goal of balancing against China's rise. There is no doubt that the United States should be challenging its partners to strengthen the alliance system in every way possible—including by enlarging their contributions where appropriate—but continuous criticism of the distribution of mutual gains hardly conduces toward the common purpose that will be required to checkmate Chinese (and Russian) ambitions. Even in the Indo-Pacific theater, for example, European support for the United States will be valuable for the defense of the traditional Western position on the freedom of the commons (not to mention for combined freedom of navigation operations), and Japanese, Australian, South Korean, and even Indian and Taiwanese contributions will make a huge difference to the ultimate success of the administration's strategy. A sensible prioritization is therefore essential: because the real challenge posed by China to the United States overwhelms all the other disagreements that Washington may have with its friends and bystanders, treating the latter with greater regard and sensitivity is vital for the success of Trump's campaign vis-à-vis Beijing.

Finally, the president needs to pay consistent attention to addressing the problems of military modernization. After close to two decades of major overseas operations, the burdens of recapitalizing the U.S. armed

---

[122] See the discussion in Ashley J. Tellis, "The Geopolitics of the TTIP and the TPP," in *Power Shifts and New Blocs in the Global Trading System*, ed. Sanjaya Baru and Suvi Dogra, Adelphi Papers, no. 450 (Abingdon: Routledge, 2015), 93–119.

[123] Aaron L. Friedberg, "Competing with China," *Survival* 60, no. 3 (2018): 7–64.

forces are huge. While the United States was expending itself in peripheral wars in Afghanistan and Iraq, China made great strides in building the capabilities necessary to limit U.S. power from being able to operate freely along the Asian rimland. After an initial and long overdue spike in the U.S. defense budget in his first year in office, Trump appears to view future budget growth as unnecessary. This turnabout now puts at risk his administration's otherwise sensible plans for a 355-ship navy and an expanded bomber force.

There is much that remains to be done with respect to strengthening U.S. military power in order to protect American primacy. The debates about how to restructure U.S. power projection for enhanced effectiveness in the face of China's investments in anti-access and area-denial, the budgetary priority that should be afforded to expeditionary warfare capabilities over land forces, and the importance of sustaining investments in high-leverage conventional forces in the face of the extremely expensive modernization of the nuclear triad have not been resolved. If these issues are not settled in ways that preserve U.S. military hegemony, Washington's ability to meet threats at some distance from the homeland and protect the global system that disproportionately advantages the United States will be at significant risk—and the dangers emerging from China to U.S. primacy will become even greater.

To its credit, the Trump administration has taken on the cause of balancing China's rise in order to protect U.S. national interests. The means that it has employed for this purpose, however, are not assured of success. This could be doubly tragic. If current efforts fail to correct the basic flaws that have enabled China's ascendency, they could reinforce the belief that China's rise is inevitable and thereby undermine any meaningful initiatives by a future administration to limit Chinese power. If that outcome were to eventually obtain, China's not so long march toward global preeminence would finally produce the bipolarity that U.S. grand strategy should be seeking to avert.

EXECUTIVE SUMMARY

This chapter examines the contributions of both Russia and the Arctic to China's quest for great-power status and highlights the constraints that China faces in its interactions with each.

MAIN ARGUMENT

The Sino-Russian partnership and China's growing role in Arctic affairs attest to the country's aspirations as a rule-maker. A comparison of its objectives with regard to Russia and the Arctic shows that China faces different challenges as an insider in its partnership with Russia and as an outsider in its Arctic activities. With Russia, China must accept some constraints (e.g., in Central Asia and the Arctic) and agree to disagree with some Russian policies (e.g., on Ukraine) in exchange for Russian diplomatic support and military cooperation. In the Arctic, China fears being left out of the evolving governance structures and seeks to position itself through diplomacy and investments to take advantage of future opportunities afforded by climate change and its observer status in the Arctic Council.

POLICY IMPLICATIONS

- Greater U.S. support for its own alliances as well as for democratic principles and institutions will be important in counteracting Sino-Russian efforts to erode their functioning.

- Russia's ability to pursue a more diversified Asia policy will constrain China's ambitions in the region.

- China's Arctic ambitions reflect its great-power and maritime-power aspirations. The U.S. should work to involve China in Arctic governance along with other observer states, while remaining mindful of Chinese efforts to increase its economic leverage in the region.

- The U.S. needs to play a more active role in Arctic affairs to better support its interests by funding scientific research, modernizing its icebreaker fleet, cooperating on the environment, and ratifying the United Nations Convention on the Law of the Sea.

Russia and the Arctic in China's Quest for Great-Power Status

Elizabeth Wishnick

Despite Russia's economic difficulties and diminished status relative to the Soviet era, the Sino-Russian partnership has played an important role in the rise of the People's Republic of China (PRC) as a great power. This has been most obvious in terms of military cooperation, where Russia was one of only a few countries willing and able to sell China the weapons systems it wanted in the aftermath of post-Tiananmen sanctions. Although China has increasingly sought to produce its own weapons since the mid-2000s, it continues to buy some Russian-made systems, which could have a considerable impact on Asian regional security. Moreover, Sino-Russian naval exercises have enabled China to show its flag more widely as it seeks to expand its maritime power well beyond its own shores.

In terms of energy, neighboring Russia has been a logical supplier of the oil and gas that China increasingly needs to power its growing economy. Although agreements for oil and gas pipelines took a long time to negotiate, Russia is now China's top oil supplier, providing about 15% of its oil in 2018.[1] After sanctions were imposed on Russia in 2014, China succeeded in investing in key upstream energy projects in the country, such as the Yamal liquefied natural gas (LNG) plant. Energy cooperation with Russia supports many key Chinese goals—reducing the risk of chokepoints in the Malacca Strait and the

Elizabeth Wishnick is a Professor of Political Science and Law at Montclair State University. She can be reached at <wishnicke@montclair.edu>.

[1] Daniel Workman, "Top 15 Crude Oil Suppliers to China," World's Top Exports, April 1, 2018, http://www.worldstopexports.com/top-15-crude-oil-suppliers-to-china.

Suez Canal, encouraging long-sought cooperation between northeast China and the Russian Far East, and highlighting China's role in the development of Arctic resources.

While China is geographically an outsider in the Arctic, it claims to be a "near-Arctic" state on the basis of its physical presence, achieved through investments, research stations, and diplomacy in the region. Russia both facilitates and restrains China's role, which is important for its great-power aspirations. Indeed, the Arctic is the only region in the world where China is an outsider, and Chinese leaders fear missing out on the bounty to be developed as the polar ice melts. Yet the Arctic is important for China not only economically, due to the promise of reduced shipping times to Europe and plentiful resources, but also politically. As the Arctic ice recedes, China wants to be a participant in the governance process that will decide how to manage the region's resources and waterways. Participation in the Arctic also requires improving China's naval and shipping capabilities to accommodate Arctic routes and projects. In addition, China's Arctic diplomacy supports its approach to Europe more broadly, where the country seeks out opportunities to engage, divide, and expand its presence. Nonetheless, in the short term, China faces many constraints in the region.

This chapter examines the contributions of both Russia and the Arctic to China's quest for great-power status and highlights the constraints that China faces in its interactions with each. In the first section on China's ambitions vis-à-vis Russia, key areas of cooperation (specifically defense and energy) are examined. This section also discusses the ties between northeast China and the Russian Far East, especially within the context of the Belt and Road Initiative (BRI), and Russian support for China's global and regional positions. While Russia provides considerable support for China's great-power aspirations, the Sino-Russian partnership also constrains China in other respects, especially in terms of its Arctic ambitions. The second main section focuses on these great-power ambitions in the Arctic, including China's efforts to establish a physical presence in the region and relations with Arctic states. The chapter concludes with a discussion of the policy consequences for the Arctic region and the United States of China's ambitions in both the Sino-Russian partnership and the Arctic.

China's Ambitions and Russia

The Sino-Russian partnership is neither an alliance nor a marriage of convenience. The focus on asymmetries and differences on some issues obscures China's interests, which are long-term and reflect the perception that the Sino-Russian partnership can help China deal with certain key threats. Indeed, this partnership has supported China's global, regional, and domestic ambitions by improving its energy security, enhancing its military capabilities, contributing to the development of its northern border provinces, and providing support on important foreign policy issues. Nonetheless, this partnership constrains Chinese ambitions in other respects—by requiring the country to be more circumspect in Central Asia and the Arctic and tolerate Russian arms sales to China's rivals in Asia. Chinese investments in Russia also have been limited by Russian caution and the imperfect business climate, especially in the eastern region of the country, where Chinese officials had high hopes for cooperation.

Enhancing Military Capabilities

Creating a strong military is a key component of Xi Jinping's "China dream." At the 19th Party Congress in November 2017, Xi declared that China's military modernization would be nearly complete in 2035 and that the PRC would have a world-class military by 2050.[2] This involves developing capabilities that allow the People's Liberation Army (PLA) to project power beyond China's borders and coastlines as well as to challenge U.S. technological superiority.[3]

Since the 1990s, security cooperation with Russia has been an important factor in China's military modernization. Unable to purchase Western military technology after the 1989 Tiananmen Square massacre, China turned to Russia to satisfy most of its military needs, spending an average of $1 billion annually in the 1990s and more than $2 billion per year in the early 2000s.[4] This was a mutually beneficial arrangement that extended a lifeline to Russia's ailing defense industries and provided China with a source of relatively affordable military technology to improve its forces.[5] Within a few years, Chinese arms purchases had declined and were limited to component parts. Indigenous industries proved capable of producing major systems, though these were largely based on older designs from Russia and other countries. At the same time, as a result of concerns over reverse engineering

---

[2] "Full Text of Xi Jinping's Report at 19th CPC National Congress," Xinhua, November 3, 2017, http://www.xinhuanet.com/english/special/2017-11/03/c_136725942.htm.

[3] U.S. Department of Defense, *Annual Report to Congress: Military and Security Developments Involving the People's Republic of China 2017* (Washington, D.C., 2017), 6, https://www.defense.gov/Portals/1/Documents/pubs/2017_China_Military_Power_Report.PDF.

[4] Paul Schwartz, "Sino-Russian Defense Relations Intensify," Asan Forum, December 23, 2015, http://www.theasanforum.org/sino-russian-defense-relations-intensify.

[5] Ethan Meick, "China-Russia Military-to-Military Relations: Moving toward a Higher Level of Cooperation," U.S. Economic and Security Review Commission, Staff Research Report, March 20, 2017, 4, https://www.uscc.gov/sites/default/files/Research/China-Russia%20Mil-Mil%20Relations%20Moving%20Toward%20Higher%20Level%20of%20Cooperation.pdf.

by Chinese manufacturers, Russia refused to sell its most advanced systems to China during this period, including some that were sold to India.[6] In 2008, China and Russia signed an agreement on intellectual property to address these concerns, paving the way for Chinese purchases of major Russian systems.[7] Moreover, Alexander Gabuev, an expert on Russian policy toward Asia, reported that a defense review conducted after the Ukraine crisis found that many of the systems Moscow believed China had reverse-engineered actually were developed indigenously thanks to improvements in Chinese defense technology.[8]

Contemporary Sino-Russian military cooperation involves arms purchases, joint production of weapons systems, policy consultations, and exercises.[9] A number of deals were under contract by 2014, including for Su-35 fighter jets, when international sanctions were imposed on Russia.[10] The sanctions accelerated ongoing negotiations and spurred a series of additional sales, such as a $1.7 billion contract for S-400 surface-to-air missiles, reached in the fall of 2014. China has long sought these systems to support its goals in Taiwan and the South China Sea. Once fully deployed, the S-400 will facilitate coastal defense and extend to the entire territory of Taiwan. Naval deployments of the system will be an important defense against U.S. long-range anti-ship missiles. The Su-35 would enable China to expand its patrolling of disputed areas in the East and South China Seas.[11]

As the Sino-Russian partnership has deepened in recent years, the two sides are increasingly collaborating on the production of military technology. China and Russia will jointly produce a number of systems, including a Chinese-financed heavy-lift helicopter for exclusive Chinese use, submarines based on the Lada-class diesel model, and aircraft engines and space components.[12] Chinese suppliers have also been able to replace some key

---

[6] Charles Clover, "Russia Resumes Advanced Weapons Sales to China," *Financial Times*, November 3, 2016, https://www.ft.com/content/90b1ada2-a18e-11e6-86d5-4e36b35c3550.

[7] Elina Sinkkonen, "China-Russia Security Cooperation: Geopolitical Signalling with Limits," Finnish Institute of International Affairs, Briefing Paper, no. 231, January 16, 2018, 6, https://storage.googleapis.com/upi-live/2018/01/bp231_china-russia.pdf.

[8] Alexander Gabuev, "China and Russia: Friends with Strategic Benefits," Lowy Institute, Interpreter, April 7, 2017, https://www.lowyinstitute.org/the-interpreter/china-and-russia-friends-strategic-benefits.

[9] Li Shuyin, "Dui ZhongE junshi hezuo de lishi kaocha yu sikao" [Historical Investigation and Reflection on the Military Cooperation between China and Russia], *Eluosi xuekan*, no. 3 (2016): 6.

[10] Alexander Lukin, *China and Russia: The New Rapprochement* (Cambridge: Polity Press, 2018), 157.

[11] Paul Schwartz, "Evolution of Sino-Russian Defense Cooperation since the Cold War (Part 1 + Part 2)," in *International Relations and Asia's Northern Tier: Sino-Russia Relations, North Korea, and Mongolia*, ed. Gilbert Rozman and Sergey Radchenko (London: Palgrave Macmillan, 2018), 42.

[12] Meick, "China-Russia Military-to-Military Relations," 16–17.

components that Russia once received from Ukraine.[13] In addition, increasing restrictions in the West on cooperation with Chinese civilian companies on dual-use technology production has encouraged greater Sino-Russian cooperation in this area.[14] China's interest in joint production also partly reflects a realization within the country that its indigenous defense industries remain weak in research and development despite their rapid development.[15]

Yet although Russian arms sales and the joint production of weapons systems contribute to the ability of China to fulfill its global, regional, and domestic ambitions, the partnership also constrains it in several important respects. As China seeks to expand its own clientele for weapons, it finds itself competing with Russia for market share in East Asia—for example, in Myanmar and the Philippines. In addition, Russian arms sales to China are counterbalanced by sales, including of more advanced components, to key regional opponents like India and Vietnam.

China and Russia have been holding joint military exercises regularly since 2005, including naval exercises since 2012. Initially these exercises provided an opportunity for China to assess Russian military technologies for potential purchase while enabling the PLA to gain operational knowledge. In recent years, however, they have emphasized interoperability and provided training in a variety of combat scenarios. The naval exercises in particular have highlighted the PLA Navy's growing capabilities and increasingly global aspirations (see **Table 1**). Chinese commentary notes the strategic importance of the exercises, given the tension over maritime issues in many regions as well as the specific sites selected.[16] The first three sets of naval exercises took place in East Asia (the Yellow Sea, Sea of Japan, and East China Sea), but subsequent rounds have taken place much farther afield in the Mediterranean (2015), the South China Sea (2016), and the Baltic Sea (2017).

In September 2018, 3,200 Chinese personnel took part for the first time in the land-based Vostok (East) exercises that Russia typically holds on its own. While many Western observers have tended to view these biannual exercises as Russian preparations against a potential Chinese threat, this time commentary focused on the large (but likely inflated) number of

---

[13] Richard A. Bitzinger and Nicu Popescu, eds., *Defence Industries in Russia and China: Players and Strategies*, ISSUE Report 38 (Luxembourg: EU Institute for Security Studies, 2017), 17.

[14] Vassily Kashin, "Industrial Cooperation: Path to Confluence of Russian and Chinese Economies," *Russia in Global Affairs*, April 18, 2016, https://eng.globalaffairs.ru/valday/Industrial-cooperation-path-to-confluence-of-russian-and-chinese-economies-18111.

[15] Bitzinger and Popescu, *Defence Industries in Russia and China*, 17.

[16] Ma Yao, "Liangguo zhanlüe cengci de xuyao: 'Ouzhou neihai' ZhongE junyan zai guoji guanzhu" [The Strategic Dimension of the Needs of the Two Countries: The Global Significance of Sino-Russian Military Exercises in European Internal Seas], *Shijie Bolan*, no. 16 (2017): 25.

TABLE 1   Chinese-Russian naval exercises

Year	Month	Host and operational area	Scale
2012	April	China – Yellow Sea	• 25 warships • 13 planes • 9 helicopters
2013	July	Russia – Sea of Japan	• 18 surface ships • 1 submarine • 3 airplanes • 5 ship-launched helicopters
2014	May	China – East China Sea	• 14 warships • 2 submarines • 9 airplanes • 6 helicopters
2015	May	Russia – Black Sea/Mediterranean Sea	• 18 warships
2015	August	Russia – Sea of Japan	• 23 vessels • 2 submarines
2016	September	China – South China Sea	• 18 ships and support vessels • 21 aircraft
2017	July	Russia – Baltic Sea	• 13 warships • Ka-27 multipurpose ship-borne helicopters • Su-24 tactical bombers
2017	September	Russia – Sea of Japan/Okhotsk Sea	• 11 ships • 2 submarines • 4 antisubmarine warfare aircraft • 4 ship-borne helicopters

SOURCE: David Scott, "Russia-China Naval Cooperation in an Era of Great Power Competition," Center for International Maritime Cooperation, June 12, 2018, http://cimsec. org/russia-china-naval-cooperation-in-an-era-of-great-power-competition/36773.

forces and the implications for an incipient Sino-Russian military alliance.[17] An opinion piece in China's usually nationalist tabloid the *Global Times* struck a measured tone, noting that fears of such an alliance reflect "old-fashioned"

---

[17] The Russian Ministry of Defense claimed that nearly 300,000 Russian soldiers participated in the exercises. Michael Kofman, "Vostok 2018 Day 4 (September 14)," Russia Military Analysis, September 15, 2018, https://russianmilitaryanalysis.wordpress.com/2018/09/15/vostok-2018-day-4-september-14.

logic and arguing that the Sino-Russian partnership was evolving so that the two countries could meet new challenges together.[18] *China Daily* further explained that it was only "natural" for two neighbors with excellent bilateral ties to cooperate and that the exercises would improve their capability to respond to regional crises.[19] Gabuev argues that exercises like Vostok serve as vehicles for confidence-building among senior Chinese and Russian officials. He further claims that in an environment where both countries feel increased pressure from the United States, they have begun to share intelligence on CIA operations and possibly even cooperate in determining U.S. vulnerabilities in cyberspace.[20]

Energy Cooperation

Chinese leaders have long touted energy cooperation as a key aspect of the Sino-Russian partnership, particularly with respect to cooperation between northeast China and the Russian Far East. In May 1992, China National Petroleum Corporation (CNPC) first proposed developing Siberian oil for the Asian market. The following year China became a net oil importer for the first time. Three years later in 1996, the same year that the Sino-Russian strategic partnership was initiated, the two countries established an intergovernmental commission on energy cooperation. In 1997, they signed an intergovernmental agreement for a pipeline that would ship Siberian natural gas to China.[21]

The East Siberia–Pacific Ocean (ESPO) pipeline spanning from Taishet in East Siberia to Kozmino on Russia's Pacific coast was completed in 2009 and began pumping oil to China via a branch line to Daqing in 2011. On January 1, 2018, a second parallel branch line from Russia to China began operating, enabling crude deliveries to double from 15 million tons to 30 million tons per year.[22] Russia has been China's top supplier of crude since 2016, surpassing Saudi Arabia. Thanks to energy cooperation with Russia, China has been able to diversify its supply sources beyond the Middle East, via land pipeline

---

[18] "Jiefangjun canjia Ejunyan tuxian jieban bu jie meng" [PLA Participation in Russian Military Exercises Highlights Partnership Not Alliance], *Huanqiu Shibao*, August 29, 2018, http://opinion.huanqiu.com/editorial/2018-08/12868870.html.

[19] "Military Exercise Should Not Be Misinterpreted," *China Daily*, August 30, 2018, http://europe.chinadaily.com.cn/a/201808/30/WS5b87f0bba310add14f388b96.html.

[20] Alexander Gabuev, "Why Russia and China Are Strengthening Security Ties," *Foreign Affairs*, September 24, 2018, https://www.foreignaffairs.com/articles/china/2018-09-24/why-russia-and-china-are-strengthening-security-ties.

[21] Keun-Wook Paik, *Sino-Russian Oil and Gas Cooperation: The Reality and Implications* (New York: Oxford University Press, 2012), 10–12.

[22] Li Fang, "New Line of China-Russian Oil Pipeline Begins Operation," Xinhua, January 1, 2018, http://www.xinhuanet.com/english/2018-01/01/c_136864998.htm.

and LNG, thereby reducing the impact of the "Malacca dilemma"—China's vulnerability to Middle East oil supplies being cut off at the chokepoint of the narrow Malacca Strait.

Gas pipelines connecting Russia and China have been slower to move forward. After years of difficult negotiations, an agreement for the $400 billion Power of Siberia gas pipeline connecting the two countries was finally signed, and the first gas is expected to be pumped in 2019. A second pipeline, spanning from the Altai region to China, remains under discussion. The western route has always been less desirable for China, which receives gas from Turkmenistan, Kazakhstan, and Uzbekistan and has highest demand in its eastern coastal areas, than for Russia, which has harbored hopes of becoming a swing producer for Europe.[23]

Energy cooperation is a key piece of BRI and an important means of involving Russia within Xi's signature initiative, despite the history of difficult bilateral negotiations. According to the 2017 white paper jointly issued by China's National Development and Reform Commission and the National Energy Administration, "the Belt and Road Initiative seeks to foster energy cooperation in order to jointly build up an open, inclusive, and beneficial community of shared interests, responsibility and destiny."[24] Initially, maps of BRI appeared to circumvent Russia, but by 2015, Xi and Vladimir Putin agreed to a "great Eurasian partnership" that would connect the initiative to the Russian-led Eurasian Economic Union (EEU).[25] Despite these grandiose plans for economic corridors and major infrastructure development, the scale of Sino-Russian cooperation has thus far been modest and mostly centered on the Russian Far East.

One exception is the Yamal LNG plant. Chinese lenders invested $12 billion in the $27 billion project operated by Novatek, a private company with connections to the Kremlin, after CNPC secured a 20% stake and the Silk Road Fund acquired 9.9%.[26] China contracted to purchase 3 million tons of

---

[23] Elizabeth Wishnick, "'The 'Power of Siberia': No Longer a Pipe Dream," PONARS Eurasia, Policy Memo, no. 332, August 18, 2014, http://www.ponarseurasia.org/memo/%E2%80%9Cpower-siberia%E2%80%9D-no-longer-pipe-dream.

[24] National Development and Reform Commission and National Energy Administration of the People's Republic of China (PRC), "Vision and Actions on Energy Cooperation in Jointly Building Silk Road Economic Belt and 21st-Century Maritime Silk Road," May 12, 2017, http://www.nea.gov.cn/2017-05/12/c_136277478.htm.

[25] Sebastien Peyrouse, "The Evolution of Russia's Views on the Belt and Road Initiative," Asia Policy, no. 24 (2017): 96.

[26] Elena Mazneva, "From Russia with Love: A Super-Chilled Prize for China," Bloomberg, October 26, 2017, https://www.bloomberg.com/news/articles/2017-10-26/china-to-get-first-yamal-lng-cargo-as-russia-says-thank-you.

LNG annually and the plant began production in December 2017.[27] As China seeks to decrease its dependence on coal, still the country's dominant energy source, LNG imports have soared, climbing 46% in 2017.[28] The Yamal investment has supported Xi's efforts to increase reliance on cleaner energy sources while providing opportunities for Chinese companies to supply equipment and gain expertise in Arctic conditions.[29]

Expanding nuclear energy has also been a key component of Xi's efforts to reduce China's reliance on fossil fuels. The Soviet Union and China had a brief period of nuclear cooperation in the late 1950s that would fall victim to the Sino-Soviet split. Chinese cooperation with Russia on nuclear energy began in 1992 with the signing of an intergovernmental agreement. Construction commenced in 1999 on the first two blocks of the two-gigawatt Tianwan Nuclear Power Station in Jiangsu Province, the first major Sino-Russian cooperative venture in the nuclear sector, and the project was completed in 2009. Russia and China then signed another agreement to cooperate at the same power station on the construction of two WWER-1000 reactors, each with a capacity of 1,060 megawatts. Construction began in 2012 on a third block and in 2015 on a fourth.[30] The two sides have signed subsequent agreements on additional blocks that will use Russia's most advanced technology.

Despite such progress, limitations on energy cooperation persist due to a variety of causes. In the area of nuclear technology, China's complaints about delivery times and Russia's concerns about competition for nuclear contracts have introduced obstacles to cooperation. Previously, Russian technology faced competition from U.S. and Japanese suppliers, but China's interest in developing its own technology poses a new threat and has constrained Sino-Russian nuclear deals. For example, a consortium of Chinese companies appears to be developing floating nuclear technology largely on their own, despite having signed agreements with Russia, which has been a leader in this area. This capability will enable China to better supply its outposts in the South China Sea independently of Russia. Similarly, fearing excessive dependence on the Chinese market, Russian officials in effect barred Chinese companies from upstream oil and gas investments in Russia in the first decade

---

[27] Viktor Katona, "Yamal LNG Is Conquering China," *Oil Price*, July 16, 2018, https://oilprice.com/Energy/Natural-Gas/Yamal-LNG-Is-Conquering-China.html.

[28] Anna Shiryaevskaya, Matthew Carr, and Dan Murtaugh, "What LNG Traders Want to Know Most Is if China Surprises Again," Bloomberg, February 13, 2018, https://www.bloomberg.com/news/articles/2018-02-13/what-lng-traders-want-to-know-most-is-if-china-surprises-again.

[29] Nadezhda Filimonova and Svetlana Krivokhizh, "China's Stakes in the Russian Arctic," *Diplomat*, January 18, 2018, https://thediplomat.com/2018/01/chinas-stakes-in-the-russian-arctic.

[30] James Henderson and Tatiana Mitrova, *Energy Relations between Russia and China: Playing Chess with the Dragon* (Oxford: Oxford Institute for Energy Studies, 2016), 72, https://www.oxfordenergy.org/publications/energy-relations-russia-china-playing-chess-dragon.

of the 2000s, even as it allowed such investment from other Asian partners like India and Vietnam. While Russian opposition had softened by the end of 2010, it was the sanctions imposed following Russia's intervention in Ukraine that finally removed any remaining caution about Chinese investments in the energy sector.[31]

Developing China's Northeast Provinces

For China, the end of the Sino-Soviet conflict in the late 1980s brought security to the border regions and led to confidence-building steps with Russia and Central Asian neighbors in the 1990s. The meetings of the Shanghai Five (China, Russia, Kazakhstan, Kyrgyzstan, and Tajikistan) became the basis for the Shanghai Cooperation Organisation (SCO), created in 2001 to foster regional economic and security cooperation. The settlement of outstanding border disputes with Russia in the 1990s and 2000s paved the way for bilateral cross-border cooperation and generated hope and enthusiasm for the development of China's northeastern provinces, which have lagged economically. Northeast China was the first region to industrialize, and successive Chinese leaders have sought to reinvigorate inefficient state-owned enterprises and address the social consequences of underemployment, including periods of worker unrest. In China, the revitalization of the northeast is now the focus of a leading group headed by Prime Minister Li Keqiang.

Since the 1990s, Russian concerns about illegal Chinese immigration to the Russian Far East and population asymmetries have served as a brake on cooperation. Another factor is the lack of Russian investment in regional development and a poor investment climate in the region for foreign investors. In recent years, Russia and China have created new institutions to oversee their regional cooperation. In 2009 the two sides developed a ten-year strategy for cooperation between northeast China and the Russian Far East, and in 2016 they set up an intergovernmental commission to discuss cooperation. Two years later, the China Development Bank, one of China's three policy banks, and the Russian Direct Investment Fund announced a plan to set up the China-Russia RMB Investment Cooperation Fund, which will invest $10 billion in joint projects.

Some joint regional projects now finally appear to be near fruition, such as the Tongjiang-Nizhneleninskoye railway bridge that is part of the China-Mongolia-Russia economic corridor and a key component of

---

[31] Lukin, *China and Russia*, 148–49.

BRI, and a high-speed rail line connecting Harbin and Vladivostok.[32] The railway bridge, expected to be completed in 2019, will be the first bridge connecting the Russian and Chinese rail lines and is expected to reduce shipping costs and time between the two countries. The long-discussed Blagoveshchensk-Heihe automobile bridge is slated for completion in 2020.[33] Other projects under the BRI umbrella include two new trade corridors that will use Russian Far East ports as hubs. Primorye-1 will serve as a conduit for Chinese goods bound for the west coast of the United States via Vladivostok, Nakhodka, and Vostochny, while Primorye-2 will focus on trade with Japan and the Korean Peninsula and connect Changchun with Zarubino.[34]

Experts in the Russian Far East hope that Pacific Russia will become integrated more broadly with the Asia-Pacific region and diversify both its partners and economy.[35] While progress on oil and gas pipeline projects is often viewed as the barometer for the vitality of the Sino-Russian partnership, over the years the two countries have quietly pursued cooperation in renewable energy, especially hydropower. As early as 1992, China's Heilongjiang Province began receiving electricity from Russian hydropower plants across the Amur River from Heihe City, and this cooperation was expanded in the 2000s. In 2014, China and Russia signed a long-term contract for the export to China of 100 billion kilowatt hours of electricity through 2036.[36] Beijing views this as a model of trans-border energy cooperation, bringing reliable and clean energy to China and improving economic ties with Russia. It has sought to replicate this success with other neighbors first through BRI and later through the Global Energy Interconnection Development and Cooperation Organization, which was established in 2017 to promote such efforts worldwide.[37]

---

[32] Chinging Chen, "Heilongjiang Highway Bridge Project Moves Ahead," *Global Times*, August 17, 2017, http://www.globaltimes.cn/content/1061888.shtml; and "Kitay nastroilsya na skorost" [China Is in the Mood for Speed], EastRussia, November 16, 2018.

[33] Ivan Zuenko, "A Milestone, Not a Turning Point: How China Will Develop the Russian Far East," Carnegie Moscow Center, November 8, 2018, https://carnegie.ru/commentary/77671.

[34] Qiyang Niu, "Can Russia Save Northeast China's Economy?" *Diplomat*, April 8, 2017, https://thediplomat.com/2017/04/can-russia-save-northeast-chinas-economy; and "Russia, China Agree On Primorye-1 Corridor; Opens Up Heilongjiang to Asia-Pacific Markets," Russia Briefing, May 15, 2017, https://www.russia-briefing.com/news/russia-china-agree-primorye-1-corridor-opens-heilongjiang-asia-pacific-markets.html.

[35] Victor Larin, "Pacific Russia in the New Regionalism of North Pacific: Cross-Border and Inter-Regional Relations," in *The Political Economy of Pacific Russia: Regional Developments in East Asia*, ed. Huang Jing and Alexander Korolev (London: Palgrave Macmillan, 2017), 42.

[36] Henderson and Mitrova, *Energy Relations between Russia and China*, 72.

[37] "Economic Watch: China Pushes for Global Energy Network to Power B&R Initiative," Xinhua, September 5, 2017, http://www.xinhuanet.com/english/2017-05/09/c_136269140.htm.

Agriculture is another promising area of cooperation between northeast China and the Russian Far East. However, this area, too, is not without controversy when Chinese farm workers are employed or lease land in the region. Although northeast China is a food-producing region, it is also home to heavily polluting industries. Consequently, around 80% of the water in the region is considered unsafe for drinking.[38] Moreover, one-fifth of the land is contaminated by soil pollution.[39] For these reasons, China's wary consumers welcome Russian agricultural products, which are produced under greener conditions. China is building a new port in Fuyuan in Heilongjiang Province on the Amur River to accommodate up to 650,000 tons of grain by September 2019. Grain exports from Russia increased 42% in the first half of 2018 compared with the previous year and reached 1.23 million tons. China's largest food processor, COFCO (China National Cereals, Oils and Foodstuffs Corporation), is prepared to import up to 4 million tons of spring wheat alone in the future.[40]

The difficulties in Sino-Russian cooperation in oil and gas reflect a broader problem—the disconnect between Chinese and Russian approaches to regional integration. While China has allocated considerable resources to BRI, Russia has only partially implemented its own agenda for the development of the Russian Far East, as outlined in its 2009 strategy document.[41] More importantly, the Chinese conception of comparative advantage, based on the asymmetric involvement of weaker neighboring economies to the benefit of its own, is very different from the Russian conception of economic development for the region, which relies on state-led industrialization.[42]

A similar mismatch of approaches is occurring in Central Asia, which Chinese leaders have long viewed as a key region economically and politically. China has needed to tread more cautiously due to Russia's long-standing view of the region as its sphere of interest and its own identity as a key player in Eurasia. Another issue is local Sinophobia, though the Ukraine events created more concern in the region about Russian intentions, perhaps reducing fear of China to some extent. China's inability to push forward multilateral economic

---

[38] "China Pollution: Over 80% of Rural Water in North-east 'Undrinkable,'" BBC News, April 12, 2016, https://www.bbc.co.uk/news/world-asia-china-36022538.

[39] Yu Zhuang, "Soil Pollution in China Threatens the Health of Its Citizens and Investment," Asian Environmental Governance Blog, May 9, 2016, http://asia-environment.vermontlaw.edu/2016/05/09/soil-pollution-in-china.

[40] "Russia's Grain Exports to China Hit Record One Million Tons," RT, May 17, 2018, https://www.rt.com/business/426971-russia-china-grain-exports.

[41] Ivan Zuenko, "A Chinese-Russian Regional Program Ends with a Whimper," Carnegie Moscow Center, September 26, 2018, https://carnegie.ru/commentary/77341.

[42] Gaye Christoffersen, "Northeast China and the Russian Far East: Positive Scenarios and Negative Scenarios," in Rozman and Radchenko, *International Relations and Asia's Northern Tier*, 220.

projects within the SCO helped motivate it to create its own institutions, such as the Asian Infrastructure Investment Bank (AIIB), and frameworks such as BRI, to engage with Central Asia, other neighbors, and partners outside the region. In pursuing these initiatives, China has had to be mindful of Russian sensitivities and has made an effort to engage Russia by signing an agreement with the EEU and urging the country to be a key stakeholder in the AIIB.

Support for Chinese Global and Regional Positions

Xi Jinping has called the partnership with Russia a "ballast stone."[43] The relationship has served as a model for China's approach to great-power relations. In their numerous interactions and joint statements, the two countries have outlined the rules of the authoritarian road, including noninterference in the domestic affairs of states and a strong emphasis on sovereignty. Together, China and Russia have put forward joint initiatives at the United Nations and resisted the widespread application of human rights norms, such as the responsibility to protect civilians and the imposition of sanctions for human rights violations. They have used their double veto to block Western initiatives and show a united front, even when a single veto would have been sufficient.[44] While China and Russia are not in a position to challenge the global order, they have been involved in rule-making and pushed back against rule-taking in situations where their own interests are threatened. By promoting alternative norms, they seek to be insiders in an evolving international system rather than outliers in the liberal order. They have sought to take advantage of information asymmetries in interactions with democracies to expand their own influence at the expense of democratic choices—what Christopher Walker and Jessica Ludwig have called projecting "sharp power."[45]

At a time when China's increasingly active role in the Asia-Pacific has caused alarm in many countries, its partnership with Russia, despite limitations on some issues, has provided an important source of support. Lacking any specific mutual defense clause, the partnership falls short of an alliance. But through their regular meetings, the two countries have outlined some key norms of behavior for East Asia. Both are opposed to the deployment of missile defense systems, and their opposition to deployment of the Terminal High Altitude Area Defense (THAAD) missile defense system

---

[43] "Xi Says China, Russia Play Role of 'Ballast Stone' in World Peace, Stability," Xinhua, May 14, 2017, http://www.xinhuanet.com/english/2017-05/14/c_136282238.htm.

[44] Sinkkonen, "China-Russia Security Cooperation."

[45] Ren Xiao, "Toward a Normal State-to-State Relationship? China and the DPRK in Changing Northeast Asia," *North Korean Review* 11, no. 2 (2015): 65.

on the Korean Peninsula led them to begin a special bilateral dialogue on Asian security issues, as well as to issue a rare statement cosigned by their foreign ministries.[46] This being said, Russian and Chinese positions on the North Korean nuclear crisis are not identical. China prefers the status quo to a united Korea with a U.S. military presence and can deal with a nuclear North Korea as long as it is not provocative. From its perspective, strengthening the Sino-Russian partnership prevents North Korea from being able to find much daylight between its two main interlocutors. Moreover, due to its leverage, China has faced more pressure from the international community to use its economic power to achieve North Korean compliance with UN resolutions, and Russia's support for Chinese positions helps alleviate this pressure. Russia, on the other hand, is more concerned about its long-term economic plans for the peninsula and becoming a part of the Asian security solution.

Interestingly, both China and Russia claim to pursue neutrality with respect to the conflicts that the other has with the international community over territory and sovereignty issues. Fu Ying, chair of the Foreign Affairs Committee of the Chinese legislature, has described the partnership as "stable, complex, and deeply rooted" but acknowledges the two countries' differences in diplomatic style: "Russia is more experienced on the global theater, and it tends to favor strong, active, and often surprising diplomatic maneuvers. Chinese diplomacy, in contrast, is more reactive and cautious."[47] On Ukraine, Fu argues that the Chinese leadership understood Russian policy in the context of the complex political, economic, and social environment in Ukraine and against the background of Western intervention in "color revolutions" and NATO expansion.[48] In her account, China's official response to the crisis in Ukraine was to urge respect for its territorial sovereignty and integrity and to outline a three-pronged proposal involving (1) international coordination to stabilize the situation, (2) an appeal for the parties to refrain from actions that might aggravate the crisis, and (3) steps to assist Ukraine economically. While Xi reportedly told Putin just after the takeover of Crimea that he understood the situation as an "inevitable accident," Fu affirms that "Beijing did not take sides" and that "impartiality has been a commitment that China has consistently honored when dealing with international affairs."[49] Indeed, China abstained from the March 2014 UN Security Council resolution condemning Russian actions in Crimea. China's ambassador to the

---

[46] Sinkkonen, "China-Russia Security Cooperation," 4–5.

[47] Fu Ying, "How China Sees Russia," *Foreign Affairs*, December 14, 2015, https://www.foreignaffairs.com/articles/china/2015-12-14/how-china-sees-russia.

[48] Fu Ying, "Are China and Russia Partnering to Create an Axis?" Valdai Discussion Club, October 24, 2016, http://valdaiclub.com/a/highlights/are-china-and-russia-partnering-to-create-an-axis.

[49] Ibid.

United Nations Liu Jieyi explained that the resolution would only exacerbate the crisis and complicate matters.[50]

China has had to accept Russian neutrality on some of its core concerns as well, particularly on territorial conflicts in the East and South China Seas. While some analysts interpret the Russian stance as a limitation on the partnership, others view Russia as largely a "bystander" in the territorial disputes.[51] Due to the Northern Sea Route (NSR) and pipeline connections to Europe and Asia, the country does not face the Malacca dilemma so acutely experienced by its resource-consuming Asian neighbors. Moreover, Russia needs to cooperate with all of its neighbors to be able to successfully develop and market the resources from its eastern regions. Regarding the East China Sea, Nikolai Patrushev, Chairman of the Security Council of Russia, stated that "Russia doesn't take any position."[52] Russia, however, gives the appearance of supporting Chinese positions by cooperating in joint naval exercises in the region, patrolling by air areas claimed by China, and issuing joint statements on World War II.

In the case of the South China Sea, Russia has a long history of partnering with Vietnam, including defense and energy cooperation. It also has sought to broaden ties with other Southeast Asian states such as the Philippines, Malaysia, and Indonesia. Although Putin went so far as to support China's position not to recognize the validity of the Permanent Court of Arbitration ruling in 2016,[53] Russia made no official expression of support for China's claims to the nine-dash line. When some Chinese media overstated the level of Russian support, the Russian Foreign Ministry pushed back to clarify.[54] In the end, the Chinese Foreign Ministry praised Putin's position for its objectivity and fairness, and Xi himself thanked the Russian president for his support.[55] Although Russia did participate in naval exercises with China in the South China Sea in 2016 not long after the court's decision, these drills took place in waters recognized by all as Chinese. Yet, as in the case of the East

---

[50] Liu Jieyi, "Statement by Ambassador Liu Jieyi after Security Council Voting on the Draft Resolution on Ukraine," Permanent Mission of the PRC to the UN, March 15, 2014, http://www.china-un.org/eng/hyyfy/t1140296.htm.

[51] For an example of the former view, see Alexander Korolev and Vladimir Portyakov, "China-Russia Relations in Times of Crisis: A Neoclassical Realist Explanation," *Asian Perspective* 42, no. 3 (2018): 422. For an example of the latter view, see Anna Kireeva, "Russia's View on the International Security in Northeast Asia," *Korean Journal of Defense Analysis* 30, no. 1 (2018): 121.

[52] Elizabeth Wishnick, "The Sino-Russian Partnership and the East Asian Order," *Asian Perspective* 42, no. 3 (2018): 367.

[53] "Russia Supports China's Stance on the South China Sea," Sputnik News, September 5, 2016, https://sputniknews.com/world/201609051044988523-russia-china-putin.

[54] Lukin, *China and Russia*, 134.

[55] Hua Xia, "China Appreciates Putin's Position on South China Sea Issue," Xinhua, September 8, 2016, http://www.xinhuanet.com/english/2016-09/08/c_135673025.htm.

China Sea, even as Russia avoids clear expressions of support, Russian weapon sales enable China to better press its claims. The first Su-35s, for example, were used by China to patrol the South China Sea in February 2018, enabling the PLA to respond to a freedom of navigation operation by the USS *Hopper* near Scarborough Shoal, which is disputed by China and the Philippines.[56]

Despite the limitations of the Sino-Russian partnership, in many respects China has no alternative to Russia as a partner either in global institutions like the UN Security Council or in East Asia, where most other states are either competing with China or fearful of its rise. The benefits of the partnership have been significant for China, particularly in the energy and defense sectors. Nonetheless, China has had to make some tradeoffs, for example, in the Arctic.

China's Ambitions in the Arctic

The Arctic and China's Great-Power Ambitions

The Sino-Russian partnership has both supported China's Arctic ambitions and at times acted as a check on them. Broadly speaking, the region serves as a testing ground for key goals of Xi Jinping's foreign policy agenda. On January 26, 2018, the Chinese State Council issued a long-awaited white paper defining its policy goals and interests in the Arctic. The document is interesting both for what aspects of China's Arctic policy it highlights and for what it omits. Focusing on climate change, sustainable development, and global governance, the white paper downplays China's security interests in the region, especially the link between the projection of power in the polar region and the development of naval capabilities needed for great-power status. The PLA, however, has been integral to the development of China's Arctic capabilities, and the changing Arctic (and China's evolving role in it) are becoming a key part of the country's maritime strategy.[57]

For several years prior to the white paper's publication, Chinese academics sought to justify their country's role as an Arctic player. They did so by pointing to China's history of involvement in the region, dating back to the Republic of China's signing of the Svalbard Treaty in 1925 and then to the PRC's participation in the International Arctic Science Committee in 1996 and in research expeditions in subsequent years. In 2003, China acquired a physical presence in the region by building a research station in Svalbard.

---

[56] Ralph Jennings, "How China Could Gradually Assume Control of Scarborough Shoal in the South China Sea," *Forbes*, December 29, 2017, https://www.forbes.com/sites/ralphjennings/2017/12/29/chinas-takeover-of-an-islet-disputed-with-the-philippines-3-scenarios/.

[57] For further discussion, see Anne-Marie Brady, *China as a Polar Great Power* (Cambridge: Cambridge University Press, 2017), 75–77.

In 2013, it finally became an observer on the Arctic Council, and the following year, Xi first referred to China as a "polar great power."[58] The new priority of the Arctic mission was reflected in its association in 2015 with BRI. Chinese officials began outlining a vision for a Polar Silk Road linking BRI to the PRC's Arctic infrastructure projects, to be built with the Arctic states, especially Russia. In June 2017 the National Development and Reform Commission and State Oceanic Administration identified the Arctic as one of three key shipping routes under BRI.

Interestingly, Chinese officials have showcased their country's Arctic credentials with a new vertical image of Sinocentrism—a vertical map of the world with China at the center of the two poles.[59] According to Zhang Xia, director of the Polar Strategy Center at the Polar Research Institute of China, the vertical map better expresses China's strategic and development goals with respect to the polar regions than horizontal maps, with their more limited land-based focus.[60] For others, however, the map exemplifies how Chinese polar policies have led to a major shift in the country's view of its own place in the world.[61]

In recent years some Chinese experts have begun referring to China controversially as a "near-Arctic state," despite the country's geographic distance from the Arctic. Yang Jian, vice president of the Shanghai Institute for International Studies, points to geography, influence, and connections to the Arctic as justification for China's near-Arctic status. The geographic factors seem the most tenuous—Yang highlights that the Ertix River begins in Xinjiang, China, before becoming the Irtysh River in Kazakhstan, which turns into the Ob River and flows into the Arctic Ocean. He also notes that birds migrate from China to the Arctic and that Chinese coastal waters flow into the Arctic.[62] Nonetheless, Harbin, one of China's northernmost cities, is still located 1,440 miles south of the Arctic Circle, on the same latitude as Venice.

Connections and influence are more readily established, in terms of China's participation in Arctic governance institutions, economic investments and resource interests in the region, scientific and technical contributions,

---

[58] Brady, *China as a Polar Great Power,* 109, 182.

[59] For an image of the map, see "A New Version of World Map Published," Chinese Academy of Sciences, Institute of Geodesy and Geophysics, 2013, http://english.whigg.cas.cn/ns/es/201312/ t20131211_114311.html.

[60] Yang Haixia, "Jing lüe Beiji jinzao xingdong—Zhuanfang Zhongguo Jidi Yanjiu Zhongxin Jidi Zhanlüe Yanjiushi zhuren Zhang Xia" [A Strategy for Passing through the Arctic as Soon as Possible: An Interview with Zhang Xia, Director of the Research Division on Polar Strategy at the Polar Research Institute of China], *Xianzhuang Qishi,* no. 7 (2018): 20.

[61] See, for example, Brady, *China as a Polar Great Power,* 4.

[62] Yang Jian, "Zhongguo de Beiji zhence" [China's Arctic Policy], *Taipingyang Xuebao* 3 (2018).

and partnerships with Arctic states.[63] Geographic evidence notwithstanding, the 2018 Arctic white paper codifies the term near-Arctic state:

> China is an important stakeholder in Arctic affairs. Geographically, China is a "Near-Arctic State," one of the continental States that are closest to the Arctic Circle. The natural conditions of the Arctic and their changes have a direct impact on China's climate system and ecological environment, and, in turn, on its economic interests in agriculture, forestry, fishery, marine industry and other sectors.[64]

The Chinese government justifies its participation in the region by virtue of its permanent seat on the UN Security Council, global economic power, and interests in Arctic energy, shipping, and infrastructure development. While recognition of the sovereignty of Arctic states was a precondition for China's observer status in the Arctic Council, the white paper emphasizes the importance of reciprocity and the rights of states outside the region:

> States from outside the Arctic region do not have territorial sovereignty in the Arctic, but they do have rights in respect of scientific research, navigation, overflight, fishing, laying of submarine cables and pipelines in the high seas and other relevant sea areas in the Arctic Ocean, and rights to resource exploration and exploitation in the Area, pursuant to treaties such as UNCLOS [United Nations Convention on the Law of the Sea] and general international law. In addition, Contracting Parties to the Spitsbergen Treaty enjoy the liberty of access and entry to certain areas of the Arctic, the right under conditions of equality and, in accordance with law, to the exercise and practice of scientific research, production and commercial activities such as hunting, fishing, and mining in these areas.[65]

The Chinese government further states its intention to "seize the historic opportunity" to participate in the development of the Arctic on the basis of the principles of respect, cooperation, and sustainability with the aim of building a "shared future of mankind," a concept that Xi began developing in 2015.[66] According to the white paper, China seeks "to understand, protect, develop and participate in the governance of the Arctic, so as to safeguard

---

[63] Yang, "Zhongguo de Beiji zhence," 33–34.

[64] Information Office of the State Council of the People's Republic of China, *China's Arctic Policy 2018* (Beijing, January 2018), https://www.chinadailyhk.com/articles/188/159/234/1516941033919.html.

[65] Ibid. Russia and Canada pressed the Arctic Council to change its rules so that members would have to agree to observe UNCLOS and respect the sovereignty of Arctic states, with their compliance being subject to review every four years. After these new rules were passed in 2011, China and other non-Arctic states succeeded in achieving observer status in 2013. For further discussion, see Elizabeth Wishnick, *China's Interests and Goals in the Arctic: Implications for the United States*, Letort Papers (Carlisle: U.S. Army War College Press, 2017), 42, https://ssi.armywarcollege.edu/pubs/display.cfm?pubID=1347.

[66] Xi Jinping, "A New Partnership of Mutual Benefit and a Community of a Shared Future" (speech at the 70th UN General Assembly, New York, September 29, 2015), in Xi Jinping, *The Governance of China II* (Beijing: Foreign Languages Press, 2017), 575.

the common interests of all countries and the international community in the Arctic, and promote sustainable development of the Arctic."[67] Polar scholar Anne-Marie Brady notes that this is a rephrasing of Xi's 2014 speech in Chinese (understand, protect, exploit) and integrates his language from the 19th Party Congress on "common interests of mankind."[68]

To justify its status as a near-Arctic state and lend credence to its aim to be a polar great power, China has sought to establish a physical presence at both poles.[69] In the Arctic, as noted earlier, the first step was the establishment of China's Yellow River research base at Svalbard in 2003. This was followed a decade later by an agreement to set up a joint research station in Iceland, which was completed in October 2018, to study the aurora borealis. China put in place its first overseas satellite-receiving ground station in Kiruna, Sweden, in December 2016, and in April 2018 it agreed with Finland to set up a joint center for satellite observation and remote sensing of the Arctic. Discussions with Greenland about the establishment of a research station have been taking place since 2015, and in 2017 a Chinese delegation held a ceremony at the Kangerlussuaq airport to celebrate the future construction of a satellite ground station there, reportedly before Greenland even authorized the project.[70] Yet while China has been a leader in investment in Arctic infrastructure and has big plans (and funds) for developing its own Arctic science capabilities, its scientific contributions remain modest.

China faces several obstacles to fulfilling its Arctic ambitions. At present, the country has limited experience in cold-water navigation and polar research, though the Chinese government has been making substantial investments, particularly in the latter. In the short term, fears about Russia in Northern Europe may contribute to greater receptivity to China's activities in the Arctic, but this may no longer be the case if China seeks to play a more substantial role. The current blowback against China in Sri Lanka, Malaysia, Djibouti, and other countries over debt incurred in BRI projects also may lead to more caution by smaller Arctic states. When questioned about this possibility, Chinese officials have been quick to dismiss concerns about China's role in the region, without much reassurance. For example, Vice Foreign Minister Kong Xuanyou stated that "some people may have misgivings over our participation in the development of the Arctic,

---

[67] State Council Information Office (PRC), *China's Arctic Policy*.

[68] Brady, *China as a Polar Great Power*, 137. An official English translation changed "exploit" to "explore." Xi Jinping, "Secure a Decisive Victory in Building a Moderately Prosperous Society in All Respects and Strive for the Great Success of Socialism with Chinese Characteristics for a New Era" (speech delivered at the 19th National Congress of the Communist Party of China, Beijing, October 18, 2017).

[69] Brady, *China as a Polar Great Power*, 137.

[70] Ibid., 3.

worried we may have other intentions, or that we may plunder resources or damage the environment," but he claimed that "these kinds of concerns are absolutely unnecessary."[71]

China's ambitions in the Arctic could also complicate its relations with Russia. China's entry into the region has been importantly facilitated by Russia's acceptance of Chinese investments and provision of Arctic navigation training (though, as discussed above, Russia was initially wary of China's quest for observer status in the Arctic Council). Yet China may not need a gatekeeper in the region for much longer if Arctic ice continues to recede. If the NSR is no longer frozen, then Russia may lose its legal rationale for administering the waterway, potentially leading to tensions with China and other users hoping to avoid Russian oversight and fees. The country currently requires a Russian ice pilot to accompany all vessels at the rate of $673 per day.[72]

Developing Arctic Transportation and Related Naval Capabilities

As one of the world's largest shipping powers, China seeks to reduce its shipping time to the Arctic by developing what Chinese scholars call the "blue passage." Using the NSR could reduce shipping times by up to two weeks from existing routes through chokepoints in the Malacca Strait and the Suez Canal.[73] This makes many Chinese observers optimistic about the prospects for polar shipping. After the first Chinese commercial ship successfully sailed through the NSR in August 2013, Yang Huigen, the director of China's Polar Research Institute, claimed that anywhere from 5% to 15% of China's trade could use the route by 2020.[74] Guo Weiping, a scholar at Ocean University of China, spoke of the northern shipping route as having the potential to "change the structure of global trade."[75] For now, this route is the most plausible, due to more variable ice conditions, inadequate infrastructure, and the multiple permissions required for sailing along the Northwest Passage, which spans

---

[71] Oki Nagai, "China and Russia Battle for North Pole Supremacy," *Nikkei Asian Review*, April 10, 2018, https://asia.nikkei.com/Spotlight/Asia-Insight/China-and-Russia-battle-for-North-Pole-supremacy.

[72] Jeroen F.J. Pruyn, "Will the Northern Sea Route Ever Be a Viable Alternative?" *Maritime Policy and Management* 43, no. 6 (2016): 665.

[73] Sherri Goodman and Elisabeth Freese, "China's Ready to Cash In on a Melting Arctic," *Foreign Policy*, May 1, 2018, https://foreignpolicy.com/2018/05/01/chinas-ready-to-cash-in-on-a-melting-arctic.

[74] Trude Pettersen, "First Chinese Merchant Ship on Northern Sea Route," *Barents Observer*, August 12, 2013, https://barentsobserver.com/en/arctic/2013/08/first-chinese-merchant-ship-northern-sea-route-12-08.

[75] Cited in Kai Sun, "Zhongguo beiji waijiao: Shizhan, liyi yu jinlu" [China's Arctic Diplomacy: Practice, Principles, and Ways Forward], *Taipingyang xuebao* 23, no. 5 (2015): 40; and Linyan Huang, Frédéric Lasserre, and Olga Alexeeva, "Is China's Interest for the Arctic Driven by Arctic Shipping Potential?" *Asian Geographer* 32, no. 1 (2015): 61.

from the Bering Strait to the North Atlantic. But as long as Russia claims the legal right to administer the NSR, Russian fees and other controls erode the projected savings. Moreover, the narrow passage through the Bering Strait is a chokepoint patrolled by U.S. as well as Russian forces.[76]

Despite more challenging conditions, the Chinese Arctic policy considers opportunities not just in the Northwest Passage but also along the Transpolar Sea Route in the event of significant ice melt there in the long term. The 40% reduction in shipping time experienced by the Canadian ore carrier *Nunavik*, which in 2014 sailed from Quebec to northeastern China through the Northwest Passage rather than the Panama Canal, fueled imaginations in China. This led the Chinese Maritime Safety Administration, which is under the Transport Ministry, to release a 365-page guidance in 2016 on navigation in the Northwest Passage in an effort to promote the route as weather conditions enable its greater use for trade.[77]

This requires investments in icebreaker technology and related naval capabilities. China currently has one ice-resistant ship, the *Xue Long* (Snow Dragon), which completed its first voyage through the NSR in 2012, and is constructing its first domestically built icebreaker in cooperation with Finland. Russian experts note that the *Xue Long* is a research vessel and would not be easily adapted to commercial shipping.

Much like northeastern Chinese provinces seized on the Deng Xiaoping–era concept of special economic zones to promote their regional interests, scholars from this part of China today view the Arctic route as a way of becoming involved in and benefiting from BRI. Thus, scholars from Ocean University of China in Dalian in Liaoning Province argue that combining the new shipping possibilities in the Arctic with BRI would have important consequences for the "greater Arctic."[78] Nonetheless, Chinese shipping companies have been as cautious as their Western counterparts, and shipping along the NSR has thus far proceeded slowly. While exports of Arctic resources from Russia to China have been increasing gradually, Russian ships have largely been used. A recent survey of Chinese shipping companies showed that they were more interested in access to these resources than in assuming responsibility for shipping due to the high risk and costs associated with Arctic shipping today.[79]

[76] Marc Lanteigne and Su Ping, "China's Developing Arctic Policies: Myths and Misconceptions," *Journal of China and International Relations* 3, no. 1 (2015): 10.

[77] Erica Haun, "China Issues Guidance on Arctic Navigation," Marine Link, May 10, 2016, http://www.marinelink.com/news/navigation-guidance409448.aspx.

[78] Zhenfu Li, Wenya Wang, and Jing Zhu, "Beiji hanxian zai wo guo 'Yidai Yilu' jianshe zhong de zuoyong yanjiu" [The Study of the Role of the Arctic Route in Belt and Road Construction], *Yatai Jingji*, no. 3 (2015): 36.

[79] Huang et al., "Is China's Interest for the Arctic Driven by Arctic Shipping Potential?" 66.

Relations with Arctic States

As discussed above, China's relationship with Russia is central to its Arctic ambitions, though Russia's positions on Arctic shipping also set limits to the Chinese role. As a part of the cooperation between BRI and the EEU, in 2017 China and Russia pledged to cooperate on developing a Polar Silk Road. In June 2018 the China Development Bank pledged $9.9 billion in new financing for Vnesheconombank to support BRI projects in Russia, particularly in the Arctic.[80] For China to take advantage of shipping opportunities via the NSR, cooperation with Russia will be essential. Article 234 of UNCLOS allows coastal states to administer and develop ice-covered waterways. China's Arctic shipping ambitions became further constrained in 2018 when Russia issued new rules limiting the shipping of energy resources through the NSR to Russian vessels. As noted earlier, Russian icebreakers also must accompany foreign ships in the waterway.

Thus far, Sino-Russian cooperation in the Arctic has involved some training for Chinese crews in polar navigation, though it was Finland that teamed up with China to build its first icebreaker. China's announcement of its plans to construct a nuclear icebreaker has raised questions about the degree to which Russia would cooperate in providing technology, given the potential military applications—for example, for the creation of the first nuclear-powered Chinese aircraft carrier. Russia is the only country with nuclear-powered ice breakers.[81] Chinese ships have already cooperated with the Russian Navy in a joint sea exercise in the Baltic Sea in 2017, and a visit by a PLA delegation to Russia's Northern Fleet in July 2018 led to speculation about a possible Barents Sea exercise in the near future.[82]

Although Russia is China's key partner in the Arctic, Chinese officials have sought to improve relations with all the Arctic states. As an observer in the Arctic Council, China depends on members to put forward its proposals and will only be able to participate in Arctic resource development in cooperation with these states. According to a 2014 report, a research institute affiliated with the PLA characterized the Arctic as a potential "lifeline" for

---

[80] Atle Staalesen, "Chinese Bank Invests in Russia's Northern Sea Route," Eye on the Arctic, June 12, 2018, http://www.rcinet.ca/eye-on-the-arctic/2018/06/12/china-russia-arctic-shipping-infrastructure-northern-sea-route.

[81] Minnie Chan, "How China Could Move Closer to Nuclear-Powered Aircraft Carriers—with Russia's Help," South China Morning Post, June 27, 2018, https://www.scmp.com/news/china/diplomacy-defence/article/2152785/how-china-could-move-closer-nuclear-powered-aircraft.

[82] Thomas Nilsen, "Chinese Navy Commander Talks Cooperation in Severomorsk," Barents Observer, July 30, 2018, https://thebarentsobserver.com/en/security/2018/07/chinese-navy-commander-talks-cooperation-severomorsk.

the growing Chinese economy and urged greater energy cooperation with Arctic countries.[83]

China's Arctic ambitions have elicited concern among regional states for two sets of reasons. First, countries like Russia that view Arctic coastal waterways as subject to their own jurisdiction are apprehensive about China's position. Second, most of the Arctic states have significant resource deposits or coastal access to such stores and are concerned about the consequences of China's investments and economic power in the region. This is particularly acute for smaller Arctic states such as Iceland, where a large infusion of Chinese funds might have an outsized political and economic impact.

Sino-U.S. relations in the Arctic have thus far been cooperative. The U.S. and Chinese coast guards have a history of joint patrols in the northern Pacific Ocean in support of a UN General Assembly resolution (46/215) prohibiting driftnet fishing in the high seas. Beginning in 2015, China joined Japan, South Korea, and the five Arctic coastal states in several rounds of negotiations that culminated in the signing of an agreement in December 2016 prohibiting fishing in the central Arctic Ocean for sixteen years. For China, which has no vote in the Arctic Council, participating in the negotiation of this fisheries agreement provided a path to participation in Arctic governance as well as a means to safeguard its future fishing interests in the region.[84] China generally supports creating mechanisms to regulate fisheries issues on the basis of UNCLOS, to which it is a signatory, as a way of maintaining its voice on the issue.[85] The Chinese government also cites UNCLOS to side with the United States on freedom of the seas in the Arctic, despite its more restrictive definitions of sovereignty on "near seas" in the South China Sea.[86] In support of this, Chinese military vessels sailed near the Aleutian Islands in 2015.

While Canada, which views the Northwest Passage as internal waters, and Russia, with its assertion of administrative rights over the still ice-covered NSR, have had some reservations about China playing a greater role in the Arctic, Nordic countries have largely welcomed its growing interest in the region. Chinese policy toward these states has involved multilateralism, as well as bilateral diplomacy and investments under BRI. China has been an

---

[83] "Junkeyuan fashi zhanlüe pinglun baogao: Zhongguo mianlin san da taikong weixie" [Army Research Institute Released a Strategic Assessment Report: China Faces Three Major Space Threats], *Sina Military*, June 19, 2014, http://mil.news.sina.com.cn/2014-06-19/1657785793.html.

[84] Min Pan and Henry P. Huntington, "A Precautionary Approach to Fisheries in the Central Arctic Ocean: Policy, Science, and China," *Marine Policy* 63 (2016): 153–57.

[85] Nengye Liu, "How Has China Shaped Arctic Fisheries Governance?" *Diplomat*, June 20, 2018, https://thediplomat.com/2018/06/how-has-china-shaped-arctic-fisheries-governance.

[86] Jingchao Peng and Njord Wegge, "China's Bilateral Diplomacy in the Arctic," *Polar Geography* 38, no. 3 (2015): 241; and Vesa Virtanen, "The Arctic in World Politics. The United States, Russia, and China in the Arctic—Implications for Finland," Harvard University, Weatherhead Center for International Affairs, July 17, 2013, 55–56.

active participant in the annual Arctic Circle Assembly, championed by Iceland. Prior to unveiling its own Arctic strategy, it regularly sent high-level delegations to this venue to explain Chinese objectives in the region. In 2013, when China achieved observer status in the Arctic Council, four Chinese academic institutes with input into Chinese policymaking on the Arctic (the Shanghai Institute for International Studies, the Polar Research Institute of China, Tongji University's Center for Polar and Oceanic Studies, and Ocean University of China's Research Institute of Polar Law and Politics) along with institutes from six Nordic countries created the China-Nordic Arctic Research Center to engage in joint research, share information, and hold annual meetings. In October 2015, three ships from the PLA Navy visited Finland, Sweden, and Denmark for the first time.[87]

More generally, Chinese diplomacy has focused on states with leadership roles in the Arctic Council, especially the United States (chair through 2016), Finland (current chair), and Iceland (next chair). Xi visited Finland in April 2017, after it had assumed the chairmanship, which was the first visit to the country by a Chinese leader since 1995. He then welcomed to Beijing the prime minister of Norway (now back on China's good side after a lengthy period of tension due to the decision by the Nobel Committee to honor a Chinese dissident), followed by the prime ministers of Denmark and Greenland.

Cooperation with Finland is now proceeding on several fronts, including plans (which also include Russia, Norway, and Japan) for a 6,500-mile fiber-optic cable on the polar seabed, a new freight rail connection to Xi'an, and a Finnish air hub for flights between Europe and Asia.[88] Iceland was the first European country to sign a free trade agreement (FTA) with China and is embarking on a new project to develop geothermal energy in the country. In addition, Chinese companies have been examining the possibility of investing in two ports in Iceland, as well as in Klaipeda, Lithuania, and Kirkenes, Norway.[89]

Chinese investments in Greenland have been especially controversial due to its strategic location and domestic pressures for political independence from Denmark. Chinese companies have been pursuing airport projects in the infrastructure-poor country, as well as a number of mining opportunities (especially for uranium, rare earths, lead, and iron). Progress has been slow

---

[87] Shannon Tiezzi, "China's Navy Makes First-Ever Tour of Europe's Arctic States," *Diplomat*, October 2, 2015, https://thediplomat.com/2015/10/chinas-navy-makes-first-ever-tour-of-europes-arctic-states.

[88] Ting Shi, "10,000 Kilometers of Fiber-Optic Cable Show China's Interest in Warming Arctic," Bloomberg, December 13, 2017, https://www.bloomberg.com/news/articles/2017-12-13/undersea-cable-project-shows-china-s-interest-in-warming-arctic.

[89] James Kynge, "Chinese Purchases of Overseas Ports Top $20bn in Past Year," *Financial Times*, July 16, 2017, https://www.ft.com/content/e00fcfd4-6883-11e7-8526-7b38dcaef614.

due to community opposition to uranium mining, political opposition to any influx of Chinese workers, and the high costs of development. The Danish government also blocked a puzzling effort by the General Nice Company, a loss-making iron and mining company, to buy the Grønnedal naval base, used by the United States during World War II. The Danish military closed the site in 2014 and then decided to reopen it in 2017 as a strategic and logistics base.[90]

While Chinese officials and analysts have been cautiously avoiding discussion of Greenland's political future, China's approach to the Nordic states is in keeping with its general approach to Europe. China has successfully taken advantage of strains within the EU, as well as differences between NATO and non-NATO members and EU and non-EU countries. According to a 2018 report, it seeks a stable but pliant and fragmented Europe.[91] This strategy is at work in the Arctic as well. As noted above, China signed its first FTA in Europe with Iceland, a non-EU state, and has assiduously courted Finland, a non-NATO country and neighbor of Russia. The Trump administration's belligerence toward Europe may make China an even more attractive partner at a time of heightened EU-Russia tension. Only Sweden is experiencing difficulties with China as a result of protests over the kidnapping of a Swedish national.

Nonetheless, economic trends and domestic political factors in the Arctic states will restrict the pace and scope of Chinese investment. For example, although a development-friendly party achieved a large majority in the April 2018 elections in Greenland, low commodity prices are an obstacle to several mining projects, including the Citronen Fjord zinc project, owned by the Australian company Ironbark. China Nonferrous Metals was supposed to build the mine, most likely with Chinese workers (at least initially), but the low price of zinc due to a global glut has led to delays.

China is playing a long game in the Arctic, slowly building up its presence, scientific capacity, and naval capabilities in anticipation of future economic bounties as the ice recedes. China has had to tread carefully as an outsider, however "near-Arctic" it claims to be, because even small steps by Chinese investors could have a big impact on small Arctic states. While somewhat wary of China's intentions and protective of its own status as an Arctic littoral state, Russia has provided an important entry point, via transit through the NSR and investment opportunities in the Russian Arctic.

---

[90] Jichang Lulu, "China, Greenland and Competition for the Arctic," Asia Dialogue, January 2, 2017, http://theasiadialogue.com/2017/01/02/china-greenland-and-competition-for-the-arctic.

[91] Thorsten Benner et al., "Authoritarian Advance: Responding to China's Growing Political Influence in Europe," Global Public Policy Institute and Mercator Institute for China Studies, February 2018, 6, https://www.merics.org/sites/default/files/2018-02/GPPi_MERICS_Authoritarian_Advance_2018_1.pdf.

Nonetheless, China has to balance its aspirations with the need to be mindful of Russian sensitivities on Arctic issues.

Conclusion

Implications for China's Great-Power Ambitions

When we typically think of China's rise as a great power we consider its role on the global stage, not its behavior on the peripheries. However, China's ambitions in the partnership with Russia and in the Arctic have a lot to say about its global aspirations. The Sino-Russian partnership has proved to be an important testing ground for Chinese foreign policy conceptions, and together the two countries have sought to challenge the United States in Asia and the Western order more broadly. For example, the new concept of great-power relations, typically ascribed to Xi's view of U.S.-China relations, was first discussed in the context of Sino-Russian relations.

While not operating in lockstep on all questions, China and Russia often act in parallel in ways that complicate U.S. foreign policy. Together they have sought to put their own imprimatur on global governance, advancing joint initiatives at the United Nations in support of information sovereignty and in opposition to the broad application of human rights norms such as the responsibility to protect. They have projected their own "sharp power" to take advantage of the vulnerabilities of open democracies and expand their own influence at the expense of democratic norms. As James Steinberg argues, the Sino-Russian partnership presents a greater challenge than the sum of their joint capabilities in that it emboldens the two countries to challenge Western interests and legitimates the existence of what Richard Ellings and Robert Sutter have termed a new "authoritarian axis" confronting the West.[92]

Nonetheless, differences between the two partners are sufficient to serve as a constraint to Chinese regional ambitions, even as Russia supports them globally. The military wherewithal that China has obtained over the years from Russia has enabled China to expand its reach well beyond its borders, but in the interest of maintaining the partnership with Russia, Xi will need to limit his ambitions in areas of key concern to Putin, such as Central Asia and the Arctic. Even in Asia, Russia has provided at best only qualified support and has traditionally developed relations with China's regional opponents, such as India and Vietnam. Countries that are uneasy about China's expanding reach,

---

[92] James B. Steinberg, "China-Russia Cooperation: How Should the United States Respond?" in *Axis of Authoritarians: Implications of China-Russia Cooperation*, ed. Richard J. Ellings and Robert Sutter (Seattle: National Bureau of Asian Research [NBR], 2018), 160–61; and Ellings and Sutter, eds., *Axis of Authoritarians*.

such as Myanmar and Malaysia, have also been expanding their relations with Russia.

The partnership with Russia has enabled China to reduce its own vulnerabilities. Thanks to Russia, China has been able to modernize its military, especially in the 1990s, a time when international sanctions prevented it from purchasing weapons from most other countries. Although China increasingly produces a growing share of its own military technology, it continues to depend on Russia for key systems that are important for its goals vis-à-vis Taiwan and the South China Sea.

A broader limitation involves the differing conceptions of economic integration in the two countries, with Russia turning inward with the EEU, and China looking outward with BRI. While Xi has been mindful of Russian sensitivities, choosing to include Russia within the initiative (after initially circumventing it) and then seeking to find some *modus vivendi* between BRI and the EEU, China will still need to tread carefully on Russia's peripheries. This has been true of the Russian Far East as well, where China hoped to encourage regional integration, while Russia has sought to limit Chinese inroads, even to its own detriment.

For China, the Arctic is a promised land of untapped resources and an opportunity to exert its influence in global governance, yet these benefits are largely promised to insiders. However loudly China proclaims itself to be a near-Arctic state, it nonetheless has to demonstrate its presence through economic, scientific, and political activities. These same activities raise concerns among Arctic states about China's intentions and willingness to accept the status quo, which for Russia means the authority to administer currently ice-covered waterways. The Arctic is not a static environment, however, and its melting ice will have profound political consequences as well as environmental ones.

For Xi, the Arctic and polar regions more broadly are the testing grounds for his global ambitions, both as a maritime power and as a participant in the development of new forms of global governance. Two of Xi's landmark concepts, used at the 19th Party Congress and now inscribed in the Chinese Communist Party's constitution, have been applied to the Arctic. China has sought to justify its role in the Arctic in order to contribute to the "shared future of mankind." Xi also endeavored to enlist Putin's cooperation with China's Arctic agenda by promising to build a joint polar Silk Road, thereby creating an Arctic route in his signature Belt and Road Initiative.

When viewed together, China's Russia policy and its Arctic strategy reveal a quest for great-power status that is more than just an effort to improve and enhance Chinese capabilities. What these two policy areas have in common is that they show that for China to be a global player means to have a voice in global governance.

Implications for the United States

Where the Sino-Russian partnership has succeeded mostly on the global level, and to a lesser extent in Europe and Asia, is in projecting a sense of common purpose and parallelism of action, which contrasts greatly with the fractious behavior of the United States in particular and Western countries as a whole. U.S. officials have struggled to make sense of the Sino-Russian partnership, and U.S. policy has tended to vacillate between two extreme positions. One view, expressed in the Trump administration's National Security Strategy, sees the United States pitted against a Sino-Russian bloc, whereas the other downplays the challenge of the Sino-Russian partnership because of differences between the two countries. Proponents of the first view argue that because the partnership is strengthening, the United States needs to counter it, and the only solution is to build up U.S. strength to counter this resurrected axis. A greater show of U.S. military might, they contend, would both deter and weaken Sino-Russian efforts to weaken U.S. positions. By contrast, others argue that Sino-Russian relations are a marriage of convenience, with more appearance of congruence than reality due to unabated historical differences and Russia's inferior economic position. Members of this group disagree over which country poses the greater threat to U.S. interests and seek to exert leverage over the more threatening state by accommodating the other.[93]

Neither of these approaches is likely to bear fruit, however, and both are rooted in past conceptions of world order that no longer apply (i.e., Cold War–era bipolarity and U.S. primacy of the 1990s). The Sino-Russian partnership is not a result of U.S. policies or policy failures but of their own shared interests and values. Thus, efforts to weaken the partnership by sanctions on Chinese military entities that purchase Russian weapons are unlikely to lead to any change in Sino-Russian military cooperation.

The question is often posed whether the United States should tilt toward Russia or China in an effort to weaken their partnership.[94] Those experts who see a greater threat from China urge greater accommodation of Russia, while those who focus on the benefits of an improved Sino-U.S. relationship argue for greater accommodation there. Nonetheless, such maneuvering by the West is unlikely to alter the domestic drivers of the Sino-Russian partnership,

---

[93] Robert Sutter, "China-Russia Relations: Strategic Implications and U.S. Policy Options," NBR, NBR Special Report, no. 73, September 2018, 17–19.

[94] Ibid.

which reflect enduring national interests and shared identities and are largely unrelated to U.S. policy choices.

For the Trump administration, the solution has been to refocus on building U.S. strength and confronting both China and Russia simultaneously. While there may be merit to enhancing U.S. capabilities where they are lacking and pushing back against various Chinese and Russian actions that challenge U.S. interests, there is little sense of priority or understanding of the need to pursue the shared interests that the United States nonetheless has with states it considers its opponents, not to mention its allies. The underlying problem for current U.S. policy is a lack of coordination with allies and engagement with multilateral institutions. This is all the more important at a time when the international community faces an increasing number of transnational threats and challenges from nonstate actors that defy state-centric logics.

China has become more involved with multilateral economic institutions of its own creation, though primarily it has been using funding from BRI and state institutions to deepen bilateral economic partnerships, largely at the expense of regional political unity and economic transparency. Here the United States needs to encourage China to work within existing multilateral governance structures and prevent its money diplomacy from filling governance gaps. To counteract this trend in the Arctic, Mark Rosen and Cara Thuringer have proposed the development of a code of conduct to govern investment in the Arctic and the creation of a multilateral Arctic Development Bank, patterned on the European Investment Bank.[95] China has aptly capitalized on the need in the Arctic for infrastructure investments, and a regional framework, led by Arctic states, would ensure that development proceeds in a transparent way and in the interests of the sustainable development of the Arctic states rather than to the primary benefit of outside investors.

In the Arctic, a focus on building U.S. capabilities, not just icebreakers but also transportation and communications infrastructure, should accompany an equal effort to engage with allies, participate in multilateral institutions, and develop new approaches to governance as climate change brings about new challenges in the region. The ratification of UNCLOS would also enable the United States to defend its sovereignty and give it greater credibility in meeting challenges elsewhere, such as China's position on the South China Sea.

As in the response to the Sino-Russian partnership, the alliances and institutions that the United States has developed in the last half century

---

[95] Mark E. Rosen and Cara B. Thuringer, "Unconstrained Foreign Direct Investment: An Emerging Challenge to Arctic Security," CNA, November 2017, 62–65.

are sources of strength that China lacks in the Arctic and globally. Despite China's great-power aspirations and growing capabilities, it faces a lonely struggle to become a global power, with only Russia at its side, and then sometimes only agreeing to disagree. With a greater focus on collaborating with allies and providing leadership in global and regional multilateral institutions, the United States would be in a much stronger position to address the challenges that China will pose, both with Russia and in the Arctic, as it pursues its quest for great-power status.

EXECUTIVE SUMMARY

This chapter examines China's efforts to expand its influence in Northeast Asia and its strategies toward South Korea, North Korea, Japan, and the East China Sea.

MAIN ARGUMENT

China seeks to build a Northeast Asian regional order centered on economic development in which it enjoys superiority across all dimensions and can freely protect its interests while retaining the respect and support of its neighbors. It is working to achieve these objectives through: (1) a public diplomacy strategy that aims to win support for its great-power ambitions, (2) an economic strategy that draws regional states into Chinese-led initiatives, and (3) a security strategy based on expanding military capabilities, strengthening territorial claims in the East China Sea, and weakening the U.S.-led alliance system. On the Korean Peninsula, Beijing seeks to maintain stability, draw Seoul away from the U.S., and keep Pyongyang closely aligned with it. China desires stable economic relations with Japan but also views Tokyo as its primary regional competitor that must be prevented from assuming a greater security role in the region.

POLICY IMPLICATIONS

- To retain influence in Northeast Asia and check destabilizing Chinese behavior, the U.S. must continue to strengthen its alliances with South Korea and Japan and advance a comprehensive and positive strategy for the region that focuses not just on balancing against China.

- To compete with China and signal commitment to the region, the U.S. must demonstrate both military and economic engagement, and continue to reaffirm the values of democratic governance, political freedom, and rule of law that have long underpinned U.S. soft power.

- The U.S. should leverage China's desire for stability by working with U.S. allies to discourage Beijing from pursuing disruptive policies and to encourage its cooperation on regional and global challenges.

China's Quest for Influence in Northeast Asia: The Korean Peninsula, Japan, and the East China Sea

Patricia M. Kim

Northeast Asia is arguably the region that is and will remain the most consequential for China's trajectory for the foreseeable future. China shares this neighborhood with Japan and the Republic of Korea (ROK, or South Korea), two states that are not only among Beijing's largest trading partners but close allies of the United States with the ability to balance against China's growing power. Also in this region is the Democratic People's Republic of Korea (DPRK, or North Korea), a state with which China shares a border and a complex history, and that ranks among the international community's top concerns due to the DPRK's advanced nuclear weapons program. North Korea has long been a source of instability at China's doorstep, and the resolution of the nuclear crisis on the Korean Peninsula, peaceful or otherwise, will have significant consequences for China and the region. Finally, the East China Sea is a critical source of contestation with overlapping territorial claims and ongoing struggles for control. Northeast Asia, in short, is a region filled with both opportunities and pitfalls that could benefit or hold back China in its quest to become a global power.

China's primary objectives in Northeast Asia consist of expanding its influence and respect for its preferences among neighboring countries; becoming the region's greatest power across all dimensions, from military and economic capabilities to soft power; and maintaining stability so as not to jeopardize its rise. Beijing seeks to accomplish these goals

Patricia M. Kim is a Senior Policy Analyst at the United States Institute of Peace. She can be reached at <pkim@usip.org>.

through (1) a vigorous public diplomacy strategy emphasizing China's indispensability for regional prosperity and its desire to create a "new type" of regional order that prioritizes economic development and noninterference, (2) an economic strategy that draws states into Chinese-led initiatives, and (3) a security strategy concerned with increasing the regional and global power-projection capabilities of the People's Liberation Army (PLA), strengthening China's territorial claims, and preventing the expansion of, and when possible rolling back, the U.S. presence and alliance system in Asia.

More specifically, China's primary objectives on the Korean Peninsula are maintaining stability and preventing war. Beijing sees Seoul as an ideal target to woo away from the U.S.-led alliance system given South Korea's extensive economic dependence on China, geographic proximity, and desire for Beijing's cooperation in reaching peace on the Korean Peninsula. As such, China believes that it can cultivate its ties with the ROK and weaken the country's alliance with the United States. China sees North Korea as a necessary ally despite their tumultuous bilateral history. It seeks to keep Pyongyang closely aligned by shielding North Korea from international pressure and serving as its primary conduit for economic development and integration into the region.

China views Japan, on the other hand, as its primary competitor in Northeast Asia. Its principal objectives with regard to Japan include maintaining relatively stable economic relations given their mutual economic interdependence as well as the growing uncertainty caused by the trade war and general economic friction between the United States and China. At the same time, China seeks to prevent Japan from expanding its military capabilities and its participation in providing regional security. In the East China Sea, China continues to increase its presence and military operations to strengthen its maritime sovereignty claims. This has led to increased tension and clashes at times with Tokyo, as well as with Seoul, over long-standing territorial disputes.

The direction and success of China's Northeast Asia strategy will be affected by both developments in its domestic political arena and the responses of regional actors. While a major crisis or economic downturn at home could force Chinese leaders to turn inward, they are more likely to continue efforts to deepen Beijing's involvement and influence in the region given the declared goal of the Chinese Communist Party (CCP) of transforming China into a world-class power by 2049. As the status quo power and traditional security provider in Northeast Asia, the United States' response to China's quest for influence will also play a decisive role in regional outcomes. Whether Washington demonstrates willingness to remain engaged in the region and leads efforts to check Beijing's destabilizing behavior will have a significant impact on the range of options available to Japan, South Korea, and even North Korea as they contemplate their own strategies toward China.

The chapter begins with an overview first of China's general strategy and activities in Northeast Asia, as well as its specific strategies toward South Korea, North Korea, and Japan. It then discusses factors that may aid or hinder China's attempt to achieve its objectives in the region and the implications of its success or lack thereof for the United States and Northeast Asia. The chapter concludes with policy recommendations based on these findings.

China's General Strategy in Northeast Asia

Under the leadership of President Xi Jinping, the CCP has largely set aside Deng Xiaoping's maxim of "keeping a low profile" (*taoguang yanghui*) to embrace a more confident and assertive role in its immediate neighborhood and beyond. According to Xi, China is now at a "historical juncture" in which it can reach for the "great rejuvenation of the Chinese nation."[1] The quest for greatness includes expanding China's leadership role in the world and protecting its "core national interests," while preventing instability that can endanger its continued rise. Beijing ultimately seeks a Northeast Asian order in which it enjoys superiority across all dimensions and can freely protect its interests while retaining the respect and support of its neighbors.

Public Diplomacy Campaign

Since the beginning of Xi's tenure, Chinese leaders have launched a vigorous public diplomacy campaign that emphasizes China's indispensability for the region's prosperity and peace, and its drive for a "new type of international relations." First, Beijing has sought to cultivate a positive image by promoting the narrative that China's economic success is good for the entire region. Chinese leaders like to emphasize, for instance, that while China's development depends on the East Asia region, the region's prosperity is also impossible without China.[2] According to the country's most recent white paper detailing its Asia-Pacific strategy, "the Chinese people are working hard to realize the Chinese dream of the great renewal of the Chinese

---

[1] "Xi Urges Breaking New Ground in Major Country Diplomacy with Chinese Characteristics," Xinhua, June 24, 2018, http://www.xinhuanet.com/english/2018-06/24/c_137276269.htm.

[2] Xi Jinping, "Shenhua gaige kaifang, gongchuang meihao Yatai" [Deepen Reform and Opening, Work Together for a Better Asia-Pacific], in *Xi Jinping tan zhiguo lizheng di yi juan* [Xi Jinping on the Governance of China, Volume 1] (Beijing: Wai wen chubanshe, 2014).

nation" and "this process will bring greater opportunities and benefits" for everyone.[3] This logic of "win-win cooperation" underpins China's regional grand strategy and is seen by Chinese leaders as the answer to creating a friendly and conducive environment for the country's rise.

In addition to stressing China's centrality for the region's economic prospects, Chinese leaders also argue that its rise should not be feared but welcomed by others because the country will practice great-power diplomacy with Chinese characteristics. This approach to diplomacy, as defined by President Xi and Foreign Minister Wang Yi at the 19th Party Congress, eschews the "traditional model" of power politics in which the strong bully the weak and seeks instead to build a "community of common destiny."[4] Chinese leaders also like to emphasize that states should pursue multilateralism and partnerships instead of alliances, which they insist are vestiges of the Cold War. They argue that "small- and medium-sized countries need not and should not take sides among big countries."[5] When speaking specifically to an Asian audience, Xi has advocated for an "Asian security concept" that takes into account Asia's "unique characteristics." He reasons that because of the diverse nature of the region, which includes states with different political systems, religions, and cultures, it is best to practice the "principle of noninterference." This principle demands that states should refrain from critiquing the internal political system of other states, while respecting each other's security interests and using dialogue to resolve differences.[6] In recent years, Chinese leaders have even begun to describe China's foreign policy as not only distinct but aimed at "occupy[ing] the commanding heights of

---

[3] Information Office of the State Council of the People's Republic of China (PRC), *China's Policies on Asia-Pacific Security Cooperation* (Beijing, January 2017), https://www.fmprc.gov.cn/mfa_eng/zxxx_662805/t1429771.shtml.

[4] Xi Jinping, "Report at the 19th Communist Party of China National Congress," 18th Central Committee of the Chinese Communist Party, October 18, 2017, http://www.china.org.cn/chinese/2017-11/06/content_41852215.htm; and Wang Yi, "Wang Yi tan xinshidai Zhongguo tese daguo waijiao zongmubiao: tuidong goujian renlei mingyun gongtongti" [Wang Yi Discusses the General Goal of Great-Power Diplomacy with Chinese Characteristics: Promoting the Construction of a Community of Common Destiny], October 19, 2017, http://www.fmprc.gov.cn/web/zyxw/t1503111.shtml.

[5] For example, see Xi Jinping's keynote address at the opening of the 2018 Boao Forum for Asia, Hainan, April 10, 2018, https://www.uscnpm.org/blog/2018/04/11/transcript-president-xi-addresses-2018-boao-forum-asia-hainan; Information Office of the State Council (PRC), *China's Policies on Asia-Pacific Security Cooperation*; and Zheng Zeguang, "Major-Country Diplomacy with Chinese Characteristics in the New Era," *China International Studies*, no. 70 (2018).

[6] See Xi Jinping, "New Asian Security Concept for New Progress in Security Cooperation" (opening speech at the Conference on Interaction and Confidence-Building Measures in Asia, Shanghai, May 21, 2014), https://www.fmprc.gov.cn/mfa_eng/zxxx_662805/t1159951.shtml; and "Xi Jinping jiu 'Yazhou anquan guan' zuochu naxie xinlunshu?" [What New Discourse Does Xi Jinping's "Asia Security Concept" Bring About?], Xinhua, April 29, 2016, http://www.xinhuanet.com/world/2016-04/29/c_128944821.htm.

human morality" by "building peace, security, common prosperity, openness and tolerance, and a world that is clean and beautiful."[7]

Despite these lofty descriptions of itself as a different kind of great power with noble intentions, China often fails to live up to its own standards. As will be discussed below, it often utilizes hard power, from its economic leverage to military capabilities, to try to influence the policy choices of neighboring countries. As a result, China's grand intentions have been met with general skepticism and its public diplomacy campaign has yet to win Beijing the region's full support.

Economic Initiatives

Under Xi's tenure, China has taken significant steps to operationalize its pledge to bring about regional prosperity. It has launched massive initiatives such as the Asian Infrastructure Investment Bank (AIIB) and the Belt and Road Initiative (BRI) in recent years, with the aim of placing China squarely in the center of the regional economy. The primary recipients of Chinese investment, however, are developing states outside Northeast Asia as Japan and South Korea are both developed economies and China's competitors in many industries. Both countries, nonetheless, have expressed interest in participating in Chinese initiatives with the hopes of pursuing joint development projects in third countries for the benefit of their domestic companies. Needless to say, Beijing has welcomed their participation, given its desire to draw its neighbors into China's economic orbit.[8]

Despite enthusiasm for bilateral and multilateral economic cooperation between China, Japan, and South Korea, the momentum for cooperation has ebbed and flowed over the years primarily due to conflicts in the security realm. For instance, when Beijing initially proposed the creation of the AIIB and invited South Korea and Japan to join, they both hesitated. The former joined at the last minute as a founding member in 2015, while the latter is still considering membership.[9] Their reluctance was due in large part to the United States lobbying its allies not to join out of concern that the AIIB would fail to meet international standards and undercut existing institutions like the World

---

[7] Yi, "Wang Yi tan xinshidai Zhongguo tese daguo waijiao zongmubiao: Tuidong goujian renlei mingyun gongtongti."

[8] China's bilateral economic relationships with South Korea, North Korea, and Japan and their strategic implications will be covered in greater detail below.

[9] "Xi Wants Japan in AIIB as Beijing and Tokyo Mend Fences," *Nikkei Asian Review*, May 17, 2017, https://asia.nikkei.com/Politics/Xi-wants-Japan-in-AIIB-as-Beijing-and-Tokyo-mend-fences.

Bank and the Asian Development Bank.[10] In addition, China's bilateral relations with the two states were not particularly warm at the time because of tensions in the security realm. Beijing and Seoul were embroiled in a dispute over the pending deployment on South Korean territory of a U.S. missile defense system known as Terminal High Altitude Area Defense (THAAD). Similarly, relations between Beijing and Tokyo had grown tense over their ongoing standoff over the Senkaku Islands (known as the Diaoyu Islands in China).

Despite serious conflicts in the security realm, the economic benefits of cooperating with China and joining its massive economic initiatives continue to incentivize South Korea and Japan to explore ways to work with China. The strong desire to secure opportunities for its infrastructure and manufacturing sectors motivated Seoul's decision to break ranks with Washington and join the AIIB, following other U.S. allies like Britain and Germany. Since coming into power in May 2017, the Moon Jae-in administration has repeatedly expressed its desire to pursue economic cooperation with China. It believes that working with China is not only essential for South Korea's economy but necessary to draw North Korea out of its isolation and firmly integrate it into the global economy.[11] Tokyo is also moving to join the AIIB and participate in BRI projects following a recent thaw in relations with Beijing. In June 2018, Prime Minister Shinzo Abe officially signaled in a speech that Japan was "ready to extend cooperation" on BRI and took a delegation of more than five hundred business leaders to Beijing during his visit to the Chinese capital in late October 2018.[12]

China, Japan, and South Korea have also pursued a trilateral free trade agreement (FTA) since March 2013. Despite all sides agreeing on the benefits of a trilateral FTA, the momentum has stalled over the years due to ongoing tensions over territorial disputes, especially between China and Japan, and over historical issues, especially between South Korea and Japan. In May 2018, Premier Li Keqiang, Prime Minister Abe, and President Moon met for a trilateral summit in Tokyo for the first time in two years. The three

---

[10] Jane Perlez, "U.S. Opposing China's Answer to World Bank," *New York Times*, October 9, 2014, https://www.nytimes.com/2014/10/10/world/asia/chinas-plan-for-regional-development-bank-runs-into-us-opposition.html.

[11] "S. Korean Leader Urges Increased Business Cooperation between S. Korea, China," Yonhap, December 16, 2017, http://english.yonhapnews.co.kr/news/2017/12/16/0200000000A EN20171216001751315.html.

[12] "Japan and 'One Belt, One Road,'" *Japan Times*, June 24, 2018, https://www.japantimes.co.jp/opinion/2017/06/24/editorials/japan-one-belt-one-road/#.W2CxlhJKi9Y; Isabel Reynolds, Takashi Hirokawa, and Emi Nobuhiro, "Japan Could Still Join China Infrastructure Bank, Abe Ally Says," Bloomberg, December 6, 2017, https://www.bloomberg.com/news/articles/2017-12-06/japan-could-still-join-china-infrastructure-bank-abe-ally-says; and Yohei Muramatsu, "Japan's Jumbo Delegation Racks Up China Deals, with Eye on Trump," *Nikkei Asian Review*, October 27, 2018, https://asia.nikkei.com/Politics/International-Relations/Japan-s-jumbo-delegation-racks-up-China-deals-with-eye-on-Trump.

leaders promised to expand economic ties by invigorating negotiations for a trilateral FTA. Premier Li also used the opportunity to rebuke the Trump administration's "America first" approach to trade, calling on the three states to stand "firmly together" to defend the "rules-based multilateral free trade system" and oppose "trade protectionism and unilateralism."[13]

While it remains to be seen whether another flare-up in the security or political realms will undo the forward momentum for economic cooperation between the three states, Beijing has already achieved half of its objective, having convinced Tokyo and Seoul of the benefit of participating in Chinese-led initiatives. Moreover, China has doubled down on maintaining progress with its neighbors in recent months in light of its growing trade war with the United States and the desire to stabilize its other bilateral relationships. As one recent *Global Times* article put it, the trilateral FTA and general economic cooperation among China, Japan, and South Korea will pave the way for an "Asia for Asians."[14]

Finally, North Korea has yet to explicitly join or benefit from China's signature economic initiatives due to the ongoing nuclear crisis and associated sanctions. Beijing and Seoul, however, are eager to integrate the DPRK into the regional economy through infrastructure projects and various joint development initiatives. Chinese and ROK leaders firmly believe, as will be discussed further below, that North Korea's economic opening and integration into the region are key to establishing peace on the Korean Peninsula.

Security Strategy

In addition to a proactive diplomatic and economic campaign to increase its influence in the region, China has ambitious plans to advance its military capabilities and create a favorable security environment for itself. Xi has explicitly tasked the PLA to complete military reform and modernization by 2035 and to become a world-class military by 2050 as part of China's "national rejuvenation" efforts.[15] The most recent white paper on China's Asia-Pacific strategy also clearly states the goal of building military capabilities that are "commensurate with China's international standing," are adequate for protecting its interests, and provide a "strong guarantee" for the country's continued rise. In addition, the white paper signals that China is no longer exclusively interested in self-defense but intends to take

---

[13] "China Urges Accelerating China-Japan-S. Korea FTA Talks, Proposes New Cooperation Mode," Xinhua, May 9, 2018, http://www.xinhuanet.com/english/2018-05/09/c_137166858.htm.

[14] Ding Gang, "China-Japan-SK FTA Key to 'Asia for Asians,'" *Global Times*, September 26, 2018, http://www.globaltimes.cn/content/1121035.shtml.

[15] See Xi, "Report at the 19th Communist Party of China National Congress."

on "greater responsibilities" and "provide public security services to the Asia-Pacific region and the world," although it has yet to articulate precisely how it seeks to do this.[16] During Xi's tenure, the PLA has undertaken significant modernization efforts. Some of the measures have included increasing the size of the navy and air force, reducing ground troops by 300,000, creating five new theater commands to boost joint operations capabilities, and establishing the Strategic Support Force, which focuses on space, cyber, and electronic warfare.[17]

Along with this boost in general capabilities, the PLA has increased its military presence in the East and South China Seas. As Xi's work report at the 19th Party Congress clearly indicated, China intends to become a "strong maritime country" through "coordinated land and marine development."[18] As part of this push, it declared an air defense identification zone (ADIZ) in November 2013 in the East China Sea, where it has territorial disputes with both Japan and South Korea. Since then, China has significantly increased its naval and air presence, sending maritime law-enforcement ships and aircraft regularly into disputed zones to assert its sovereignty claims.[19] As Oriana Skylar Mastro writes in the previous volume of *Strategic Asia*, the PLA's modernization efforts and activities all point toward China's interest in strengthening its regional power projection capabilities.[20]

In addition to upgrading its military capabilities, China has sought to create a more favorable security environment by opposing any strengthening of the U.S. alliance system. Chinese leaders routinely protest that the United States and its allies are trying to contain China, and a majority of Chinese citizens agree that the United States is attempting to block the country's rise.[21]

---

[16] Information Office of the State Council (PRC), *China's Policies on Asia-Pacific Security Cooperation*.

[17] For more on China's military modernization, see Patricia M. Kim, "Understanding China's Military Expansion and Implications for U.S. Policy," testimony before the House Permanent Select Committee on Intelligence, Washington, D.C., May 17, 2018, available at https://www.cfr.org/report/understanding-chinas-military-expansion-and-implications-us-policy; Joel Wuthnow and Phillip C. Saunders, *China's Military Reforms in the Age of Xi Jinping: Drivers, Challenges, and Implications*, China Strategic Perspectives, no. 10 (Washington, D.C.: National Defense University Press, 2017); Oriana Skylar Mastro, "Ideas, Perceptions, and Power: An Examination of China's Military Strategy," in *Strategic Asia 2017–18: Power, Ideas, and Military Strategy in the Asia-Pacific*, ed. Ashley J. Tellis, Alison Szalwinski, and Michael Wills (Seattle: National Bureau of Asian Research, 2017), 19–43; and Ronald O'Rourke, "China Naval Modernization: Implications for U.S. Navy Capabilities—Background and Issues for Congress," Congressional Research Service, CRS Report for Congress, RL 33153, December 13, 2017.

[18] See Xi, "Report at the 19th Communist Party of China National Congress."

[19] For more details on China's ADIZ, see Edmund J. Burke and Astrid Stuth Cevallos, *In Line or Out of Order? China's Approach to ADIZ in Theory and Practice* (Santa Monica: RAND Corporation, 2017).

[20] Mastro, "Ideas, Perceptions and Power," 24–27.

[21] Richard Wike, "6 Facts about How Americans and Chinese See Each Other," Pew Research Center, March 30, 2016, http://www.pewresearch.org/fact-tank/2016/03/30/6-facts-about-how-americans-and-chinese-see-each-other.

According to the latest defense white paper released by Beijing in 2015, the United States' efforts to enhance its military presence and alliances in the region are issues of "grave concern."[22]

Chinese leaders are particularly sensitive about the rise of a U.S.-led missile defense system in the region that could be used to limit China's capabilities during a contingency in the East and South China Seas. They complain that a boost in U.S. missile defense capabilities will negate China's relatively small nuclear arsenal and embolden the United States to do as it wishes in the Asia-Pacific without having to worry about sparking a nuclear war with China. Because China's nuclear doctrine is premised on maintaining a minimum nuclear deterrent with a second-strike capability, Chinese strategists insist that the expansion of the United States' missile defense gives China no choice but to enhance its own retaliatory-strike capabilities instead of focusing on disarmament.[23] According to the white paper on Asia-Pacific strategy, "Cold War style military alliances" and global and regional missile systems are to blame for decreasing strategic stability and mutual trust in the region.[24] In addition to regularly repeating this message at diplomatic venues, Beijing has used its economic leverage to deter the expansion of a U.S.-led missile defense system, with South Korea experiencing significant economic retaliation for allowing U.S. Forces Korea to deploy THAAD batteries to ROK territory.

China has also tried to dilute the importance of the U.S. alliance system in Northeast Asia and to increase its own influence by calling on states to prioritize the use of multilateral mechanisms as the primary means to address regional issues. For instance, Beijing has been an ardent advocate of the six-party talks as the appropriate mechanism to resolve the DPRK nuclear crisis. The talks, which were first hosted by Beijing in 2003, have been suspended since 2009 due to North Korea's nuclear and missile tests and the lack of progress in negotiations. While most of the other participants long lost faith in the format, Beijing insisted until recently that all six parties should return to the talks.[25] A large part of China's interest in this multilateral mechanism is rooted in its desire not to be sidelined from developments on

---

[22] Information Office of the State Council (PRC), *China's Military Strategy* (Beijing, May 2015), http://english.gov.cn/archive/white_paper/2015/05/27/content_281475115610833.htm.

[23] For an overview of China's nuclear posture, see Patricia M. Kim, "Chinese Perceptions on Nuclear Weapons, Arms Control, and Nonproliferation," testimony before the Subcommittee on Terrorism, Nonproliferation, and Trade, U.S. House Foreign Affairs Committee, June 21, 2018, https://docs.house.gov/meetings/FA/FA18/20180621/108459/HHRG-115-FA18-Wstate-KimP-20180621.pdf.

[24] Information Office of the State Council (PRC), *China's Policies on Asia-Pacific Security Cooperation.*

[25] See PRC, "Position Paper of the People's Republic of China for the 72nd Session of the United Nations General Assembly," September 12, 2017, 4–6, http://www.fmprc.gov.cn/mfa_eng/zxxx_662805/P020170904435053466190.pdf.

the Korean Peninsula, since any negotiated agreements will have significant consequences for China's immediate security environment.[26]

China's Ideal Order in Northeast Asia

When China's diplomatic, economic, and security strategies toward the region are examined together, a general picture emerges of the kind of order that Beijing seeks to create in Northeast Asia. First, it seeks a stable neighborhood in which China is the greatest power across all dimensions, and neighbors, whether individually or in an alliance, cannot challenge its primacy. This is why Beijing opposes any efforts by Japan, a neighbor with the potential to be a true peer competitor, to expand its military capabilities or role in contributing to regional security. This is also why Beijing seeks to weaken the United States' alliances with South Korea and Japan and to prevent trilateral cooperation between these three states. China, in short, wants the freedom to advance its interests—from asserting its claims over disputed maritime territories to pursuing reunification in some form with Taiwan—without facing a balancing response from its neighbors.

Despite its desire for regional supremacy, China seems to have no intention of taking over the United States' traditional model of providing security for the region. Instead, Beijing rather wishfully envisions a conflict-free Northeast Asia where all countries peacefully pursue economic development together and leave politics off the table. This is precisely the kind of neighborhood that the CCP finds safe—a region in which no country questions the domestic political system of others.

Finally, China seeks to be a central and indispensable economic player in the region so that states have no choice but to adjust their policies to accommodate its interests. In addition, China wants not only to be accommodated because of its economic importance, but to be respected and liked by its neighbors for practicing a "different" type of great power diplomacy that brings about "win-win benefits" to all.

---

[26] In addition to the six-party talks, the China-Japan-ROK Trilateral Summit mechanism is in theory the primary venue for trilateral dialogue and cooperation among the three major powers of Northeast Asia. This summit series, which first began in December 2008, was devised to discuss regional security, trilateral economic cooperation, and other relevant issues. In practice, however, the summits have yet to yield any significant agreements or outcomes, with the three sides forgoing meetings from 2013 to 2014 and again from 2016 to 2017 due to various historical and territorial disputes. The leaders of the three states agreed at the latest summit in Tokyo in May 2018 to hold meetings on "a regular basis" and to deepen trilateral cooperation. Nonetheless, this particular trilateral mechanism is unlikely to take precedence over Japan's and South Korea's respective coordination with the United States anytime soon, given the overwhelming importance of their alliances for security, as well as the reality that the deep-rooted historical and territorial disputes among the three states are not likely to be fully resolved in the near future.

In short, Beijing seeks an alliance-free Northeast Asia that it can rule as a benevolent hegemon among admiring neighbors. This idealized vision clearly has many contradictory elements. For instance, the region somehow remains stable without China stepping in to provide regional security that the United States and its allies have historically provided. Furthermore, in this vision Beijing freely pursues the full range of its strategic interests, while other states refrain from similar behavior and focus solely on regional economic cooperation. And finally, despite unilaterally pursuing its interests, Beijing is well-liked and respected in this ideal world. While Chinese leaders hope to realize all of these conflicting goals, Beijing is most likely to prioritize certain goals over others based on its changing needs and on shifts in the regional environment.

China's Strategy toward Neighboring Countries

South Korea

China's primary objectives on the Korean Peninsula include maintaining stability and preventing war, ensuring that it has a voice in any negotiations about the future of the peninsula, and weakening the United States' influence and presence in the area. With regard to South Korea specifically, Beijing seeks to cultivate Seoul's deference for Chinese preferences and to pull it away from Washington and the broader U.S. alliance system. China sees the ROK as a promising target for such efforts given the two countries' historical ties and geographic proximity, shared historical grievances against Japan, the presence of anti-American sentiment among South Korea's liberal factions, Seoul's awareness of China's importance in resolving the North Korean nuclear crisis, and most significantly, its growing dependence on trade with China.

Despite the ROK's reliance on the United States for its security, its economic prosperity has become largely dependent on China. Since the early 2000s, China has been South Korea's largest trade partner, and as of 2017 is the destination for a quarter of South Korea's total exports.[27] Many South Korean businesses, from street vendors to major conglomerates, have benefited immensely in recent years from Chinese interest in South Korean products, culture, and entertainment. This reality often puts South Korean leaders between a rock and a hard place, having to balance between Washington's and Beijing's conflicting preferences and choose between maximizing either their economic or security interests.

---

[27] From "Republic of Korea," World Trade Organization, Statistics Database, http://stat.wto.org/CountryProfile/WSDBCountryPFView.aspx?Country=KR&Language=F.

China is well aware of this dilemma and has not shied away from using its economic leverage in attempts to influence ROK decision-making. The conflict over the deployment of THAAD serves as a prime illustration of China's strategy in pulling South Korea away from its traditional ally. The THAAD dispute first arose in 2014 when U.S. Forces Korea recommended the missile defense system be deployed to South Korean territory to defend against North Korea's short- and medium-range ballistic missiles. Despite U.S. and ROK assurances that the system would be purely configured to defend against North Korean threats, Beijing protested that THAAD's radar could be used to monitor Chinese airspace and would expand a U.S.-led missile defense system designed to contain China. Beijing reasoned that because THAAD compromised China's own security interests, it was detrimental to "the regional strategic balance" and counterproductive for peace on the Korean Peninsula.[28]

From 2014 onward, China's top leaders, from Xi to his deputies, aggressively lobbied their ROK counterparts to reject THAAD. Seoul, torn between Beijing and Washington, maintained for two years that it had yet to formally review the proposal. Following North Korea's fourth nuclear test and long-range rocket test in 2016, however, Washington and Seoul ultimately decided to deploy the system on South Korean territory. Beijing, as a result, unleashed an extensive economic retaliation campaign, banning Chinese tour groups to the ROK, barring South Korean celebrities and entertainment companies from operating inside China, and increasing regulatory barriers for South Korean firms that rely on the Chinese market. Boycott campaigns against South Korean products by Chinese consumers also had a significant impact on businesses.[29] Despite China's economic retaliation, the South Korean government ultimately stood by its decision to accept the deployment of THAAD, driven in large part by a desire to strengthen the U.S.-ROK alliance amid the DPRK's increasingly aggressive behavior. But the incident sparked debate in South Korea about the costs of the alliance with the United States. Others also reasoned that Seoul should find ways to accommodate

---

[28] Information Office of the State Council (PRC), *China's Policies on Asia-Pacific Security Cooperation.*

[29] Tom Hancock and Wang Xueqiao, "South Korean Consumer Groups Bear Brunt of THAAD Ire," *Financial Times*, August 20, 2017, https://www.ft.com/content/f3c78afe-821d-11e7-94e2-c5b903247afd; and Javier C. Hernández, Owen Guo, and Ryan McMorrow, "South Korean Stores Feel China's Wrath as U.S. Missile System Is Deployed," *New York Times*, March 9, 2017, https://www.nytimes.com/2017/03/09/world/asia/china-lotte-thaad-south-korea.html.

Beijing's demands for the sake of South Korea's economic welfare, as well as progress toward peace on the peninsula.[30]

After months of effort by the newly elected president Moon Jae-in to smooth relations with Beijing, the two sides declared that they would seek a "new start" in bilateral relations at a summit in December 2017. According to Chinese reports, in order to reset relations, Moon assured Xi that South Korea would not join the United States' missile defense network, form a trilateral military alliance with the United States and Japan, or deploy additional THAAD batteries.[31] South Korean officials have insisted that these are not new concessions and are actually long-standing policies that predate the THAAD dispute with China. Beijing, however, has characterized these as new commitments and will most likely use Seoul's words to pressure South Korean leaders when they engage in trilateral activities with the United States and Japan or increase cooperation with the United States on missile defense in the future. In addition, fears of renewed economic retaliation will always hang over Seoul and will continue to factor into its foreign policy decision-making.

Finally, as discussed in the preceding section, China has prioritized asserting its maritime sovereignty claims and continues to increase its presence in the East China Sea. This has led to growing tension between Beijing and Seoul due to their long-standing territorial dispute over a submerged rock known as Socotra Rock, or Ieodo in Korean and Suyan Jiao in Chinese. While South Korea currently exercises administrative control over the rock, both states claim that it falls within their respective exclusive economic zones (EEZs). Since South Korea's construction of a research station on the rock in 2003, China has increased its surveillance activities in the area and included the rock in the ADIZ it declared in the East China Sea in November 2013.[32] While China's incursions into South Korea's ADIZ are less frequent than its incursions into Japan's ADIZ, it nonetheless continues to

---

[30] During the special presidential elections that followed the impeachment of President Park Geun-hye in early 2017, how to handle the row over THAAD and improve relations with China featured as a major topic of debate between the candidates. South Koreans were especially worried at the time that the United States and China would cut a deal regarding the future of the Korean Peninsula without involving Seoul, and saw rapprochement with Beijing as a critical step in ensuring that South Korea's voice would be heard.

[31] "Foreign Ministry Spokesperson Hua Chunying's Regular Press Conference," Ministry of Foreign Affairs (PRC), October 31, 2017, https://www.fmprc.gov.cn/mfa_eng/xwfw_665399/s2510_665401/t1506230.shtml.

[32] China was criticized by many East Asian states for unilaterally declaring the ADIZ and drafting vague rules that seemed to imply that it was creating a no-fly zone for foreign military aircraft across a vast swath of airspace. Following the announcement, Seoul asked for but failed to secure Beijing's agreement to adjust the contours of the ADIZ. South Korea responded by conducting sea and air drills near Socotra Rock and expanding its own ADIZ by 186 miles. For more details on this case, see Michael J. Green et al., *Countering Coercion in Maritime Asia: The Theory and Practice of Gray Zone Deterrence* (Washington, D.C.: Center for Strategic and International Studies, 2017), 148–68.

periodically conduct such exercises. For instance, in December 2017, just days after the summit that reset bilateral relations, five Chinese military aircraft flew near Socotra Rock as part of a "routine training."[33] The move signaled that regardless of overall improvements in bilateral relations, China intends to continue to assert its territorial claims.[34]

China's strategy toward South Korea and especially its efforts to shape Seoul's strategic decisions are unlikely to change in the foreseeable future given South Korea's proximity to China and the fact that it is a major U.S. ally. Even if the U.S.-ROK alliance were to be dissolved—following the denuclearization of North Korea and the establishment of a peace regime on the Korean Peninsula, for instance—China would most likely continue its attempts to influence Seoul's decision-making as it has throughout the history of the two states.

North Korea

China's primary objective with regard to North Korea is to help it become a stable, economically open authoritarian state that remains closely aligned with Beijing. While Chinese leaders want to see a nuclear-free Korean Peninsula, they prioritize stability over the speed of denuclearization. Beijing also seeks to prevent North Korea's drift from its orbit, and endeavors, therefore, to always have a seat at the table in any discussion that involves the future of the Korean Peninsula. Despite the problems North Korea has created for China and the entire region, Beijing continues to view Pyongyang as a necessary ally and seeks to keep it closely aligned by becoming its primary conduit for economic development and integration into the region.

Beijing and Pyongyang's complex relationship stretches back to the start of the Cold War when the two sides fought alongside each other in the Korean War. Despite the fact that Pyongyang benefited immensely from Beijing's support during and after the war, their relationship has always been strained. North Korean leaders have long bristled at what they see as Chinese meddling in their internal affairs, and Chinese leaders have been frustrated

---

[33] Andrew Jeong, "China Flies Military Aircraft into Airspace Claimed by Seoul," *Wall Street Journal*, December 18, 2017, https://www.wsj.com/articles/china-appears-to-provoke-south-korea-with-warplanes-after-summit-1513593977.

[34] In addition to the dispute over Socotra Rock and overlapping ADIZs, the primary source of maritime disputes between Seoul and Beijing involves illegal fishing by Chinese vessels in South Korea's EEZ. Despite an agreement between the two countries signed in 2001, incursions have increased in recent years. Violent standoffs between Chinese fishermen and South Korean Coast Guard officers have led to deaths on both sides. In 2016 an estimated 1,500 Chinese fishing boats illegally operated in South Korea's EEZ. Elizabeth Shim, "U.S. North Korea Bill Could Push China to Scale Back Illegal Fishing," UPI, March 29, 2017, https://www.upi.com/Top_News/World-News/2017/03/29/US-North-Korea-bill-could-push-China-to-scale-back-illegal-fishing/2071490807616.

by North Korea's blatant disregard for China's interests.[35] Today, the DPRK is overwhelmingly economically dependent on China, which accounts for 90% of its total trade volume.[36] In addition, China has long served as North Korea's door to the outside world, with Chinese intermediaries often assisting North Korean entities in evading sanctions.[37]

While Pyongyang has never directly threatened Beijing with its nuclear weapons, North Korea's nuclear program and provocations throughout the years have created numerous headaches for its patron. Specifically, North Korea's nuclear ambitions have undercut Chinese interests by raising the chances of military conflict in the region; exacerbating threat perceptions in Japan and South Korea, leading these states to engage in their own internal balancing and even inspiring calls by some for the need to develop their own nuclear weapons; and sparking fears of radiation among Chinese citizens given the proximity of North Korea's nuclear tests to their shared border. North Korea's open disregard for Chinese interests has sparked a debate inside China in recent years about the wisdom of continuing to shield North Korea. Some Chinese analysts have called on their government to rethink its long-standing tradition of viewing North Korea as a necessary partner.[38]

From the beginning of Xi's tenure, Beijing seemed to be distancing itself from Pyongyang. Xi, for instance, visited Seoul and invited South Korean president Park Geun-hye to Beijing years before meeting with North Korean leader Kim Jong-un. China also supported increasing UN sanctions as North Korea began to conduct nuclear and missile tests under Kim's leadership. In early 2018, however, it quickly returned to its original policy of extolling the "profound revolutionary friendship" between China and North Korea and lending support to Pyongyang's negotiating positions once Kim began his diplomatic outreach in attempts to strike a nuclear deal.[39] In addition to consistently stressing that it will not allow "war and

---

[35] For greater detail on the history of China–North Korea relations, see Patricia M. Kim, "How China Sees North Korea: Three Critical Moments in History and Future Directions," Chicago Council on Global Affairs, January 17, 2018, https://www.thechicagocouncil.org/publication/how-china-sees-north-korea-three-critical-moments-history-and-future-directions.

[36] See Stephen Haggard, "The KOTRA Report," Peterson Institute for International Economics, September 13, 2016, https://piie.com/blogs/north-korea-witness-transformation/kotra-report.

[37] Anna Fifield, "China is Putting the Squeeze on North Korea. But for How Long?" *Washington Post*, November 18, 2016. https://www.washingtonpost.com/world/asia_pacific/china-is-putting-the-squeeze-on-north-korea-but-for-how-long/2016/11/18/752137a6-a049-11e6-8864-6f892cad0865_story.html?utm_term=.d4cdd212f915.

[38] See Kim, "How China Sees North Korea."

[39] Patricia M. Kim, "Did Kim's Visit Just Hand China a Trump Card?" *Foreign Policy*, March 29, 2018, https://foreignpolicy.com/2018/03/29/did-kims-visit-just-hand-china-a-trump-card.

chaos" on the Korea Peninsula, Beijing has also endorsed Kim's desire for a "synchronous and phased" approach to denuclearization.[40]

China's own proposal for the denuclearization of the peninsula involves what it calls a "suspension for suspension" and "dual track" approach. The former refers to the idea that the United States and South Korea should suspend their military exercises in exchange for North Korea's suspension of its nuclear and missile tests; the latter refers to the idea that a peace treaty and denuclearization should be negotiated at the same time in a "synchronized and reciprocal manner."[41] The first part of this proposal was largely implemented following the summit between President Donald Trump and Kim Jong-un in Singapore,[42] and the dual track approach is currently being pushed by Beijing, Pyongyang, and Seoul. Beijing has also insisted that it must be included in any negotiations to end the Korean War and in drafting a peace treaty. While the Chinese proposal is favored by both Koreas, it also involves a heavy dose of self-interest for Beijing as establishing a peace regime on the Korean Peninsula and rolling back the U.S.-ROK alliance advances China's own goals for the region.[43]

Beijing ultimately wants North Korea to follow in its footsteps by adopting the Chinese model of reform and opening—that is, economic but not political opening. Although North Korea has long resisted such change, Kim has signaled his desire to shift his country's focus from building military capabilities to promoting economic development since the spring of 2018. Both Xi and Moon have eagerly welcomed Kim's stated new direction, given their shared belief that North Korea must be economically engaged in order to build trust and work toward peace on the Korean Peninsula. While economic engagement will remain limited until sanctions are fully lifted, Beijing and Seoul already have grand plans for the integration of North Korea into the regional economy. For instance, Moon reportedly shared with Kim a blueprint for the "new economic map of the Korean Peninsula" when the two leaders met for the first time at Panmunjom in April 2018. This plan involves linking North and South Korea through three belts extending to China, Russia, and

---

[40] See, for example, "Foreign Ministry Spokesperson Geng Shuang's Remarks on the United Nations Security Council's Adoption of Resolution 2375," Ministry of Foreign Affairs (PRC), September 12, 2017, http://www.fmprc.gov.cn/mfa_eng/xwfw_665399/s2510_665401/t1492131.shtml.

[41] Wang Yi, "Stay Committed to the Goal of Denuclearization, Uphold Peace and Stability on the Peninsula" (statement at the UN Security Council Ministerial Session on the Nuclear Issue on the Korean Peninsula, New York, April 28, 2017), http://www.fmprc.gov.cn/mfa_eng/zxxx_662805/t1458508.shtml.

[42] Since the summit, several U.S.-ROK military exercises have been suspended or modified in scale. It is unclear how long this policy will be in place. "S. Korea, U.S. Still Reviewing Military Exercise Plans: Pentagon," Korea Herald, December 5, 2018, http://www.koreaherald.com/view.php?ud=20181205000111.

[43] Patricia M. Kim, "U.S.-China Relations," Asan Forum, June 20, 2018, http://www.theasanforum.org/us-china-relations/?dat=.

Europe and fits nicely, at least conceptually, with China's BRI.[44] A *Global Times* article demonstrates Chinese enthusiasm for the plan, arguing that linking South and North Korea's development to China's would stimulate growth for China's northeastern provinces, speed up North Korean reforms, and reduce security tensions on the peninsula by "altering the regional structure from a hostile balance of power" to a peaceful one where "cooperation and non-competition become the norm."[45]

China's vision for the Korean Peninsula is thus one in which North and South Korea are firmly integrated with the Chinese economy. Barring dramatic changes or crises, Beijing will continue to push this vision for the foreseeable future. Beijing is likely to continue to serve as North Korea's economic lifeline, shielding Pyongyang from international pressure so that the regime is not destabilized and encouraging its pursuit of economic modernization. This does not mean that China will defend North Korea at all costs. Beijing, for instance, is unlikely to stand by Pyongyang if it were to launch an unprovoked attack. If the attack were to spark a war on the Korean Peninsula, however, China would most likely intervene in some fashion in order to have a hand in the changing dynamics on the peninsula.

Japan

China views Japan as its primary competitor in Northeast Asia, as opposed to a partner that can be pulled into its orbit like South or North Korea. Its objectives with regard to Japan include maintaining relatively stable economic relations, given the interdependence of their economies; preventing Japan from strengthening its military capabilities and influence in the security realm; and challenging Japan's territorial claims while asserting China's own.

China and Japan have maintained a robust trade relationship since normalizing relations in 1972, with China benefiting from Japanese FDI and the import of Japanese technology, particularly in the earlier phases of its development. As China has moved up the value chain, however, the two states have become economic competitors, most notably in the infrastructure sector, where Chinese and Japanese companies are now competing to secure contracts in Southeast Asia.[46] Their rivalry is likely to increase as China strives to advance its manufacturing sector and become a leader in the high-tech

---

[44] Tara Francis Chan, "Kim Jong Un Received a USB from South Korea's President with a Blueprint for Connecting North Korea with the World," *Business Insider*, May 6, 2018, https://www.businessinsiderom/kim-jong-un-received-a-usb-from-south-koreas-president-2018-5.

[45] Ding Rongjun, "Belt and Road Initiative Meshes with South Korea's Northern Policy," *Global Times*, July 18, 2018, http://www.globaltimes.cn/content/1056917.shtml.

[46] Chietigj Bajpaee, "Japan and China: The Geo-economic Dimension," *Diplomat*, March 28, 2016, https://thediplomat.com/2016/03/japan-and-china-the-geo-economic-dimension.

industry through state-led initiatives like Made in China 2025. Yet despite their increasing competition, the two states remain highly interdependent, with both ranking as each other's second-largest export market after the United States.[47] China is likely to continue to value Japanese FDI, which peaked at $7.3 billion dollars in 2012 before declining due to political tensions over territorial disputes. Tokyo also seeks to reinvigorate economic cooperation with China for the benefit of its domestic firms.[48]

The Trump administration's America-first approach to trade has also driven the two countries together. With the trade war between the United States and China escalating in recent months, China has sought to deepen its economic ties with Japan and has called on Japanese leaders to join together to defend free trade and multilateralism.[49] Tokyo, too, has looked to China amid growing uncertainty in the U.S.-Japan economic relationship. The United States' withdrawal from the Trans-Pacific Partnership (TPP) was a blow to Prime Minister Abe, who had promoted the TPP as a means to strengthen the Japanese economy and keep U.S. involvement in the region.[50] Now Japan is looking to sign the Regional Comprehensive Economic Partnership (RCEP), an FTA that has been led by China and includes fifteen other potential signatories.[51] With Tokyo signaling its willingness to cooperate on BRI, the AIIB, and RCEP, and given China's enthusiasm for Japanese involvement in these initiatives, economic cooperation between the two sides is likely to increase barring an unexpected political crisis.

While China seeks to maintain stable economic relations with Japan, it has been much more aggressive in the two countries' territorial dispute over the Senkaku/Diaoyu Islands, which are administered by Japan. Beijing has exponentially increased incursions into Japanese waters since the Japanese government purchased three of the islands from a private citizen

---

[47] "Japan Exports, Imports and Trade Balance by Country 2016," World Bank, World Integrated Trade Solution, https://wits.worldbank.org/CountryProfile/en/Country/JPN/Year/2016/TradeFlow/EXPIMP/Partner/by-country.

[48] Shunsuke Tabeta, "Regional Leaders from China Hunt for More Japanese Investment," *Nikkei Asian Review*, May 18, 2018, https://asia.nikkei.com/Business/Business-Trends/Regional-leaders-from-China-hunt-for-more-Japanese-investment.

[49] Oki Nagai, "Xi Courts Friends Worldwide as Trade War Drags On," *Nikkei Asian Review*, September 13, 2018, https://asia.nikkei.com/Politics/International-Relations/Xi-courts-friends-worldwide-as-trade-war-drags-on; and Yoichi Funabashi and Harry Dempsey, "Trump Threat Drives Japan and China Closer," East Asia Forum, July 9, 2017, http://www.eastasiaforum.org/2017/07/09/trump-threat-drives-japan-and-china-closer.

[50] Terada Takashi, "How and Why Japan Has Saved the TPP: From Trump Tower to Davos," *Asan Forum*, February 19, 2018, http://www.theasanforum.org/how-and-why-japan-has-saved-the-tpp-from-trump-tower-to-davos.

[51] Kenneth Rapoza, "Will Japan Go against U.S. and Sign China's 'Free Trade' Deal?" *Forbes*, September 3, 2018, https://www.forbes.com/sites/kenrapoza/2018/09/03/will-japan-go-against-u-s-and-sign-chinas-free-trade-deal/#42b205c33ad6.

in September 2012. The number of Chinese government vessels that entered Japanese seas peaked in 2016 at 147, including 23 in the month of August alone.[52] In addition, China's declaration of an ADIZ over the disputed area in November 2013 is thought to have been motivated by the "nationalization" of the islands by Japan. Since declaring the East China Sea ADIZ, the number of Chinese aircraft operating near Japan's airspace has steadily increased.[53] While the two sides have most recently set up an emergency communication system known as the Maritime and Aerial Communication Mechanism, any resolution of the territorial dispute seems out of reach in the foreseeable future.[54] To defend its sovereignty claim, China will most likely continue regular patrols in the East China Sea.

In addition to pushing Japan over the Senkaku/Diaoyu Islands, Beijing seeks to prevent Tokyo from increasing its military capabilities and involvement in regional security issues. Chinese leaders often protest the expanding mission and growing budget of the Japan Self-Defense Forces (JSDF), bilateral efforts by Washington and Tokyo to increase Japan's security role in the U.S.-Japan alliance, and moves by Abe to revise Japan's peace constitution. Chinese observers insist that a militarily advanced Japan will destabilize the region and bring back the "militarism" from which China and other countries suffered during the twentieth century. Beijing is especially concerned about the implications of Japan's growing military capabilities and willingness to take on greater defensive responsibilities in the U.S.-Japan alliance for its ability to win a war in the Taiwan Strait.[55]

While protesting Japan's moves to expand the mission and capabilities of the JSDF, China has also vehemently opposed Japan's attempts to obtain a permanent seat on the UN Security Council. Since 2005, Tokyo has called for the council to be reformed to "reflect the realities of the 21st century." It has argued that Japan should be granted a permanent seat because of the country's

---

[52] "Senkakushoto shuhen kaiiki ni okeru Chugoku kosen-to no doko to wagakuni no taisho" [Trends in Public Shipping, etc. in the Sea Area around the Senkaku Islands and Japan's Response], Japan Coast Guard, June 8, 2018, http://www.kaiho.mlit.go.jp/mission/senkaku/senkaku.html.

[53] Jesse Johnson, "Chinese Military Aircraft Flew over Strategic Waterway Record Number of Times in Fiscal 2017, Japan Defense Ministry Says," *Japan Times*, April 14, 2018, https://www.japantimes.co.jp/news/2018/04/14/national/chinese-military-aircraft-flew-strategic-waterway-record-number-times-fiscal-2017-defense-ministry-says/#.W9IWaH_QaUk.

[54] Shinichi Fujiwara and Hirotaka Kojo, "Japan-China Communications Start Up to Avoid Air, Sea Clashes," *Asahi Shimbun*, June 8, 2018, http://www.asahi.com/ajw/articles/AJ201806080061.html.

[55] See, for example, Wu Xinbo, "The End of the Silver Lining: A Chinese View of the U.S.-Japanese Alliance," *Washington Quarterly* 29, no. 1 (2005): 117–30, available at https://www.brookings.edu/wp-content/uploads/2016/06/xinbo20060101.pdf; Zhu Feng and Lan Jianzhong, "Who Will Pay for Abe's 'Dream of Militarism?'" *China Daily*, December 6, 2016, http://www.chinadaily.com.cn/opinion/2016-12/06/content_27582724.htm; and Liu Lulu, "Asia Needs to Be Wary of Militarism Revival in Japan," *Global Times*, April 8, 2018, http://www.globaltimes.cn/content/1097003.shtml.

outsized contributions to the UN budget and peacekeeping missions.[56] Beijing has pushed back, however, with the argument that Japan should not be given a seat because it has not fully recognized or atoned for its history of imperialism.[57] An obvious but unspoken reason for China's opposition also lies in its desire to block a country with which it often has very different interests from shifting the balance in the UN Security Council.

China has primarily employed strong rhetoric and anti-Japanese sentiment at home to oppose Japan's security reforms. For instance, Chinese newspapers and officials often cast doubt on these reforms by highlighting Japanese public opposition to the Abe administration's efforts to alter the country's pacifist postwar orientation.[58] In addition, Beijing utilizes nationalistic rhetoric and state-controlled media, as well as patriotic education, to animate anti-Japanese sentiment among Chinese citizens. Major protests and boycotts of Japanese products have occurred in China as a result, most notably in 2005 following the approval of a controversial Japanese textbook and in 2012 following the Japanese government's purchase of the Senkaku/Diaoyu Islands. The latter episode is believed to have cost Japanese businesses over $100 million due to physical damage to assets in China, as well as reduced sales.[59]

Beijing's strategy toward Japan will likely remain consistent as Chinese leaders balance between the conflicting goals of maintaining stable economic relations with Japan and applying pressure in the security realm. For now the pendulum has swung toward the first of these goals as Chinese leaders face economic uncertainty and find ways to weather the trade war with the United States. The pendulum could quickly swing in the other direction, however, if Tokyo begins to adopt more assertive policies in the security realm.

Evaluating China's Northeast Asia Strategy

China's Northeast Asia strategy demonstrates that Beijing has a clear vision for how it can become the leader of the region, and what kind of regional order it would like to lead. Just like the United States believes it is exceptional because of its unique history, political system, and culture, China

---

[56] "Japan's Position on the United Nations Security Council for the 21st Century," Ministry of Foreign Affairs (Japan), March 2011, https://www.mofa.go.jp/policy/un/sc/pdfs/pamph_unsc21c_en.pdf.

[57] "China Opposes UNSC Enlargement with Japan," *China Daily*, June 3, 2005, http://www.chinadaily.com.cn/english/doc/2005-06/03/content_448242.htm.

[58] Amy King, "China's Response to Japan's Constitutional Reinterpretation," East Asia Forum, July 27, 2014, http://www.eastasiaforum.org/2014/07/27/china-responds-to-japans-constitutional-reinterpretation.

[59] "China Anti-Japan Protest Damage May Be over US$100M," *South China Morning Post*, November 13, 2012, https://www.scmp.com/news/china/article/1081778/china-anti-japan-protest-damage-may-be-over-us100m.

believes that it is exceptional for these same reasons. Chinese exceptionalism, or "great-power diplomacy with Chinese characteristics," as Xi calls it, draws from China's recent history of economic reform and opening that has remarkably lifted hundreds of millions out of poverty and brought about rapid economic growth over the last four decades. Beijing seeks to create an "Asian community of common destiny" that focuses on joint development, prioritizes economic but not political openness, and upholds the "principle of noninterference," by which Beijing means no state should have the right to criticize the domestic political systems of other states. China also desires the ability to assert greater influence over the policy choices made by its neighbors. It seeks to cultivate such influence by deepening its economic relationships and increasing its central role in the regional economy; strengthening its military capabilities; weakening the United States' alliances with South Korea and Japan, as well as preventing trilateral cooperation between the three countries; and prioritizing stability on the Korean Peninsula over North Korea's rapid denuclearization.

Factors Influencing China's Northeast Asia Strategy

Chinese leaders find it difficult to believe that anyone would regard their concept of win-win cooperation, i.e., setting aside politics to get rich together, as objectionable. The arrival of the Trump administration and its America-first policies have inspired confidence among Chinese leaders that the time has come for China to claim greater regional and global leadership roles. According to Xi's address in June 2018 at the Central Conference on Work Relating to Foreign Affairs, the CCP's most important meeting on its foreign policy held once every five to ten years, China is currently experiencing its "best period of development," while the world is undergoing "its greatest change in the past century." Xi asserts that if China works to grasp this opportunity and manages its foreign affairs well in the near future, it can create "favorable conditions" for itself in the international arena.[60]

The success of China's attempts to increase its influence in Northeast Asia and to shape the region's norms and *modus operandi* will be affected both by dynamics in the country's domestic political arena and by the response of its neighbors. As of late 2018, the triumphant mood in Beijing has somewhat diminished, given a months-long trade war with the United States that has no quick resolution in sight and a growing hard-line consensus in Washington on the strategic threat posed by China. Despite the CCP's general faith in

---

[60] "Xi Jinping: Nuli kaichuang Zhongguo tese daguo waijiao xinjumian" [Xi Jinping: Diligently Initiate New Aspects of Great-Power Diplomacy with Chinese Characteristics], Xinhua, June 23, 2018, http://www.xinhuanet.com/politics/2018-06/23/c_1123025806.htm.

economic development and cooperation as the key to China's domestic and international success, not all Chinese approve of Xi's grandiose application of this principle. Many Chinese experts privately grumble that by ostentatiously launching massive initiatives like BRI and prematurely abandoning Deng's maxim of keeping a low profile while biding one's time, Xi has unnecessarily stoked U.S. fear and balancing. The Chinese middle class has also grown increasingly critical of the leadership in the midst of growing economic uncertainty at home, questioning Beijing's many foreign projects and handling of bilateral relations with the United States.[61]

The CCP, however, has doubled down on its message that continuing to open up and deepen economic engagement with the outside world, and especially with Northeast Asian countries, is necessary for the prosperity of both China and the region. Chinese leaders are also turning to nationalism in attempts to rally the public and win its support. They are telling Chinese citizens to "be confident" and to expect animosity as China continues to rise.[62] Such messaging suggests that the CCP, at least for the time being, has not been discouraged from and is likely to continue its proactive posture in the region despite some misgivings about Xi's approach among the Chinese public. However, a severe economic downturn or extreme societal discontent over the party's mismanagement of issues in realms like public health and environmental safety could push Chinese leaders to turn their attention inward. But the CCP is unlikely to adopt a fully hands-off approach in the region as developments in the immediate neighborhood often have direct strategic implications for China. Furthermore, the CCP desires observable indications of China's growing influence, and successful foreign projects are useful for boosting Xi and the party's support at home. Chinese leaders are aware that consistently failing to show progress will increase their domestic political vulnerability and raise questions about the utility of the CCP's monopoly over power.

In addition to domestic politics, Washington's response to China's pursuit of influence will also have a decisive impact on whether or not the latter achieves its objectives in Northeast Asia. Whether the United States continues its traditional role as Northeast Asia's security provider, or reduces its involvement in the region, will affect the range of options Japan, South Korea, and even North Korea can consider as they craft their

---

[61] See Chris Buckley, "As China's Woes Mount, Xi Jinping Faces Rare Rebuke at Home," *New York Times*, July 31, 2018, https://www.nytimes.com/2018/07/31/world/asia/xi-jinping-internal-dissent.html; and Cheng Li, "How China's Middle Class Views the Trade War," *Foreign Affairs*, September 10, 2018, https://www.foreignaffairs.com/articles/china/2018-09-10/how-chinas-middle-class-views-trade-war.

[62] "China Must Open Up Despite External Risks," *Global Times*, September 19, 2018, http://www.globaltimes.cn/content/1120312.shtml; and "Time for Northeast Asia to Steer Regional Growth by Cooperation," *Global Times*, September 13, 2018, http://www.globaltimes.cn/content/1119422.shtml.

own strategies toward China. If the United States' interest in the region and commitment to its allies show signs of wavering, South Korea and Japan will inevitably feel the need to strengthen their ties with China and face greater pressure to accommodate its interests. North Korea, too, will find a land of limited diplomatic and economic options if and when it begins to open up and engage with the outside world. Such developments are in fact already evident in the economic realm. As discussed above, the Trump administration's confrontational approach on trade vis-à-vis allies and rivals alike has cast doubts on the United States' reliability as a stable partner and brought China, Japan, and South Korea together to pursue regional cooperation amongst themselves.

How the region responds will also have critical implications for the realization of China's Northeast Asia strategy. Although the Trump administration's disruptive approach to foreign policy has helped China's efforts to present itself as a responsible leader and champion of economic globalization, Beijing has also set a very high bar for itself by promising to eschew the "traditional model" of power politics and guaranteeing that everyone can win together. Many have yet to buy into these claims and remain wary of China's intentions, especially in its immediate neighborhood. For instance, according to polling data, most Asians have low confidence that Xi will "do the right thing" in world affairs. Liberal democracies are especially critical of China's authoritarian system and the lack of personal freedoms its people enjoy at home.[63] Similarly, while South Korean and Japanese citizens have mixed views on the benefits of China's growing economic power, overwhelming majorities believe that the country's rising power and influence, and especially its expanding military capabilities, pose grave threats.[64] Furthermore, a vast majority of South Korean and Japanese citizens perceive the territorial disputes between their country and China as threatening.[65]

While China's economic importance has ensured that its neighbors will pay attention to its preferences, states have yet to fully align themselves with Beijing. In fact, Beijing's willingness to use its economic leverage in a coercive manner has perhaps brought about short-term results but

---

[63] Richard Wike et al., "Globally, More Name U.S. than China as World's Leading Economic Power," Pew Research Center, July 13, 2017, http://www.pewglobal.org/2017/07/13/more-name-u-s-than-china-as-worlds-leading-economic-power.

[64] Laura Silver, "How People in Asia-Pacific View China," Pew Research Center, October 16, 2017, http://www.pewresearch.org/fact-tank/2017/10/16/how-people-in-asia-pacific-view-china.

[65] Bruce Drake, "As Tensions Rise in Asia, a Look at How Japanese, South Koreans and Chinese View Each Other," Pew Research Center, December 2, 2013, http://www.pewresearch.org/fact-tank/2013/12/02/as-tensions-rise-in-asia-a-look-at-how-japanese-south-koreans-and-chinese-view-each-other.

undermined China's long-term interests by arousing fear among its neighbors and pushing them to look elsewhere for economic opportunities, such as in Southeast Asia. Seoul, for instance, is now promoting its New Southern Policy, which seeks to reduce South Korea's economic dependence on China by finding opportunities to cooperate with Southeast Asian nations as well as India and Pakistan.[66] Tokyo has a similar strategy of increasing engagement and investment in Southeast Asia, and Japanese businesses now practice a "China plus" strategy to diversify their investments.[67]

Similarly, while China's expanding presence and activities in the East China Sea have sent the message that the country intends to defend its territorial claims, this assertive approach has stimulated Japan and South Korea to increase their own maritime patrolling and reinforced the need to further invest in their alliances with the United States. In short, while China may have amplified its ability to influence the policy choices of its neighbors, it has yet to earn the region's allegiance or admiration, nor has it fundamentally weakened the U.S. alliance system. Such pushback undoubtedly affects China's strategic decision-making and is helpful for signaling to Beijing that its coercive actions will not be met with acquiescence in the region.

Implications of China's Northeast Asia Strategy for the Region

If China were to succeed in becoming the most powerful country across all dimensions in the region, having successfully rolled back the U.S. alliance system and created a regional order with Beijing at the center of all economic activity, it would likely pursue its interests in a less restrained manner. For instance, Beijing might advance some form of reunification with Taiwan or freely operate and exploit resources in the East China Sea with little concern about facing a response from the U.S.-led alliance system. The CCP would also get a major boost at home from having delivered on its promise to restore China's status as a global power. While strong domestic support could inspire Chinese authorities to relax their exercise of absolute control at home, it might also embolden them to further pursue some of the party's more repressive policies.

As for others in the region, life in a Northeast Asia dominated solely by China could in theory be economically prosperous and peaceful, as long as a state does not have any conflicting interests with China. But given the many disagreements that already exist, including long-standing historical and territorial disputes, and the fact that new conflicts will inevitably arise, such

---

[66] "S. Korean Minister Promotes 'New Southern Policy' in Singapore," *Korea Herald*, August 1, 2018, http://www.koreaherald.com/view.php?ud=20180801000795&ACE_SEARCH=1.

[67] Bajpaee, "Japan and China."

a benign outcome is highly unlikely. In fact, although China has yet to reach hegemonic status in the region, it has already used its economic and military prowess to intimidate its neighbors at times when diplomatic lobbying has proved ineffective. In a region dominated by China, with no commensurate power or alliance to balance against it, states would more likely acquiesce to Beijing's demands, given its ability to hold their economies and security hostage.

Conversely, if China were to experience continuous setbacks in its Northeast Asia policy, such a development would not necessarily be great for regional stability and prosperity either. If, for instance, Chinese citizens judged that their leaders were not sufficiently tough or had been humiliated by their South Korean or Japanese counterparts, the CCP would become much more vulnerable to patriotic criticism at home. Such criticism could in turn force Chinese leaders to adopt more extreme foreign policies, ultimately leading to greater tension in the region. Or if China's major economic initiatives were to prove financially disastrous, this would not only have ripple effects on the entire regional economy, but also force China to turn inward, depriving the region of much-needed infrastructure and development. Furthermore, a China uninterested in tackling global problems, such as climate change or nonproliferation, would be disastrous for the prospects of addressing pressing international concerns.

Policy Implications for the United States[68]

Given the desire among Northeast Asian states to keep the United States engaged in the region, China's objective of creating a regional order with itself at the center and a diminished role for the U.S.-led alliance system is still far from being achieved. If the United States seeks to retain its influence in Northeast Asia, however, it will need to work to inspire confidence in the region that it is a committed and credible partner.

As discussed above, if the United States were to withdraw from the region, neglecting or even abrogating its alliances with South Korea and Japan, Washington would have little if any influence over the rules and norms of the region, or the strategic choices made by regional states. Its former allies and friends, whose security would no longer depend on maintaining strong ties with the United States, would prioritize their relationship with the power next door and refrain from challenging China's preferences. Furthermore, they would be much less likely to vote with the United States in the United Nations or to join Washington in its various global initiatives.

---

[68] The policy implications in this section draw on Kim, "Understanding China's Military Expansion and Implications for U.S. Policy."

The current U.S. president's tendency to characterize U.S. troops in Asia simply as an economic burden, his willingness to speak of U.S.-ROK exercises as "provocative" and "expensive," and his decision to cancel them following a meeting with Kim Jong-un before fully consulting Seoul has already hurt U.S. credibility in the eyes of its allies and partners.[69] Such rhetoric and behavior by a U.S. leader ultimately helps Beijing's cause in weakening trust and cohesion in the U.S. alliance system in Asia.

To compete with China, the United States first must uphold and strengthen its alliances with South Korea and Japan. These two long-standing alliances are invaluable assets that enable Washington to lead collective challenges against Chinese aggression and to generally shape outcomes in the global arena. As the primary security partner for Seoul and Tokyo, the United States receives many strategic benefits, including their willingness to consult, coordinate, and adjust their policies with Washington, or at the very least to keep U.S. leaders informed on any decisions of consequence. These allies also provide access to foreign bases that allow the United States to project its power far and wide, and they contribute forces and political support for various U.S. endeavors. The United States, therefore, should continue to work with these Northeast Asian allies to boost their individual military capabilities as well as the ability to operate together. Furthermore, it should endeavor to resolve any disagreements with them discreetly and in a manner that does not undermine the credibility of its commitments.

An outright containment strategy toward China, however, is unlikely to generate much support given the importance that Japan and especially South Korea place in maintaining stable economic relations with China. Seoul, for instance, has been circumspect about endorsing the "free and open Indo-Pacific" strategy,[70] which broadly calls on Asian states, and especially members of the Quadrilateral Security Dialogue, or Quad (which includes Australia, India, Japan, and the United States), to advance a free and open regional order in the Indo-Pacific through joint economic development and

---

[69] Choe Sang-Hun and Motoko Rich, "Trump's Talk of U.S. Troop Cuts Unnerves South Korea and Japan," *New York Times*, May 4, 2018, https://www.nytimes.com/2018/05/04/world/asia/south-korea-troop-withdrawal-united-states.html; and Dan Lamothe, "Trump Pledged to End Military Exercises with South Korea. But Will It Ever Happen?" *Washington Post*, June 12, 2018, https://www.washingtonpost.com/news/checkpoint/wp/2018/06/12/trump-pledged-to-end-military-exercises-with-south-korea-but-will-it-ever-happen.

[70] Rachel Le, "Moon Cautious about Indo-Pacific Proposal," *Korea Times*, November 10, 2017, https://www.koreatimes.co.kr/www/nation/2017/11/120_239062.html.

the enforcement of a rules-based maritime order.[71] While this strategy has yet to be fully developed or institutionalized, if it begins to look purely like a mechanism to counter China, states like South Korea are unlikely to support the strategy. Furthermore, China's rhetoric calling for win-win diplomacy and a new type of international relations could start to sound much more reasonable in contrast with a call for Cold War–style containment. Instead of leading the charge against *China*, the United States should lead its allies in challenging unacceptable Chinese *behavior*.

Second, the United States must present a comprehensive and positive agenda for Northeast Asia and beyond, instead of merely reacting to Chinese initiatives like BRI and the AIIB. The free and open Indo-Pacific strategy is one such attempt at positive agenda-setting, but it has largely been overshadowed by the destabilizing rhetoric and policy choices by the current U.S. president. The United States should continue to fill out this strategy and consider other measures, such as rejoining the TPP, to signal its willingness to remain economically engaged and to generally maintain a constructive presence in East Asia.

Furthermore, U.S. leaders should continue to support the liberal world order that the United States helped build and the values of democratic governance, political freedom, and rule of law that underpin U.S. soft power. These values resonate with South Korean and Japanese audiences, and even inside China, where many elites and citizens alike are disturbed by the increasingly authoritarian turn of their government. While Beijing touts its value-free diplomacy as a pragmatic and attractive model, its claims ring hollow when benefits either do not materialize or are lopsided. There is also a limit to how much trust and loyalty can be built through relationships devoid of shared values. The United States, therefore, should continue to reaffirm the importance of liberal values among its Northeast Asian allies. And the United States must also put its own house in order so that it can stand as a beacon that inspires citizens and elites in China and elsewhere to push for greater openness in their own political systems.

Finally, Washington should work with Seoul and Tokyo to leverage Beijing's desire for stability and prosperity at home to discourage destabilizing behavior and encourage instead its contributions to tackling regional and global challenges. As discussed above, Chinese leaders have set out multiple ambitious targets for their country, many of which will be very difficult to

---

[71] The "free and open Indo-Pacific" is a concept first advanced by Abe in a speech at the Indian parliament in 2007, although the United States has now adopted the terminology. For more details, see "Briefing on the Indo-Pacific Strategy," U.S. State Department, April 2, 2018, https://www.state.gov/r/pa/prs/ps/2018/04/280134.htm. For Abe's speech, see Shinzo Abe, "Confluence of the Two Seas" (speech at the Indian parliament, New Delhi, August 22, 2007), https://www.mofa.go.jp/region/asia-paci/pmv0708/speech-2.html.

achieve if the region is beset with chaos and instability, such as conflict on the Korean Peninsula or in the East China Sea. Rather than engaging in transactional bargains, U.S. leaders should continue to make the case to their Chinese counterparts that China should refrain from provocative behavior, such as militarizing disputed territories, and instead cooperate to solve global challenges, such as the North Korean nuclear crisis, because it is in China's long-term strategic interests to do so. Chinese leaders have reiterated over the years in speeches and in major strategic documents that China seeks to contribute to peace and stability in the world. The United States and its allies should hold them accountable to these promises through persistent diplomatic engagement and collective resolve.

EXECUTIVE SUMMARY

This chapter examines the evolution of Beijing's approach to Taiwan as China transitions to a major-power role in the international system and concludes by assessing the implications of broader trends associated with China's growing power and influence for the cross-strait relationship.

MAIN ARGUMENT

Taiwan is central to China's core interests not only due to Beijing's emphasis on sovereignty and territorial integrity and the island's salience in Chinese domestic politics but also because of the implications it holds for a rising China's broader strategic aims. Xi Jinping has clearly linked the goal of unification with Taiwan to his larger pursuit of "the great rejuvenation of the Chinese nation." Since Taiwan's 2016 election, which resulted in Tsai Ing-wen of the Democratic Progressive Party (DPP) becoming president and the DPP gaining control of the island's legislature, China has carried out an escalating, multidimensional pressure campaign that includes diplomatic isolation, military intimidation, economic coercion, and influence operations. At the same time, it has offered a set of enhanced incentives, the "31 measures," in an effort to entice key groups in Taiwan, with a focus on young people and the business community.

POLICY IMPLICATIONS

- China's intensified pressure campaign presents serious challenges, but it also risks backfiring by further alienating people in Taiwan, many of whom are increasingly skeptical of the benefits of a closer cross-strait relationship.

- If Beijing wants to maintain a stable and constructive cross-strait relationship, it will need to adopt a more creative and flexible approach to dealing with Taiwan.

- The U.S. will need to think more broadly about the island's security needs, including helping increase its resilience in the face of Chinese pressure on a variety of fronts.

A Rising China's Challenge to Taiwan

Michael S. Chase

Although maritime disputes in the East and South China Seas have dominated much of the discussion about a rising China's security policy in recent years, Taiwan still occupies a central place among Beijing's strategic priorities. The evolution of China's approach to Taiwan as it continues its transition to a major-power role in the international system will have important implications for the cross-strait relationship. Broader trends associated with the growing power and influence of the People's Republic of China (PRC), coupled with recent developments such as Xi Jinping securing indefinite tenure as the country's top leader with the removal of term limits, point to important questions about China's Taiwan policy and what it could mean for regional security and stability more generally.

For Beijing, when it comes to Taiwan, the stakes could not be higher. Chinese leaders would undoubtedly see failure to prevent *de jure* independence for Taiwan as a disaster politically. At the same time, however, armed conflict over Taiwan would entail exceptionally grave risks for Beijing. Even if China won, a cross-strait conflict would likely result in tremendous costs, especially if it triggered a wider regional war involving the United States. Whatever the outcome, a cross-strait conflict could fundamentally alter China's broader international trajectory. Peaceful unification, on the other hand, would represent a tremendous political victory for Beijing and might facilitate China's achievement of its broader international ambitions. But that outcome is not a realistic prospect in the near term, especially given recent trends in domestic politics in Taiwan. For now, Beijing may be left with little choice but to muddle through, relying on its growing military

Michael S. Chase is a Senior Political Scientist at the RAND Corporation and an Adjunct Professor at the Johns Hopkins University's Paul H. Nitze School of Advanced International Studies (SAIS). He can be reached at <michael_chase@rand.org>.

power and other sources of leverage to prevent Taiwan from moving toward independence, and attempting to employ a combination of coercion and inducements to push Taiwan in the desired direction over a longer period of time. The ultimate outcome is uncertain, but it is clear that Taiwan is central to what China considers to be its core interests. This is not only due to what Taiwan means in terms of sovereignty and territorial integrity but also because of the implications it holds for a rising China's broader strategic aims in terms of its regional and global power. Indeed, Xi has clearly linked the goal of unification with Taiwan to the larger pursuit of "the great rejuvenation of the Chinese nation." For all these reasons, Taiwan is also a central consideration in Chinese domestic politics, which could increase the risks that China is willing to take in order to secure its aims with respect to the island, especially if Xi and other leaders in Beijing perceive the prospects for unification to be slipping away.

Since the election of Tsai Ing-wen of the Democratic Progressive Party (DPP) as president of Taiwan in 2016, China has carried out an escalating, multidimensional pressure campaign that includes military intimidation, economic coercion, diplomatic isolation, and influence operations against Taiwan. At the same time, it has offered a set of enhanced incentives, the "31 measures," in an effort to entice key groups in Taiwan, with a focus on young people and the business community. Despite these new incentives, however, China's intensified pressure campaign appears to risk backfiring by further alienating people in Taiwan.

Looking ahead, China's removal of presidential term limits will allow Xi to remain in power indefinitely. Some observers assess that he has become a strongman leader subject to few constraints, and that his consolidation of power will embolden him to pursue a Taiwan strategy that involves exercising growing levels of pressure against the island.[1] Indeed, China could further increase its pressure if Xi and other leaders believe domestic trends in Taiwan or developments in the U.S.-Taiwan relationship necessitate a tough response. Chinese leaders might also apply greater pressure if they calculate that they need to look strong domestically when it comes to the politically sensitive issue of the cross-strait relationship. Another possibility is that Xi's elimination of term limits and the incorporation of "Xi Jinping Thought on Socialism with Chinese Characteristics for a New Era" into the Chinese Communist Party charter and the PRC constitution could lead him to pursue a major breakthrough on Taiwan as a means of justifying his extraordinary status.[2] As Jessica Drun points out, however, views among China watchers in Taiwan

---

[1] See Claudia Liu and Flor Wang, "China's Saber Rattling on Taiwan in Vain: Defense Minister," Focus Taiwan, May 19, 2018, http://m.focustaiwan.tw/news/aipl/201805190004.aspx.

[2] The author thanks an anonymous reviewer for raising this possibility.

and the United States are divided, "with some viewing Xi's consolidation of power as allowing for a greater mandate on hardening Beijing's approach to the island, while others view it as generating space for greater flexibility."[3] In any case, with China's growing power and the consolidation of Xi's position, the future of Beijing's approach to Taiwan remains uncertain. China does not appear to have set a deadline for unification with Taiwan, but Xi has suggested that the issue cannot remain unresolved indefinitely.[4]

The rest of this chapter is organized as follows. The first main section considers recent developments in cross-strait relations in the context of China's rise and Xi's pursuit of national "rejuvenation." The second section then examines key aspects of the country's current approach to dealing with Taiwan, including diplomatic, military, economic, and informational components of Chinese strategy. The third section offers some conclusions and considers the implications of a rising China's challenge to Taiwan.

China's Rise, National Rejuvenation, and Cross-Strait Relations

China's Goals and Recent Developments

China's overall long-term objective with respect to Taiwan is clear: Beijing seeks unification. Since the establishment of the PRC in 1949, successive Chinese leaders have viewed Taiwan as an inalienable part of China that must eventually be returned to the motherland. Official Chinese statements describe Taiwan's continued separation from the mainland largely as the result of the actions of external enemies. For instance, China's 1993 Taiwan white paper highlights the loss of Taiwan to Japan as a result of the 1894–95 Sino-Japanese War and describes defeated nationalist forces taking refuge on the island as they were fleeing the mainland following their defeat in the Chinese Civil War. The white paper also criticizes the intervention of the United States to protect Chiang Kai-shek and the position of the Kuomintang (KMT) on Taiwan after the outbreak of the Korean War. It asserts that after the United States and Taiwan signed a mutual defense treaty in 1954 "the erroneous policy of the U.S. government of continued interference in China's internal affairs" led to a "prolonged and intense

---

[3] Jessica Drun, "Dwindling Confidence: Is the CCP's View of the KMT Changing," Project 2049, Party Watch Initiative, October 16, 2017, https://www.ccpwatch.org/single-post/2017/10/16/Dwindling-Confidence-Is-the-CCPs-View-of-the-KMT-Changing.

[4] Richard C. Bush, "What Xi Jinping Said about Taiwan at the 19th Party Congress," Brookings Institution, October 19, 2017, https://www.brookings.edu/blog/order-from-chaos/2017/10/19/what-xi-jinping-said-about-taiwan-at-the-19th-party-congress.

confrontation" across the Taiwan Strait and made Taiwan an issue of dispute in the U.S.-China relationship.[5]

In pursuit of its goal of unification, Beijing has adhered to its long-standing "one-China principle," which holds that Taiwan is a part of China and the PRC is the sole legitimate government representing the whole of China.[6] Since 1979, Beijing has asserted that it pursues a policy of "peaceful reunification" and has promised that after unification Taiwan would enjoy a high degree of autonomy under a policy of "one country, two systems." Nonetheless, China has also reiterated that it reserves the right to use force if necessary. Indeed, in 2005 it underscored this point by passing the Anti-Secession Law, which articulates the conditions under which it would use force against Taiwan.[7]

Taiwan is clearly a core interest for Beijing in its own right, but China's approach to Taiwan must also be viewed in the context of the country's broader strategic goals, including the pursuit of the "China dream" and national rejuvenation. Yet given the widening gulf between Taiwan and the mainland politically, even as the cross-strait economic relationship has expanded dramatically over the years, this important component of these strategic objectives is likely to prove elusive. Even though the cross-strait relationship warmed considerably from 2008 to 2016, culminating in the historic November 2015 meeting between Xi and Taiwan's then president Ma Ying-jeou in Singapore, domestic political realities on the island limited what was possible in terms of Chinese objectives. This was starkly illustrated by the backlash to some of Ma's policies promoting greater economic and cultural integration with the mainland, which was embodied in the student-led Sunflower Movement in spring 2014 and ultimately led to the DPP's victory in the January 2016 elections.[8]

Within this context, China's fundamental policy goals have remained unchanged, and there has been considerable continuity in the broad outlines of its strategy. Under Hu Jintao, China focused more on preventing Taiwan independence than on compelling movement toward unification. Yet although Xi has continued to adhere to this basic approach since assuming power in 2012, comments and speeches by Xi and other Chinese officials tasked

---

[5] Taiwan Affairs Office of the State Council of the People's Republic of China (PRC), *The Taiwan Question and the Reunification of China* (Beijing, August 1993), http://www.china.org.cn/english/7953.htm.

[6] Taiwan Affairs Office of the State Council (PRC), *The One China Principle and the Taiwan Issue* (Beijing, February 2000), http://en.people.cn/features/taiwanpaper/taiwan.html.

[7] For more information on these conditions, see "Full Text of Anti-Secession Law," March 14, 2005, https://www.fmprc.gov.cn/zflt/eng/zt/asl/t187776.htm.

[8] The DPP's performance in the election effectively left the KMT to wander in the political wilderness, an observation for which the author wishes to thank one of the anonymous reviewers.

with managing the cross-strait relationship suggest that China is adjusting its methods. As noted above, Xi has not set a deadline for unification with Taiwan, but some of his remarks suggest that he has sought to push harder for progress in that direction. In October 2013, during a meeting with the former vice president of Taiwan, Vincent Siew, at the Asia-Pacific Economic Cooperation (APEC) leaders forum, Xi went beyond the usual language about China's Taiwan policy, stating that the two sides should make progress and the issues between them must not be "passed down from generation to generation."[9] Much of what Xi said was not new, but his "generation to generation" comment suggested he might be preparing to increase the pressure on Taiwan to achieve results in the short term.[10]

Subsequent comments indicated that Xi intended to focus on movement toward Beijing's long-term goals rather than press for a more hurried timeline. In a February 2014 meeting with KMT honorary chair and former vice president Lien Chan, he appealed to shared cultural and historical bonds: "compatriots on both sides of the Taiwan Strait are family, rooted in common blood and spirit, and common history and culture."[11] Xi also stated that both sides of the strait would benefit from China's "rejuvenation" and that they should work together to achieve the China dream.

In the wake of the Sunflower Movement, Beijing adjusted its tactics, but it continued to follow basically the same overall strategy. In September 2014, Xi told a pro-unification delegation from Taiwan that China would continue to adhere to "peaceful reunification" and "one country, two systems."[12] However, this formulation is unacceptable to many people in Taiwan and has become even more unattractive because of Beijing's heavy-handed implementation of "one country, two systems" in Hong Kong.[13] By late 2014, it was becoming clear that the mainland might face the prospect of a DPP victory in Taiwan's

---

[9] "Xi Jinping zongshuji huijian Xiao Wanchang yixing" [General Secretary Xi Jinping Meets with Xiao Wanchang and Delegation], Taiwan Affairs Office of the State Council (PRC), October 6, 2013, http://www.gwytb.gov.cn/wyly/201310/t20131007_4979072.htm.

[10] Alan D. Romberg, "From Generation to Generation: Advancing Cross-Strait Relations," Hoover Institution, China Leadership Monitor, no. 43, Spring 2014, 1, https://www.hoover.org/research/generation-generation-advancing-cross-strait-relations.

[11] See "Xi Jinping: Liang'an tongbao yao xieshou tongxin gong yuan Zhongguo meng" [Xi Jinping: Compatriots on Both Sides Must Work Together to Unite in Pursuit of the Chinese Dream], Taiwan Affairs Office of the State Council (PRC), February 18, 2014, http://www.gwytb.gov.cn/wyly/201402/t20140218_5693296.htm.

[12] Zhao Bo and Xu Xueyi, "Xi Jinping zong shuji huijian Taiwan heping tongyi tuanti lianhe canfangtuan" [General Secretary Xi Jinping Meets with Taiwan Peaceful Reunification Groups], Xinhua, September 26, 2014, http://news.xinhuanet.com/politics/2014-09/26/c_1112641354.htm.

[13] Alan D. Romberg, "Cross-Strait Relations: Portrayals of Consistency—Calm on the Surface, Paddling Like Hell Underneath," Hoover Institution, China Leadership Monitor, no. 45, Fall 2014, 6, https://www.hoover.org/research/cross-strait-relations-portrayals-consistency-calm-surface-paddling-hell-underneath.

2016 presidential and legislative elections, and analysts in China were considering how to respond if the DPP rejected "one China," as well as what to do if the party instead chose to adopt a more flexible approach.[14] Xi and other officials repeatedly emphasized that adhering to the 1992 Consensus and opposing Taiwan independence would be the prerequisites for the mainland to engage with the island. He also added a sharply worded warning: "It is frequently said that 'if the foundation is not sturdy, the earth will move and the mountains will shake.'"[15] In November 2015, Ma and Xi held their historic meeting in Singapore, with both leaders emphasizing the importance of the 1992 Consensus and the one-China principle. Xi not only underscored the mainland's insistence on this principle but also briefly alluded to the dangers of Taiwan failing to accept it as the basis of the cross-strait relationship. Without agreement on this common foundation for cross-strait ties, he warned that "the boat of peaceful development will encounter terrifying waves or even capsize."[16]

Just about two months later, the victory of Tsai and the DPP in the presidential and legislative elections presented a sharp challenge to China's approach. In March 2016, Xi discussed cross-strait relations with the Shanghai National People's Congress delegation, once again highlighting the importance of the 1992 Consensus and the one-China principle as essential components of a positive cross-strait relationship.[17] He stated that China's policy was clear and consistent and would not change as a result of political developments in Taiwan.[18] Xi's statement, however, did not repeat his threatening language from the previous year.[19]

Beijing reportedly distrusts Tsai in part because she served in the administrations of two previous presidents, Chen Shui-bian and Lee Teng-hui, whom Beijing viewed as bent on moving Taiwan toward

---

[14] Alan D. Romberg, "Cross-Strait Relations: 'The Times They Are A-Changin,'" Hoover Institution, China Leadership Monitor, no. 46, Winter 2015, https://www.hoover.org/research/cross-strait-relations-they-are-changin.

[15] Sung Ping-chung and Lu Su-mei, "Xi bu dianming xiang Lü han hua: Rentong yi Zhong" [Without Mentioning It by Name, Xi Sends a Message to the Green Camp: Acknowledge One China], China Times, March 5, 2015, http://www.chinatimes.com/newspapers/20150305000881-260301.

[16] See Alan D. Romberg, "The '1992 Consensus'—Adapting to the Future?" Hoover Institution, China Leadership Monitor, no. 49, Winter 2016, https://www.hoover.org/research/1992-consensus-adapting-future.

[17] For an analysis of Xi's remarks, see Richard C. Bush, "Decoding Xi Jinping's Latest Remarks on Taiwan," Brookings Institution, March 17, 2016, https://www.brookings.edu/blog/order-from-chaos/2016/03/17/decoding-xi-jinpings-latest-remarks-on-taiwan.

[18] "President Xi Warns against 'Taiwan Independence' in Any Form," Xinhua, March 5, 2016, http://news.xinhuanet.com/english/2016-03/05/c_135159093.htm.

[19] It is unclear why Xi has refrained from repeating this phrase. Nonetheless, some observers have characterized this as a relatively positive development, despite the overall tough stance on the part of the mainland. See, for example, Christie Chen, "Cross-Strait Opportunities and Challenges," Commercial Times, March 7, 2016.

formal independence. Chinese leaders associate her with what they see as unacceptable pro-independence policies, such as Lee's statement that the relationship between China and Taiwan was a "special state-to-state relationship." Beijing was also concerned about the DPP majority in the Legislative Yuan and its implications for cross-strait relations.[20] As a demonstration of its willingness to use economic and diplomatic leverage to punish Taiwan, China reduced the number of mainland tourists visiting Taiwan, established official diplomatic relations with Gambia, and pressured the Kenyan government into deporting Taiwan nationals involved in a telephone fraud case to the mainland.[21] Additionally, the statements of Chinese experts in the months leading up to Tsai's inauguration signaled that Beijing was preparing to break off official and semiofficial cross-strait exchanges unless she accepted the 1992 Consensus and its core implication of one China in her May 2016 inauguration speech.[22]

Although President Tsai used conciliatory language to describe her goals for cross-strait relations in her speech, she did not endorse the 1992 Consensus and one-China principle in the way China demanded, and Beijing was quick to dismiss the speech as falling short of its expectations. An official statement from the Taiwan Affairs Office of the State Council likened Tsai's speech to an "incomplete answer sheet" and charged that it was "ambiguous about the fundamental issue, the nature of cross-Straits relations, an issue that is of utmost concern to people on both sides of the Taiwan Straits."[23] Following Tsai's inauguration, the mainland made good on its threat to suspend official and semiofficial mechanisms for cross-strait communications,[24] ushering in a new period of cooler relations between the two sides of the Taiwan Strait.

---

[20] Joseph Yeh, "Lawmakers Allow 'Republic of Taiwan' Passport Stickers," *China Post*, April 7, 2016.

[21] Chen Yuxuan, "Tai zhapian fan bei Kenya qiansong Zhongguo, Waijiaobu yanzheng kangyi" [Taiwan Fraud Suspects Deported by Kenya to China, Ministry of Foreign Affairs Strongly Protests], *Liberty Times*, April 11, 2016, http://news.ltn.com.tw/news/politics/breakingnews/1660492.

[22] "Recognise 'One China' or Risk Deep Rift in Cross-Strait Ties, Beijing Think Tank Warns Taiwan's Tsai," *South China Morning Post*, March 10, 2016, http://m.scmp.com/news/china/policies-politics/article/1922768/recognise-one-china-or-risk-deep-rift-cross-strait-ties.

[23] For the Chinese text, see "Zhonggong zhongyang Taiban, guuwuyuan Taiban fuzeren jiu dangqian liang'an guanxi fazhan tanhua" [Central Committee Taiwan Office, State Council Taiwan Affairs Office Gives a Talk on Current Cross-Strait Relations], Taiwan Affairs Office of the State Council (PRC), May 20, 2016, http://www.gwytb.gov.cn/topone/201605/t20160520_11463138.htm. For an English summary of the response, see "Tsai's Speech on Cross-Straits Ties Offers 'an Incomplete Answer Sheet': Mainland Official," Xinhua, May 20, 2016, http://en.people.cn/n3/2016/0520/c90785-9060973.html.

[24] "Zhongguo Guotaiban: Liang'an lianxi goutong jizhi yijing tingbai" [China TAO: Cross-Strait Communication Mechanism Already Stopped], BBC (Chinese), June 26, 2016, http://www.bbc.com/zhongwen/trad/china/2016/06/160626_taiwan_china.

Looking Ahead: Implications for China's Objectives

Since President Tsai assumed office, Xi's strategy has evolved to include both an intensified pressure campaign against Taiwan and enhanced incentives to entice key groups on the island to embrace opportunities presented by the mainland. China was also concerned by Tsai's congratulatory phone call with Donald Trump after his surprise victory in the 2016 U.S. presidential election, and probably even more so by Trump's subsequent statements that suggested he might view the one-China policy as a bargaining chip. But China's overall policy toward Taiwan does not appear to have changed. Indeed, Xi's remarks on Taiwan at the 19th Party Congress in 2017 reflected a substantial amount of continuity.[25] He pledged to "uphold the principles of 'peaceful reunification' and 'one country, two systems,' work for the peaceful development of cross-Straits relations, and advance the process toward the peaceful reunification of China." He underscored the centrality of the 1992 Consensus and the one-China principle as "the political foundation of cross-Straits relations." After highlighting the theme that people on both sides of the Taiwan Strait are part of the "same family" and pledging to expand cross-strait economic and cultural exchanges, Xi foreshadowed the increased incentives China would later offer to people from Taiwan in the form of the 31 measures, a set of policies announced in 2018 to promote cross-strait economic integration. The toughest part of Xi's remarks dealt with deterring Taiwan independence:

> We stand firm in safeguarding China's sovereignty and territorial integrity, and will never allow the historical tragedy of national division to repeat itself. Any separatist activity is certain to meet with the resolute opposition of the Chinese people. We have the resolve, the confidence, and the ability to defeat separatist attempts for "Taiwan independence" in any form.[26]

Following these more strident comments, Xi turned in a more optimistic direction, one that underscored Taiwan's importance in the context of China's pursuit of national rejuvenation.[27] He did not set a deadline for unification, but his remarks underscored Taiwan's importance as part of his broader policy agenda and suggested that he sees unification with Taiwan as a key element of the ultimate realization of his vision.

---

[25] Bush, "What Xi Jinping Said about Taiwan at the 19th Party Congress."

[26] "Full Text of Xi Jinping's Report at 19th CPC Congress," *China Daily*, November 4, 2017, http://www.chinadaily.com.cn/china/19thcpcnationalcongress/2017-11/04/content_34115212.htm. Some of the language about Taiwan in Xi's 19th Party Congress speech appears to echo Article 2 of the Anti-Secession Law, which states that China's sovereignty and territorial integrity "brook no division" and warns that China "shall never allow the 'Taiwan independence' secessionist forces to make Taiwan secede from China under any name or by any means."

[27] "Full Text of Xi Jinping's Report at 19th CPC Congress."

Xi's speech at the closing of the 13th National People's Congress in March 2018 reiterated the importance of upholding the one-China principle and 1992 Consensus and promoting the peaceful development of cross-strait relations. Xi also called for the expansion of economic and cultural exchanges.[28] At the same time, however, he once again delivered a firm message about deterring independence and achieving unification:

> It is the shared aspiration of all Chinese people and in the fundamental interests of the Chinese nation to safeguard China's sovereignty and territorial integrity and realize China's complete reunification. In front of the great national interests and the tide of history, any actions and tricks to split China are doomed to fail. They are certain to meet with the people's condemnation and the punishment of history.[29]

Recent Chinese statements continue to reflect these goals. For example, during a meeting between China's Taiwan Affairs Office and a delegation of KMT members of the Legislative Yuan, the head of the office Liu Jieyi reiterated China's determination to achieve ultimate "unification of the motherland," push Taipei to accept the 1992 Consensus, and oppose any "secessionist activities that promote Taiwan independence."[30] Liu also stated that "the two sides of the Taiwan Strait are one family," a vision that would guide Beijing when trying to bring together "the hearts of compatriots" on both sides and promoting exchanges between the mainland and the island. In addition, Liu highlighted the 31 measures unveiled earlier in the year to appeal to students and businesspeople in Taiwan.

Looking to the future, however, China could face an increasingly difficult situation. Interviews with Chinese specialists on Taiwan and articles published by Chinese scholars indicate that Beijing is becoming more and more concerned about trends in public opinion in Taiwan, particularly among the island's youth. Chinese scholars are well aware that opinion polls show that young people in Taiwan increasingly see themselves as Taiwanese rather than Chinese and view Taiwan and China as separate countries, a situation that does not bode well for China's ambitions and objectives with regard to Taiwan.[31] These concerns are reflected by Beijing's evolving approach to achieving its policy goals. The next section examines the key elements of this approach.

---

[28] "Speech Delivered by President Xi at the NPC Closing Meeting," *China Daily*, March 22, 2018, http://eng.chinamil.com.cn/view/2018-03/22/content_7980317.htm.

[29] Ibid.

[30] Cheng Hung-ta and Tseng Wei-chen, "KMT Lawmakers Meet with TAO Head," *Taipei Times*, June 3, 2018, http://www.taipeitimes.com/News/taiwan/archives/2018/06/03/2003694245.

[31] See, for example, Tong Liqun, "Taiwan qingnian liang'an guanxi renzhi yanjiu" [Research on Perceptions of Cross-Strait Relations among Young People in Taiwan], *Journal of United Front Science* 5 (2017): 96–102.

Key Components of China's Taiwan Policy: Political, Economic, and Security Activities

This section explores the different aspects of China's policy toward Taiwan, with particular attention to recent developments under Xi's leadership. Since Tsai took office in Taiwan, China has intensified its campaign of diplomatic isolation, military intimidation, economic coercion, and influence operations against Taiwan. Along with these steps, China has increased the incentives it offers to key groups in Taiwan, especially the island's youth and business community. Although Beijing has not been entirely clear about what it expects to accomplish, the available evidence suggests that this pressure campaign is aimed at constraining Taiwan by reducing its diplomatic space, limiting its economic options, and influencing public opinion. The campaign probably also aims to undermine President Tsai and the DPP politically. The rest of this section examines each of the major components of China's pressure campaign: diplomatic isolation, military intimidation, economic coercion, and influence operations.

Diplomatic Isolation

China eased its diplomatic pressure campaign during Ma's presidency, adhering to a truce that resulted in a pause in the competition for the allegiance of Taiwan's remaining diplomatic allies and allowing Taiwan to participate in the World Health Assembly (WHA). Since the election of Tsai as president, however, Beijing has renewed and intensified its efforts to isolate the island diplomatically.

One important component of this campaign involves preventing Taiwan from participating in meetings of international bodies such as the World Health Organization. From 2009 to 2016, Taiwan participated in the WHA as an observer under the name Chinese Taipei, a development that was possible with the support of the United States and because of warmer cross-strait relations under Ma's KMT administration.[32] However, this changed after Tsai entered office. In 2017, China used its leverage to exclude Taiwan from participation in the WHA, and in 2018 Beijing froze Taiwan out of the WHA for the second year in a row.[33] Ma Xiaoguang, the spokesperson for the PRC's Taiwan Affairs Office, reiterated Beijing's position that it would only permit

---

[32] Taiwan's invitation to participate is issued on a year-by-year basis.

[33] Joseph Yeh, "Taiwan Regrets Latest Exclusion from World Health Assembly," Focus Taiwan, May 8, 2018, http://m.focustaiwan.tw/news/aipl/201805080005.aspx.

Taiwan to participate in international events if it accepts the 1992 Consensus and the one-China principle.[34]

Another part of China's diplomatic isolation of Taiwan is its renewed exclusion of Taipei from the International Civil Aviation Organization (ICAO). In 2013, when cross-strait relations were warmer, Beijing allowed the ICAO to invite Taiwan to participate in its triennial assembly. In 2016, however, after cross-strait relations cooled, it blocked Taiwan from participation in the meeting. China's exclusion of Taiwan from the ICAO is not only a matter of squeezing its international space for symbolic reasons. This action also has practical consequences. Indeed, it appears to have enabled Beijing to unilaterally change flight routes over the Taiwan Strait.[35] In January 2018 the PRC's Civil Aviation Administration unilaterally expanded the M503 flight route, which previously consisted of southbound flights over the strait from Shanghai to Hong Kong. Without consulting Taiwan, China announced its expansion of the route to include northbound flights and added extension routes with flights to three cities: Xiamen, Fuzhou, and Dongshan. China justified its actions by claiming that because the route lies entirely within the Shanghai flight information region, it was under no obligation to consult with Taiwan. However, Taipei argued that it should have been consulted as a concerned party in accordance with ICAO rules because the M503 route is so close to the Taiwan flight information region and crosses other flight routes from Taiwan to the Kinmen and Matsu island groups.[36]

China's attempts to isolate Taiwan diplomatically go beyond restricting its participation in international organizations. Indeed, perhaps the most high-profile action involves persuading the island's dwindling number of official diplomatic allies to break off official ties with Taiwan and shift diplomatic recognition to the PRC. This competition was largely frozen from 2009 to 2016. However, following Tsai's election, Beijing quickly returned to its practice of using a combination of pressure and inducements to persuade Taiwan's diplomatic allies to shift recognition to the mainland. First, in March 2016 China announced the establishment of official diplomatic relations

---

[34] "Mainland Official Reiterates One-China Principle as Prerequisite for Taiwan's Global Event Attendance," Xinhua, April 25, 2018, http://www.xinhuanet.com/english/2018-04/25/c_137136280.htm.

[35] For an overview of the changes to the flight route and potential consequences, see "A Primer on M503 and Civil Aviation in Asia," Center for Strategic and International Studies, Asia Maritime Transparency Initiative, March 14, 2018, https://amti.csis.org/primer-m503-civil-aviation-asia.

[36] Ibid.

with Gambia.[37] Gambia had severed its official ties with Taiwan in November 2013, but Beijing did not move to establish formal diplomatic relations with Gambia at that time. Although the PRC Foreign Ministry spokesperson avoided directly answering a question about whether the decision to do so in March 2016 marked the end of the so-called diplomatic truce, many observers in Taiwan and elsewhere interpreted it as a clear signal that Beijing was returning to its policy of diplomatic isolation.[38] Beijing proved that interpretation correct in December 2016 when it persuaded São Tomé and Príncipe to switch recognition to the mainland.[39] Then in June 2017, China convinced Panama to change sides, delivering a heavy diplomatic blow to Taiwan. This move, in particular, seemed to be designed to embarrass Tsai, who had traveled to Panama to attend a ceremony marking the expansion of the Panama Canal a year earlier. Her visit to Panama in June 2016 was widely seen as underscoring Panama's importance to Taiwan, particularly as it was Tsai's first overseas trip after her inauguration.[40]

China has since accelerated its diplomatic isolation campaign. On May 1, 2018, the Dominican Republic severed official ties with Taiwan and established diplomatic relations with China.[41] Less than a month later, on May 24, 2018, Burkina Faso announced its decision to sever official ties with Taiwan and switch recognition to China, leaving eSwatini (known as Swaziland until April 2018) as Taiwan's sole remaining official partner in Africa and another obvious target for Beijing.[42] In August 2018, El Salvador broke off diplomatic relations with Taiwan and established official ties with the PRC. In all, China's renewed campaign to isolate Taiwan diplomatically has reduced the number of countries with which Taiwan maintains official

---

[37] See "Foreign Ministry Spokesperson Lu Kang's Remarks on Resumption of Diplomatic Ties between China and Gambia," Ministry of Foreign Affairs (PRC), March 17, 2016, http://www.fmprc.gov. cn/mfa_eng/xwfw_665399/s2510_665401/t1348635.shtml; and "Joint Communiqué between the People's Republic of China and the Islamic Republic of the Gambia on Resumption of Diplomatic Relations," Ministry of Foreign Affairs (PRC), March 17, 2016, http://www.fmprc.gov.cn/mfa_eng/zxxx_662805/t1348575.shtml.

[38] Stacy Hsu, "Gambia, China Resume Ties in Lieu of Taiwan," *Taipei Times*, March 18, 2016, http://www.taipeitimes.com/News/front/archives/2016/03/18/2003641843.

[39] "China Resumes Ties with São Tomé, Which Turned Away from Taiwan," *New York Times*, December 26, 2016, https://www.nytimes.com/2016/12/26/world/asia/china-taiwan-sao-tome-diplomatic-relations.html.

[40] Simon Denyer, "Taiwan Reacts Defiantly as Panama Switched Diplomatic Ties to China," *Washington Post*, June 13, 2017, https://www.washingtonpost.com/world/panama-establishes-ties-with-china-abandoning-taiwan-as-beijing-steps-up-the-pressure/2017/06/13/0a3bc8f0-4ff5-11e7-a973-3dae94ed3eb7_story.html.

[41] See "Wang Yi tan Zhong-Duo jianli waijiao guanxi" [Wang Yi Discusses the Establishment of China–Dominican Republic Diplomatic Relations], Ministry of Foreign Affairs (PRC), May 1, 2018, http://www.fmprc.gov.cn/web/wjbzhd/t1555856.shtml.

[42] "China, Burkina Faso Resume Diplomatic Ties," Xinhua, May 26, 2018, http://www.xinhuanet.com/english/2018-05/26/c_137208642.htm.

diplomatic relations by five since Tsai's inauguration. At the time of writing, Taiwan maintains official diplomatic relations with just sixteen countries and the Vatican (see **Table 1**).

China has also pressured a number of Taiwan's unofficial diplomatic partners to change the names of Taiwan's representative offices in their countries and replace references to the Republic of China or Taiwan. For example, in May 2018, after months of pressure from China, the government of Papua New Guinea insisted that Taiwan change the name of its representative office in the country from the Trade Mission of the Republic of China (Taiwan) in Papua New Guinea to the Taipei Economic

TABLE 1   Taiwan's official diplomatic allies (18 as of June 2018)

Region	Country
East Asia and Pacific (6)	Kiribati
	Marshall Islands
	Nauru
	Palau
	Solomon Islands
	Tuvalu
Africa (1)	eSwatini
Europe (1)	Holy See
Latin America and Caribbean (9)	Belize
	Guatemala
	Haiti
	Honduras
	Nicaragua
	Paraguay
	Federation of Saint Christopher and Nevis
	Saint Lucia
	Saint Vincent and the Grenadines

SOURCE: Ministry of Foreign Affairs (Taiwan), "Diplomatic Allies," https://www.mofa.gov.tw/en/AlliesIndex.aspx?n=DF6F8F246049F8D6&sms=A76B7230ADF29736; and Chris Horton, "El Salvador Recognizes China in Blow to Taiwan," *New York Times*, https://www.nytimes.com/2018/08/21/world/asia/taiwan-el-salvador-diplomatic-ties.html.

and Cultural Office in Papua New Guinea.[43] This followed similar changes under Chinese pressure in Ecuador, Bahrain, Nigeria, Jordan, and the United Arab Emirates. In Nigeria, a combination of pressure and incentives (in the form of $40 million in promised investment) also resulted in a demand to move Taiwan's renamed representative office from Abuja, the capital, to the commercial city of Lagos.[44]

Military Intimidation

Military displays aimed at intimidating Taiwan are another important and long-standing element of China's pressure campaign, albeit one that has often backfired in certain respects. The most intense example of military intimidation to date took place during the 1995–96 Taiwan Strait crisis, when the People's Liberation Army (PLA) conducted a show of force that included military exercises and missile launches. Although it has not repeated such a high-intensity display of military power since that time, the PLA has carried out a series of military exercises over the years, including some with a focus on amphibious operations of the type that would be part of an invasion campaign, to underscore its growing military capabilities and send a message to Taiwan.

More recently, China has added a new means of demonstrating its growing military power to Taiwan. Starting in March 2015, it has conducted a series of long-range strategic bomber flights throughout the region, including over the South China Sea, near Japan, and around Taiwan. The flights appear to be modeled on U.S. and Russian employment of bombers for strategic signaling purposes. These flights have mostly occurred through the Miyako Strait (between Okinawa and Taiwan) and the Bashi Channel (between Taiwan and the Philippines) and over the South China Sea.[45]

Beginning in late 2016, Beijing turned its attention to Taiwan and directed the PLA Air Force (PLAAF) to begin circumnavigating the island, simultaneously incorporating at least six different types of supporting aircraft, including early-warning, fighter, electronic warfare, and intelligence,

---

[43] Stacy Hsu, "PNG Demands New Name for Taiwan Office," *Taipei Times*, June 2, 2018, http://www.taipeitimes.com/News/taiwan/archives/2018/06/02/2003694174.

[44] "Nigeria Trims Ties with Taiwan as It Courts China," Reuters, January 12, 2017, https://www.reuters.com/article/us-taiwan-nigeria-idUSKBN14W1BI.

[45] This section draws on Mark R. Cozad and Nathan Beauchamp-Mustafaga, *People's Liberation Army Air Force Operations over Water: Maintaining Relevance in China's Changing Security Environment* (Santa Monica: RAND Corporation, 2017); Nathan Beauchamp-Mustafaga et al., "China Signals Resolve with Bomber Flights over the South China Sea," War On the Rocks, August 2, 2016, https://warontherocks.com/2016/08/china-signals-resolve-with-bomber-flights-over-the-south-china-sea; and Nathan Beauchamp-Mustafaga et al., "Chinese Bomber Flights around Taiwan: For What Purpose?" War On the Rocks, September 13, 2017, https://warontherocks.com/2017/09/chinese-bomber-flights-around-taiwan-for-what-purpose.

reconnaissance, and surveillance aircraft. Bomber flights around Taiwan continued through the summer of 2017 with an increased operational tempo, featuring seven flights during that summer alone. More recently these bomber flights have continued to focus on Taiwan, and the flights around the island appear to be designed, at least in part, to ratchet up the pressure against Tsai over policies to which China objects. Some recent flights have been accompanied by statements that appear to reflect this messaging. For example, in December 2017, when H-6K bombers, Su-30 and J-11 fighters, and several support aircraft flew around Taiwan from north to south,[46] the PLAAF spokesperson referred to the flight as an "island encirclement patrol."[47]

In April 2018, the PLAAF conducted flights on three days in a row for the first time, with a fourth flight occurring several days later. These flights varied between solo H-6K flights and flights accompanied by other support aircraft. In May 2018, China for the first time dispatched advanced Su-35 fighters to accompany H-6K bombers on Taiwan-related flights, according to the PLAAF. Spokesperson Shen Jinke described the flights as representing a "new breakthrough" because it was the first time Su-35 fighters crossed the first island chain, flying over the Bashi Channel with H-6K bombers. The PLAAF spokesperson also noted that the flights included early-warning and surveillance aircraft along with the bombers and fighters.[48] The spokesperson from the PRC Taiwan Affairs Office, An Fengshan, indicated that the flights were meant to send "a strong warning to Taiwan independence separatist forces and their activities" and demonstrate China's "determination and capabilities to safeguard national sovereignty and territorial integrity."[49]

As another part of its campaign to intimidate Taiwan with displays of military power, China has regularly used official media to send messages associated with military activities around Taiwan or opposite the island. Sometimes Beijing has also highlighted Taiwan-focused drills held in other

---

[46] People's Liberation Army Air Force (PLAAF), Weibo, December 11, 2017, https://m.weibo.cn/status/4184072500922480; and "Chugokuki no higashishinakai oyobi taiheiyo niokeru hikonitsuite" [On the Flight of Chinese Aircraft in the East China Sea and the Pacific Ocean], Ministry of Defense (Japan), Press Release, December 11, 2017, http://www.mod.go.jp/js/Press/press2017/press_pdf/p20171211_01.pdf.

[47] PLAAF Weibo, December 11, 2017. For one example of a PLAAF spokesperson implicitly suggesting photos posted to Weibo from flights near Taiwan were of Chinese territory, see PLAAF Weibo, December 12, 2017, https://weibo.com/tv/v/FyZRGCeYG?fid=1034:0e50a3232e762b320adbba4df67e74d2. For Taiwan's reaction, see Michael Martina and Jess Macy Yu, "China Angered as U.S. Considers Navy Visits to Taiwan," Reuters, December 13, 2017, https://af.reuters.com/article/worldNews/idAFKBN1E808I.

[48] See "Su-35 Fighter Jets Join Patrol around Taiwan," Global Times, May 11. 2018, http://www.globaltimes.cn/content/1101857.shtml; and Matthew Strong, "Chinese Su-35 Jets Fly over Bashi Channel South of Taiwan for the First Time," Taiwan News, May 11, 2018, https://www.taiwannews.com.tw/en/news/3428186.

[49] "China Admits Military Exercises Intended to Threaten Taiwan," Japan Times, May 16, 2018.

parts of China. For example, in July 2015, the official China Central Television (CCTV) broadcast a video of the PLA's Stride 2015 exercise, held at the Zhurihe Training Base in Inner Mongolia, complete with a scene showing troops storming a structure that closely resembled Taiwan's presidential palace. The video was broadcast in Taiwan as well as internationally, illustrating how China's military messages can be quickly transmitted to the public.[50]

More recently, China has supplemented its official media coverage with postings on social media, including official Chinese-language microblogs (*weibo*) and Twitter accounts. The diversification of messaging channels appears to allow Beijing to amplify the signals sent by its military activities around Taiwan. Indeed, in addition to official media reports, social media postings have highlighted many of the bomber flights. Some have been prominently featured on the PLAAF's official Chinese-language microblog and on the Twitter accounts of the *People's Daily* and the State Council Information Office. Indeed, a number of postings have incorporated photos and videos of the bombers and accompanying aircraft. For example, after the December 2017 flight mentioned above, PLAAF Weibo posted photos of an H-6K against the backdrop of an unnamed island and asked Chinese netizens to guess which it was (unsurprisingly, they correctly guessed Taiwan).[51] The flight was front page news on the *People's Daily*, was the top story on CCTV News, and was featured in the *PLA Daily*, all of which the PLAAF reposted on its official microblog account.[52]

Sometimes Beijing has even used official media outlets to exaggerate the scale and scope of some of its military exercises, presumably in order to amplify their psychological effects on people in Taiwan. Perhaps most notably, in April 2018, Chinese official media played up what appeared to be a small, routine military exercise opposite Taiwan, apparently in response to Premier Lai Ching-te's statement characterizing himself as a "political worker

---

[50] Emily Rauhala, "Watch: China Soldiers Storm What Looks Like a Replica of Taiwan's Presidential Palace," *Washington Post*, July 24, 2015, https://www.washingtonpost.com/news/worldviews/wp/2015/07/24/watch-chinese-soldiers-storm-what-looks-like-a-replica-of-taiwans-presidential-palace; and Lo Tien-pin and Jake Chung, "China Simulates Attack on Presidential Office," *Taipei Times*, July 23, 2015, http://www.taipeitimes.com/News/front/archives/2015/07/23/2003623689.

[51] PLAAF Weibo, December 11, 2017, https://m.weibo.cn/status/4184081916589933.

[52] Su Yincheng, "Kongjun duoxing zhanji cheng tixi 'rao dao xunhang'" [Multiple Types of Aircraft Form System for "Around the Island Cruise"], *People's Daily*, December 12, 2017, http://paper.people.com.cn/rmrb/html/2017-12/13/nw.D110000renmrb_20171213_6-01.htm; Li Jianwen, "Kongjun duoxing zhanji cheng tixi 'rao dao xunhang'" [Multiple Types of Aircraft Form System for "Around the Island Cruise"], *PLA Daily*, December 12, 2017, http://www.81.cn/jfjbmap/content/2017-12/13/content_194273.htm; PLAAF Weibo, December 13, 2017, available at https://m.weibo.cn/status/4184594699505559; and "News Broadcast," CCTV-13, December 13, 2017, available at https://weibo.com/tv/v/FzuFWgaAj?fid=1034:a62198dd48c59c867f3971a2f7f91486.

for Taiwan independence."[53] The exercise was a routine coastal artillery drill, but China's official media promoted it heavily to magnify its psychological impact. Following the exercise, a spokesperson for Taiwan's Ministry of National Defense characterized the activity as "small-scale" and charged that "Chinese official media calling this a so-called 'military exercise' in the Taiwan Strait is an exaggeration." The spokesperson also said that the activity was part of a series of annual drills China has carried out almost every year since 2007 "to create a feeling of panic."[54] According to Chieh Chung, a research fellow at National Policy Foundation, a KMT-affiliated think tank, "Beijing has regularly taken advantage of these cheap, routine, small-sized, regional drills to serve its purpose of psychological warfare against Taiwan."[55]

Economic Coercion

At the outset of China's reform and opening era there was virtually no economic contact between the mainland and Taiwan. Beginning in the early 1980s, however, their economic relationship expanded rapidly. By 2001, China had replaced the United States as Taiwan's top export market. Cross-strait trade has continued to increase over the past fifteen years, despite the ups and downs in the bilateral relationship, making the mainland Taiwan's most important trade partner. In 2017, trade between Taiwan and China was $139 billion, constituting 24% of Taiwan's total trade and more than double its trade with the United States, the island's second-largest trading partner. Specifically, Taiwan's exports to the mainland in 2017 amounted to almost $89 billion, accounting for 28% of its total exports, and imports from China reached $50 billion, amounting to 19% of its total imports.[56] Additionally, China has become the top destination for investment. According to official statistics from Taiwan, in 2017 investment in mainland China was more than $8.7 billion. This increase in cross-strait investment reflects China's emergence as a key manufacturing base for many Taiwanese companies, including in the information technology sector, which plays an important role in the island's economy.

---

[53] Ku Chuan and Evelyn Kao, "Premier Reiterates Taiwan-Independence Approach as 'Pragmatic,'" Focus Taiwan, April 15, 2018, http://focustaiwan.tw/news/acs/201804150010.aspx.

[54] Te-Ping Chen, "Taiwan Plays Down Chinese Military Exercises," *Wall Street Journal*, April 18, 2018, https://www.wsj.com/articles/taiwan-downplays-chinese-military-exercises-1524055670.

[55] Joseph Yeh, "Beijing's Routine Exercises Psychological Warfare: Expert," Focus Taiwan, April 22, 2018, http://m.focustaiwan.tw/news/acs/201804220010.aspx.

[56] It is important to note that Taiwan counts trade with Hong Kong separately. In 2017, its total trade with Hong Kong amounted to about $42.7 billion, including about $41.2 billion in exports and about $1.5 billion in imports. See Bureau of Foreign Trade, Ministry of Economic Affairs (Taiwan), "Trade Statistics," https://cus93.trade.gov.tw/FSCE040F/FSCE040F.

The dramatic increase in the level of cross-strait economic interaction could be seen as a force for stability in cross-strait relations, but it could also create vulnerabilities. As Murray Scot Tanner observes, "the two economies are now in a deep, wide-ranging relationship of 'asymmetric interdependence' in which each side relies upon the other for important contributions to its economy, and each would suffer great economic pain and dislocation in the event of a major disruption in that relationship."[57] Some in Taiwan have argued that Taiwan is far more dependent on the mainland than the mainland is on Taiwan. For example, although China is Taiwan's largest trading partner, Taiwan was only the mainland's seventh-largest trading partner in 2017.[58] Additionally, Chinese companies have invested very little in Taiwan, where Chinese investment is restricted for national security reasons.[59] On the other hand, the two sides are interdependent in ways that are not easily captured by such statistics. Notably, the island's substantial investment in China's high-tech industry means that Beijing is reliant on Taiwan to continue developing what it views as an important sector of the Chinese economy.[60] Nonetheless, the rapid growth of cross-strait economic ties has intensified concerns in Taiwan that such increasing economic connections could give the mainland the ability to employ economic coercion. China has certainly attempted to do so, and it has made no secret of its intentions over the years.[61]

Although skepticism about the dangers of giving China greater leverage has curtailed the further expansion of the cross-strait economic relationship that was envisioned under the Ma administration from 2008 to 2016, China has a number of tools at its disposal to apply economic pressure on Taiwan. The most prominent example is the reduction of Taiwan-bound tourists from China. Beijing denies that it has been restricting the number of tourists visiting the island in the wake of Tsai's victory, but many observers in Taiwan see the decline in tourist arrivals as a means of warning Tsai and the DPP that China would use its economic leverage unless they agree to meet the mainland's political demands.[62] According to official statistics from Taiwan's Tourism Bureau, the number of mainland tourists dropped from 4.18 million in 2015 to 3.51 million in 2016, a decline of 16%. In 2017 the decline in

---

[57] Murray Scot Tanner, *Chinese Economic Coercion against Taiwan: A Tricky Weapon to Use* (Santa Monica: RAND Corporation, 2007), xiii.

[58] "SCIO Briefing on China's Imports and Exports in 2017," Information Office of the State Council (PRC), January 15, 2018, http://www.scio.gov.cn/32618/Document/1616896/1616896.htm.

[59] Jan Knoerich, "When It Comes to Outward Direct Investment, Mainland Chinese Firms Are Ignoring Taiwan," Taiwan Insight, April 9, 2018, https://taiwaninsight.org/2018/04/09/when-it-comes-to-foreign-direct-investment-china-is-ignoring-taiwan.

[60] The author thanks an anonymous reviewer for raising this point.

[61] For further discussion, see Tanner, *Chinese Economic Coercion against Taiwan*, xiii–xiv.

[62] Shelley Shan, "Minister Sees Drop in Chinese Tourism," *Taipei Times*, April 6, 2016.

mainland tourist arrivals was even more pronounced, falling to 2.73 million, down 22% from 2016.[63] For complete figures on mainland tourist arrivals from 2008 (the first year mainland tourists could fly directly to Taiwan) to 2017, see **Table 2**.

Although Beijing has not officially acknowledged that it is reducing the number of tourists to punish Tsai and the DPP, Chinese sources have privately confirmed that this is the case.[64] Indeed, according to media reports, tour operators assert that Beijing has limited the issuance of travel permits to visit Taiwan as part of tour groups.[65] In response, Taiwan has attempted to reduce the island's reliance on mainland tourists by attracting more visitors from other locations. In particular, it has been trying to attract more tourists from South Korea, Japan, and countries in Southeast Asia, resulting in substantial increases in recent years. Table 2 also shows complete figures on tourist arrivals from these countries from 2008 to 2017.

Additionally, some observers have suggested that a decline in the number of undergraduate students from the mainland studying in Taiwan in 2018 might be another form of Chinese economic pressure.[66] Other reports, however, indicate that China's apparent effort to reduce the number of undergraduate students in Taiwan might be motivated primarily by concerns that they could be "easily liberalized" while attending universities in Taiwan.[67]

Influence Operations

China's pressure campaign has also featured some key elements that do not fit neatly into the above categories. These are best characterized as various types of political influence operations, ranging from traditional "united front" operations to the manipulation of social media. Most of these operations are aimed at Taiwan, but some are aimed at influencing how international actors characterize or deal with Taiwan. In particular, the international component of China's political influence campaign includes attempts to pressure international companies to refer to Taiwan as Chinese territory.

China has a long history of employing "united front" tactics and conducting political influence operations as a means of advancing its

---

[63] Statistics on mainland Chinese tourist arrivals are drawn from the Tourism Bureau, Ministry of Transportation and Communications (Taiwan), "Yearly Statistics," http://admin.taiwan.net.tw/statistics/year_en.aspx?no=15.

[64] Author's interviews.

[65] Shan, "Minister Sees Drop in Chinese Tourism."

[66] Author's interviews.

[67] Duncan DeAeth, "Chinese Undergrads in Taiwan on Steady Decline," *Taiwan News*, June 13, 2018, https://www.taiwannews.com.tw/en/news/3456319. There also appears to have been a slight increase in the number of Chinese graduate students in Taiwan in 2018, which further complicates the picture.

TABLE 2 Visitor arrivals in Taiwan from mainland China, South Korea, Japan, and select Southeast Asian countries, 2008–17

	2008	2009	2010	2011	2012	2013	2014	2015	2016	2017
China	329,204	972,123	1,630,735	1,784,185	2,586,428	2,874,702	3,987,152	4,184,102	3,511,734	2,732,549
South Korea	252,266	167,641	216,901	242,902	259,089	351,301	527,684	658,757	884,397	1,054,708
Japan	1,086,691	1,000,661	1,080,153	1,294,758	1,432,315	1,421,550	1,634,790	1,627,229	1,895,702	1,898,854
Vietnam	76,786	60,476	72,352	95,837	89,354	118,467	137,177	146,380	196,636	383,329
Thailand	84,586	78,405	92,949	102,902	97,712	104,138	104,812	124,409	195,640	292,534
Malaysia	155,783	166,987	285,734	307,898	341,032	394,326	439,240	431,481	474,420	528,019
Singapore	205,449	194,523	241,334	299,599	327,253	364,733	376,235	393,037	407,267	425,577
Philippines	87,936	77,206	87,944	101,539	105,130	99,698	136,978	139,217	172,475	290,784
Indonesia	110,420	106,612	123,834	156,281	163,598	171,299	182,704	177,743	188,720	189,631

SOURCE: Tourism Bureau, Ministry of Transportation and Communications (Taiwan), "Tourism Statistics Database," http://stat.taiwan.net.tw/system/country_years_arrival.html.

strategic objectives.[68] Such operations may be secretive, but China's goals are relatively straightforward: promoting the one-China principle and defeating the pro-independence movement.[69] Beijing has often seen members of Taiwan's business community as targets that can be leveraged to oppose any pro-independence moves that could risk undermining cross-strait economic relations. Likewise, China has sought to use its party-to-party relationship with the KMT to advance its interests and influence politics in Taiwan.[70]

Since Tsai assumed office as president, Beijing has continued to pursue this relationship with the KMT, at least partly in hopes of bolstering its prospects in Taiwan's 2020 elections. This has included holding a number of meetings with KMT and other pan-Blue politicians visiting the mainland.[71] For example, in April 2018, Liu Jieyi, director of the Taiwan Affairs Office, held meetings with former KMT chair Hung Hsiu-chu and New Party chair Yok Mu-ming when they visited Xi'an for an event commemorating the legendary Yellow Emperor Huangdi, who the CCP has promoted as a common ancestor for all Chinese people, including residents of Taiwan.[72] Official media reported that Liu expressed his appreciation for efforts by Hung, Yok, and other like-minded politicians and organizations in Taiwan to uphold the one-China principle and oppose Taiwan independence.[73] However, such efforts to bolster the prospects of pan-Blue politicians could backfire by making them less appealing to voters in Taiwan.

Most recently, China has turned to social media as a new arena for political influence operations, adapting its traditional approach to propaganda and disinformation to take advantage of opportunities presented by the evolving media environment in Taiwan. This new element of China's strategy

---

[68] China refers to a variety of types of political warfare and influence operations as "united front" work, but the CCP's United Front Work Department is not the only organization that carries out such activities. The PLA and Chinese intelligence services are also involved in various types of influence operations.

[69] On China's approach to political warfare in general and the roles of the United Front Work Department in particular, see Thomas G. Mahnken, Ross Babbage, and Toshi Yoshihara, "Countering Comprehensive Coercion: Competitive Strategies Against Authoritarian Political Warfare," Center for Strategic and Budgetary Assessments, 2018, 25–52.

[70] For further discussion, see Ian Forsyth, "Analyzing China's 31 Measures for Taiwan," China-US Focus, April 24, 2018, https://www.chinausfocus.com/political-social-development/analyzing-chinas-31-measures-for-taiwan.

[71] In Taiwan, "pan-Blue" is the term sometimes applied to a loose coalition consisting of the KMT and several smaller parties such as the People First Party and New Party that favor closer relations with the mainland. "Pan-Green" is sometimes used to refer collectively to the DPP and several smaller parties that are more independence-leaning.

[72] For a brief overview of the CCP's efforts to promote the Yellow Emperor as a common ancestor for political reasons, see "China's Communist Party Turns to Mythical Yellow Emperor to Bolster Legitimacy," Straits Times, May 18, 2016, https://www.straitstimes.com/asia/east-asia/chinas-communist-party-turns-to-mythical-yellow-emperor-to-bolster-legitimacy.

[73] "Mainland Official Calls for Jointly Advancing Peaceful Cross-Strait Relations," Global Times, April 5, 2018, http://www.globaltimes.cn/content/1096661.shtml.

includes spreading false or misleading information via channels such as Facebook and the popular messaging app LINE.[74]

Importantly, Chinese influence operations related to Taiwan take place not only in Taiwan but also in other countries where China seeks to influence attitudes or policies toward the island.[75] China has also pressured a number of international companies to list Taiwan as Chinese territory on their websites, in their mobile apps, and even on product packaging. Perhaps the most widely reported incident involved China shutting down Marriott's Chinese website and mobile phone app until the company apologized for an online survey identifying Taiwan as a separate country and complied with Beijing's demands.[76] Likewise, in April 2018, China started pressuring international airlines, including American Airlines, Delta Airlines, and United Airlines, to stop listing Taiwan as a country on their websites. By July 2018, all three U.S. carriers had complied.[77] In addition, China has targeted retailers that sell items in packaging that lists Taiwan as the "country of origin." For example, in April 2018, it announced a 200,000 yuan fine against the Japanese retailer Muji for carrying clothes hangers in packaging listing the originating country as Taiwan. This followed a previous incident in which Muji had to withdraw a catalogue with maps of China that did not include Taiwan and the Senkaku Islands, which China disputes with Japan and calls the Diaoyu Islands.[78]

China's Enhanced Incentives

Even as China has intensified its multifaceted pressure campaign, it has also sought to win over key groups in Taiwan with a variety of economic incentives. Recently, it has enhanced these incentives, issuing new measures that appear to be targeted primarily at the island's youth and business community.

On February 28, 2018, China's Taiwan Affairs Office announced the enactment of the 31 measures, a set of incentives intended to facilitate cross-strait contacts and increase opportunities for Taiwanese individuals and

---

[74] Russell Hsiao, "CCP Propaganda against Taiwan Enters the Social Age," Jamestown Foundation, China Brief, April 24, 2018, https://jamestown.org/program/ccp-propaganda-against-taiwan-enters-the-social-age.

[75] For further discussion, see Mahnken et al., "Countering Comprehensive Coercion," 44.

[76] Marriott also attracted China's ire because the administrator of one of its social media accounts "liked" a post about Tibet. See "China Shuts Marriott's Website over Tibet and Taiwan Error," BBC, January 12, 2018, http://www.bbc.com/news/business-42658070.

[77] Sui-Lee Wee, "Giving In to China, U.S. Airlines Drop Taiwan (in Name, at Least)," New York Times, July 25, 2018, https://www.nytimes.com/2018/07/25/business/taiwan-american-airlines-china.html.

[78] "China Fines Retailer Muji for Listing Taiwan as a Country," BBC, May 24, 2018, http://www.bbc.com/news/world-asia-china-44234270.

businesses in China.[79] The measures are divided into two broad categories, with one containing 19 measures aimed at enticing young people from Taiwan to study, start a business, or seek employment in China and the other consisting of 12 measures focused on increasing opportunities for Taiwan's business community to invest in or engage in other forms of economic cooperation with the mainland. The latter incentives include opportunities for Taiwanese companies to participate in the "Made in China 2025" program, become involved in infrastructure projects, and take advantage of tax breaks. In addition, following the announcement of the 31 measures, the city of Xiamen enacted its own set of 60 additional incentives enabling people and businesses from Taiwan to compete on an equal footing with mainland individuals and companies.[80]

China appears to have enacted the 31 measures as a way to reach key groups in Taiwan without having to work with the current government.[81] This approach was also reflected by Xi Jinping's direct appeal to Taiwan's business community during the 2018 Boao Forum for Asia. He stated that "friends in the island's business community should take a stand and firmly maintain the '1992 consensus,' oppose 'Taiwan independence' and firmly promote the peace and stability of cross-straits relations."[82] In addition, in August 2018, Beijing announced that work permits would no longer be required for residents of Taiwan, making it easier for China to lure skilled workers from the island to the mainland.[83]

Not surprisingly, the Tsai administration reacted to the announcement of the 31 measures with a considerable amount of concern. The Mainland Affairs Council suggested that the incentives were intended to absorb talent and resources from Taiwan and buy the political loyalty of key constituencies.[84] Similarly, a number of experts indicated that they view the measures as aimed at hollowing out Taiwan's economy and gaining even greater economic leverage over the island at a time when there are calls for greater examination and monitoring of the national security implications of cross-strait trade

---

[79] Taiwan Affairs Office of the State Council (PRC), "Guanyu yinfa 'guanyu cujin liang'an jingji wenhua jiaoliu hezuo de ruogan cuoshi de tongzhi" [Notice Pertaining to the Publication of Certain Measures Concerning the Promotion of Cooperation in the Fields of Cross-Strait Economic and Cultural Exchanges], February 28, 2018, http://www.gwytb.gov.cn/wyly/201802/t20180228_11928139.htm.

[80] Flor Wang, "Xiamen Comes Up with More Incentives to Woo Taiwanese People," Focus Taiwan, April 11, 2018, http://focustaiwan.tw/news/acs/201804110024.aspx.

[81] For further discussion, see Forsythe, "Analyzing China's 31 Measures for Taiwan."

[82] Christian Shepherd, "China's Xi Urges Taiwan Business Community to Shun Independence," Reuters, April 10, 2018, https://www.reuters.com/article/us-china-boao-taiwan/chinas-xi-urges-taiwan-business-community-to-shun-independence-idUSKBN1HH0H4.

[83] This change also applies to people from Hong Kong and Macau.

[84] Chiu Kuo-chiang and Flor Wang, "MAC Responds to China's Incentives Measures for Taiwanese People," China Post, March 1, 2018, https://chinapost.nownews.com/20180301-243932.

and financial ties. The Tsai government quickly responded by setting up a task force aimed at reviewing its own policies in relevant areas. It remains to be seen how much the 31 measures will help Beijing achieve its political goals, but the approach is clearly representative of China's determination to offer increasingly attractive carrots to key groups in Taiwan, even as the country wields more imposing sticks in executing its military, economic, and diplomatic pressure campaign against the island.

Conclusion and Implications

China's Approach in the Run-Up to Taiwan's 2020 Elections

China's current approach to Taiwan likely offers some clues about how its strategy might evolve in the run-up to Taiwan's 2020 elections. China seems unlikely to ramp up pressure with a large-scale show of force reminiscent of the military exercises and missile launches it conducted during the 1995–96 Taiwan Strait crisis or through the use of threatening language similar to Premier Zhu Rongji's March 2000 statement that voters in Taiwan had better not "act on impulse" when choosing Taiwan's future course or they "won't get another opportunity to regret."[85] Beijing probably recognizes that such heavy-handed tactics would almost certainly be counterproductive. However, that does not mean that it will stand down ahead of the election. China could continue its current campaign of military intimidation, diplomatic isolation, economic coercion, and influence operations. It could also escalate one or more components of the pressure campaign to new levels. For example, China could attempt to use influence operations—including ones based on computer hacking and exploitation of social media like Russia employed during the 2016 U.S. presidential election—to try to damage the prospects of the DPP or boost its preferred candidates in the KMT.

If the DPP wins and remains in power after 2020, China could finally be convinced that it needs to find a way to work with Taiwan that is acceptable to both sides. Unfortunately, however, Beijing seems more likely to further escalate its pressure campaign to try to compel the DPP to accept the "1992 Consensus" and one-China principle, or at least to further weaken and isolate Taiwan. If the KMT regains power, Beijing would probably expect to make progress on cross-strait issues, but it could be disappointed if it believes that the relationship would be easy. If the KMT moves closer to the center of the political spectrum to win the election and is unwilling to negotiate on

---

[85] Clay Chandler, "China Threatens Voters in Taiwan: Premier Issues Warning Near Election," *Washington Post*, March 16, 2000, http://www.washingtonpost.com/wp-srv/WPcap/2000-03/16/032r-031600-idx.html.

Beijing's terms, which are increasingly unpopular in Taiwan, China might need to adjust its approach.

Longer-Term Challenges for China's Taiwan Policy

China's campaign of diplomatic, military, and economic pressure and influence operations seems more likely to backfire than compel concessions from Taiwan. Indeed, this approach already appears to be alienating many people. For example, after Burkina Faso severed ties with Taiwan in May 2018, Foreign Minister Joseph Wu said China's diplomatic pressure campaign was angering many people in Taiwan and repeated President Tsai's pledge that Taiwan's people "will never succumb to Beijing's pressure."[86] There is also widespread dismay in response to Beijing's economic coercion and other actions seen as demeaning, including its aggressive attempts to pressure international companies to list Taiwan as a part of China on their websites. Indeed, public opinion polls in Taiwan show increases in the percentage of people who indicate that they identify as Taiwanese rather than Chinese.[87] For example, according to the Election Study Center at National Chengchi University, as of June 2018, around 56% of people in Taiwan consider themselves to be Taiwanese, up from around 18% when the survey began in 1992. The polling data indicates that around 37% currently identify as both Taiwanese and Chinese, down from around 46% in 1992, and around 4% see themselves as Chinese, down from around 26%.[88] In addition, recent polling found that 68% of respondents (including more than 71% in the 20–39 age group) would be willing to fight for Taiwan if China were to attempt to achieve unification through military force.[89]

China's efforts to intimidate Taiwan with displays of its growing military power also seem to be leading to greater resentment among its population, particularly since Beijing began conducting bomber flights around Taiwan and stepped up its use of official media, including official social media accounts, to amplify these activities and other military exercises aimed at Taiwan. In May 2018, Taiwan's minister of defense Yen De-fa stated that China's saber

---

[86] See Hsu, "Burkina Faso Severs Ties."

[87] Fang-Yu Chen et al., "The Taiwanese See Themselves as Taiwanese, Not as Chinese," *Washington Post*, January 2, 2017, https://www.washingtonpost.com/news/monkey-cage/wp/2017/01/02/yes-taiwan-wants-one-china-but-which-china-does-it-want.

[88] "Taiwanese/Chinese Identification Trend Distribution in Taiwan (1992/06-2018/06)," Election Study Center, National Chengchi University, https://esc.nccu.edu.tw/course/news.php?Sn=166#.

[89] Shih Hsiu-chuan, "Taiwanese People Willing to Fight for Democracy: Surveys," Focus Taiwan, April 19, 2018, http://focustaiwan.tw/news/aipl/201804190036.aspx.

rattling "will have almost no effect, but will only stir up resentment among Taiwan's people."[90]

The incentives China is offering to members of key groups may promote greater interaction across the Taiwan Strait, but they are unlikely to counteract the political trends in Taiwan that Beijing finds most worrisome. Moreover, China's coercion campaign will very likely exacerbate the problems the mainland faces in terms of public opinion in Taiwan. If Beijing genuinely wants to improve the cross-strait relationship, it will probably need to adopt a much more creative and flexible approach. This is essential if China wants to repair its relationship with Taiwan under a DPP government. Moreover, because the DPP's position on China is more reflective of public opinion in Taiwan, the KMT may find that it needs to shift some of its positions closer to those of the DPP over time to be more competitive in future elections. Indeed, there are indications that China is already worried about the possibility that the KMT may move in the direction of greater "localization" or "Taiwan-ization." According to Drun, "the KMT may be finding itself in the same unenviable position as its domestic political rival—struggling to balance the preferences of Taiwan's electorate while treading a thin line with the Mainland."[91] Indeed, from Beijing's point of view, the worst-case scenario is that this might ultimately result in the KMT moving away from a cross-strait policy centered on the 1992 Consensus and one-China principle.

Taken together, these trends suggest that Beijing may need to rethink its current approach. China's combination of coercion and incentives may be adequate to deter Taiwan from pursuing major moves toward independence, but it appears to be further alienating many people on the island. Consequently, it is probably undermining rather than advancing China's long-term objectives. If Beijing decides to change its approach, however, it could be more likely to double-down on coercion than to opt for more flexible engagement with Taiwan. For example, Beijing might attempt to further intensify its pressure campaign against Taiwan by persuading more of the island's remaining diplomatic partners to switch recognition to the PRC, using economic leverage against Taiwan more aggressively, conducting large-scale naval exercises around the island, or escalating its efforts to influence Taiwan politics or interfere with elections.

Looking to the future, most people in Taiwan will likely continue to reject unification on Chinese terms, while Beijing will probably respond with increased pressure instead of greater flexibility. This raises questions about the lengths to which China will be willing to go to achieve unification with Taiwan

---

[90] Yen made these remarks at a Tamkang University forum on Taiwan's national security strategy. See Liu and Wang, "China's Saber Rattling on Taiwan in Vain."

[91] Drun, "Dwindling Confidence."

as part of its broader objective of "national rejuvenation." China obviously prefers to avoid a cross-strait conflict. Achieving unification with Taiwan peacefully would be a major political achievement for Beijing, and it could facilitate China's pursuit of its broader regional and global objectives. But the prospects appear highly remote given trends in Taiwan. Conversely, Chinese use of force against the island would carry extremely serious political, military, and economic risks. Armed conflict across the Taiwan Strait could lead to U.S. military intervention and might result in a major regional war. Even if China prevailed, a major conflict would likely result in significant military and economic losses. Notably, it could also damage China's international standing and lock in adversarial relationships with the United States, Japan, and other countries. But there are circumstances under which Beijing would be willing to use force to attempt to resolve the situation on its terms, or at least to prevent Taiwan from moving in a direction that it sees as gravely imperiling Chinese interests and goals, some of which are highlighted in the 2005 Anti-Secession Law. Analysts in Taiwan frequently suggest that domestic political factors in China, such as social unrest or a sharp struggle in elite politics, could also prompt Beijing to adopt a much more aggressive approach.

For now, China is likely to continue employing a mix of pressure and inducements to try to manage its relationship with Taiwan. Over the longer term, it is unclear whether Chinese leaders will conclude that they can continue to expand China's regional and global influence in pursuit of the broader goal of national rejuvenation while leaving unresolved the issue of Taiwan unification. Much will depend on how they weigh the practical and political consequences of doing so against the risks inherent in attempting to compel unification on China's terms. As long as the implications of leaving the issue unresolved do not seem to seriously imperil China's most important interests or impede its overall international trajectory, and the grave dangers inherent in a sharp crisis or conflict over Taiwan appear daunting, China can be expected to refrain from using force unless it concludes that some action by Taiwan (or perhaps by the United States) crosses a line that requires a military response despite the risks. Even if China maintains its current approach indefinitely, however, its intensified pressure and influence campaign presents major challenges that Taiwan and its unofficial security partners will need to address.

Implications for Taiwan, Japan, and the United States

Taiwan. Beijing's "carrot and stick" approach presents serious challenges to Taiwan, as a number of the island's officials have pointed out.[92] Even as China has been stepping up its attempts at diplomatic isolation, military

---

[92] See Liu and Wang, "China's Saber Rattling on Taiwan in Vain."

intimidation, and economic coercion, it is also offering more incentives to Taiwan's people in the form of the 31 measures. From the point of view of the Tsai government, both the coercive components of China's policy and the enhanced incentives threaten to further undermine Taiwan's position.

Taiwan's national security establishment clearly sees China as the principal threat to its security. According to Taiwan's 2015 National Defense Report, for example, "the PRC remains the major security threat to our country as it has yet to renounce the use of force against Taiwan and can employ more diverse and flexible array of military means against the island."[93] Taiwan's leading defense experts also judge that the PLA seeks to attain a more comprehensive capability to compel unification by force while deterring third-party intervention within the next few years.[94] The threat is increasingly multifaceted, however, incorporating not only military power but also a variety of diplomatic, economic, and informational levers. Consequently, Taipei needs to develop and implement a strategy that accounts for all the challenges presented by China's approach to Taiwan.

Strengthening Taiwan's military capability is essential to help maintain deterrence and an adequate defense posture. One important institutional challenge is the transition to a volunteer force, which has been delayed due to recruitment difficulties. Another is the development of Taiwan's reserve force, which will become increasingly important as the size of the active duty force declines from about 275,000 to 175,000 under a streamlining plan.[95] Additionally, many observers have raised doubts about the adequacy of Taiwan's defense budget, which was about $11 billion in 2018, falling well short of President Tsai's campaign target of 3% of GDP.[96] Finally, Taiwan recognizes the need to pursue a more "innovative and asymmetric" approach to its defense strategy, but further changes may be required to maintain a credible defense and deterrence posture sufficient to deal with China's growing military power.

Taiwan should also continue to pursue efforts to deepen strategic dialogues with the United States and Japan and expand exchanges with other democracies. Officials and experts in Taiwan should also continue to aim to diversify the island's economic relationships to reduce its dependence on China. The centerpiece of this effort is the DPP's implementation of the New Southbound Policy to promote economic links to the Association of Southeast Asian Nations, India, Australia, and other countries. The policy is enjoying

---

[93] Ministry of National Defense (Taiwan), *National Defense Report 2015* (Taipei, 2015), 24.

[94] Ibid., 57.

[95] Ian Easton et al., *Transformation of Taiwan's Reserve Force* (Santa Monica: RAND Corporation, 2017).

[96] Lo Tien-pin and Jonathan Chin, "Defense Budget Fails to Meet Tsai Campaign Pledge," *Taipei Times*, July 16, 2018, http://www.taipeitimes.com/News/front/archives/2018/07/16/2003696762.

some notable successes as reflected by increases in trade, investment, tourism, and people-to-people exchanges, especially with countries in Southeast Asia.[97] In addition to these military, diplomatic, and economic steps, Taiwan should explore ways to increase its ability to resist and counter Chinese influence operations. For example, experts from Taiwan might learn from efforts to respond to Chinese influence operations in Australia.[98]

Japan. China's policy toward Taiwan also has important implications for Japan. Many Japanese analysts view stability in the Taiwan Strait as directly linked to Japan's national security. Moreover, many have argued that unification would threaten Japan's national security interests, especially if achieved through China's use of force or coercion. In addition, China's assertive behavior around the Senkaku/Diaoyu Islands and island building and construction of military facilities in the South China Sea reinforce these concerns in Tokyo.

Although it does not sell arms to Taiwan or engage in security cooperation with Taiwan's military like the United States does, Japan maintains a close, albeit unofficial, relationship with Taiwan.[99] Japan is widely viewed as Taiwan's most important unofficial ally after the United States, and it has been working to strengthen its ties with Taiwan under Prime Minister Shinzo Abe. Expanded economic ties with Japan could help mitigate the effects of Chinese economic pressure, and Tokyo could also become more involved in helping Taiwan participate in the international community. Additionally, as Japan continues to improve its military capabilities with an eye on the threat posed by an increasingly capable PLA, it could play a more important role in deterrence or defense of Taiwan alongside the United States. Nonetheless, Japan's willingness to engage more directly with Taiwan on sensitive military issues will very likely be limited by the desire to maintain a relatively stable relationship with China.

The United States. China's approach to Taiwan will also have important implications for the United States as long as it remains interested in regional stability in general and the security of Taiwan in particular. Accordingly, Washington should continue to focus on maintaining a stable situation across the Taiwan Strait and expanding and deepening the unofficial

---

[97] Hunter Marston and Richard C. Bush, "Taiwan's Engagement with Southeast Asia Is Making Progress under the New Southbound Policy," Brookings Institution, July 30, 2018, https://www.brookings.edu/opinions/taiwans-engagement-with-southeast-asia-is-making-progress-under-the-new-southbound-policy.

[98] Taiwan might also learn from efforts to resist Russian influence operations and interference in elections in the United States, France, and other countries, though there appear to be some important differences between Chinese and Russian practices.

[99] See Jeffrey W. Hornung, "Strong but Constrained Japan-Taiwan Ties," Brookings Institution, March 13, 2018, https://www.brookings.edu/opinions/strong-but-constrained-japan-taiwan-ties.

U.S.-Taiwan relationship. Indeed, there is much that can be done within the boundaries of Washington's long-standing one-China policy. At the broadest level, the United States should continue to emphasize publicly that it welcomes Taiwan's exercise of democracy, protection of human rights, and rule of law. Some specific means of doing so include statements by senior U.S. officials and occasional high-level visits to Taiwan. Washington should also continue to express support for Taiwan's desire to make a greater contribution on international issues, such as humanitarian assistance and disaster relief, global health, and the development of civil society. Additionally, the United States should work with Taiwan to further strengthen relationships between the people of both countries, such as through tourism and educational exchanges.

Because of China's multifaceted pressure campaign, the United States will increasingly need to think more broadly about the island's security needs. It should continue to support Taiwan's defense requirements, not only through arms sales but also through other security cooperation initiatives designed to strengthen deterrence and increase Taiwan's resilience. The United States can do much to assist Taiwan and strengthen the bilateral relationship by focusing its efforts on relatively low-profile, but potentially very important, areas. One important area of emphasis for further deepening security cooperation could include supporting Taiwan's plans for the development of its domestic defense industry, which center on expanding the island's aerospace, shipbuilding, and information security sectors. Another important area for U.S. assistance is the reform of Taiwan's military service system. Still another is strengthening Taiwan's reserve forces, which will become more important to the defense of the island and its ability to deter China, as the number of troops on active duty decreases under the reforms.

It is equally important for the United States to help Taiwan enhance its ability to resist Chinese economic coercion, diplomatic isolation, and influence operations. On the economic front, the United States should seek ways to assist Taiwan in achieving its objectives. Ideally, the United States should try to facilitate its participation in multilateral agreements like the Trans-Pacific Partnership (TPP), which is moving forward without the United States following President Trump's decision to withdraw. Taiwan still wants to join the TPP, but the prospects dimmed after the United States' withdrawal from the agreement. To help resist China's intensifying diplomatic isolation campaign, the United States could not only encourage Taiwan's remaining supporters to retain their ties to the island but also continue to facilitate its international participation through initiatives like the Global Cooperation and Training Framework. The United States should also consider options for working with Taiwan on evaluating and responding to Chinese influence operations. Such options could include expanded intelligence and law enforcement cooperation, as well as facilitation of exchanges with other countries that have relevant experiences and expertise to share with Taiwan.

Taiwan is an important economic and security partner for the United States, and its emergence as a vibrant democracy underscores that the bilateral relationship is based on shared values as well as common interests. Moreover, Washington has broader interests at stake in the sense that its support for Taiwan could be seen as a bellwether for its willingness and ability to uphold its security commitments in the region more generally. In a worst-case scenario, if China were to attempt to use military power to coerce Taiwan into unification, failure to prevent China from absorbing Taiwan through the use of force would seriously undermine U.S. credibility. It might also increase China's ability to threaten the security interests of the United States and its regional allies, especially Japan, given Taiwan's proximity to the Senkaku/Diaoyu Islands and the Ryukyu Islands.[100] Because of Taiwan's importance to U.S. interests as part of a strong and well-rounded, albeit unofficial, relationship, the United States should continue to work with Taiwan to help the island address a broad range of defense, economic, diplomatic, and national security challenges. As those challenges continue to evolve, Washington will need to think in terms that go well beyond arms sales. It will need to place substantial emphasis not only on helping Taiwan modernize its armed forces but also on pursuing other forms of cooperation aimed at increasing Taiwan's resilience and enhancing its ability to resist Chinese military pressure, economic coercion, diplomatic isolation, and influence operations.

---

[100] Additionally, unification in any form could pose some challenges to the interests of the United States and Japan. Indeed, even if unification is peaceful and takes place with the assent of Taiwan's people, it could still adversely affect some U.S. and Japanese security interests. The extent to which it would do so would depend on the nature of China's relationships with the United States and Japan at that time, as well as on the specific terms of peaceful unification, such as whether the PLA Navy and PLA Air Force would be able to use military bases on Taiwan. It is difficult to imagine peaceful unification taking place under current circumstances. However, if the appropriate conditions were to exist in the future, and peaceful unification were preceded by some combination of major changes in China's political system, improvements in the cross-strait relationship, and improvements in China's ties with other countries, including the United States and Japan, or did not involve basing Chinese forces on Taiwan, the adverse effects on U.S. and allied interests would be limited. Such a scenario would remove Taiwan as a flashpoint and diminish the risk of major-power war in the region. It is difficult to imagine that the United States would try to stand in the way if at some point in the future the situation changed so dramatically that unification became an appealing option for Taiwan's people. See Nancy Bernkopf Tucker, "If Taiwan Chooses Unification, Should the United States Care?" *Washington Quarterly* 25, no. 3 (2002): 15–28.

EXECUTIVE SUMMARY

This chapter examines China's growing influence in Southeast Asia and the South China Sea, addressing implications for the region and the U.S.

MAIN ARGUMENT

China's growing economic, strategic, and political prominence have put it in a stronger position to shape developments in Southeast Asia. Beijing's apparent disinterest in strategic restraint, the region's inability to resolve collective action problems, and uncertainty over the future U.S. role in the region bolster China's influence and preeminence there. Such trends reflect not just historically close ties between China and Southeast Asia but also China's recent attempts to take the initiative in these relationships and divide the unity of the Association of Southeast Asian Nations (ASEAN). Should the U.S. wish to retain an active forward presence in Southeast Asia, more direct, frequent, and intense friction with China is likely. Robust regional partnerships and a credible rules-based order are key to weathering such tensions.

POLICY IMPLICATIONS

- China's resurgence in the region, coupled with uncertainty about U.S. regional leadership, implies the continued erosion of ASEAN centrality, which in the past has helped promote regional calm. If Southeast Asian states wish to maintain regional autonomy and avoid being torn between the U.S. and China, they must overcome collective action problems.

- ASEAN's challenges in managing contentious U.S.-China relations mean there is mounting urgency for member states to decide whether to engage in serious organizational reform or adopt alternative institutional arrangements, including ones that may facilitate Chinese primacy.

- The U.S. must more concretely articulate and implement its Indo-Pacific strategy in Southeast Asia. The viability of the U.S. position in the region depends on clarity, consistency, and direction with ASEAN, individual Southeast Asian states, and other regional actors.

Shifting Winds in Southeast Asia: Chinese Prominence and the Future of the Regional Order

Ja Ian Chong

The past decade has witnessed the People's Republic of China (PRC) becoming increasingly assertive and abrasive in Southeast Asia, with the most recent example being its efforts to disrupt proceedings and block a joint statement at the November 2018 APEC summit in Papua New Guinea.[1] The PRC has become the top trading partner for all members of the Association of Southeast Asian Nations (ASEAN) and a major regional investor. It is now a significant influence on politics as well as security across the region and a dominant military presence in the South China Sea. These developments are the culmination of Beijing's push for eminence over a spectrum of issues in Southeast Asia. Unless the United States and other actors in Southeast Asia are willing to accept a PRC veto, they need to invest in mechanisms and processes that enhance the current rules-based order.

Growing PRC involvement and preeminence in Southeast Asia is, at best, a mixed blessing for the region. Mainland Southeast Asia borders the country's historically difficult-to-govern southern and southwest border regions, while the South China Sea provides access to seaborne trade with points west

---

Ja Ian Chong is an Associate Professor in the Department of Political Science at the National University of Singapore. He can be reached at <polcji@nus.edu.sg>.

[1] Josh Rogin, "Inside China's 'Tantrum' Diplomacy at APEC," *Washington Post*, November 20, 2018, https://www.washingtonpost.com/news/josh-rogin/wp/2018/11/20/inside-chinas-tantrum-diplomacy-at-apec.

as well as to the southern perimeter of the so-called first island chain.[2] Reaching into Southeast Asia and ensuring that developments are favorable to Chinese concerns is a natural extension of Beijing's interests. Cooperation with the PRC promises economic growth and wealth for many countries in Southeast Asia but also can sharpen domestic political contestation and intensify Sino-U.S. competition. However, the PRC has not yet shown strategic restraint or supported a more equitable distribution of the costs and benefits of its engagement. In contrast with the United States after World War II, it has refused to bind itself to institutional mechanisms that limit its ability to exercise power arbitrarily.[3]

Compounding the above risks are the weakness of the main regional organization, ASEAN, and the unpredictability of the Trump administration. Beijing's headway into Southeast Asia and the consolidation of its forward-leaning posture in the South China Sea add to the rising trade and political tensions between the PRC and the United States. Centripetal pressures on ASEAN mean that the organization and its members struggle to exert even the limited moderating effect on great-power competition in the region that they exercised late in the Cold War. Individual ASEAN members seem increasingly taken by what Beijing has to offer and less confident in the United States' ability to continue contributing to the region, thereby weakening the U.S. position in Asia.

To make this case, this chapter will begin by laying out long-standing Chinese interests in Southeast Asia, followed by a discussion on the growing economic integration between China and Southeast Asia and its implications for regional politics. The chapter then turns to examine the features of contestation over the South China Sea between China and various Southeast Asian claimants and user states before explaining the limitations that ASEAN faces in addressing the challenges posed by an increasingly powerful and pushy China. The penultimate section looks at possible ways forward in the management of relations between Southeast Asia and China, and the conclusion considers the implications of the dynamics addressed in the chapter for the United States.

---

[2] Pamela Kyle Crossley, Helen F. Siu, and Donald S. Sutton, eds., *Empire at the Margins: Culture, Ethnicity, and Frontier in Early Modern China* (Berkeley: University of California Press, 2006); and Toshi Yoshihara, "China's Vision of Its Seascape: The First Island Chain and Chinese Seapower," *Asian Politics and Policy* 4, no. 3 (2012): 293–314.

[3] G. John Ikenberry, *After Victory: Institutions, Strategic Restraint, and the Rebuilding of Order after Major Wars* (Princeton: Princeton University Press, 2001).

China's Perennial Interests in Southeast Asia

Geography largely explains the PRC's interest in Southeast Asia. The region's general accessibility, proximity to the PRC's southeastern seaboard, and contiguity with its southern land border means that Southeast Asia has a natural importance to Beijing. The historical involvement of the Chinese Communist Party (CCP) in the region bears out this fact. The CCP actively supported the Vietnamese Communist Party during the First and Second Indochina Wars (1945–75), and the PRC was a belligerent in the Third Indochina War (1979–80).[4] In addition, the CCP was a key patron of Khmer Rouge in Cambodia through the 1980s and partnered with Sukarno's Indonesia, as well as with revolutionary Communist parties in Borneo, Burma, Indonesia, Malaya, the Philippines, and Thailand that had been active since the 1930s.[5]

China has a long history of engagement with Southeast Asia, predating the establishment of the PRC. The Han, Yuan, and Ming empires all occupied Vietnam and led military expeditions extending to Java. During the Ming Dynasty, Zheng He undertook naval voyages to establish regional dominance.[6] Imperial records also note trade and pilgrimage routes between what today is southern China and the Southeast Asian kingdoms of Funan, Angkor, Srivijaya, Majapahit, and Malacca.[7] These locations form a larger East Asian trading network with links to ports in Honshu, Kyushu, Taiwan, Luzon, and Borneo. Early migration from China to Southeast Asia followed these same routes.[8] Lingering apprehensions from these historical ties and interactions partly explain why various Southeast Asian governments and populations have treated their ethnic Chinese communities with some suspicion over the years.

What historically has made Southeast Asia important for China has not fundamentally changed. To the contrary, the region's salience for today's PRC has only risen. Its most efficient routes for seaborne trade with Europe,

---

[4] Ang Cheng Guan, *Southeast Asia's Cold War: An Interpretive History* (Honolulu: University of Hawaii Press, 2018); and Andrew Mertha, *Brothers in Arms: China's Aid to the Khmer Rouge, 1975–1979* (Ithaca: Cornell University Press, 2014).

[5] Ang, *Southeast Asia's Cold War*; and Norman G. Owens, ed., *The Emergence of Modern Southeast Asia: A New History* (Honolulu: University of Hawaii Press, 2015).

[6] Geoff Wade, "The Zheng He Voyages: A Reassessment," *Journal of the Malaysian Branch of the Royal Asiatic Society* 78, no. 1 (2005): 37–58.

[7] Martin Stuart-Fox, *A Short History of China–Southeast Asia Relations: Tribute, Trade, and Influence* (Crows Nest: Allen and Unwin, 2013).

[8] Tonio Andrade and Xing Hang, eds., *Sea Rovers, Silver, and Samurai: Maritime East Asia in Global History, 1550–1700* (Honolulu: University of Hawaii Press, 2016).

the Middle East, Africa, and South Asia pass through the South China Sea.[9] This includes the energy imports so important to the Chinese economy. The strategic significance of the region has given rise to discussions about a "Malacca dilemma,"[10] and the need to find alternative westward routes has arguably informed Beijing's infrastructure-focused Belt and Road Initiative (BRI). Potential hydrocarbon deposits and fishing grounds in the South China Sea, as well as rice production in mainland Southeast Asia, amplify the importance of the region, considering the PRC's concerns about energy and food security.[11]

Establishing a dominant position in the South China Sea thus makes strategic sense for Beijing. A strong presence in those waters permits the PRC to secure the southern section of the first island chain.[12] Acquiring such strategic depth enables the country to hold potential threats and challenges at greater distances, reducing the potential of attacks on its industrial coast. Safeguarding access to the South China Sea also means that nuclear ballistic submarines based at Hainan, which are an integral leg of the PRC's nuclear triad, enjoy safer passage to the deeper waters of the Pacific Ocean.[13] The enhanced survivability of the PRC's sea-based nuclear arsenal increases the credibility of its nuclear deterrence.

These incentives for the PRC to shape developments in Southeast Asia will grow as it becomes a major global power, especially given the increasing competition with the United States. The ability to block access to the South China Sea would allow the PRC to pressure key U.S. allies and partners in Northeast Asia, such as Japan, South Korea, and Taiwan, which also depend on those waters for trade and energy imports. Likewise, the ability to disrupt the United States' free use of the South China Sea would put the PRC in a position to impose costs on U.S. military operations in the Indian Ocean and Persian Gulf and complicate its Indo-Pacific strategy. Acquiring such advantages is relatively straightforward for Beijing because of the inability of Southeast Asian states to respond collectively to imposition and enticement by the PRC. Such developments allow Beijing to complicate the U.S. forward presence in Asia should it choose to do so and even potentially acquire an ability to veto the United States' actions in the region.

---

[9] "Maritime Vessel Traffic Density (July 2016)," National Bureau of Asian Research (NBR), Maritime Awareness Project, http://maritimeawarenessproject.org/interactivemap.

[10] "Nengyuan anquan zaoyu 'Maliujia kunjing' Zhong Ri Han nengfou xieshou" [Energy Security Faces "Malacca dilemma" Can China, Japan, and Korea Cooperate], *People's Daily*, June 15, 2004, http://www.people.com.cn/GB/guoji/14549/2570978.html.

[11] Nicholas Thomas, "Going Out: China's Food Security from Southeast Asia," *Pacific Review* 26, no. 5 (2013): 531–62.

[12] Yoshihara, "China's Vision of Its Seascape."

[13] James R. Holmes, "Defend the First Island Chain," *Proceedings Magazine*, April 2014.

Economic Integration, Prosperity, and Their Downsides

Given its rapid economic growth since the 1990s, the PRC has become ASEAN's largest trading partner, both collectively and for each individual member state. Such a development is unsurprising given the integration of global production networks. Southeast Asia exports raw materials, components, and semi-finished products to the PRC for final assembly and re-export to other markets such as the United States, Europe, and Japan. Consumers in the PRC and Southeast Asia also provide markets for Chinese manufactures. Although trade with the PRC has undoubtedly stimulated economic growth in Southeast Asia, such economic integration has cross-cutting political consequences for the region, ranging from unintended local backlash to interference in domestic political processes.

Figures 1 and **2** summarize the PRC's trade relationship with ASEAN between 2007 and 2016. Given that the relationship with each member state clearly varies, it is somewhat misleading to aggregate Southeast Asia into ASEAN. Nonetheless, these figures provide an overall sense of PRC trade ties.

FIGURE 1   Trade in goods: Inter-ASEAN and ASEAN's top five partners ($ million)

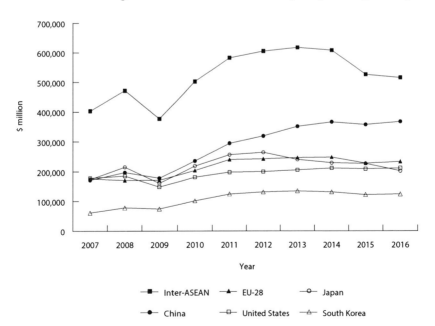

SOURCE: *ASEAN Statistical Yearbook 2016/2017* (Jakarta: ASEAN Secretariat, 2017), chap. 5.

FIGURE 2   Trade in goods: Inter-ASEAN and ASEAN's top five partners (%)

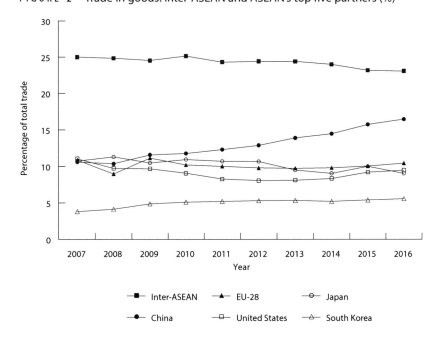

SOURCE: *ASEAN Statistical Yearbook 2016/2017*, chap. 5.

Chinese capital is increasingly prominent in Southeast Asia following the launch of BRI. Chinese FDI in the region increased to $11.3 billion in 2017 from $6.6 billion in 2015, with a focus on infrastructure projects.[14] That said, a significant proportion of the PRC's investment commitments await full realization—planned FDI for 2015 was more than $14 billion, for example.[15] Notably, Chinese investment in Southeast Asia still lags investment by the developed economies. The largest source of FDI in Southeast Asia remains the European Union, followed by the United States and Japan, with most coming in the form of private capital toward commercial facilities rather than infrastructure.[16] **Figures 3** and **4** provide an official ASEAN overview of investment trends in Southeast Asia from 2007 to 2016.

---

[14] ASEAN Statistics Division, "Flow of Inward Foreign Direct Investment (FDI) by Host Country and Source Country (in million US$)," ASEAN Stats Data Portal, https://data.aseanstats.org/fdi-by-hosts-and-sources.

[15] Edward Ng, "The Rise of Chinese FDI into ASEAN," *Nikkei Asset Management*, October 5, 2017, https://www.nikkoam.com.sg/articles/2017/10/the-rise-of-chinese-fdi-into-asean.

[16] ASEAN Statistics Division, "Flow of Inward Foreign Direct Investment (FDI)."

FIGURE 3   Inbound FDI: Inter-ASEAN and ASEAN's top five investors ($ million)

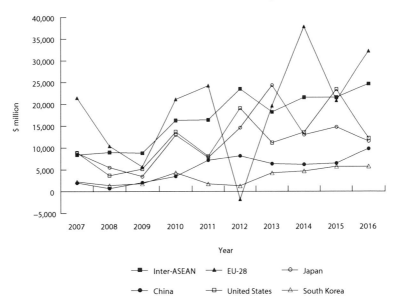

SOURCE: ASEAN Statistics Division, "Flow of Inward Foreign Direct Investment (FDI) by Host Country and Source Country (in million US$)," ASEANstatsDataPorta.

Enhanced economic ties in recent years have reduced the appetite for friction with the PRC among Southeast Asian governments. Notably, expectations that Beijing could impose economic costs for disagreement dampened Southeast Asian reactions to the PRC's construction and militarization of artificial features in the South China Sea. Even after the Arbitral Tribunal on the United Nations Convention on the Law of the Sea (UNCLOS) ruled that Beijing's most extensive South China Sea claims lacked standing, most regional governments either kept silent or gave muted responses.[17] Singapore faced diplomatic and commercial

---

[17] ASEAN, "Joint Statement of the Foreign Ministers of ASEAN Member States on Maintenance of Peace, Security, and Stability in the Region," July 25, 2016, https://asean.org/wp-content/uploads/2016/07/Joint-Statement-of-the-Foreign-Ministers-of-AMS-on-the-Maintenance-of-Peace-Security-and-Stability-in-the-Region-AGREED.pdf; "Malaysia, Singapore, Indonesia React to S. China Sea Ruling," *Kyodo News*, July 13, 2016, https://news.abs-cbn.com/overseas/07/13/16/malaysia-singapore-indonesia-react-to-s-china-sea-ruling; "Ruling Hailed, Philippines Thanks All Responsible Nations," *Philippine Star*, July 13, 2016, https://www.philstar.com/headlines/2016/07/13/1602360/ruling-hailed-philippines-thanks-responsible-nations-support; and "Vietnam Welcomes Hague Ruling on East Vietnam Sea Disputes," *Tuoi Tre*, July 13, 2016, https://tuoitrenews.vn/politics/35827/vietnam-welcomes-.

FIGURE 4 Inbound FDI: Inter-ASEAN and ASEAN's top five investors (%)

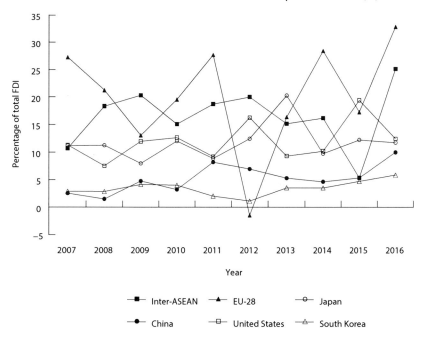

SOURCE: ASEAN Statistics Division, "Flow of Inward Foreign Direct Investment (FDI)."

pressure from the PRC for its open support for applying the rule of law to the South China Sea dispute, despite the fact that this has been Singapore's long-standing position.[18] Fear of further pressure likely has discouraged Singaporean officials from being more candid about the PRC's noncompliance with international rule of law at sea and supporting more robust enforcement mechanisms.[19]

Not surprisingly, this desire to conform with Beijing's foreign policy preferences is especially acute among Southeast Asia's smaller and least-developed economies, given their heavy dependence on PRC investment

[18] Minnie Chan, "How Singapore's Military Vehicles Became Beijing's Diplomatic Weapon," *South China Morning Post*, December 3, 2016, https://www.scmp.com/week-asia/politics/article/2051322/how-singapores-military-vehicles-became-beijings-diplomatic; and Tan Weizhen, "S'pore Businesses Quizzed by Chinese Counterparts over Stand on South China Sea," *Today* (Singapore), October 3, 2016, https://www.todayonline.com/business/spore-businesses-quizzed-chinese-counterparts-over-their-stand-south-china-sea-issue.

[19] Ng Eng Hen, "Adapting to the Changing Rules of the Game" (speech at the Shangri-La Dialogue, Singapore, June 3, 2018), https://www.mindef.gov.sg/web/portal/mindef/news-and-events/latest-releases/article-detail/2018/june/03june18_speech.

and trade.[20] Particularly susceptible are Cambodia, Laos, and Myanmar, which also happen to be among the poorest states in the region. The governments of these states see the basic infrastructure development proposed under BRI as integral to their economic futures. As a result of economic, diplomatic, and domestic political support from the PRC, Hun Sen's Cambodian government supposedly obstructed the formulation of clearer ASEAN positions on the South China Sea territorial disputes on several occasions.[21] These moves from Phnom Penh were important in helping Beijing minimize diplomatic pressure from its southern neighbors.

Another consequence of close economic ties with the PRC is the unintended domestic pushback that can result from the various commercial, social, and environmental externalities involving Chinese-backed projects. The PRC's winning bid to construct a high-speed railway in Thailand met with disputes over exorbitant interest rates and questionable quality, while similar projects in Indonesia and Malaysia ran into disputes over land acquisition, cost, and progress.[22] Myanmar's Myitsone dam project sparked local political disputes and unrest that resulted in a stoppage of construction, with Naypyidaw accusing Beijing of harboring armed rebels across border trading towns.[23] Hydroelectric projects financed by the PRC face accusations of damaging the environment and the livelihoods of riverine communities in Laos, Vietnam, and Cambodia.[24]

The unequal distribution of costs and benefits of economic development between the PRC and Southeast Asian host governments can itself become a source of dispute. The current Thai military government, for instance, faces

---

[20] Ng, "The Rise of Chinese FDI into ASEAN."

[21] Ananth Baliga and Vong Songkeng, "Cambodia Again Blocks ASEAN Statement on South China Sea," *Phnom Penh Post*, July 25, 2016, https://www.phnompenhpost.com/national/cambodia-again-blocks-asean-statement-south-china-sea.

[22] Om Jotikasthira, "Talks Hit Wall over Delay Clause," *Bangkok Post*, June 2, 2018, https://www.bangkokpost.com/news/general/1477265/talks-hit-wall-over-delay-clause; Jeffrey Hutton, "A Catch-22 from China That Could Derail Indonesia's Widodo," *South China Morning Post*, May 12, 2018, https://www.scmp.com/week-asia/politics/article/2145806/catch-22-china-could-derail-indonesias-widodo; Stefania Palma," Malaysia Suspends $22bn China-Backed Projects," *Financial Times*, July 5, 2018, https://www.ft.com/content/409942a4-7f80-11e8-bc55-50daf11b720d; and Jun Suzuki, "Securing Land Still a Problem for Indonesia's Rail Project," *Nikkei Asian Review*, August 7, 2017, https://asia.nikkei.com/Business/Securing-land-still-a-problem-for-Indonesia-rail-project.

[23] Mark Ives, "A Chinese-Backed Dam Project Leaves Myanmar in a Bind," *New York Times*, March 31, 2017, https://www.nytimes.com/2017/03/31/world/asia/myanmar-china-myitsone-dam-project.html; and Wai Moe, "Why Kokang Rebels Are Giving Fits to Burma's Military," *Foreign Policy*, May 6, 2015, https://foreignpolicy.com/2015/05/06/why-kokang-rebels-are-giving-fits-to-burmas-military-myanmar.

[24] Marcus W. Beck, Andrea H. Claassen, and Peter J. Hundt, "Environmental and Livelihood Impacts of Dams: Common Lessons across Development Gradients that Challenge Sustainability," *International Journal of River Basin Management* 10, no. 1 (2012): 73–92; and Samantha Page, "Damming the Future? Livelihoods at Stake on Mekong River," *Public Radio International*, July 25, 2012, https://www.pri.org/stories/2012-07-25/damming-future-livelihoods-stake-mekong-river.

the criticism that its engagement in BRI-related projects such as high-speed rail aims to enrich associated individuals and groups rather than bring broader economic benefit.[25] Critics further claim that the project, with its escalating interest rates, could trap Thailand in long-term indebtedness.[26] According to many in and outside the region, Chinese financing is a form of "debt-trap diplomacy" that will lead to the loss of control over key national and strategic assets.[27] Beijing's response to such criticism so far has been to emphasize that the agreements are voluntary and based on mutual consent.[28] Yet, even though the PRC has set up arbitral courts to deal with disputes, the regulations under which these courts operate, their independence, and their ability to effectively deal with disputes remain in doubt.[29]

The risks of corruption, exploitation, and repression are high for BRI-related projects given the absence of transparent bidding, oversight, and arbitration. Lingering questions over environmental degradation and labor exploitation surrounding PRC-related projects in Cambodia, Laos, Malaysia, and Myanmar allegedly stem from such problems.[30] Another issue is that the PRC's "no strings attached" approach to economic cooperation and assistance enables repression and human rights abuses by the governments of the recipient countries. Cambodia's Hun Sen and the Philippines' Rodrigo Duterte, for example, face allegations of such behavior.[31]

Another contentious issue relating specifically to BRI projects is that insufficient transparency means that PRC firms receive, or appear to win, the

---

[25] Eli Elinoff, "Concrete and Corruption: Materializing Power and Politics in the Thai Capital," *City* 21, no. 5 (2017): 587–96.

[26] Yukako Ono and Apornrath Phoonphongphiphat, "Thailand Welcomes Chinese Investment but Is Cautious on Financing," *Nikkei Asian Review*, June 12, 2018.

[27] Ailto L. Malinao, "China's Debt Trap Diplomacy: Inquirer Columnist," *Straits Times*, January 25, 2018, https://www.straitstimes.com/asia/se-asia/chinas-debt-trap-diplomacy-inquirer-columnist.

[28] "2018 nian 7 yue 3 ri Waijiaobu fayanren Lu Kang zhuchi lixing jizhe hui" [Regular Press Conference by Foreign Ministry Spokesperson Lu Kang on July 3, 2018], Ministry of Foreign Affairs of the People's Republic of China (PRC), http://www.mfa.gov.cn/web/fyrbt_673021/t1573569.shtml.

[29] "'Yidai yilu' (Zhongguo) zhongcaiyuan chengli" ["Belt and Road" (China) Arbitration Court Established], Xinhua, November 1, 2016, http://www.xinhuanet.com/silkroad/2016-11/01/c_129345689.htm.

[30] Yun Sun, "Winning Projects and Hearts? Three Cases of Chinese Mega-Infrastructure Projects in Southeast Asia," Asan Forum, November 3, 2017, http://www.theasanforum.org/winning-projects-and-hearts-three-cases-of-chinese-mega-infrastructure-projects-in-southeast-asia; Darren Touch, "What Does Chinese Investment Mean for Cambodia?" *Diplomat*, February 2, 2018, https://thediplomat.com/2018/02/what-does-chinese-investment-mean-for-cambodia; and "Malaysia's Regime Change Puts at Risk Infrastructure Projects Involving Chinese Firms," *South China Morning Post*, June 17, 2018, https://www.scmp.com/news/china/diplomacy-defence/article/2151169/malaysias-regime-change-puts-risk-infrastructure.

[31] Hannah Beech, "Embracing China, Facebook, and Himself, Cambodia's Leader Digs In," *New York Times*, March 19, 2018, https://www.nytimes.com/2018/03/17/world/asia/hun-sen-cambodia-china.html; and Shannon Tiezzi, "Duterte's China Convergence Continues," *Diplomat*, April 13, 2018, https://thediplomat.com/2018/04/dutertes-china-convergence-continues.

bulk of the most lucrative contracts, leading to suspicions that they crowd out firms in host countries.[32] Worsening matters is the fact that Chinese firms on BRI projects reputedly import labor from their home country rather than hire local workers, possibly because of the need to avoid communication difficulties and the availability of relevant skills.[33] Even the rumor of such phenomena can fuel long-standing communal tensions relating to ethnic Chinese communities in Southeast Asian host countries, especially when mixed with local expectations of employment.[34] These indirect effects that result from BRI projects are unfortunately not issues to which Beijing or its partner governments seem to pay sufficient attention in their haste to advance infrastructure construction.

Economic ties with the PRC can thus be highly politicized in Southeast Asia and ensnare Beijing in domestic political disputes. A reason for the fall of the Najib Razak government in the 2018 Malaysian general elections was its cozy relationship with Beijing, which led to widespread blaming of the administration for selling out the country both literally and figuratively.[35] PRC complicity supposedly enabled groups on the Yunnan-Kokang border to challenge the Myanmar central government in Naypyidaw.[36] Likewise, unrealized PRC investment in the Philippines under the Duterte government has led to local criticism that Beijing is issuing empty promises, on the one hand, and pursuing an agenda of economic imperialism, on the other.[37] Chinese leaders and businesses may come to learn that hitching their economic wagons to political figures in places where the rule of law and politics are fluid can invite blowback and exacerbate local political contestation as political fortunes shift.

Moreover, Beijing faces suspicion about its efforts to actively cultivate and acquire support from political leaders and ethnic Chinese populations to

---

[32] Economics Intelligence Unit, "Participation of Foreign Firms in the BRI," HSBC, June 18, 2018, https://www.business.hsbc.com/belt-and-road/participation-of-foreign-firms-in-the-bri.

[33] Jonathan E. Hillman, statement before the U.S.-China Security and Economic Review Commission for a hearing on "China's Belt and Road Initiative: Five Years Later," Washington, D.C., January 25, 2018, https://www.csis.org/analysis/chinas-belt-and-road-initiative-five-years-later-0.

[34] Eveline Danubrata and Gayatri Suroyo, "In Indonesia, Labor Friction and Politics Fan Anti-Chinese Sentiment," Reuters, April 18, 2017, https://www.reuters.com/article/us-indonesia-election-china/in-indonesia-labor-friction-and-politics-fan-anti-chinese-sentiment-idUSKBN17K0YG.

[35] Liz Lee, "Selling the Country to China? Debate Spills into Malaysia's Election," Reuters, April 27, 2018, https://www.reuters.com/article/us-malaysia-election-china/selling-the-country-to-china-debate-spills-into-malaysias-election-idUSKBN1HY076.

[36] Zhiding Hu and Victor Konrad, "In the Space between Exception and Integration: The Kokang Borderlands on the Periphery of China and Myanmar," Geopolitics 23, no. 1 (2017): 147–79; and Oliver Ward, "China's Dirty Secret: Funding Myanmar's 'Other' Border War," ASEAN Today, April 12, 2017, https://www.aseantoday.com/2017/04/chinas-dirty-secret-funding-myanmars-other-border-war.

[37] John Nery, "Duterte: Make China Great Again," Inquirer, April 24, 2018, http://opinion.inquirer.net/112691/duterte-make-china-great.

buttress its influence and advance its preferences. This includes accusations that the PRC targets investment to extend preferential treatment to politicians who can sway key policies in its favor. Former Malaysian prime minister Najib Razak, for example, is facing criminal proceedings for accepting Chinese investments to cover up his alleged corruption and taking public positions partial to Beijing.[38] The PRC also faces charges of trying to use ethnic Chinese populations in Southeast Asia to weaken resistance to its more controversial policies in ways that could prove domestically destabilizing.[39] Such sway was allegedly key in compelling Thai authorities to permit the abduction of Chinese dissidents on Thai territory as well as in the Cambodian government extraditing Taiwanese fraud suspects to the PRC.[40]

In summary, although economic integration with the PRC offers to boost prosperity in Southeast Asia, it comes with serious long-term risks for both the entire region and individual partner states. Market access to the PRC and Chinese capital may prove especially important for the region at a time when traditional economic partners such as the United States and Europe are under internal political pressure to become more protectionist. This creates a perception that the region needs the PRC to sustain its prosperity, even if actual trade with and FDI from the United States and Europe have not actually declined. Indeed, Chinese president Xi Jinping has exploited this situation by publicly committing support to international economic openness on several occasions.[41] The lure of such wealth could prevent ASEAN countries from working together more effectively at a time when it is more important than ever for the grouping to carry its collective weight and could even contribute to domestic political uncertainty. Whatever the PRC's intentions, economic integration with Southeast Asia could also ironically expose Beijing to the

---

[38] Ida Lim, "Where Are the China Benefits Tied to the RM9.4b Scandal, Guan Eng Asks Najib," *Malay Mail*, June 11, 2018, https://www.malaymail.com/s/1640768/najibs-us2t-china-import-claim-untrue-says-guan-eng.

[39] Amy Qin, "Worries Grow in Singapore over China's Calls to Help 'Motherland,'" *New York Times*, August 5, 2018, https://www.nytimes.com/2018/08/05/world/asia/singapore-china.html; and Charissa Yong, "S'poreans Should Be Aware of China's Influence Ops: Bilahari," *Straits Times*, June 28, 2018, https://www.straitstimes.com/singapore/sporeans-should-be-aware-of-chinas-influence-ops-bilahari.

[40] Zach Dorfman, "The Disappeared," *Foreign Policy*, March 29, 2018, https://foreignpolicy.com/2018/03/29/the-disappeared-china-renditions-kidnapping; and "Cambodia Arrests Nearly 400 Chinese and Taiwanese Nationals over Telecom Fraud," Reuters, August 16, 2017, https://www.reuters.com/article/cambodia-china-taiwan/cambodia-arrests-nearly-400-chinese-and-taiwanese-nationals-over-telecom-fraud-idUSL4N1L31MK.

[41] Wang Zihui, "Xin shidai quanmian shenhua gaige kaifang, Xi Jinping xia yibu daqi" [Next Generation Comprehensive Deepening of Reform and Opening, Xi Jinping Makes a Big Move], Xinhua, April 13, 2018, http://www.xinhuanet.com/politics/2018-04/14/c_1122682904.htm; and "Xi Jinping bamai shijie jingji Zhongguo zhuzhang zhangxian daguo zeren" [Xi Jinping Takes the Pulse of the World Economy, China Proposed to Expand Great-Power Responsibilities], CCTV Online, July 10, 2018, http://news.cctv.com/m/index.shtml?article_id=ARTIoXbZ8fkVjutOIb62bc2z170710.

same accusations of economic exploitation and neoimperialism that it used to hurl at the United States, Europe, and Japan decades ago.

South China Sea Entanglements

An area of significant interaction and contestation between the PRC and Southeast Asia is the South China Sea. Beijing claims most of the South China Sea based on an older position marked out by the Republic of China (ROC) in charts from 1947 and purportedly ancient "historical rights" that predate even the Qing empire.[42] These assertions of sovereignty follow a nine-dash line extending south of Taiwan, past the western coastlines of the Philippines and Borneo, just north of the Natuna Islands, past the eastern coastline of Vietnam, and ending with Hainan. Neither the PRC nor the ROC's successor government on Taiwan has officially clarified the nature of the nine-dash line and the area it encompasses.[43] Beijing's claims are identical to Taipei's and overlap with competing claims from the Philippines, Malaysia, Brunei, Vietnam, and Indonesia.

Much is at stake for the PRC in the dispute over the South China Sea apart from just ownership. In addition to the right to exploit prospective hydrocarbon deposits and fish stocks, a chief concern is the control of the waters and airspace though which vital sea lanes of communication (SLOCs) and air routes pass. This understanding partially led the Philippines under the Benigno Aquino III administration to seek international arbitration over the nature of the various maritime features in the South China Sea as stipulated under UNCLOS provisions.[44] The PRC's rejection of the arbitral tribunal ruling in the case brought by the Philippines, continued militarization of the artificial islands it occupies, and insistence that these reclaimed features can generate territorial waters in contravention of UNCLOS enforce a new and more unstable precedent for handling maritime disputes. Such behavior, in combination with the unwillingness of other disputants and interested parties to challenge the PRC, is indicative of the weakness of UNCLOS and related mechanisms.

Under UNCLOS, only legally recognized islands can possess the full complement of rights over territorial waters and exclusive economic

---

[42] Bill Hayton, "Calm and Storm: The South China Sea after the Second World War," Center for Strategic and International Studies (CSIS), Asia Maritime Transparency Initiative, August 13, 2015, https://amti.csis.org/calm-and-storm-the-south-china-sea-after-the-second-world-war.

[43] "Why Is the South China Sea Contentious?" BBC News, July 12, 2018, https://www.bbc.com/news/world-asia-pacific-13748349.

[44] Peter Dutton, "Three Disputes and Three Objectives—China and the South China Sea," *Naval War College Review* 64, no. 4 (2011): 1–26.

zones (EEZs). Other maritime features like reefs, atolls, and rocks that are not naturally above the high-tide water level permanently and do not support permanent human habitation cannot have such rights.[45] The Arbitral Tribunal at The Hague decided in 2016 that features disputed by the PRC, Philippines, and Taiwan are not legally islands. This implies that even if the PRC were to have undisputed ownership of these features, they could not give it full control of waters and EEZs within the nine-dash line in areas disputed with the Philippines. Beijing refused to participate in the proceedings and still does not recognize the ruling.[46] The PRC now reportedly occupies up to 28 maritime features in the South China Sea that it has reclaimed into artificial islands.[47] Despite Xi repeatedly denying any desire to militarize these features, several now feature airstrips capable of supporting medium-range bombers, advanced anti-aircraft capabilities, radar facilities, and electronic intelligence emplacements.[48] Beijing insists that foreign military vessels maintain a distance of twelve nautical miles from these features and sometimes uses naval vessels and military aircraft to enforce this buffer, even though the features cannot generate such territorial claims under UNCLOS.[49] Such behavior has resulted in dangerous encounters between U.S. and People's Liberation Army (PLA) vessels that risked collision or other forms of escalation, including an incident between a U.S. Navy and a PLA Navy vessel in early September 2018.[50]

Abetting Beijing in this process is the silence of the Duterte administration, which entered office in 2016. Some suspect that the PRC helped with Duterte's campaign in exchange for aid, investment, and silence

---

[45] *United Nations Convention on the Law of the Sea* (1982) Article 121, Part VIII, 1982, http://www.un.org/depts/los/convention_agreements/texts/unclos/part8.

[46] Feng Zhang, "Assessing China's Response to the South China Sea Arbitration," *Australian Journal of International Affairs* 71, no. 4 (2017): 440–59.

[47] See "Island Features of the South China Sea," CSIS, Asia Maritime Transparency Initiative, https://amti.csis.org/scs-features-map; and NBR, Maritime Awareness Project, http://maritimeawarenessproject.org/interactivemap.

[48] "Chinese Power Projection Capabilities in the South China Sea," CSIS, Asia Maritime Transparency Initiative, 2018, https://amti.csis.org/chinese-power-projection; David Brunnstrom and Michael Martina, "Xi Denies Turning Artificial into Military Bases," Reuters, September 26, 2018, https://www.reuters.com/article/us-usa-china-pacific/xi-denies-china-turning-artificial-islands-into-military-bases-idUSKCN0RP1ZH20150925; and Thomas Gibbons-Neff and Steven Lee Myers, "China Won't Yield 'Even One Inch' of South China Sea, Xi Tells Mattis," *New York Times*, July 27, 2018, https://www.nytimes.com/2018/06/27/world/asia/mattis-xi-china-sea.html.

[49] Eli Meixler, "U.S. Navy Sails Near Disputed Islands amid Escalating Tensions with China," *Time*, October 1, 2018, http://time.com/5411238/u-s-navy-decatur-south-china-sea.

[50] John Power and Catherine Wong, "Exclusive Details and Footage Emerge of Near Collision between Warships in the South China Sea," *South China Morning Post*, November 4, 2018, https://www.scmp.com/week-asia/geopolitics/article/2171596/exclusive-details-and-footage-emerge-near-collision-between.

over the Philippines' territorial dispute.[51] Periodic freedom of navigation operations (FONOPs) by the United States, Australia, the United Kingdom, and France that began in 2016 notwithstanding, the PRC has established a dominant military presence in the South China Sea. Aircraft and missiles based on these artificial islands allow the PRC to complicate military operations, shipping, and aviation over much of the South China Sea, even given the most determined and well-equipped of adversaries. **Figure 5** gives a sense of PRC aircraft and missile ranges from the South China Sea features it has reclaimed, constructed, and militarized.

Making matters more challenging is China's proclivity to use paramilitary and civilian-registered vessels to enforce its maritime claims, including civilian-registered fishing vessels reportedly with reinforced hulls and military-trained crews—its so-called maritime militia.[52] These vessels often disrupt operations by official vessels from other governments operating in disputed waters and are known to ram vessels that do not comply with demands to depart.[53] Such actions come in addition to the interdiction of non-PRC-registered fishing vessels in PRC-claimed waters by Chinese paramilitary and other government vessels as well as the use of oil exploration platforms by the PRC to mark claims over an area.[54] The scale and frequency of such behavior complicates responses by other actors, owing to their more limited maritime capacities and general desire to avoid escalation through the use of better-equipped and better-armed naval forces.

One factor in the PRC's success in achieving the preeminent position it now enjoys in the South China Sea has been the inconsistent and piecemeal response by ASEAN and its member states. The official ASEAN position is that the grouping neither supports nor opposes any claims but insists that the disputes be resolved through peaceful, noncoercive means and based on mutual consent.[55] This approach guides the ASEAN-initiated 2002 Declaration

---

[51] See, for example, Trisha Macas, "Duterte Says Anonymous Chinese Donor Partially Paid for Initial Pol Ads," GMA News, March 10, 2016, http://www.gmanetwork.com/news/news/nation/558539/duterte-says-anonymous-chinese-donor-partially-paid-for-initial-pol-ads/story; and "Did China Bankroll Duterte Campaign? Trillanes Wants to Know," Politiko, June 13, 2018, http://politics.com.ph/did-china-bankroll-duterte-campaign-trillanes-wants-to-know.

[52] Conor M. Kennedy and Andrew S. Erickson, "China's Third Sea Force, the People's Armed Forces Maritime Militia: Tethered to the PLA," U.S. Naval War College, China Maritime Report, March 2017.

[53] Ibid.

[54] Michael Green et al., "Counter-Coercion Series: China-Vietnam Oil Rig Stand-off," CSIS, Asia Maritime Transparency Initiative, June 17, 2017, https://amti.csis.org/counter-co-oil-rig-standoff.

[55] Yee Kwang Heng, "ASEAN's Position on the South China Sea and Implications for Regional Peace and Security," in Territorial Disputes in the South China Sea: Navigating Rough Waters, ed. Jing Huang and Andrew Billo (Basingstoke: PalgraveMacmillan, 2015), 69–81; and Siew Mun Tang, "The ASEAN Way on the South China Sea Speaks Volumes," ISEAS–Yusof Ishak Institute, Commentary, May 7, 2018, https://www.iseas.edu.sg/medias/commentaries/item/7469-the-asean-way-on-the-south-china-sea-speaks-volumes-by-tang-siew-mun.

FIGURE 5   China's land, air, and missile presence in the South China Sea

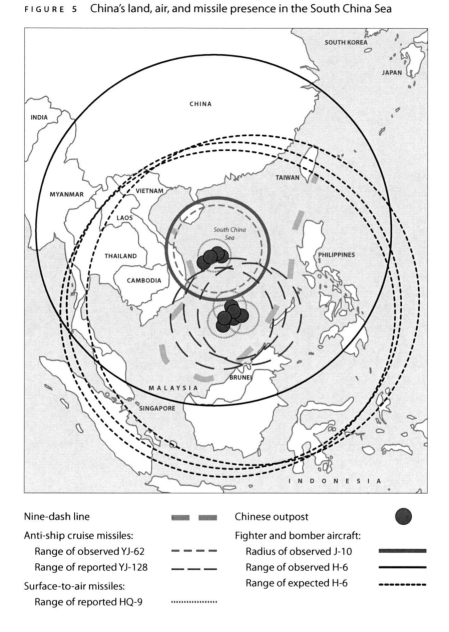

Nine-dash line		**— —**
Anti-ship cruise missiles:		
Range of observed YJ-62		**– – – –**
Range of reported YJ-128		**— – — –**
Surface-to-air missiles:		
Range of reported HQ-9		**·················**
Chinese outpost		●
Fighter and bomber aircraft:		
Radius of observed J-10		**▬▬▬**
Range of observed H-6		**——**
Range of expected H-6		**---------**

SOURCE: Center for Strategic and International Studies, Asia Maritime Transparency Initiative, 2018. See also NBR, Maritime Awareness Project, http://maritimeawarenessproject. org/interactivemap.

on the Conduct of Parties in the South China Sea, the 2012 implementation guidelines for the Declaration, and the draft code of conduct currently under negotiation. They follow the spirit of nonconfrontation and negotiation established under one of ASEAN's key founding documents, the 1976 Treaty of Amity and Cooperation—of which the PRC is a signatory in virtue of being an ASEAN dialogue partner. Such thinking is also behind other ASEAN approaches to managing security, such as the 1971 Zone of Peace Freedom and Neutrality declaration, the 1995 Southeast Asian Nuclear-Weapon-Free Zone Treaty, and the ASEAN Regional Forum.

ASEAN and its members ultimately proved unable to adhere to their stated principles and goals on handling differences with the PRC over the South China Sea, however. The PRC's construction and militarization of islands stands in some tension with the Declaration on the Conduct of Parties and its implementation guidelines, but ASEAN offered no tangible response. Beijing allegedly worked through Cambodia to veto any mention of the South China Sea in joint statements after the ASEAN meetings in 2012 and 2016.[56] It again apparently prevented mention of the South China Sea in another joint statement in 2017, forcing the chair of ASEAN at the time, Malaysia, to issue a separate chair's statement.[57] Even the Philippines' submission to arbitration in 2012 and the 2016 arbitral tribunal ruling were met with lukewarm responses, and even silence, from other Southeast Asian claimant states and interested parties.[58]

Part of the challenge facing ASEAN when it comes to having a coherent and effective response to PRC military encroachment in the South China Sea is the different priorities of its membership. Claimants obviously have a direct interest in staking their positions but vary widely in their approaches. Vietnam is most consistently active in demonstrating resolve over its claims, including by deploying its own maritime militia, naval vessels, and military aircraft to disputed areas.[59] The Philippines is less consistent. It was more willing to confront PRC pressure under the Aquino administration through the use of the arbitral tribunal at The Hague but became reticent under the Arroyo and

---

[56] Baliga and Vong, "Cambodia Again Blocks ASEAN Statement on South China Sea"; and Carl Thayer, "Revealed: The Truth behind ASEAN's Retracted Kunming Statement," *Diplomat*, June 19, 2016, https://thediplomat.com/2016/06/revealed-the-truth-behind-aseans-retracted-kunming-statement.

[57] Tan See Seng, "Claims of ASEAN Disunity at Summit Unfounded," *Straits Times*, November 26, 2015, https://www.straitstimes.com/opinion/claims-of-asean-disunity-at-summit-unfounded.

[58] Ian Storey, "Assessing Responses to the Arbitral Tribunal's Ruling on the South China Sea," *ISEAS Perspective*, July 28, 2016, https://www.iseas.edu.sg/images/pdf/ISEAS_Perspective_2016_43.pdf.

[59] Derek Grossman and Nyugen Nhat Ahn, "Deciphering Vietnam's Evolving Military Doctrine in the South China Sea," CSIS, AMTI Update, May 11, 2018, https://amti.csis.org/deciphering-vietnams-doctrine-south-china-sea.

Duterte administrations.[60] Brunei and Malaysia tend to assiduously avoid open friction with the PRC, given the large economic stakes they have in continued and undisrupted cooperation.[61]

Non-claimant ASEAN members with interests in the South China Sea likewise diverge on their approaches to the increasingly aggressive Chinese behavior in those waters. Indonesia is by far the most willing to risk confrontation and has challenged the PRC over fishing rights in the waters around the Natuna Islands where its EEZ overlaps with the nine-dash line. The China Coast Guard reportedly rammed towlines after the Indonesian Coast Guard tried to impound Chinese vessels suspected of illegal fishing in one incident, prompting Jakarta to lodge a protest.[62] Another skirmish over fishing in the same waters three months later saw the Indonesian Navy fire warning shots at a Chinese fishing vessel, injuring a crew member and drawing a diplomatic protest from Beijing.[63] Moreover, the Indonesian fisheries administration has made public displays of sinking emptied vessels it impounds for illegal fishing, including those from the PRC.[64] Singapore has insisted on respect for existing maritime laws and better mechanisms for managing tensions, while Thailand, Myanmar, Laos, and Cambodia have kept silent.

Other non-claimants for which the South China Sea is an important SLOC periodically signal their disagreement with the abrasive way in which Beijing is pursuing its claims over those waters. The United States has conveyed disapproval of the escalation and militarization of the disputes, insisted on conformity to prevailing international laws, and initiated arrangements like the 2014 Code for Unplanned Encounters at Sea.[65] It also on occasion has sailed naval vessels and flown military aircraft within twelve nautical miles of PRC-occupied features to demonstrate its rejection of Beijing's claim that

---

[60] Jay Batongbacal, "South China Sea: The Philippines Fissure," Lowy Institute, Interpreter, March 27, 2018, https://www.lowyinstitute.org/the-interpreter/south-china-sea-philippine-fissure.

[61] Elina Noor and Thomas Daniel, "Key Issues and Dilemmas for Malaysia and Brunei in the South China Sea Dispute," National Asian Studies Security Program, Issue Brief, December 2016.

[62] See, for example, Ristian Atriandi Supriyanto, "Breaking the Silence: Indonesia vs China in the Natuna Islands," Diplomat, March 23, 2016, https://thediplomat.com/2016/03/breaking-the-silence-indonesia-vs-china-in-the-natuna-islands.

[63] "Indonesian Navy Fires on Chinese Fishing Boat in Disputed Waters," BBC, June 20, 2016, https://www.bbc.com/news/world-asia-36573291.

[64] "Indonesia Sinks 125 Mostly Foreign Illegal Fishing Vessels," Associated Press, August 22, 2018, https://www.apnews.com/adf6b8342a874823abb5a4998eb7ff6a.

[65] Ahn Duc Ton, "Code for Unplanned Encounters at Sea and Its Practical Limitations in the East and South China Seas," Australian Journal of Maritime and Ocean Affairs 9, no. 4 (2017): 227–39; and Western Pacific Naval Symposium, "Code for Unplanned Encounters at Sea: Version 1.0," 2014, http://www.jag.navy.mil/distrib/instructions/CUES_2014.pdf.

these features could possess territorial waters.[66] These FONOPs risk collision or escalation when the PRC responds with close passes by its own naval ships and military aircraft to discourage such activity. Other non-claimants such as Australia, France, India, Japan, and the United Kingdom appear willing to send their naval vessels into disputed waters to test PRC claims, sometimes in apparent coordination with the U.S. Navy.[67]

However, these efforts to signal disapproval of the PRC's actions in the South China Sea through FONOPs have at best had a limited effect in slowing Beijing's consolidation of its position. The risk of escalation from near collisions and encounters involving military vessels creates incentives to establish protocols for managing such incidents but does not fundamentally challenge the PRC's claims or its actions to protect them. Even at the height of the Obama administration's "rebalance to Asia," regional states lacked confidence in the United States' willingness to mount a sustained response. Washington remains vague on the matter even as the Trump administration confronts the PRC over trade. As critical as FONOPs are in underscoring the importance of freedom of navigation, they do not alter the PRC's effective control over South China Sea features nor diminish its growing ability to coerce regional actors. The fact that there simply are no discernable consequences for Beijing should it continue to contravene Washington's preferences and those of other interested parties is an invitation for the PRC to forge ahead.

ASEAN's Apathy and Atrophy

Institutional Weakness

A key constraint on Southeast Asia's ability to effectively address the challenges posed by a PRC that is more willing and able to impose its preferences on regional countries is ASEAN's institutional weakness. ASEAN originated through coordination among states that shared aversions to Communist rule, external domination, and restrictions on their autonomy. These principles are at the heart of its emphasis on consensus, autonomy,

---

[66] U.S. Department of Defense, "Freedom of Navigation Program," Fact Sheet, March 2015, https://policy.defense.gov/Portals/11/Documents/gsa/cwmd/DoD%20FON%20Program%20--%20Fact%20Sheet%20(March%202015).pdf.

[67] Euan Graham, "Australian Warships Challenged in South China Sea," Lowy Institute, Interpreter, April 20, 2018, https://www.lowyinstitute.org/the-interpreter/australian-navy-challenged-south-china-sea; Tuan Ahn Luc, "Are France and the UK Here to Stay in the South China Sea?" *Diplomat*, September 14, 2018, https://thediplomat.com/2018/09/are-france-and-the-uk-here-to-stay-in-the-south-china-sea; and Ryan Pickrell, "U.S. and Japanese Warships Are Drilling in the South China Sea in a Show of Force in China's Backyard," *Business Insider*, September 1, 2018, https://www.businessinsider.com/us-japanese-warships-put-on-show-of-force-in-south-china-sea-2018-9.

and nonintervention as the "ASEAN way."[68] In the organization's early years, collective action over specific issues could be managed on an *ad hoc* basis given the small number of members, which was how it handled Vietnam's occupation of Cambodia. Today's ASEAN is far more diverse and less cohesive, putting it in a much weaker position to respond robustly to the PRC's pressure. The end of the Cold War, regime transitions, and a series of financial crises eroded the common interests shared by the older ASEAN members. Moreover, membership expansion in the 1990s brought former adversaries such as Cambodia, Laos, and Vietnam into the grouping alongside Myanmar. As a result, ASEAN is more imbalanced than before in terms of economic development and more sharply divided between the divergent mainland and maritime orientations of its membership. As consensus remains key to its decision-making, meaningful agreements have become more difficult to forge, especially if they involve commitments to collective action.

Complicating matters is the chronic lack of political will for institutional investment and reform that could both restore ASEAN's ability to address coordination problems and introduce new capacities for collective action. Managing difference within the grouping could become easier with more efficient coordination through the secretariat and adjustments to procedural arrangements on common positions. However, member countries generally claim that giving the secretariat the capacity to become better at its current responsibilities without any increase in authority is already a bridge too far and would set the body on a path to overreach.[69] No ASEAN state is prepared to limit its own veto power on any issue, and all seem quite ready to exercise this right, which means that decision-making procedures are unlikely to change. Thus, any reform of ASEAN to meet contemporary needs will be difficult, except on the most mundane matters, which could hollow out ASEAN centrality and corrode the organization's usefulness.

Contributing to this inertia is ASEAN's long-standing position of "not choosing sides" between the United States and PRC.[70] A focus on simultaneously seeking opportunities with both Beijing and Washington

[68] Rodolfo C. Severino, "The ASEAN Way and the Rule of Law" (address at the International Law Conference on ASEAN Legal Systems and Regional Integration, Kuala Lumpur, September 1, 2001), https://asean.org/?static_post=the-asean-way-and-the-rule-of-law.

[69] Dewi Fortuna Anwar, "Indonesia, ASEAN, and Regional Stability" (lecture to Social Science Commission of the Indonesian Academy of Sciences, Jakarta, February 16, 2017), http://admin.thcasean.org/assets/uploads/file/2017/03/Indonesia,_ASEAN_and_Regional_Stability_compress.pdf; and Bilahari Kausikan, "Thinking about ASEAN Realistically," *Nikkei Asian Review*, November 16, 2015, https://asia.nikkei.com/Location/Southeast-Asia/ASEAN/Thinking-about-ASEAN-realistically2.

[70] Angaindrankumar Gnanasagaran, "Between Great Powers, ASEAN Need Not Choose," *ASEAN Post*, January 25, 2018, https://theaseanpost.com/article/between-great-powers-asean-need-not-choose; and Cheng-Chwee Kuik, "How Do Weaker States Hedge? Unpacking ASEAN States' Alignment Behavior towards China," *Journal of Contemporary China* 25, no. 100 (2016): 500–514.

made sense when interests in the two major powers overlapped significantly and areas for collaboration were easy to find. This is less the case now that the PRC and the United States increasingly diverge in their outlook.[71] Consequently, nonalignment has become an excuse for various ASEAN members to look out for their immediate short-term interests rather than work to consolidate the position of the grouping. Brunei, the Philippines under the Duterte administration, Cambodia, and post-coup Thailand appear to be tacking toward Beijing, while Laos, Malaysia, and Myanmar seem ambivalent in their external policies. Successive Indonesian administrations have tried to maintain greater autonomy, while Singapore and Vietnam have pursued economic cooperation with both China and the United States but prioritized security ties with the latter.

This lack of coherence in Southeast Asia means that Beijing can entice those states already amenable to its preferences away from supporting common ASEAN positions while increasing pressure on those that complicate the PRC's attempts to extend its interests across the region. Given its perennial concerns about potential encirclement and containment by the United States and its allies and partners, the PRC's efforts to consolidate its advantages in Southeast Asia to reduce U.S. influence are logical.[72] ASEAN's current disarray, coupled with U.S. inattention, has provided Beijing with an opening to block developments that it deems potentially disadvantageous. This aggressive behavior in Southeast Asia is consistent with the overall ambitious and bold approach of the Xi Jinping leadership. If member countries' handling of the South China Sea disputes is any indication, ASEAN is unlikely to muster a clear response to the PRC.[73]

Domestic Political Uncertainty

The domestic political uncertainty in Southeast Asia discussed previously is another constraint on the ability of ASEAN members to collectively respond to the challenges posed by the PRC. Local pushback against PRC-linked

---

[71] Paul Dibb, "Why Southeast Asia and ASEAN Are a Strategic Problem," East Asia Forum, July 28, 2017, http://www.eastasiaforum.org/2017/07/28/why-southeast-asia-and-asean-are-a-strategic-problem.

[72] Chou Chaobing, "Zhongguo, Meiguo yu Dongnanya: Jingzhen yu hezuo yantaohui zongshu" [General Report on the Seminar on China, the United States, and Southeast Asia: Competition and Cooperation], Institute of American Studies, Chinese Academy of Social Sciences, August 15, 2014, http://ias.cass.cn/xsyj/mgwj/201506/t20150615_2702148.shtml; and Du Lan, "Zhongguo zai Dongnanya de jingji, junshi shuangchong jingzheng jiaju" [China's Dual Economic and Military Competition in Southeast Asia Intensifies], Chinese Institute of International Studies News, March 7, 2016, http://www.ciis.org.cn/chinese/2016-03/07/content_8617503.htm.

[73] Ian Storey, "ASEAN's Failing Grade in the South China Sea," in International Relations and Asia's Southern Tier, ed. Gilbert Rozman and Joseph Chinyong Liow (Basingstoke: PalgraveMacmillan, 2017), 111–24; and Suisheng Zhao, "China and the South China Sea Arbitration: Geopolitics versus International Law," Journal of Contemporary China 27, no. 109 (2017): 1–15.

projects and the resulting instability has put governments on the defensive and discouraged cooperation through ASEAN and with other member states on these matters. Protests in Indonesia and the Philippines over PRC projects allegedly not hiring enough local workers have not spurred greater urgency in those countries to reform ASEAN and improve its ability to respond to the PRC.[74] Likewise, electoral backlash against allegations of Chinese support for corrupt officials in the 2018 Malaysian general election resulted in the suspension of bilateral projects rather than efforts to work with ASEAN and other members on related issues.[75] The same is true of social tension in Singapore between locals and Chinese migrants.[76]

Uncertainty over the U.S. Role

Sharpened uncertainty over the role that the United States now plays in the region provides another series of challenges for ASEAN and its members. Since the middle of the twentieth century, the United States has helped support the economic and security order in Southeast Asia, even if this role was not always peaceful and was clearly based in U.S. self-interest. There used to be reasonably consistent and stable expectations that the United States—along with its allies—would provide the region with capital and markets, while protecting against rapid changes to the political and security status quo.[77] These features of the U.S.-backed system provided the foundations for rapid economic growth for much of non-Communist and later post–Cold War Southeast Asia. For all its problems—and there have been many—the U.S. presence in the region used to bring the promise of prosperity, if nothing else.

The Trump administration's unpredictability and ambivalence have shaken confidence in Southeast Asia over Washington's reliability as a partner. One of the first actions of the Trump administration was to withdraw the United States from the Trans-Pacific Partnership (TPP). This action amplified existing concerns about the robustness of the U.S. commitment to Asia following the Bush administration's focus on terrorism after September 11 and the Obama administration's early description of its Asia policy as a

---

[74] See, for example, Danubrata and Suroyo, "In Indonesia, Labor Friction and Politics Fan Anti-Chinese Sentiment."

[75] C.K. Tan, "Malaysia's Rural Voters See More China and Less Mahathir," *Nikkei Asian Review*, May 2, 2018, https://asia.nikkei.com/Politics/Malaysia-in-transition/Malaysia-s-rural-voters-see-more-China-and-less-Mahathir.

[76] Brenda S.A. Yeoh and Weiqiang Lin, "Chinese Migration to Singapore: Discourses and Discontents in a Globalizing Nation-State," *Asian and Pacific Migration Journal* 22, no. 1 (2013): 31–54.

[77] G. John Ikenberry, "Between the Eagle and the Dragon: America, China, and Middle State Strategies in East Asia," *Political Science Quarterly* 131, no. 1 (2016): 9–43.

"pivot."[78] Such behavior creates an impression that Asia, and Southeast Asia in particular, is increasingly an afterthought in Washington.

Just as worrisome to many Southeast Asian states is the Trump administration's willingness, even enthusiasm, for crises that have the potential to spiral out of control. This includes the acrimony with North Korea and China, as well as threats to traditional U.S. allies like Japan, South Korea, Australia, and Europe. The latest crisis is the escalating trade war between China and the United States. The prevailing assumption among policymakers in Southeast Asia prior to the Trump administration was that Washington wished to limit major-power competition in Asia and act as a force for stability in the region.[79] There is much more apprehension today over whether this remains the case.

Growing friction and even confrontation between the United States and PRC puts further pressure on ASEAN by sharpening internal differences within and across the grouping. Unless Washington is willing to cede its current forward presence in Southeast Asia, it is likely to lean on friends and allies in the region to resist real and anticipated actions by Beijing that may hurt U.S. interests. Under Xi, the PRC is unlikely to accept U.S. attempts to hem in its position in Southeast Asia.[80] To counter the possibility of ASEAN becoming a tool for any perceived or nascent U.S. containment strategy, Beijing will have incentives to prevent the coalescence of positions that can harm its interests,[81] including offering further side payments to ASEAN members as well as politicians, political parties, and other groups within member states that can support Beijing's position. Moreover, the PRC can apply its economic clout to threaten or impose costs on recalcitrant ASEAN members, especially in response to military and security cooperation with the United States that Beijing finds potentially troublesome.[82] Such conditions mean that ASEAN members have good reason to temper their enthusiasm for U.S. initiatives and outreach efforts, while playing down or even avoiding any cooperation with Washington that Beijing may find sensitive.

---

[78] "U.S.-ASEAN Relations: From Rebalance to Reset?" *Straits Times*, November 5, 2016, https://www.straitstimes.com/opinion/us-asean-relations-from-rebalance-to-reset; Alyssa Ayers, Elizabeth Economy, and Daniel Markey, "Rebalance the Rebalance: China, India, and the United States," *Foreign Affairs*, July 13, 2016, https://www.foreignaffairs.com/articles/china/2016-07-13/rebalance-rebalance; and Satu P. Limaye, "Minding the Gaps: The Bush Administration and U.S.–Southeast Asia Relations," *Contemporary Southeast Asia* 26, no. 1 (2004): 73–93.

[79] Ikenberry, "Between the Eagle and the Dragon."

[80] Gibbons-Neft and Myers, "China Won't Yield 'Even One Inch' of South China Sea."

[81] Personal communication with a scholar at a PRC think tank.

[82] Jethro Mullen, "China Can Squeeze Its Neighbors When It Wants. Ask South Korea," CNN Money, August 30, 2017, https://money.cnn.com/2017/08/30/news/economy/china-hyundai-south-korea-thaad/index.html.

Outlook for ASEAN Unity

ASEAN's initiative and autonomy will likely decline as the grouping's internal complications persist and Sino-U.S. rivalry intensifies. The absence of effective tools for managing major-power contestation and obstacles to collective action mean that ASEAN and its members face decreasing scope for action. The growing zero-sum quality of U.S.-PRC relations means that the policy sweet spot of "not choosing sides" is more difficult to sustain, as decreasing common ground exists between the two sides. Sharpened internal discord, pressure from Beijing and Washington, and ASEAN's reliance on consensus mean that anything except the most innocuous and mundane issues requires members to compromise on substantive positions for uncertain returns. This suggests that ASEAN will increasingly converge around an unambitious agenda that reflects the lowest common denominator.

Current conditions thus suggest that ASEAN is unlikely to repeat its limited Cold War success in managing major-power competition in Southeast Asia. During the Cold War, the grouping included fewer members, all of which were unequivocally part of the U.S.-backed liberal economic order and depended on both the U.S. market and U.S. investments. They shared a common concern with promoting economic liberalization and protecting liberal international institutions.[83] Today's ASEAN is more pluralistic and contains economies that are closely tied with both the United States and PRC, whose economies and politics are pulling regional countries in different directions. ASEAN and its members face far greater obstacles in overcoming the collective action problems to corral the major powers than they did during the Cold War.

Such pessimism about ASEAN reflects a recognition of the grouping's limitations in responding to increased pressure from the PRC and heightened Sino-U.S. competition in Southeast Asia. This view is borne out by observations of the failure of ASEAN's collective approach to curb aggressive behavior by the PRC, as well as by various member states, over the past decade. Instead of simply being content with avoiding confrontation among ASEAN members, states with an interest in fostering autonomy and regional stability going forward would do well to be open to exploring alternatives to ASEAN itself. Such action obviously risks further marginalizing the grouping's ability to anchor the regional order in Southeast Asia, but a clear-eyed appreciation that it is incapable of the robust collective action the region presently requires is critical. This perspective points toward the need for alternative tools of collaboration to achieve common interests in the region, instead of simply focusing on shared aversions so much that they come at the expense of ASEAN's effectiveness.

---

[83] Ikenberry, "Between the Eagle and the Dragon."

Possible Paths Ahead

Southeast Asian governments are by and large receptive to Beijing's economic overtures even if doubts remain over the long-term implications. The promises of wealth and prosperity through the opportunity and largesse that the PRC offers are just too alluring. This is especially true of developing economies in Southeast Asia seeking to build their basic infrastructure, but it is also true for middle- and high-income countries. Powerful individuals, corporations, and other elite groups in these various localities stand to profit as well.

The PRC's willingness to publicly impose costs on actors that do not show sufficient deference further weakens the resolve of Southeast Asian states to challenge it. Since 2010, Beijing has shown that it is willing to sanction Japan over territorial disputes, South Korea over the deployment of a missile defense system, and Taiwan for not being more receptive to unification, in addition to challenging the United States on trade.[84] These incidents remind political, business, and other elites of the immediate interests at stake in resisting PRC preferences and influence broader strategic considerations in the region. They encourage Southeast Asian governments to prioritize their own economic ties with the PRC, which offer immediate benefits, rather than insist on claims with longer-term gains. The success of such efforts by the PRC to muscle its way through when regional countries' preferences diverge from its own suggests to leaders in Beijing that coercion is the best way to resolve difference in Southeast Asia and perhaps elsewhere.

With the partial exception of Indonesia, Southeast Asian states are indeed "small countries" next to China. Yet this need not be an obstacle for ASEAN as it interacts with China, so long as the grouping is still capable of banding together to bargain collectively. Unfortunately, as discussed in the previous section, divergent interests among ASEAN members, and Beijing's eagerness to exploit these differences, have exacerbated collective action problems, complicating negotiation on the very issues that require the most attention. Beijing's formula for economic cooperation and investment is inadvertently reminiscent of Soviet and U.S. behavior during the Cold War, as well as other prior efforts of indirect dominance. High-value deals are struck with political elites with limited regard for local resentment and second- and third-order consequences, which Beijing claims is acceptable

---

[84] Robert Ayson and Manjeet A. Pardesi, "Asia's Diplomacy of Violence: China-U.S. Coercion and Regional Order," *Survival* 59, no. 2 (2017): 85–124; Christina Lai, "Acting One Way and Talking Another: China's Coercive Economic Diplomacy in East Asia and Beyond," *Pacific Review* 31, no. 2 (2018): 169–87; and Robert S. Ross, "On the Fungibility of Economic Power: China's Economic Rise and the East Asian Security Order," *European Journal of International Relations* (March 16, 2018), https://journals.sagepub.com/doi/abs/10.1177/1354066118757854.

because two or more sides have an agreement. Just as was the case during the Cold War, such arrangements create conditions that can easily foster domestic political instability for host states that do not have the institutional capacity to absorb such shocks should something go wrong. Because major infrastructure projects are often inherently risky, PRC investments and economic engagement inadvertently raise the possibility of unrest in Southeast Asia.

A more even-keeled relationship between ASEAN and the PRC requires that member countries credibly commit to overcoming the problems of collective action. However, as discussed above, the current trajectory of the grouping is not promising for such an outcome. Given the stark asymmetry in resources and material capacity, as well as concerns over domestic political needs, no Southeast Asian state, again with the possible partial exception of Indonesia, is able to resist PRC pressure on its own. Achieving regional preferences requires ASEAN to serve as an effective platform for collective bargaining, particularly owing to the PRC's attempts to maximize the advantages of size by insisting on bilateral negotiations on difficult issues. Doing so means that ASEAN members must develop a common negotiating position to which they adhere even when enticed by side payments or threatened with individualized costs. Divergence in priorities and other differences within ASEAN prevent the realization of such a position, especially given that ASEAN as an organization has neither the legitimacy nor the capacity to enforce compliance among its members.

Although substantive reform to address collective action problems is an obvious means of preserving ASEAN's autonomy considering the PRC's dominance, this option may be impracticable at this point. Convincing member states to accept limitations on their autonomy, even in the pursuit of collective benefits, is a difficult proposition to broach because of the entrenched proclivity toward freedom of action in ASEAN. Movement in this direction requires political will from leaders around the region, including a commitment to risk and bear domestic criticism for "selling out" their country's policy independence to foreigners and bureaucrats with dubious local mandates. Another obstacle is the PRC and other major powers active in Southeast Asia stymieing enhanced intra-ASEAN cooperation if they believe it will be deleterious to their competitive positions. As has happened in the South China Sea disputes, Beijing and others can simply peel away members with threats or promises in order to break the consensus that is so critical for the grouping to move ahead on major issues of common concern.

An alternative is for Southeast Asian states that continue to have a preference for autonomy to work around ASEAN and establish more robust substitute mechanisms for collaboration. Such a move effectively admits that the grouping is of decreasing usefulness going forward. States that share a preference for limiting major-power contestation and PRC pressure must take issues off the table for competition, be they over states' behavior in contested waters or terms for economic cooperation. Should these like-minded states be able to overcome problems of collective action and withstand PRC pressure, they would be able to bargain and respond to issues collectively, including over the extension of benefits and imposition of costs resulting from engagement. This could help at least somewhat mitigate individual disadvantages in resources and capability. Likely candidates to initiate such an arrangement include Indonesia, Malaysia, Singapore, Vietnam, and possibly Thailand, given their greater consistency in insisting on restraints to major-power pressure in Southeast Asia. That said, any exploration of alternatives surely risks further undermining confidence in the grouping's ability to manage regional issues.

Beijing is pressing ahead with its interests in Southeast Asia and will continue to do so as long as its economy can sustain such behavior. This situation is unsurprising considering the region's natural strategic importance, coupled with the PRC's increasing ability to direct resources and capabilities to shape Southeast Asia according to its preferences. Given limited local efforts to regulate the PRC's economic outreach and ineffective resistance to Beijing's assertion of its South China Sea claims, Chinese leaders will have little reason to hold back on other issues. The perceived ineffectiveness of U.S. policy toward Southeast Asia further encourages Beijing to consolidate its advantages in the region as much and as quickly as possible.

Even though the PRC benefits from the economic stability and security that the United States historically provides, this means accepting a system and set of rules established by Washington to reinforce U.S. advantages. Moreover, the current uncertainties surrounding the Trump administration's foreign and economic policy provide strategic opportunities that the PRC can possibly exploit to curtail Washington's influence. As illustrated by its continued militarization of artificial features in disputed waters of the South China Sea, Beijing can reasonably expect little effective resistance to its efforts to shape a new reality in Southeast Asia, and this may encourage it to do so more boldly. Likewise, through BRI, the Asian Infrastructure Investment Bank, and other initiatives, the PRC has publicly advanced itself as the defender of economic openness and a new "rules-based order."[85]

However, should these efforts fail to reshape the substantive content of the rules, norms, and practices that undergird the regional order, Southeast

---

[85] Wang, "Xin shidai quanmian shenhua gaige kaifang"; "'Yidai Yilu' (Zhongguo) Zhongcaiyuan chengli"; and "Xi Jinping bamai shijie jingji Zhongguo zhuzhang zhangxian daguo zeren."

Asia may end up without any clear organizing principles and become less stable than before. The alternative economic arrangements and free trade agreements created by Beijing have the long-term potential to wean the region's economy away from the United States and toward the PRC. But they have yet to do so given the challenges of extensive domestic bad debt and the trade war with the United States. At the same time, Beijing continues to apply pressure to regional organizations such as ASEAN and individual Southeast Asian governments to deter them from obstructing or embarrassing the PRC over sensitive issues such as the South China Sea disputes. A scenario is thus possible where PRC efforts inadvertently undermine regional cooperative mechanisms before alternatives can emerge, leaving the region with a weakened ability to avoid tension and conflict.

Considerations for the United States

A net effect of the PRC's efforts in Southeast Asia, abetted by pliant regional actors and U.S. ambivalence, is a regional environment that ultimately presents more complications for the United States. The international norms, practices, and even laws that are supposed to undergird a rules-based order favoring the United States are now less credible than before. A hollowing out of ASEAN means that the centrality of the grouping, which is at any rate a collection of states rather than a collective, may be of little consequence. Allies, friends, and potential partners of the United States in Southeast Asia may no longer be able to pull as much weight as before, placing more of the burden of collaboration on Washington should it wish to take a stand. Diminished influence is less an issue for Washington should it seek to become less involved in Asia going forward, but the United States has an interest in a more coherent and consistent policy in the region if it wishes to maintain a continued forward presence.

Unless Washington effectively adjusts its current policies in Southeast Asia, future recalibration of the United States' Asia policy toward re-engagement will face significant challenges. Chinese influence within Southeast Asia will increase as Washington ponders its long-term strategic direction. Should events play out along the current trajectory, there is likely to be far greater suspicion of U.S. intentions and less goodwill toward Washington among regional countries. Beijing would be in a strong position to limit and perhaps channel some of the terms under which Washington interacts with Southeast Asia over issues ranging from economic cooperation to security and military collaboration. Efforts to re-establish U.S. influence and importance at the same level that the United States enjoyed even just a few years ago are likely to be less well-received in the region and face more PRC resistance, a situation that lends itself to sharper major-power contestation.

ASEAN's institutional difficulties imply that Washington should not expect the grouping to play a large role in moderating PRC behavior, much less to act as a buffer for U.S.-China friction. To be sure, working with ASEAN and seeming supportive of its members remain important for the United States in signaling its benign intent, respect for regional actors, and desire for continued collaboration in the region. Overt displays of cooperation and interest in participation at ASEAN-related events enable the United States to maintain the strong working relationships that buttress its relative position in Southeast Asia. However, the passivity of the grouping, alongside its insistence on ASEAN centrality, may provide cover for Beijing to complicate the U.S. presence in Southeast Asia and potentially develop a veto over the region. This possibility means that ASEAN and its members may be inadvertently drawn into the contest between the United States and PRC should Washington seek to retain or enhance a forward presence in Asia while Beijing tries to restrict and counter such options.

Rather than the United States continuing to rely on ASEAN and the vagaries of its "centrality," a way forward in Southeast Asia is to find and invest in another group of like-minded partners that are more willing to commit to holding their own despite PRC pressure. Identifying and supporting states that have a demonstrable record in maintaining autonomy and working with this subset of regional states to this end may be a way for Washington to limit unnecessary confrontation with Beijing. If these partners successfully manage those regional issues within their purview, they can take key areas of U.S.-PRC competition off the table and reduce the risks of escalatory tensions between the two major powers. U.S. support in these instances would translate into promoting and participating in enhanced cooperation in areas ranging from economics and security to social-cultural activities. A downside in exercising this option is that promoting extra-ASEAN regional cooperation would accelerate the erosion of confidence in the grouping. However, this may be a necessary cost of fostering more effective collaboration and management of regional affairs.

The Trump administration's overall actions thus far have created unease in the region. Governments apprehensive about the United States could begin to see validation of their reservations about the U.S. commitment and may seek to work more closely with Beijing. Even states originally more inclined toward working with the United States, such as Vietnam and Singapore, may find themselves with few options and less ability to resist PRC overtures, even if they remain unsure of Beijing's intentions.

To avoid such a scenario, the United States needs to articulate its concept of a "free and open Indo-Pacific" with more specificity, explain how Southeast Asia fits within this approach, and target economic and other forms of cooperation to promote the outcomes it prefers. Apart from geography—Southeast Asia sits astride the Indian and Pacific Oceans—how the region and the various states within it fit into the United States' Indo-Pacific strategy remains unclear, despite major speeches and policy documents.[86] Southeast Asian states obviously desire the best of all worlds, which undergirds their original desire to "not choose sides," so they must understand why it is worth risking Beijing's ire for closer cooperation with Washington. Initiatives like the proposed U.S. International Development Finance Corporation could gain traction in the region if Washington is able to articulate a clearer strategy—something BRI lacks—and mitigate against potential loss of opportunity from the PRC.

Other elements of U.S. engagement with Southeast Asia would benefit from a more definitive direction and greater resoluteness as well. Partners and formal treaty allies in the region are more likely to support the U.S. claims and positions if there are tangible goals and benefits from doing so, given their fear of acting in ways that simply invite punishment from Beijing. These gains and objectives need not be strictly material. They could include a guarantee of prosperity and security combined with the freedom to enjoy these advantages without having to worry about an arbitrary veto. U.S. ratification and active adherence to UNCLOS, together with support of mechanisms like the Code for Unplanned Encounters at Sea, its extension to other vessels and aircraft, and a South China Sea code of conduct alongside regional states, would be particularly helpful. Subtle but clear reminders of the potential loss of investments, trade, and technological access for harming U.S. interests could be other means to encourage cooperation among regional actors, especially with effective enforcement.

A consistent and robust U.S. military presence that engages regional partners to help uphold the current rules-based order would also be welcome if it provides tangible, substantive, and widespread gains. A more regularized U.S. military presence in the South China Sea and engagement with regional partners and allies would discourage overly assertive behavior and contribute more to U.S. interests in the region than occasional FONOPs, accompanied by periodic crises or escalation with the PRC. A commitment from other U.S. friends and allies with an interest in a stable Southeast Asia, including

---

[86] White House, *National Security Strategy of the United States of America* (Washington, D.C., 2017), 2, https://www.whitehouse.gov/wp-content/uploads/2017/12/NSS-Final-12-18-2017-0905.pdf; and Mike Pence (remarks at the Hudson Institute, New York, October 4, 2018), https://www.whitehouse.gov/briefings-statements/remarks-vice-president-pence-administrations-policy-toward-china.

Japan, Australia, South Korea, the United Kingdom, and European allies, to a long-term forward presence would provide a further calming effect. Such a move would invite a strong initial reaction from Beijing, but unequivocal Southeast Asian and international opposition to actions that are threatening and undermine the existing order is likely to elicit less provocative PRC behavior eventually.

The PRC is only likely to adjust unwelcome policies when its leaders understand that a course of action elicits real, substantive costs. No Southeast Asian government seeks sharp or prolonged confrontation with the PRC, as seen from their desire to avoid choosing sides. To the extent that Beijing views such a perspective as translating into an overriding desire by other parties to back down on difficult issues, it has an incentive to press for more extensive demands. Encouraging less coercive Chinese behavior is more likely to succeed when several actors, ideally including the United States, pursue this goal concurrently and consistently. Sustaining positions that are separate and distinct from Beijing's preferences will require the acceptance of friction and the risk of escalation—otherwise these claims will simply be cheap talk.

Constitutional moments when the characteristics of a world or regional order take shape—or not—tend to be rare events that only occur once every few generations. Southeast Asia is facing just such a moment as the PRC is working to consolidate its position in the region at the same time that the United States ponders its future role. Southeast Asian states now must face the long-term consequences of not previously investing more heavily in institutions and arrangements to manage regional challenges and shocks more effectively. The United States must decide whether it wants to maintain its long-established position as the leading actor in Southeast Asia—and if it does, what degree of confrontation with China it is willing to accept. Whether China succeeds in creating a new order in the region or the current U.S.-led system can adapt and survive will be consequential for Southeast Asia and the world in the decades ahead. Actions taken or forgone today will prove decisive.

EXECUTIVE SUMMARY

This chapter examines China's growing strategic presence in the Indian Ocean region (IOR), with a particular focus on its future military role.

MAIN ARGUMENT

China's military presence in the IOR is likely to grow significantly in coming years, principally driven by the country's expanding economic interests. But China's military presence will be limited. Achieving military predominance in the IOR would be a major undertaking requiring decades of sustained expansion of military capabilities and local security partnerships. Instead, in the short to medium term, China's military capabilities on land and at sea will principally reflect its imperatives to protect nationals and assets. These capabilities will likely evolve over time to provide Beijing with options in respect to a wider range of contingencies.

POLICY IMPLICATIONS

- China's future military presence in the IOR will grow as a function of its unique strategic imperatives, which include the protection of its sea lines of communication and the protection of Chinese nationals and economic interests.

- China's naval presence will likely evolve to provide capabilities to respond to an increasingly broad range of contingencies. It would be a major challenge, though, for China to achieve sea control across the Indian Ocean, even in the long term.

- To protect Chinese nationals and assets, Beijing will primarily rely on local security forces and private security contractors and will deploy ready-response units such as the Chinese marines only as necessary.

- The U.S. should not assume that China's military presence in the IOR will necessarily resemble the U.S. presence. The U.S. will need to craft a strategy that addresses a sizeable but not predominant Chinese military presence within a multipolar strategic environment.

The Red Flag Follows Trade:
China's Future as an Indian Ocean Power

David Brewster

Historically, China has had virtually no presence in the Indian Ocean region (IOR). This is changing quickly, however, as a result of its growing economic relationships with regional states. China's presence in the IOR has the potential to change the basic strategic geography of the region: in the long term, China might in some ways come to look more like a resident power of the Indian Ocean than an extraregional one.

China's interests in the IOR are principally driven by economics, including the Belt and Road Initiative (BRI). Wherever possible, the country is leveraging its economic power into greater political and strategic influence. The extent to which this is opportunistic or part of a predetermined grand strategy is debatable, but in any event it should be seen as the outcome of China's political and economic system.

China's economic engagement in the region is creating a new and unique set of strategic imperatives for Beijing. Ensuring the security of its sea lines of communication (SLOCs) across the Indian Ocean is one. But at least in the short to medium term, China's military presence may be driven more by other imperatives, such as the need to protect Chinese nationals and assets, as well as a desire to expand its political influence through soft power and naval diplomacy.

As China pursues these goals, the People's Liberation Army Navy (PLAN) will likely play a leading regional role among China's armed forces. The PLAN is now pursuing a two-ocean strategy in the IOR that includes

David Brewster is a Senior Research Fellow with the National Security College at the Australian National University. He can be reached at <dhbrewster@bigpond.com>.

The author would like to thank Melanie Berry and Alicia Fawcett from the National Bureau of Asian Research for their research assistance.

supporting elements such as doctrine, capabilities, local access arrangements and logistics support facilities, and associated land and air elements. Given China's growing economic and strategic interests in the region, it is almost certain that the PLAN's presence in the IOR will be not only sustained but significantly expanded. In the short to medium term, the PLAN is likely to be primarily focused on military operations other than war (MOOTW), including antipiracy, noncombatant evacuation operations (NEOs), and the protection of maritime economic interests. The PLAN's capabilities may evolve to include limited contingency and sea-denial capabilities, particularly in the northwest Indian Ocean. But any bid to achieve naval predominance across the ocean to protect China's SLOCs and potentially control the maritime trade of competitors would be a major undertaking. It would require many years of sustained expansion of the PLAN and the development of multiple local military partnerships in the IOR.

China will also have land-based security requirements in connection with the protection of Chinese people and assets in the region. The country will seek to limit its security footprint as much as possible, leading it to rely heavily on local security forces, preferably assisted by private Chinese security contractors. Chinese marines, based in China or forward-deployed, will be available as a ready-response force where necessary. China will also need to develop its long-range and expeditionary air-power capabilities to support naval operations and MOOTW.

This chapter examines the drivers of China's strategic role in South Asia and the IOR and the future shape of its military presence in the region. It argues that China's role in the Indian Ocean will be principally driven by its material interests, which are mainly economic. This will create a set of unique strategic imperatives that will, in turn, shape the nature of China's military presence. The United States and its partners in the IOR will need to calibrate their responses to China's military presence with this in mind.

The chapter is divided into five parts. The first section provides an overview of the changing strategic geography of the Indian Ocean, while the next section considers the growth of China's economic role in the region, including in connection with BRI. Third, the chapter elucidates China's key strategic imperatives in the IOR, which will be derived primarily from its material and economic needs. It then considers how China's military presence in the region will likely grow to meet its strategic imperatives. This fourth section will first examine China's land-based security needs and then the possible evolution of its naval presence. The chapter concludes that although its regional presence will grow, China may be subject to significant strategic constraints and vulnerabilities in the IOR. There are several ways in which the United States could limit China's economic, political, and military role in the region, if it so chooses.

China and the Strategic Geography of the IOR

Despite being a major Eurasian continental power, China has lacked direct access to South Asia and the Indian Ocean for most of its history. High mountain ranges, deserts, and jungles extend across southern Asia, cutting off much of the continent from easy access to the sea. These formidable barriers meant that there are few overland pathways between the continental hinterland and the Indian Ocean. Indeed, until well into the twentieth century, there were no major transport routes—roads, railways, or rivers—between China and South Asia, or the Indian Ocean.[1] China might only be four hundred miles from the Indian Ocean, but it may as well be four thousand miles.

This geographic disconnect has contributed to China's historical orientation away from the Indian Ocean. China saw its sphere of influence as largely confined to East Asia on its Pacific coast. Beijing's recent efforts to promote the exploits of Zheng He, a Chinese mariner and explorer who made several expeditions to the Indian Ocean in the fifteenth century, only underline the country's historical absence from the IOR.

But this is now changing, principally driven by China's growing economic role, with potentially fundamental consequences for the strategic and political dynamics of the region. China's economic interests (and an accompanying demographic presence) are now increasingly shaped by BRI. The initiative includes the development of new overland pathways through Pakistan and Myanmar that will, for the first time ever, provide substantial direct connections between China and the Indian Ocean.[2] BRI also involves the development of ports to support China's maritime pathways across the Indian Ocean to the Pacific. Overall, it expands China's economic links and connectivity south and westward into the Indian Ocean, making the Pacific and Indian Ocean theaters a much more connected strategic space. Indeed, BRI might be seen as the "Indo-Pacific with Chinese characteristics."[3]

---

[1] David Brewster, "Silk Roads and Strings of Pearls: The Strategic Geography of China's New Pathways in the Indian Ocean," *Geopolitics* 22, no. 2 (2017): 1–23.

[2] China's only previous overland link to the Indian Ocean was the tenuous Burma Road, built between southern China with Rangoon in the 1930s. Its role as the only overland connection between China and the Western allies led Burma to become one of the biggest battlegrounds in the Pacific theater during World War II.

[3] Rory Medcalf, "Mapping Our Indo-Pacific Future" (speech at Australian National University, Canberra, June 5, 2018), https://www.policyforum.net/mapping-our-indo-pacific-future-rory-medcalfs-speech.

Since the 1970s, the United States has held military predominance in the IOR as an extraregional power. Its focus has been on ensuring the security of the production and transportation of energy from the Persian Gulf, but its security interests in the broader region have otherwise been relatively limited. Strategic competition between the United States and China in the IOR has been relatively muted to date, although Washington is slowly responding to BRI with its own infrastructure funding proposals. Current proposals to expand the size of the U.S. Navy could also provide opportunities to increase the U.S. naval presence in the IOR.

But the United States is also far away from the Indian Ocean, and it is quite possible that the U.S. military presence could be reduced in the future. If the United States becomes a net exporter of oil in a few years' time as expected, Washington may have more strategic options than in the past, including the option of not indefinitely maintaining a large military force in the Persian Gulf that now essentially protects oil bound for China. These uncertainties have only grown under the current U.S. administration. From the standpoint of IOR states, whether it be sooner or later, a day may come when the U.S. fleet will sail for home, just as the Royal Navy departed from the region in the late 1960s. Whether or not the U.S. military commitment to the IOR changes in the short term, there can be little doubt that the future of the Indian Ocean is much more multipolar than at any time before, with China jostling for position with the United States, India, and several middle powers.

Importantly, the impact of BRI may over time lead China to assume a quite different role in the region as compared with the extraregional presence of the United States. China's close physical proximity to the Indian Ocean, the new direct overland connections being built between China and the ocean, and the growing presence of large numbers of Chinese nationals may in effect make it act more like a resident state of the Indian Ocean, almost as if it were a littoral state.

In the long run, the biggest single constraint on China's role in the IOR may be India, which sees itself as a potential peer competitor. India has historically dominated South Asia and aspires to become the leading power across the IOR. In any realistic scenario, its naval power for the foreseeable future will far exceed that which China can deploy to the Indian Ocean. India's relations with China are difficult, and there are numerous points of strategic friction. Underlying these is the refusal by Beijing to recognize India's claim to special rights as the leading regional power. For its part, New Delhi refuses to countenance a significant role for China in the Indian Ocean. The largely negative dynamics of this relationship may become an increasingly important driver of China's actions in the IOR.

China's future role in the IOR will also be constrained by other players. There are several resident middle powers in the Indian Ocean, including Australia, Indonesia, Iran, Saudi Arabia, and France, as well as several active extraregional powers besides the United States, such as Japan and Britain, all of which have large or capable militaries and strong interests in the region. Many of these countries are building new networks with each other (and with India) with an eye to stabilizing and diffusing power across the region in light of the changing strategic environment, including the growing Chinese presence and concerns about the future U.S. role. Whatever may be the wishes of the major powers, the future of the IOR looks much more multipolar than its past.

Although China's strategic behavior in the IOR will be predominantly driven by economic considerations, ideology may still be a factor. Marxism is no longer relevant to China's engagements in the region. But a new ideational factor—the need to demonstrate its status as a major power—could increasingly become a factor in China's calculations beyond the mere advancement of material interests. Considerations of international status may, for example, contribute to China's assertiveness in protecting Chinese citizens and assets abroad. An important role in the IOR would also complement the country's power in East Asia and support its claim to a leading role in Asia as a whole. A major Chinese military role in the Persian Gulf—if, or more likely when, that occurs—would further enhance its role in the international system.

China's Economic Engagement in the IOR

The role of China in the IOR is underpinned, and primarily driven, by its economic engagement with the region. These interests create a new set of strategic imperatives that in turn will drive its future military presence.

As in many parts of the world, over the space of a few short years China has become a major trading partner for most countries in the IOR. These tend to fall into two groups. The first group comprises a handful of energy- and resource-rich countries, including Australia, Iran, Oman, and Saudi Arabia, that run large trade surpluses with China. Some, such as Australia, have become highly reliant on China as a customer, creating concerns about overexposure to the Chinese economy (and, potentially, to Chinese political influence).[4] But for many IOR states, trade runs strongly in the other direction. Countries such as India, Pakistan, Bangladesh, Sri Lanka, Tanzania, and

---

[4] See, for example, Rory Medcalf, "Australia and China: Understanding the Reality Check," *Australian Journal of International Affairs* (2018), https://doi.org/10.1080/10357718.2018.1538315.

Djibouti all run major trade deficits with China.[5] These countries have found it difficult to penetrate the Chinese market with their own products and may also compete with China in other markets. Although such trade imbalances are not necessarily problematic, they can strain bilateral relationships, even in the case of a close political partner such as Pakistan. In any event, China is playing an ever-more important role in regional trade.

Chinese companies (state-owned and private) have also become important investors in many IOR states. The overall size of Chinese investment, however, should not be overstated: while growing, it still only exceeds 10% of total foreign investment stock in a handful of countries such as Eritrea, Kenya, Mauritius, Myanmar, and Pakistan.[6] But the nature of these investments is important. In many countries, Chinese direct investment has so far been focused on infrastructure and resources rather than manufacturing, which largely reflects the poor state of infrastructure across the region and the need to develop connectivity. As basic infrastructure improves, there may be greater Chinese investment in the manufacturing sector, including in the development of manufacturing production and value chains that connect IOR states with China.[7]

BRI potentially raises a qualitatively different set of issues from China's normal trade and investment relationships. The initiative represents an attempt by Beijing to reshape the world around China. It involves huge expenditures—more than $1 trillion according to some sources—in developing connectivity and other essential infrastructure in Eurasia, the IOR, Africa, the South Pacific, and indeed across the world.[8] But the strategic impact of BRI may be most profound in the IOR, where it has the potential to fundamentally reshape the strategic dynamics of the region.

To some extent, BRI is just a grab bag of Chinese investments of many different types, some of which are unremarkable or of little strategic significance.[9] But some elements have considerable consequences in terms

---

[5] International Monetary Fund, *Direction of Trade Statistics Quarterly*, 2018.

[6] These figures are through the end of 2016 and are based on data for FDI flows from 2003 using figures supplied by the Chinese Ministry of Commerce. UN Conference on Trade and Development (UNCTAD), http://unctadstat.unctad.org. FDI stock is the value of the share of capital and reserves (including retained profits) attributable to the parent enterprise, plus the net indebtedness of affiliates to the parent enterprises. It is approximated by the accumulated value of past FDI flows.

[7] Over time, this could develop into a system analogous with Japan's "flying geese" system in East Asia in the 1970s.

[8] "Will China's Belt and Road Initiative Outdo the Marshall Plan?" *Economist*, May 8, 2018, https://www.economist.com/finance-and-economics/2018/03/08/will-chinas-belt-and-road-initiative-outdo-the-marshall-plan.

[9] Jonathan E. Hillman, "China's Belt and Road Is Full of Holes," Center for Strategic and International Studies (CSIS), CSIS Brief, September 4, 2018, https://www.csis.org/analysis/chinas-belt-and-road-full-holes.

of expanding China's political and military role in the region. As noted, the extent to which these consequences are part of a predetermined strategy or instead may be opportunistic outcomes of an authoritarian regime desperate to export excess economic capacity is debatable. The growth of China's political influence in countries that participate in BRI has led many to deduce that strategic outcomes are a key motivation of the initiative. Others might argue that growing political influence is just a natural and obvious consequence of China's massive spending as part of BRI. Ultimately, the opaque nature of China's political system makes the mix of its motivations a matter of speculation.

What are the potential strategic consequences of BRI? One concern centers on the massive amounts of debt funding that China typically uses for infrastructure projects. When large amounts of debt are offered on a nontransparent basis, often in connection with economically unfeasible projects, it has the potential to create so-called debt traps. Many weak or unstable states in the region are beginning to suffer debt distress, making them potentially open to undue influence from China. Although BRI projects are often advertised by Beijing as a form of "aid,"[10] they rarely meet the concepts of official development assistance put forth by the Organisation for Economic Co-operation and Development (OECD), and interest rates on loans often exceed those offered by international funding agencies. Several IOR states such as Djibouti, Maldives, and Pakistan have been identified as at high risk of debt distress as a result of BRI-related projects, and Sri Lanka, Ethiopia, and Kenya are considered at significant risk.[11] The inability of borrower states to repay funds is sometimes used by Beijing to extend influence in political and security affairs or (as discussed below) to gain control of strategic infrastructure. The degree to which highly indebted Pakistan, for example, is becoming increasingly beholden to China is just one example of the way in which debt can be used to create political and strategic influence. Countries such as Sri Lanka have faced problems in trying to rebalance their political alignment away from Beijing; indebtedness has significantly constrained their options, forcing them to ask Beijing for more funding.

Another concern is the potential for Chinese military use of strategic infrastructure such as ports and airports. Chinese investments in the IOR has been oriented toward infrastructure, particularly transport infrastructure. As part of BRI, China has constructed ports at Gwadar

---

[10] Eva Dou, "The Big Winner from China's Foreign-Aid Frenzy: China," *Wall Street Journal*, October 11, 2017.

[11] John Hurley, Scott Morris, and Gailyn Portelance, "Examining the Debt Implications of the Belt and Road Initiative from a Policy Perspective," Center for Global Development, Policy Paper, no. 121, March 2018.

in Pakistan, Hambantota in Sri Lanka, and Bagamoyo in Tanzania and is currently building ports at Kyaukpyu in Myanmar and Payra in Bangladesh. China has also constructed or upgraded airports at Gwadar, Hambantota, Malé in Maldives, and many locations across Africa. There are concerns that China may gain access to or control over this infrastructure for military purposes. The case of the Hambantota port in Sri Lanka is a salutary example. A Chinese state-owned company allegedly bribed then president Mahinda Rajapaksa to construct a $1 billion port in his home town.[12] When the associated debt could not be repaid, the company acquired effective ownership of the port under a 99-year lease. Although the current Sri Lankan government vehemently denies that the PLAN will ever be permitted to establish a base at Hambantota, there are real concerns that Sri Lanka's debt to China may ultimately force it to allow the port to be used for military purposes.

The potential strategic impact of BRI is most apparent in Pakistan and Myanmar, where China is effectively carving new corridors across those countries to the Indian Ocean. In Pakistan, the China-Pakistan Economic Corridor (CPEC) has become the flagship project of the entire initiative. The plan involves building a series of roads, railways, and pipelines between the Chinese autonomous region of Xinjiang, through the Karakoram mountain range, to a new port city at Gwadar on the Indian Ocean. (The route traverses Pakistan's northern and frontier territories and Baluchistan, where there are active extremist or separatist insurgencies.) The scale of China's investments in CPEC, claimed to be more than $60 billion,[13] has led Islamabad to see it as a "game changer" for Pakistan.[14] Although the economic unfeasibility of many projects has provoked concerns that Pakistan will find itself in a debt trap, the magnitude of Chinese investment in CPEC and its geopolitical importance to China may also lock in Beijing to ensuring the corridor's success.

Another part of BRI with great geostrategic significance is the China-Myanmar Economic Corridor, which includes a series of new overland connections between China's Yunnan Province and a new port at Kyaukpyu in Myanmar's Rakhine State. This includes proposals for a $7.3 billion port, with a $2.7 billion special economic zone, and oil and gas pipelines to China.[15]

---

[12] Maria Abi-Habib, "How China Got Sri Lanka to Cough Up a Port," *New York Times*, June 25, 2018, https://www.nytimes.com/2018/06/25/world/asia/china-sri-lanka-port.html.

[13] "Massive Chinese Investment Is a Boon for Pakistan," *Economist*, September 9, 2017, https://www.economist.com/asia/2017/09/09/massive-chinese-investment-is-a-boon-for-pakistan.

[14] "China-Pakistan Economic Corridor, a Game Changer for Pakistan: PM Abbasi," *Indian Express*, April 9, 2018.

[15] Jason Koutsoukis, "The Fishing Port That May Become a $10 Billion Chinese Debt Bomb," Bloomberg, May 10, 2018, https://www.bloomberg.com/news/articles/2018-05-10/the-fishing-port-that-may-become-a-10-billion-chinese-debt-bomb.

Much of this corridor will traverse regions of Myanmar where there are active insurgencies or civil unrest. But China's influence in that country is somewhat shakier than in Pakistan, and successive governments have jealously protected Myanmar's sovereignty. In fact, Sri Lanka's experience with Hambantota port is leading the Myanmar government to scale back the Kyaukpyu port project.[16]

The scale of these projects may also create significant interests in the internal security of Pakistan and Myanmar. In past decades, Beijing could afford to build cordial political relationships with their authoritarian leaders without having to involve itself with domestic security issues. As discussed below, Beijing's growing interests in the stability and security of those countries may make that approach no longer tenable.

Another related, and little discussed, geostrategic consequence of BRI and China's economic expansion in the IOR is its demographic impact. According to one estimate, there may be more than 1 million recent Chinese economic migrants in Africa.[17] Likewise, around 250,000 Chinese nationals arrive in Pakistan each year, many of them connected with CPEC. These numbers are expected to grow significantly in Pakistan and other countries in connection with the construction and operation of various BRI projects.[18]

Potential strategic consequences of these developments flow not only from the large numbers of Chinese citizens migrating to the region but also from the locations of projects. Many BRI projects include plans for major residential developments, likely including large numbers of Chinese nationals. At Gwadar, a Chinese company has announced plans to build housing for up to 500,000 Chinese workers.[19] The (now likely canceled) Forest City development in Malaysia had included plans for 700,000 residents, which Prime Minister Mahathir Bin Mohamad claimed was being "built for foreigners."[20] Other big

---

[16] Kanupriya Kapoor and Aye Min Thant, "Myanmar Scales Back Chinese-Backed Port Project Due to Debt Fears," Reuters, August 2, 2018, https://uk.reuters.com/article/us-myanmar-china-port-exclusive/exclusive-myanmar-scales-back-chinese-backed-port-project-due-to-debt-fears-official-idUKKBN1KN106.

[17] "Empire of the Sums," *Economist*, August 23, 2014, https://www.economist.com/books-and-arts/2014/08/23/empire-of-the-sums. Africa may be the continent with the greatest relative increases in overseas Chinese in coming decades. Dudley L. Poston Jr. and Juyin Helen Wong, "The Chinese Diaspora: The Current Distribution of the Overseas Chinese Population," *Chinese Journal of Sociology* 2, no. 3 (2016): 348–73.

[18] "CPEC: Business, Security Headache for China, Pak" *Business Standard*, April 23, 2018, https://www.business-standard.com/article/news-ani/cpec-business-security-headache-for-china-pak-118042300083_1.html.

[19] Murtaza Ali Shah, "500,000 Chinese Professionals Expected in Gwadar by 2023," *News* (Pakistan), October 21, 2017, https://www.thenews.com.pk/print/238644-500000-Chinese-professionals-expected-in-Gwadar-by-2023.

[20] Fathin Ungku and Joseph Sipalan, "Mahathir Takes Aim at Country Garden's Giant Development in Southern Malaysia," Reuters, August 27, 2018, https://www.reuters.com/article/forest-city-development/rpt-focus-mahathir-takes-aim-at-country-gardens-giant-development-in-southern-malaysia-idUSL3N1VJ041.

residential developments are planned for Sri Lanka, Maldives, and Tanzania, which could include large numbers of Chinese nationals. As will be seen later, the presence of Chinese nationals around the Indian Ocean littoral could become an increasingly important factor in China's security role in the region.

Finally, it should be noted that BRI is not an unstoppable juggernaut. To the contrary, China has already suffered several reverses where the perceived benefits from BRI for local populations were insufficient. Popular backlash against BRI projects and corrupt local leaders have been material factors in changes of government in Sri Lanka (2015), Myanmar (2015), Malaysia (2018), and most recently Maldives (2018). In each of these cases, the newly elected governments vowed to review corrupt or unfeasible projects (although their ability to actually do so may sometimes be questionable). These are important lessons for China about the possible consequences of becoming too close to corrupt and authoritarian regimes.

China's Strategic Imperatives in the IOR

China's military role in the IOR will almost certainly grow in conjunction with the expansion of its material interests. However, it should not be assumed that China's presence in the region will resemble that of the United States, which initially developed its military presence during the Cold War when traditional threats were at the fore. For one thing, compared with the United States, China lacks many regional allies, and the PLA's ability to unilaterally project power at a distance is highly limited.[21] More importantly, the shape and nature of China's military presence in the Indian Ocean will likely evolve as a function of its unique strategic imperatives, many of which differ significantly from the United States' strategic imperatives in the region. China's strategic imperatives include the following:

- the security of SLOCs against state and nonstate actors
- the need to evacuate Chinese nationals in response to local crises
- the provision of on-the-ground security for Chinese nationals and investments
- the protection of maritime economic interests
- the exercise of soft power such as support for UN peacekeeping and humanitarian assistance and disaster relief (HADR) operations
- use of naval diplomacy and demonstrations for political influence and coercion

---

[21] Timothy R. Heath, "China's Pursuit of Overseas Security," RAND Corporation, 2018, x.

- the need to undertake military actions or interventions in support of political objectives

These imperatives must be understood in order to fully appreciate the breadth of the drivers of China's future presence in the IOR.

SLOC Protection

China's most crucial strategic imperative in the IOR is the protection of its SLOCs across the Indian Ocean. This most critically involves the protection of energy imports from the Persian Gulf and northwest Indian Ocean as well as from West Africa (which now account for around 20% of its total oil imports).[22] Beijing understands that Indian Ocean SLOCs for energy imports are vulnerable to threats, especially at the narrow chokepoints through which most maritime trade must pass, including the Hormuz, Bab-el-Mandeb, and Malacca Straits.[23] These threats may arise from nonstate actors such as pirates and terrorists or from state adversaries that may try to use China's vulnerabilities as a bargaining chip in a wider dispute. Overall, this vulnerability is growing. In 2017, China imported some 67% of its oil requirements (with around 80% of that transported via the Indian Ocean). Its oil import requirements are expected to grow to 80% of total need by 2035. However, China's efforts to diversify its energy mix and its sources of hydrocarbon imports (e.g., through gas and oil imports from Russia) likely will have only a limited impact on its high reliance on hydrocarbons transported across the Indian Ocean.[24]

However, it is not yet entirely clear how this vulnerability will shape China's future military presence in the IOR. The U.S. Navy is currently the leading provider of SLOC security for the region, and there are no real indications, for example, that China is actively seeking to challenge or replace the public goods provided by the U.S. Fifth Fleet in the Persian Gulf.[25] But this could change quickly if there were a reduced commitment of U.S. defense resources (particularly in the Persian Gulf) or other major developments

---

[22] Ma Shikun, "The Truth about China-Africa Relations," *China Daily*, April 25, 2018, http://www.chinadaily.com.cn/a/201804/25/WS5adfdaf0a3105cdcf651a58f.html.

[23] In 2017, some 80% of China's oil imports transited the Strait of Malacca. Office of the Secretary of Defense, *Annual Report to Congress: Military and Security Developments Involving the People's Republic of China 2018* (Washington, D.C., May 2018), 54.

[24] U.S. Department of Defense, *Annual Report to Congress: Military and Security Developments Involving the People's Republic of China 2018*, 54.

[25] However, China may be developing relationships in the Persian Gulf for such a contingency. See Debasish Roy Chowdhury, "China a Pillar of Strength in Qatar's Fightback against Arab Blockade," *South China Morning Post*, June 9, 2018, https://www.scmp.com/week-asia/geopolitics/article/2149915/china-pillar-strength-qatars-fightback-against-arab-blockade.

adversely affecting China's interests that the United States is unwilling or unable to address.

China also takes quite a different view toward India's aspirations to be the leading provider of maritime security in the Indian Ocean, which is considered in Beijing as unrealistic in light of India's perceived lack of comprehensive national power. China is therefore unlikely to accept any attempts by India to replace the United States as the dominant provider of SLOC security in the region.

On the other hand, an attempt by China to unilaterally protect its Indian Ocean SLOCs against a major adversary would also come with significant problems that might make such a strategy unrealistic. In coming years, China might be in a position to achieve local naval superiority for limited periods (as could several other navies in the IOR). But it would face major problems in protecting the entire length of its SLOCs across the ocean against interdiction by major naval powers such as the United States or India. Securing only a part of the SLOCs against a major adversary is insufficient. To protect SLOCs, they must be secured in their entirety, often for lengthy periods. During World War II, Britain and the United States, the world's two greatest naval powers, were only barely able to protect the relatively shorter Atlantic Ocean SLOCs directly between them against a far-off adversary. Protecting SLOCs across the Indian Ocean would be an extraordinary challenge for China, especially given India's central location and the length of the routes (6,000 kilometers between the Hormuz and Malacca Straits and 9,500 kilometers between Cape Town and the Sunda Strait).

Yet there are also several reasons (which have little or nothing to do with a Chinese naval presence) to doubt the ability of the United States, India, or any other country to enforce a selective blockade against China in the Indian Ocean. Problems include the consequences for the global economy (probably severe, including negative impacts on the blockader), the availability of sufficient naval resources for the job (difficult, even for the United States), and knowing which ships to interdict. Short of sinking every tanker, would-be blockaders may find it very difficult to determine the final destination of shipments, particularly when cargoes can be sold while in transit. Not the least of the problems, however, would be China's response to such actions, which could include the ability to interfere with energy supplies to its adversaries.

Nevertheless, Beijing appears to take the possibility of a distant blockade sufficiently seriously for this scenario to be an important driver in its strategic thinking about the Indian Ocean. Chinese president Hu Jintao began publicly talking about China's "Malacca dilemma" as long ago as 2003.[26] The threat of

---

[26] Marc Lanteigne, "China's Maritime Security and the 'Malacca Dilemma,'" *Asian Security* 4, no. 2 (2008): 143–61.

a blockade may also be a convenient justification for China's increased naval expenditures and investment in projects such as overland energy pipelines that might not otherwise be financially viable (even if such pipelines would themselves be highly vulnerable).

China also faces localized threats to its Indian Ocean SLOCs from nonstate actors. The threat of Somali-based piracy, for example, led China to establish a naval presence in the northwest Indian Ocean in 2008. Although this threat has largely been addressed, the potential for its resurgence provides a justification for China to continue to deploy its naval task force in the northwest Indian Ocean.

Noncombatant Evacuation Operations

Another important imperative will come from the growing presence of Chinese nationals in the IOR, including many economic migrants and temporary workers on Chinese-sponsored projects. There are also many older diasporic Chinese communities in the region that could potentially come under threat.

In the past China took a relatively passive approach to the safety of Chinese nationals and diasporic communities. But this is changing rapidly as part of a new diplomatic imperative of "overseas citizen protection."[27] This reflects China's growing material capabilities, a desire to prove the value and status of Chinese citizenship, and the government's need to respond to domestic political pressures. The angry reaction of the relatives of Chinese nationals lost on Malaysian Airlines Flight 370 in the Indian Ocean in 2014 was likely a big factor in the government's heightened response to that incident compared with previous accidents.[28] Chinese social media may also have been an important factor in Beijing's decision to evacuate 35,000 citizens from Libya in 2011.[29] Importantly, domestic political pressures could narrow the government's options in responding to crises and potentially drive a military response where Beijing may prefer to respond in other ways.

An indication of the growing importance of the protection of Chinese nationals across the Indo-Pacific and elsewhere is indicated by the NEOs conducted by China in recent years, which are shown in **Table 1**.[30]

---

[27] Shaio H. Zerba, "China's Libya Evacuation Operation: A New Diplomatic Imperative—Overseas Citizen Protection," *Journal of Contemporary China* 23, no. 90 (2014): 1093–1112.

[28] Huey Fern Tray, "MH370: Chinese Families of Missing Passengers React Angrily to Formal Announcement of No Survivors," ABC (Australia), January 30, 2015, http://www.abc.net.au/news/2015-01-30/malaysian-government-rules-no-survivors-of-missing-mh370/6056380.

[29] Zerba, "China's Libya Evacuation Operation," 1099.

[30] "Backgrounder: China's Major Overseas Evacuations in Recent Years," *China Daily*, March 30, 2015, http://www.chinadaily.com.cn/china/2015-03/30/content_19954649.htm.

TABLE 1   Chinese noncombatant evacuation operations

Year	Region	Evacuations
2006	Solomon Islands	325 Chinese nationals evacuated by chartered aircraft
2006	Timor-Leste	246 Chinese nationals evacuated by chartered aircraft
2006	Tonga	300 Chinese nationals evacuated by chartered aircraft
2008	Chad	210 Chinese nationals evacuated
2008	Thailand	3,000 Chinese nationals evacuated by chartered aircraft
2009	Haiti	48 Chinese nationals evacuated
2010	Kyrgyzstan	1,299 Chinese nationals evacuated by aircraft
2011	Egypt	1,848 Chinese nationals evacuated by chartered aircraft
2011	Libya	35,000 Chinese nationals and 2,100 others evacuated by sea and air
2014	Iraq	1,200 Chinese nationals evacuated from northern Iraq to Baghdad
2015	Yemen	570 Chinese nationals and 270 others evacuated by the PLAN via Djibouti

SOURCE: "Backgrounder: China's Major Overseas Evacuations in Recent Years," *China Daily*, March 30, 2015, http://www.chinadaily.com.cn/china/2015-03/30/content_19954649.htm.

Several of these operations (including in Timor-Leste, Thailand, Egypt, Libya, and Yemen) involved evacuations from or staging in the IOR. The 2011 evacuation from Libya is China's largest and most logistically complex NEO (and is significantly larger than any recent U.S. NEO). It involved the use of chartered merchant vessels under the protection of a PLAN vessel and PLA Air Force (PLAAF) aircraft staging through Khartoum, Sudan. According to Christopher Yung, the PLA will likely prefer to use only military assets for future evacuation operations.[31]

---

[31] Christopher D. Yung, "China's Expeditionary and Power Projection Capabilities Trajectory: Lessons from Recent Expeditionary Operations," testimony before the U.S.-China Economic and Security Review Commission, Washington, D.C., January 21, 2016.

The inclusion of 2,100 non-Chinese in the Libyan evacuation and 270 non-Chinese in the 2015 Yemen evacuation is an indicator that NEOs may also increasingly become an expression of China's ability to provide public goods for the IOR. In addition, such operations could be a way for Beijing to emphasize its role as protector of the broader Chinese diaspora, whether or not they are Chinese nationals. Further large-scale operations, from or staged in the IOR, should be expected in the future as the numbers of Chinese nationals grow in West Asia and Africa.[32] China may use chartered or PLAAF aircraft where there is permissive access to airports, while operations may involve the PLAN or Chinese special forces in less permissive environments. Importantly, the ability to conduct large-scale NEOs on short notice will require assured access to port and air facilities for staging. It will also require the development of China's still nascent long-range and expeditionary air-power capabilities, as well as the prepositioning of assets such as amphibious vessels within the region.

The possible need to conduct NEOs in nonpermissive environments, including the extraction of hostages, means that armed interventions in support of such operations may become more likely. The potential for interventions far from home is being normalized in China by recent films such as *Wolf Warrior 2* (in which Chinese special forces rescue Chinese and U.S. nationals from an unnamed African country) and *Operation Red Sea* (in which Chinese naval commandos operating from a PLAN ship rescue Chinese hostages and otherwise save the day against a terrorist group located in a fictional Arabian country).

The need for assured access to facilities from which to conduct or stage NEOs and other MOOTW was an important driver in the establishment of a Chinese base in Djibouti. As discussed later, the nature of that base's facilities and its location limit its suitability for warfighting. The need for proximate locations to support NEOs and other MOOTW may drive the establishment of new facilities elsewhere in the region.

Provision of On-the-Ground Security for Chinese Nationals and Investments

China's growing investments in the IOR, including as part of BRI, and a large Chinese workforce associated with many projects may drive the country to increase its on-the-ground security presence. Many BRI projects are being undertaken in highly insecure regions, making them vulnerable to attack by nonstate actors. Chinese companies, and quite possibly the Chinese

---

[32] Michael S. Chase, "The PLA Prepares for Future Non-combatant Evacuation Operations," Jamestown Foundation, China Brief, February 15, 2013.

government, may have underestimated the security threats involved in many countries. There already have been several instances of actual or threatened attacks on Chinese projects or workers in Sudan and Pakistan (including a suicide attack on a bus full of Chinese workers in August 2018 and an attack on the Chinese consulate in Karachi in November 2018).[33]

The protection of BRI projects is thus becoming an increasingly important factor in China's engagement in the region. Several Chinese military exercises in the IOR are openly focused on the protection of these projects.[34] China may also increasingly find itself drawn into local conflicts to protect its investments, whether it be in Pakistan, Myanmar, or Africa. As the *Global Times* argued in connection with Myanmar, "China has always adhered to the principle of non-interference in the internal affairs of other countries, but that doesn't mean Beijing can turn a deaf ear to the demands of Chinese enterprises in protecting their overseas investments."[35] Similarly, the *Global Times* commented in connection with Africa: "It's natural that the Chinese troops stationed at Djibouti must be always prepared for combat, which is what a military is supposed to do....By the end of 2016, China had already invested more than $100 billion in Africa. This entails the duty of the Chinese military to safeguard China's interests in the continent, parts of which can be unstable."[36]

These comments suggest a fundamentally new mission for Chinese security forces. Never before in its history has the People's Republic of China publicly contemplated using the PLA beyond its borders for the protection of Chinese citizens and assets. The provision of sustained on-the-ground security, or at least the ability to respond quickly to contingencies involving people or assets, will require the maintenance of adequate ready-response forces based in China or forward-deployed in the region.

---

[33] "China Warns Its Citizens in Pakistan of Possible Militant Attacks," *Hindu*, December 8, 2017, https://www.thehindu.com/news/international/china-warns-citizens-in-pakistan-of-possible-terror-attacks/article21310684.ece; Gul Yousafzai, "Five Wounded in Attack on Bus Ferrying Chinese Workers in Pakistan," Reuters, August 11, 2018, https://www.reuters.com/article/us-pakistan-blast-china/five-wounded-in-attack-on-bus-ferrying-chinese-workers-in-pakistan-idUSKBN1KW05B; and "Karachi Attack: China Consulate Attack Leaves Four Dead," BBC News, November 23, 2018.

[34] One example is the China–Sri Lanka counterterrorism exercises titled "Silk Road Cooperation 2015." Ankit Panda, "Sri Lanka and China Wrap Up Silk Route 2015 Military Exercise," *Diplomat*, July 18, 2015, https://thediplomat.com/2015/07/sri-lanka-and-china-wrap-up-silk-route-2015-military-exercise.

[35] Hu Weijia, "China Ready to Play a Greater Role in Resolving Conflicts in South & Southeast Asia," *Global Times*, May 1, 2017, http://www.globaltimes.cn/content/1044849.shtml.

[36] Su Tan, "Military Drill in Djibouti Will Not Change China's Defensive Strategy," *Global Times*, November 26, 2017, http://www.globaltimes.cn/content/1077295.shtml.

Protection of Maritime Economic Interests

In addition to the imperative to protect its investments on land, China must secure its maritime economic interests, including in fishing and offshore hydrocarbon and mineral extraction. In recent years, China's fishing fleet has been at the forefront of disputes in the South China Sea, where vessels operating under state protection have brought fish stocks to the point of collapse. The decline in fish stocks near Chinese waters may have prompted Xi Jinping's exhortations to his nation's fishermen in 2013 to "build bigger ships and venture even farther into the oceans and catch bigger fish."[37] This presaged a major expansion in China's fishing fleet that is pushing ever farther into international waters, including in the Indian Ocean.[38] In September 2018, the Madagascar president announced a deal to allow 330 Chinese fishing boats to exploit Madagascar's waters for ten years. The deal was awarded in questionable circumstances.[39]

A report by the U.S. National Intelligence Council finds that the sustainability of Indian Ocean fisheries is under serious threat.[40] As fish stocks in the Indian Ocean come under increasing pressure, there is a significant risk that fishing will become a much more contested activity involving Chinese security interests. This could arise in several ways. Chinese fishing fleets may refuse to comply with local quotas, or they may operate illegally or in areas of contested jurisdiction.[41] This could lead to conflicts between local and Chinese fishermen or with local states seeking to enforce their maritime jurisdictions. There are already several instances (in the South China Sea and the Atlantic Ocean) of Chinese fishing vessels responding with force or claiming protection from the PLAN or other Chinese maritime agencies

---

[37] "Trawling for Trouble," *Economist*, April 14, 2016, https://www.economist.com/asia/2016/04/14/trawling-for-trouble.

[38] Anthony Bergin, "China's Distant Water Fisheries: It's Not Just about the Fish," Australian Strategic Policy Institute, Strategist, June 15, 2015, https://www.aspistrategist.org.au/chinas-distant-water-fisheries-its-not-just-about-the-fish; and Lucy Hornby, "A Bigger Catch: China's Fishing Fleet Hunts New Ocean Targets," *Financial Times*, March 28, 2017, https://www.ft.com/content/e7bd4094-ff34-11e6-96f8-3700c5664d30.

[39] Edward Carver, "Fishermen Oppose $2.7 Bn Deal Opening Madagascar to Chinese Fishing," *Asia Times*, November 10, 2018.

[40] Office of the Director of National Intelligence, "The Future of Indian Ocean and South China Sea Fisheries: Implications for the United States," National Intelligence Council Report, NICR 2013-38, July 30, 2013, https://www.dni.gov/files/documents/nic/NICR%202013-38%20Fisheries%20Report%20FINAL.pdf.

[41] For example, in 2016 the regional government of the renegade Somali province of Puntland sold $10 million in fishing licenses to a Chinese company in violation of Somali federal law.

against attempts by local authorities to enforce EEZs.[42] Fishing-related disputes could also be complicated by the use of private security contractors to protect Chinese fishermen and the PLAN's practice of using Sea Phantom intelligence vessels disguised as fishing boats.[43]

China's other maritime economic interests in the Indian Ocean are also growing. These include in the extraction of hydrocarbons (off the coast of East Africa and in the Bay of Bengal) and in undersea mining (where China has been one of the most active countries in seabed mining exploration in international waters). The economic value of these activities could easily turn them into security interests if they become contested.

Support for UN Peacekeeping and HADR Operations

Another important driver of China's presence in the broader IOR is gaining status and influence through the exercise of soft power. Beijing has significantly increased its commitment to UN peacekeeping operations, including the establishment of a permanent standby force of 8,000 troops.[44] As of May 2018, China had 2,654 troops deployed in Africa and the Middle East on ten UN operations, including in South Sudan, Côte d'Ivoire, Liberia, and Western Sahara.[45] Requirements to support peacekeeping activities were an important justification put forward by Beijing for establishing a base at Djibouti.

The provision of HADR may be another driver in China's regional presence. Perceptions that China responded inadequately to previous major natural disasters, including the Indian Ocean tsunami in 2004 and Typhoon Haiyan in the Philippines in 2013, have led to a greater understanding in Beijing of HADR operations as a form of soft power. In 2010, the Chinese

---

[42] In 2016, for example, China Coast Guard vessels intervened in Indonesian territorial waters to free a Chinese fishing vessel that had been detained by Indonesian authorities for illegal fishing. Joe Cochrane, "China's Coast Guard Rams Fishing Boat to Free It from Indonesian Authorities," *New York Times*, March 21, 2016, https://www.nytimes.com/2016/03/22/world/asia/indonesia-south-china-sea-fishing-boat.html.

[43] Borges Nhamire and Matthew Hill, "Erik Prince to Partner with Mozambique Hidden-Debt Companies," Bloomberg, December 13, 2017, https://www.bloomberg.com/news/articles/2017-12-12/erik-prince-to-partner-with-mozambique-s-hidden-debt-companies; and Koh Swee Lean Collin, "China's 'Sea Phantom' Fleet Prowls the Open Waters," *National Interest*, February 4, 2016, https://nationalinterest.org/feature/chinas-sea-phantom-fleet-prowls-the-open-waters-15105.

[44] Sarah Zheng, "China Completes Registration of 8,000-Strong UN Peacekeeping Force, Defence Ministry Says," *South China Morning Post*, September 29, 2017, https://www.scmp.com/news/china/diplomacy-defence/article/2113436/china-completes-registration-8000-strong-un; and Logan Pauley, "China Takes the Lead in UN Peacekeeping," *Diplomat*, April 17, 2018, https://thediplomat.com/2018/04/china-takes-the-lead-in-un-peacekeeping.

[45] U.S. Department of Defense, *Annual Report to Congress: Military and Security Developments Involving the People's Republic of China 2018*, 21.

hospital ship *Daishan Dao* (Peace Ark) deployed on a three-month mission to the Gulf of Aden to provide medical treatment in Djibouti, Tanzania, Kenya, the Seychelles, and Bangladesh. Deployments of Chinese assets in response to future natural disasters in the IOR can be expected.

Naval Diplomacy and Demonstrations

Since the establishment of its counterpiracy naval task force in the western Indian Ocean in 2008, the PLAN has had an active naval diplomacy program in the IOR. Naval diplomacy is recognized as a valuable way of developing soft power as part of a narrative about the provision of public goods in the Indian Ocean.[46]

The PLAN also participates in locally hosted and unilateral naval exercises in the Indian Ocean as a demonstration of its role in the region and to familiarize itself with local conditions. It is a regular participant in bilateral and multilateral naval exercises hosted by Pakistan and has participated in exercises hosted by South Africa, Tanzania, and Bangladesh, among other countries.[47] The PLAN also conducts an increasing number of unilateral exercises in the region, including annual exercises by task groups in the eastern Indian Ocean since 2014. The 2018 exercise involved eleven ships, including an amphibious vessel.[48]

The PLAN is also increasingly conducting naval demonstrations in support of political objectives as a form of coercive diplomacy. In 2014, for example, a PLAN submarine and support vessel visited Colombo in conjunction with an incursion by the PLA in the Himalayas, only a few days prior to President Xi's first visit to India (although these actions apparently failed in the intended effect of enhancing China's negotiating position). In August 2017, during the standoff with India at Doklam in the Himalayas, the PLAN reportedly conducted live-fire exercises near Maldives.[49] It should be expected that the PLAN will conduct further demonstrations in the context of disputes with India or other countries.

---

[46] Yen-Chiang Chang, "The '21st Century Maritime Silk Road Initiative' and Naval Diplomacy in China," *Ocean and Coastal Management* 153 (2018): 148–56.

[47] The PLAN also participated in the Indian Ocean Naval Symposium's first search-and-rescue exercises hosted by Bangladesh in November 2017.

[48] "Chinese Warships Enter East Indian Ocean amid Maldives Tensions," Reuters, February 20, 2018, https://www.reuters.com/article/us-maldives-politics-china/chinese-warships-enter-east-indian-ocean-amid-maldives-tensions-idUSKCN1G40V9.

[49] Ankit Panda, "Chinese Navy Holds Rare Live-Fire Drill in Western Indian Ocean," *Diplomat*, August 28, 2017, https://thediplomat.com/2017/08/chinese-navy-holds-rare-live-fire-drill-in-western-indian-ocean.

Military Interventions in Support of Political Objectives

The expansion of China's economic and political interests in the IOR, together with China's growing military capabilities, may increase the likelihood of China undertaking military interventions in support of political objectives. China may undertake actions against terrorist groups that threaten Chinese interests either domestically or within the region.[50] There may also be greater temptations to deploy military power in support of friendly regimes. Recent intense competition between China and India to influence elections in countries such as Sri Lanka and Maldives could take on a military dimension.

China's Future Military Presence in the IOR

Strategic imperatives will drive the nature and extent of China's military presence in the IOR. The shape of its future land-based security presence in the region will be addressed first. The importance of the maritime domain will then be discussed, with the PLAN likely playing a leading role in China's regional presence.

The Shape of China's Future Land-Based Security Presence

Some of China's strategic imperatives in the IOR, particularly the provision of security for Chinese nationals and investments, will require a land-based security presence in one form or another. Beijing will likely seek to address this need in several ways:

- reliance on local security forces (with Chinese training and advice, as required)
- use of private security contractors, where possible
- use of Chinese marines and special forces, where necessary

Beijing's preference will be to minimize its on-the-ground security footprint, meaning that it will rely on the security forces of local partners to the extent that it can. This will of course depend on the local security environment, the quality of local security forces, and the nature of China's relationship with the host government. This has been most evident in Pakistan, where, as part of the CPEC, China was able to negotiate the establishment of a special Pakistani security force of around 15,000 troops

---

[50] This includes unconfirmed reports of the deployment of special forces to Syria against Uighur extremists. Michael Clarke, "Is China's Uyghur Challenge Changing Its Calculus on Syria?" *Diplomat,* December 7, 2017, https://thediplomat.com/2017/12/is-chinas-uyghur-challenge-changing-its-calculus-on-syria.

exclusively to protect Chinese projects.[51] It is not yet clear whether this approach will provide an acceptable level of security for Chinese people and assets. Nevertheless, lessons learned from its success (or failure) could be applied in other countries.

Chinese companies operating as part of BRI may also seek to rely as much as possible on private security contractors for local security, especially Chinese contractors that employ former PLA personnel or security officers. State-owned companies prefer to employ Chinese contractors not only for language and cultural reasons but also to safeguard the companies' confidential information.[52] In Pakistan, Chinese private security contractors cooperate with local contractors, with Chinese personnel acting as security managers inside Chinese compounds while Pakistani soldiers and foreign private security contractors work on the outside.[53] Chinese private security contractors have also been particularly active in Sudan and South Sudan, including on one occasion participating in a Sudanese army mission to rescue 29 kidnapped Chinese nationals.[54]

Such reliance on private security contractors would follow similar trends of the United States and European countries operating in difficult environments. This approach, however, carries the risk that unregulated, relatively inexperienced Chinese private security contractors could make mistakes that exacerbate security problems or otherwise have adverse consequences for China's reputation.[55] Despite obvious links between private security contractors and the Chinese security apparatus, it should not be assumed that they will always have unalloyed allegiance to Beijing's interests.[56]

The inability of local security forces or private security contractors to adequately protect Chinese nationals and investments could necessitate the direct involvement of Chinese military personnel. This appears to have already occurred in Pakistan, where there are reports of a Chinese security presence in Pakistan-occupied Kashmir to protect transport infrastructure and PLAN construction units.[57] Given the PLAN's leading role in the IOR, the PLAN Marine Corps may become China's principal ready-response force in

[51] Syed Irfan Raza, "15,000 Military Personnel Protecting CPEC," *Dawn*, February 21, 2017.

[52] Alessandro Arduino, *China's Private Army: Protecting the New Silk Road* (London: Palgrave, 2018).

[53] Foreign private security contractors were nominally banned from Pakistan after a 2011 shooting by a private contractor working for the CIA. However, Chinese private security contractors now operate through "joint ventures" with Pakistani companies.

[54] Helena Legarda and Meia Nouwens, "Guardians of the Belt and Road: The Internationalization of China's Private Security Companies," Mercator Institute for China Studies, China Monitor, August 16, 2018.

[55] Ibid.

[56] Arduino, *China's Private Army*, 167.

[57] Monika Chansoria, "China Makes Its Presence Felt in Pak Occupied Kashmir," *Sunday Guardian*, December 17, 2017.

the region. The PLAN Marine Corps, which in some respects is modeled on the U.S. Marines Corps, is under the command of the South Sea Fleet, which has responsibility for the IOR.[58] It is currently undergoing a major expansion from 20,000 to 100,000 personnel in seven brigades (including transfers of elite units from the PLA). It may also incorporate an organic aviation brigade.[59] A PLAN Marine company has already been forward-deployed to Djibouti,[60] which has facilities to accommodate up to 10,000 personnel. There is also considerable speculation about future deployments to Gwadar.[61] Large-scale deployments from China would also require access to airfields by PLAAF transport aircraft. The need for air access to the region (including control over airports) will become yet another front for strategic competition, as well as driving changes in the PLAAF's long-range and expeditionary capabilities.[62]

These types of operations will also require much greater jointness between the Chinese armed services than currently exists. Beijing has recognized this, at least in theory. The U.S. Defense Department noted in its Annual Report to Congress that the PLA is undergoing major reforms to advance its ability to conduct joint operations.[63] The forward-deployment of Chinese marines in the IOR may well be an important testing ground for those reforms. However, the PLA's challenges in achieving adequate jointness are great and will likely constrain China's military effectiveness in the region for many years to come.

PLAN Marine Corps or marine commando contingents based in China or forward-deployed in the IOR, with effective support from the PLAAF, would allow the country to respond to contingencies throughout the region. Based on past behavior, China might be expected to try to avoid direct involvement in counterinsurgency or counterterrorism operations to protect

---

[58] Grant Newsham, "Can China Copy the U.S. Marine Corps?" *National Interest*, January 29, 2016.

[59] U.S. Department of Defense, *Annual Report to Congress: Military and Security Developments Involving the People's Republic of China 2018*, 28.

[60] Ibid., ii.

[61] Minnie Chan, "As Overseas Ambitions Expand, China Plans 400 Per Cent Increase to Marine Corps Numbers, Sources Say," *South China Morning Post*, March 13, 2017. Claims in that report about deployments to Djibouti and Gwadar were repeated on the Chinese Ministry of Defense official website. "China Responds to Rumored Marine Corps Expansion," Ministry of National Defense of the People's Republic of China, March 15, 2017, http://eng.mod.gov.cn/DefenseNews/2017-03/15/content_4775559.htm

[62] David Brewster, "Air Traffic Control: China and India Compete," Lowy Institute, Interpreter, September 25, 2015, https://www.lowyinstitute.org/the-interpreter/air-traffic-control-china-and-india-compete; and Cristina L. Garafola and Timothy R. Heath, *The Chinese Air Force's First Steps toward Becoming an Expeditionary Air Force* (Santa Monica: RAND Corporation, 2017), 30. The PLAAF has also been exploring the use of private contractors for air logistics functions. "PLAAF Exploring New Logistics Solutions with Chinese Commercial Companies," Air Recognition, October 27, 2027.

[63] U.S. Department of Defense, *Annual Report to Congress: Military and Security Developments Involving the People's Republic of China 2018*, 115.

Chinese people and assets, but there will be a risk of mission creep. The existence of these capabilities may create temptations to use them to protect and advance other Chinese interests.

The Shape of China's Future Naval Presence in the IOR

The PLAN will likely play a leading role in China's military presence in the IOR for several reasons. For a start, many of China's strategic imperatives in the IOR lie primarily in the maritime domain. In addition, compared with armies, navies generally have a much smaller and more transient footprint, something highly desirable from Beijing's perspective. The PLAN's deployment in the Gulf of Aden since 2007 has given it a decade's head start on the other armed services in expeditionary experience. Even now, the PLA and the PLAAF have only negligible experience beyond Chinese territory. There is no reason to believe that they could not catch up, but it will take quite some time.

According to the U.S. Department of Defense, the PLAN's ability to perform missions beyond the first island chain is "modest but growing."[64] As noted earlier, the PLAN is currently pursuing a two-ocean strategy that has involved revising its doctrine and developing new capabilities, facilities, and arrangements with host countries.[65] But while some elements of the PLAN's modernization program appear to be modeled on the U.S. Navy (including, for example, its aircraft carrier construction program), it would be incorrect to assume that the PLAN's presence in the IOR will necessarily grow to resemble that of the U.S. Navy. During the height of the Cold War, the Soviet Union developed a large naval presence in the Indian Ocean of up to 22 vessels.[66] Yet despite the large size of the Soviet Indian Ocean fleet, its mission remained very different from that of the U.S. Navy. The Indian Ocean remained a secondary theater for the Soviet Union, and the Soviet fleet had limited SLOC protection capabilities, while its sea-denial capabilities in the Indian Ocean were highly localized. Instead, the Soviet Union's naval presence in the Indian Ocean reflected its own imperatives, which included countering a perceived threat from U.S. nuclear missile submarines, interdicting the movement of U.S. forces into the region, protecting the Soviet fishing fleet,

---

[64] U.S. Department of Defense, *Annual Report to Congress: Military and Security Developments Involving the People's Republic of China 2018*, 65.

[65] You Ji, "The Indian Ocean: A Grand Sino-Indian Game of 'Go,'" in *India and China at Sea: Competition for Naval Dominance in the Indian Ocean*, ed. David Brewster (Oxford: Oxford University Press, 2018), 90–110.

[66] Bruce W. Watson, *Red Navy at Sea: Soviet Naval Operations on the High Seas, 1956–1980* (Boulder: Westview Press, 1982), 148; and Paul H. Nitze and Leonard Sullivan, *Securing the Seas: The Soviet Naval Challenge and Western Alliance Options* (Boulder: Westview Press, 1979), 69–70.

potentially threatening U.S. energy supplies (at least in part), and generally reinforcing Soviet regional influence in the western Indian Ocean.

As discussed above, Beijing has its own strategic imperatives in the IOR, some of which bear closer resemblance to Soviet imperatives than U.S. objectives. China's growing naval presence should be understood as a function of those imperatives. The possible future evolution of China's naval presence in the region can be understood in terms of three basic scenarios:[67]

- Scenario 1: Limited Chinese naval presence with an emphasis on MOOTW

- Scenario 2: A limited contingency or sea-denial strategy

- Scenario 3: A sea-control strategy

Importantly, these three scenarios are not fixed or mutually exclusive; rather, they provide some guidance as to key focus areas and consequences for necessary capabilities.

Scenario 1: Limited Chinese Naval Presence with an Emphasis on MOOTW

The PLAN's presence in the Indian Ocean over the last decade has been overwhelmingly focused on MOOTW, including the conduct of antipiracy operations, NEOs, and naval diplomacy. These tasks will likely continue to be a major focus of China's regional concerns. MOOTW missions might increasingly evolve to also include limited coercive diplomacy or naval support for limited military interventions in the region.

There are several reasons that Beijing might for some years elect to limit the nature and size of its naval presence in the Indian Ocean. First, the principal maritime threats faced by China remain overwhelmingly in the Pacific, including the Taiwan Strait, South China Sea, and East China Sea, which will require the overwhelming majority of the PLAN's attention. Indeed, Beijing might be well advised to avoid dispersing its naval forces to what is essentially a secondary theater. The second reason is geographic. In strategic jargon, the Indian Ocean represents "exterior lines" for China, where it suffers from considerable natural disadvantages compared with India. Deployments to the Indian Ocean from Chinese ports must be made at long distance through Southeast Asian chokepoints, with limited logistical support upon arrival. They thus may involve a disproportionate commitment of naval

---

[67] The following discussion draws on David Brewster, "Understanding China's Naval Strategy in the Indian Ocean," in "Policy Recommendations by the Quadripartite Commission on the Indian Ocean Regional Security," Sasakawa Peace Foundation, 2017, chap. 8, https://www.spf.org/en/global-image/units/upfiles/27201-1-20180717120639_b5b4d5d3f616ca.pdf.

resources for uncertain return. Third, given the impracticality of protecting the entirety of its Indian Ocean SLOCs against the United States and India (as discussed earlier), China may have little reason to develop its capabilities in the Indian Ocean other than for limited protection against local threats. A focus on MOOTW would allow the PLAN to gradually develop and expand its capabilities, regional familiarity, and logistical access, which could provide it with more options in the case of contingencies.

Although the size of its naval and military presence in the IOR has been growing, China has so far been relatively cautious and incremental in its approach. Its naval presence is currently limited to around four to five surface vessels and occasional submarine deployments, although this number occasionally spikes during a crossover between transiting vessels.[68] This is far below the Soviet naval presence in the Indian Ocean in the late 1970s and early 1980s. Currently, the level and nature of China's naval presence in the Indian Ocean are more appropriate for MOOTW than other purposes. Even fulfilling this objective will likely require additional replenishment and amphibious vessels. As noted, China could potentially supplement its naval presence with elements of its coast guard for some MOOTW duties such as the protection of Chinese fishing vessels.[69]

China's development of a base in Djibouti is consistent with a focus on MOOTW, including support for antipiracy, UN peacekeeping, and NEOs in the western Indian Ocean, Africa, the Middle East, and the Mediterranean. The base could also be used as a hub to support counterterrorism operations and training for forward-deployed forces.[70] The facilities will allow for the docking of up to four vessels, including replenishment and amphibious vessels.[71] But the Djibouti base has limitations. Although it has a heliport, it lacks a dedicated airfield suitable for manned fixed-wing aircraft, meaning that China must share Djibouti's international airport with the United States, France, and others. In addition, the proximity of the Chinese base to U.S., French, and Japanese facilities will reduce its value in the event

---

[68] Shaurya Karanbir Gurung, "14 Chinese Navy Ships Spotted in Indian Ocean, Indian Navy Monitoring Locations," *Economic Times*, December 1, 2017, https://economictimes.indiatimes.com/news/defence/14-chinese-navy-ships-spotted-in-indian-ocean-indian-navy-monitoring-locations/articleshow/61882634.cms.

[69] The Chinese Coast Guard fleet currently includes some 130 vessels of more than 1,000 tonnes. Office of the Secretary of Defense, *Military and Security Developments Involving the People's Republic of China 2018*, 71.

[70] Deng Xiaoci, "Claims China Turning Djibouti Base into Military Foothold 'Groundless,'" *Global Times*, May 16, 2018.

[71] Minnie Chan, "China Plans to Build Djibouti Facility to Allow Naval Flotilla to Dock at First Overseas Base," *South China Morning Post*, September 27, 2017, https://www.scmp.com/news/china/diplomacy-defence/article/2112926/china-plans-build-djibouti-facility-allow-naval.

of a major conflict, while the distance from Djibouti to the Strait of Hormuz (around 1,600 nautical miles) reduces its value for protecting that chokepoint.

Scenario 2: A Limited Contingency or Sea-Denial Strategy

A second scenario involves the development of capabilities, in addition to the MOOTW capabilities discussed above, sufficient to provide Beijing with limited or asymmetrical options to respond to contingencies. This could include capabilities sufficient to create transient local superiority, respond to a selective distant blockade, or conduct limited sea-denial operations. Such an approach, which is again in some ways analogous to the Soviet Union's Indian Ocean strategy in the late 1970s and early 1980s, could provide China with options to respond to certain contingencies at a fraction of the cost of a full sea-control strategy.

Although Beijing is very unlikely to pursue an anti-access/area-denial strategy in the IOR to the extent that it has in the western Pacific, an enhanced submarine presence or land-based missile systems could provide some of those capabilities in the Indian Ocean. In recent years, China has increased submarine deployments to the Indian Ocean (both conventional and nuclear) to familiarize the PLAN with local conditions. But without access to dedicated submarine logistics facilities in the region, the PLAN would have only a limited ability to surge submarines into the Indian Ocean in a contingency. Among other obstacles, submarines based in China would need to negotiate the narrow chokepoints through the Indonesian archipelago where they can be tracked relatively easily. Although the PLAN may already have access to Pakistani facilities in Karachi, the development of Chinese-operated submarine-support facilities in other Indian Ocean ports would be an important indicator of Beijing's strategy.

A sea-denial strategy might also involve some land-based capabilities. Missiles based on Chinese territory could, at least in theory, already cover some parts of the Arabian Sea and Bay of Bengal, although the distances involved would limit their effectiveness. China would therefore need to deploy such systems locally.[72] Pakistan is often cited as the most likely location for these capabilities near the Arabian Sea.[73] China already supplies Pakistan with some relevant technologies such as anti-ship cruise missiles, but it currently has no other reliable partners in the region, including in the central and eastern Indian Ocean.

---

[72] U.S. Department of Defense, *Annual Report to Congress: Military and Security Developments Involving the People's Republic of China 2018*, 371.

[73] See, for example, ibid., 5.

Scenario 3: A Sea-Control Strategy

The third scenario involves a bid by China to achieve naval predominance in the Indian Ocean for the purposes of protecting its SLOCs and potentially controlling maritime trade of its competitors. This would be more or less analogous to the U.S. strategy in the western IOR since the late 1970s. As discussed earlier, the protection of SLOCs would be a major undertaking over many years, if not decades, requiring the sustained deployment of large numbers of ships, including aircraft carriers and submarines, and land-based aircraft, including long-range maritime surveillance and strike aircraft. These in turn would require several naval and air bases in the region, as well as the development of multiple local military partnerships.

Such a strategy would likely focus on the Persian Gulf and northwest Indian Ocean, just as the United States currently does. But SLOC protection would also require the development of a significant Chinese naval presence in the southwestern, central, and eastern parts of the Indian Ocean, including near the Southeast Asian maritime chokepoints. Unlike the United States, which can access the Persian Gulf by either the "west about" route (via Southeast Asia) or the "east about" route (via Suez or the Cape), China can only access the Persian Gulf by transiting the northern Indian Ocean and the Southeast Asian chokepoints. Overland oil and gas pipelines (including pipelines through Myanmar and proposed pipelines through Pakistan) will not provide a substantial alternative: they provide only a fraction of the necessary volume of energy imports and are themselves highly vulnerable to interdiction. Moreover, energy for such pipelines would still need to transit the Strait of Hormuz (and in the case of the Myanmar pipelines, the Indian subcontinent also).

The pursuit of such a sea-control strategy would be indicated by the sustained deployment of multiple aircraft carrier task groups in the IOR, including the development of relevant logistical support facilities and facilities to project land-based air power. The development of such capabilities in the IOR should not be confused with likely short-term goodwill visits by a PLAN aircraft carrier, as a symbol of China's newfound international status (a development that could well occur within the next few years).

China's Basing Strategy in the IOR

The huge size of the Indian Ocean and its long distance from Chinese territory mean that access to naval and air bases or other logistics facilities will play a key role in any sustained Chinese naval presence in the IOR. During the Cold War, the United States was able to significantly constrain the effectiveness of the Soviet fleet in the Indian Ocean by denying the Soviet

Navy access to significant support facilities outside the Horn of Africa. As a result, around 50% of the Soviet fleet in the IOR comprised logistics ships. Given the relative economic strength of China and its relationships in the region, such a strategy would be more difficult to pursue today, though not impossible. Beijing might be in a position to develop large and sophisticated naval support facilities with associated airfields in the western Indian Ocean, although its options may be more limited in the central and eastern Indian Ocean, where there are fewer weak or vulnerable states that would be amenable to a Chinese military presence.

Each of the strategies discussed above would involve different naval basing requirements. A strategy primarily focused on MOOTW could be largely satisfied through relying as much as possible on a "places not bases" approach of negotiating assured access rights to commercial facilities, while minimizing the need for dedicated bases.[74] In addition to its current dedicated facilities in Djibouti, China could negotiate preferential access to Chinese-built ports or airports around the region, such as Gwadar, Khartoum, Hambantota, and in Tanzania (although these locations should not be assumed).[75]

Any significant sustained Chinese naval presence in the Indian Ocean that goes much beyond MOOTW will likely require a "place and base" strategy that includes not only access rights but also dedicated support facilities with associated airfields.[76] The acquisition of dedicated full-service naval facilities would signal a significant new phase in China's regional ambitions. In the northwest Indian Ocean, there are several locations where China now has dedicated but limited facilities (Djibouti), assured access to naval facilities of a security partner (Karachi), or regular access to commercial facilities on a nonpreferential basis. Although China does not yet have dedicated air force facilities in the IOR, it presumably would have access to facilities in Pakistan, at least for limited purposes. China also has no assured port or airfield access arrangements inside the Persian Gulf or in the eastern, central, or southwest Indian Ocean. It is difficult to imagine a credible Indian Ocean sea-control strategy, or even anything other than a limited contingency or sea-denial

[74] Christopher D. Yung et al., "'Not an Idea We Have to Shun': Chinese Overseas Basing Requirements in the 21st Century," Institute for National Strategic Studies, China Strategic Perspectives, no. 7, October 1, 2014.

[75] Apolinari Tairo, "Tanzania Surrenders Bagamoyo Port Project to Chinese Firm," East African, October 3, 2017, http://www.theeastafrican.co.ke/business/Tanzania-Bagamoyo-port-project-to-Chinese/2560-4122244-rxa9wtz/index.html.

[76] Michael McDevitt, "Great Power Competition in the Indian Ocean: The Past as Prologue?" CNA, March 2018, 2, https://www.cna.org/CNA_files/PDF/DOP-2017-U-015750-Final2.pdf.

strategy in the northwest Indian Ocean, without a high degree of control over such air facilities.[77]

Pakistan is frequently cited as a likely location of another Chinese naval base in the region, and Gwadar, located around 700 nautical miles west of the Strait of Hormuz, would be an obvious location. But China has so far been relatively cautious about developing an overt naval presence in Gwadar, and Pakistan's new government under Prime Minister Imran Khan seems keen to emphasize the purely commercial nature of the port.[78] There have also been unconfirmed reports of discussions over the development of naval facilities at Jiwani, around 60 kilometers west of Gwadar.[79]

Any significant naval presence in the IOR likely also will require assured access to facilities in the southwest Indian Ocean. There has been speculation that China has sought naval access arrangements of some type in the Seychelles and at Walvis Bay in Namibia, neither of which has come to pass.[80] Tanzania is another possible location. China is Tanzania's biggest supplier of defense equipment and built its military academy. In October 2017, a Chinese company took over full ownership of the newly built port of Bagamoyo, north of Dar es Salaam, after the Tanzanian government was unable to meet funding commitments.[81] China's good relations with Mozambique and Madagascar could also develop into security partnerships. In short, there are many weak states in and around the southwest Indian Ocean that may be susceptible to offers of Chinese economic assistance.

Crucially, any sea-control strategy in the IOR would require naval facilities in the central and eastern Indian Ocean to protect trading routes that pass through Southeast Asia. There are several potential host countries. Hambantota in southern Sri Lanka is frequently cited as a likely candidate, especially after China gained effective control of the port in 2017.[82] But although it is located close to major east-west sea lanes, the port's proximity to

[77] David Brewster, "China's New Network of Indian Ocean Bases," Lowy Institute, Interpreter, January 30, 2018, https://www.lowyinstitute.org/the-interpreter/chinas-new-network-indian-ocean-bases.

[78] David Brewster, "Will Pakistan's CPEC Dream Turn into a Nightmare?" Lowy Institute, Interpreter, June 14, 2018, https://www.lowyinstitute.org/the-interpreter/will-pakistan-cpec-dream-turn-nightmare.

[79] Minnie Chan, "First Djibouti...Now Pakistan Port Earmarked for a Chinese Overseas Naval Base, Sources Say," South China Morning Post, January 5, 2018, https://www.scmp.com/news/china/diplomacy-defence/article/2127040/first-djibouti-now-pakistan-port-earmarked-chinese.

[80] Adam Hartman, "Chinese Naval Base for Walvis Bay," Namibian, November 19, 2017.

[81] Tairo, "Tanzania Surrenders Bagamoyo Port Project."

[82] In December 2017 a Chinese state-owned company gained a 70% equity interest in the company that holds a 99-year lease over the port. Although the Sri Lankan government has claimed to have created a separate management company in which it has retained a majority interest, the details of ownership and control remain murky. Abhijit Singh, "Sri Lanka's Hambantota Gambit," Livemint, August 16, 2017, http://www.livemint.com/Opinion/qKTtTf3S4UwaFrSnD3KDJJ/Sri-Lankas-Hambantota-gambit.html.

Indian air bases would make it a vulnerable location.[83] The Indian government is also proposing to acquire control over the nearby Hambantota airport, which would limit the usefulness of the port to the PLAN.[84]

China is also building a new port at Kyaukpyu in Myanmar, which would make an excellent base for the PLAN in the eastern Indian Ocean, potentially challenging India's naval dominance over the Bay of Bengal and pre-empting the potential use of the bay as a future "bastion" for India's nuclear missile submarines.[85] But the Myanmar government is wary of losing control of the port or allowing it to be used for noncommercial purposes.[86] In the past, Myanmar's leaders, famously protective of the nation's sovereignty, refused China permission to undertake military activities from Myanmar territory.[87]

Another possible location may be Maldives, which has experienced significant financial problems, weak governance, and political instability for some time. In recent years, Maldives has become the scene of considerable strategic competition between China and India, as they jostle for influence in the tiny country. The election of a new president in September 2018 has tilted the scales toward India for the time being. Nevertheless, the worst-case scenario, which is still possible, would involve Maldives granting the PLAN or the PLAAF access to the former British port and air base on the island of Gan, located only 740 kilometers north of Diego Garcia.

Importantly, any enhanced Chinese military strategy in the IOR, and particularly any enhanced naval strategy, will require substantial air-power support, including from maritime surveillance and strike aircraft. China's lack of maritime domain awareness in the Indian Ocean places it at a major tactical disadvantage to potential adversaries.[88] This gap cannot be adequately filled with satellites, ship-based aircraft, or land-based aircraft operating from Chinese territory, especially given China's limited long-range and air-refueling capabilities. The PLAAF's maritime surveillance capabilities are still very

---

[83] Daniel J. Kostecka, "Places and Bases: The Chinese Navy's Emerging Support Network in the Indian Ocean," Jamestown Foundation, China Brief, July 22, 2010, 3–5.

[84] David Brewster, "Why India Is Buying the World's Emptiest Airport," Lowy Institute, Interpreter, July 14, 2018, https://www.lowyinstitute.org/the-interpreter/why-india-buying-world-s-emptiest-airport.

[85] There are reports that China has sought to dredge Kyaukpyu port much deeper than would be required for commercial or surface vessels. David Brewster, "China's Play for Military Bases in the Eastern Indian Ocean," Lowy Institute, Interpreter, May 15, 2018, https://www.lowyinstitute.org/the-interpreter/china-s-play-military-bases-eastern-indian-ocean.

[86] Koutsoukis, "The Fishing Port That May Become a $10 Billion Chinese Debt Bomb."

[87] Gregory P. Poling, "Kyaukpyu: Connecting China to the Indian Ocean," CSIS, Brief, March 2018, https://www.csis.org/analysis/kyaukpyu-connecting-china-indian-ocean.

[88] Raja Menon, "Scenarios for China's Naval Deployment in the Indian Ocean and India's Naval Response," in Brewster, India and China at Sea, 125–36.

rudimentary,[89] and its experience in expeditionary operations beyond Chinese territory is "nascent."[90] To pursue an enhanced maritime strategy in the IOR beyond MOOTW, China will require capabilities for land-based maritime air surveillance to cover at least three quadrants of the IOR (the southwest, northwest, and northeast). Accordingly, its lack of long-range maritime surveillance capabilities and local air basing would be a major constraint on its ability to pursue an expansive naval strategy.

Conclusion

Despite being located almost next door to the Indian Ocean, China has had little or no presence there for centuries because of geographic constraints. That is now changing quickly as the country develops its presence. The new overland connections from Chinese territory effectively change China's proximity to the Indian Ocean. The presence of large numbers of Chinese nationals could also substantially alter the nature of the country's regional role. In the long term, these developments could effectively make China act more like a resident power of the Indian Ocean as part of an increasingly multipolar region.

China's Military Presence in the IOR

China's role in the IOR is principally underpinned, and driven, by its economic engagement. These economic interests drive China's political role and its growing strategic imperatives in the region, which in turn will drive its future military presence. China's military role in the IOR will almost certainly grow in conjunction with the expansion of these interests, including interests in the internal security of other countries. The shape and nature of its military presence in the IOR will likely evolve as a function of its unique strategic imperatives, many of which differ significantly from those of the United States. Like the United States in past years, China now relies heavily on Persian Gulf oil, but it also has other important imperatives.

On land, China will face significant pressures to protect Chinese nationals and investments, while also seeking to minimize its security footprint. This will likely lead Beijing to rely on local security forces (with Chinese training and advice, as required) and private security contractors, where possible. Chinese forces (most likely marines, forward-deployed or

---

[89] Mark R. Cozad and Nathan Beauchamp-Mustafaga, *People's Liberation Army Air Force Operations over Water: Maintaining Relevance in China's Changing Security Environment* (Santa Monica: RAND Corporation, 2017).

[90] Garafola and Heath, *The Chinese Air Force's First Steps*, 1.

deployed from China) would only be used in contingencies. Given the poor security environment in the region, Beijing may find that local security forces and private contractors are not able to provide adequate levels of protection for Chinese nationals and investments, leading to a Chinese security footprint that exceeds its preferences.

The PLAN will likely play a leading role in China's military strategy in the IOR, in part because of the relatively limited and transient security footprint of navies. China's naval presence in the Indian Ocean over the last decade has been overwhelmingly focused on MOOTW, including the conduct of antipiracy operations, NEOs, and naval diplomacy. However, the PLAN is currently pursuing a two-ocean strategy in the IOR that points to an expanded and sustained naval presence in the region, which will likely include limited contingency or sea-denial capabilities. The pursuit of a full sea-control strategy to protect China's SLOCs and potentially control the maritime trade of competitors would be a major undertaking, requiring many years of sustained expansion of the PLAN and Chinese security relationships in the region, with very uncertain benefit. Despite the ambitions of some naval planners, there may be good reasons for China to limit the expenditure of its naval resources in the Indian Ocean, where it suffers from considerable strategic disadvantages.

Whatever missions the PLAN pursues in the IOR, a large and sustained naval presence will require local support facilities in several locations. The development of limited basing facilities in Djibouti was a relatively uncontroversial first step internationally, although it was a significant strategic shift for China, which had long considered the U.S. overseas basing model as an ideological anathema and strategically imprudent.[91] The mixture of bases, assured access to partner facilities, and access to commercial facilities will reflect the nature of the PLAN's mission. Importantly, any significant naval presence will also require PLAAF access to airfields in several locations.

Implications for Regional States

China's changing role has major implications for regional states. One implication, already being seen, is the impact of growing strategic competition between China and India (with the support of the United States and others). The jostle for power and influence over smaller and weaker IOR states is fast coming to resemble the strategic competition that occurred between the Soviet Union and the United States during the Cold War. Just as was the case in the 1970s and 1980s, this could have significant adverse effects

---

[91] Kristen Gunness and Oriana Skylar Mastro, "A Global People's Liberation Army: Possibilities, Challenges, and Opportunities," *Asia Policy*, no. 22 (2016): 145.

on the stability and integrity of political systems in many IOR countries, as China, India, and others support their favored leaders and oppose others. This dynamic has played out in recent years in countries such as Sri Lanka and Maldives. As an outsider to the region, China has particular reasons to disrupt the political status quo in support of its strategic objectives and will likely show little respect for democratic institutions.

It should be noted that many regional states will have a degree of agency in responding to this competition. Some countries may be tempted to use major-power competition to obtain economic or other benefits from one side or the other (or both), or to use security relationships with one side to hedge against perceived threats from the other. Other countries may seek to insulate themselves by declaring themselves neutral or nonaligned. Although it is not yet evident, based on the experience of the Cold War, there is even the potential for proxy conflicts within the region, stoked by China and other powers.

Another set of consequences of China's growing role and the decline in the relative power of the United States is that the region will almost certainly be more multipolar than ever before. China will likely become one of several major-power players in the IOR, alongside the United States and India, as well as several middle powers (including Australia, France, Indonesia, Iran, Japan, Saudi Arabia, and South Africa) that will actively pursue their own interests and agendas across the region. Several of these powers are already building new security relationships in contemplation of this emerging multipolarity. This likely will make strategic interactions within the region far more complex than at any time in centuries, potentially leading to greater strategic instability than was historically the case. There may also be a tendency for these major and middle powers to form ad hoc coalitions for different purposes (which may give an advantage to states that are more adept at coalition-building).

Implications for the United States

China's growing role in the IOR also naturally has profound implications for the United States. China's increasing economic presence, particularly through BRI, is leading to significant changes in the balance of economic, political, and military power. Many IOR states have, rightly or wrongly, come to see China as providing a pathway for their own economic development, even if there is growing skepticism about the strings that are sometimes attached to Chinese investment. Any U.S. effort to limit Chinese influence in the region would require a multipronged strategy. The United States may not choose to compete directly with China's trading relationships, but it could play an important role in providing regional states with alternatives to development projects promoted by China. But Washington will only be able to convince IOR states that there are alternative pathways to economic development through its actions and not through rhetoric. Whether it likes it or not, that will almost inevitably involve a major financial commitment.

China's military presence, on land and at sea, is set to grow in conjunction with its economic presence. Although China is years away from being in a position to directly challenge U.S. military predominance in the IOR, the U.S. military may still find it increasingly difficult to assume unencumbered freedom of action in the region. This is initially occurring around the Horn of Africa, but future Chinese naval deployments in the southwestern and eastern Indian Ocean will also increasingly affect U.S. freedom of action in those areas.

How should the United States respond? This chapter has argued that it would be an error to assume that China's military presence in the IOR will develop as a mirror of the U.S. presence. China may be rising as a global power, but it will seek to do so in its own way.[92] China's unique strategic imperatives in the region may lead to a sizeable but still limited Chinese military presence in what is ultimately a secondary theater.

The experience of the Cold War may be instructive to any U.S. efforts to limit the size and nature of China's military presence. Then, the United States and its allies used the geographic disadvantages faced by the Soviet Union to impose severe logistical constraints and drastically limit the effectiveness of its military presence. China also faces significant geographic disadvantages in the Indian Ocean. Its home ports are far away, the Indian Ocean can be reached by sea only through narrow and vulnerable chokepoints, and local logistical support is limited. China's local partnerships are currently thin—it has no historical presence in the region and only one strategic partner (Pakistan) that might be regarded as anything close to a reliable ally. But China's economic power means that many countries in the IOR are now more or less in play.

It may not be realistic (or indeed appropriate) for Washington to pursue a containment strategy against China analogous to that it pursued against the Soviet Union. But China is still subject to many important constraints and vulnerabilities that the United States may choose to leverage. Compared with the Pacific theater, the geography of the Indian Ocean provides the United States and its strategic partners with options to limit China's military power in the region. This would involve limiting military access not only to maritime ports (much discussed in recent years) but also to airfields and air-staging points around the region. Limitations on China's ability to properly support naval and military operations with land-based air power would, for example,

---

[92] Oriana Skylar Mastro, "The Stealth Superpower: How China Hid Its Global Ambitions," *Foreign Affairs*, January/February 2019.

significantly constrain its strategic options in the IOR. China may be much more vulnerable in the region than many assume.

Importantly, any U.S. strategy directed toward limiting China's influence in the IOR will be vitally dependent upon U.S. partnerships across the region, not just those in the Persian Gulf area. While the Persian Gulf will continue to be important, strategic competition is expanding across the IOR. This will require the United States to enhance its regional partnerships, including with key partners such as India, Australia, France, and Indonesia and important extraregional partners such as Japan, Britain, and even relative newcomers such as Germany. Diversified partnerships are likely to become increasingly important as the IOR becomes a more multipolar region, where several powers compete and cooperate, but where no single power predominates.

EXECUTIVE SUMMARY

The chapter finds that the Belt and Road Initiative (BRI) reflects both China's global aspirations and domestic economic and political imperatives but will have to overcome a range of challenges and uncertainties.

MAIN ARGUMENT

BRI is one of the most notable manifestations of China's rising global power, yet its drivers and implications remain clouded in uncertainty. BRI is composed of three distinct strategies, each with its own goals, tools, and sets of challenges. Politically, it enhances the image of both Xi Jinping and the Chinese Communist Party but has to contend with public ambivalence and distorted bureaucratic incentives. Economically, BRI benefits a number of Chinese interest groups, including select provinces and cities, as well as state-owned enterprises, but faces a panoply of economic, legal, and governance risks. Geopolitically, the initiative strives to create a more stable frontier, advance key partnerships, diversify energy sources, and position China to compete more effectively with the U.S. Yet it has been hobbled by hedging among recipients and growing international skepticism about its purposes and ramifications.

POLICY IMPLICATIONS

- BRI illustrates a number of lessons about China's status as an emerging global power, including its strategic flexibility, use of economic statecraft, multilayered goals and motivations, and contradictions within its own bureaucratic system.

- If left unchecked, BRI could threaten the sovereignty of recipients and undermine U.S. strategic interests. This outcome, however, is not preordained. China's own limitations, hedging by partners, and financing alternatives may all work in the opposite direction.

- The U.S. cannot compete symmetrically with BRI due to resource and political constraints. A better approach is to leverage U.S. comparative advantages, including alliances, security partnerships, and values, to retain regional balance, market access, and liberal norms.

China's Belt and Road:
One Initiative, Three Strategies

Joel Wuthnow

The international discussion of China's Belt and Road Initiative (BRI) has been a study in contrasts. It has been variously described as a driver of Asia's economic dynamism, a massive boondoggle, and a strategic ploy to dominate the Eurasian heartland through debt diplomacy and other means.[1] One reason for these differing assessments has been a journalistic focus on specific cases—such as Sri Lanka's troubled Hambantota port—that tell only part of the story.[2] Understanding the larger context has been difficult since Beijing has offered limited data at the project level, and the statistics it has provided are often designed to improve public perception of the initiative rather than to elucidate the full dimensions of this wide-ranging enterprise. Another problem is that BRI has been a moving target, originally focused on

Joel Wuthnow is a Research Fellow in the Center for the Study of Chinese Military Affairs in the Institute for National Strategic Studies at the National Defense University. He can be reached at <joel.wuthnow.civ@ndu.edu>.

This chapter represents only the author's views and not those of the National Defense University in the Department of Defense or the U.S. government. Phillip C. Saunders, Teresa Sebonis-Helf, Shirley Kan, and two anonymous reviews provided helpful feedback. Ian McManus provided valuable research assistance.

[1] For example, see "Beijing's 'Belt and Road Initiative' Will Benefit the World," *South China Morning Post*, February 12, 2018, https://www.scmp.com/comment/insight-opinion/article/2132943/beijings-belt-and-road-initiative-will-benefit-world; Sean Keeley, "One Belt, One Road, One Boondoggle?" *American Interest*, May 11, 2017, https://www.the-american-interest.com/2017/05/11/one-belt-one-road-one-boondoggle; and Jane Perlez and Yufan Huang, "Behind China's $1 Trillion Plan to Shake Up the Economic Order," *New York Times*, May 13, 2017, https://www.nytimes.com/2017/05/13/business/china-railway-one-belt-one-road-1-trillion-plan.html.

[2] Maria Abi-Habib, "How China Got Sri Lanka to Cough Up a Port," *New York Times*, June 25, 2018, https://www.nytimes.com/2018/06/25/world/asia/china-sri-lanka-port.html. For a comprehensive study on China's port investments, see Devin Thorne and Ben Spevack, "Harbored Ambitions: How China's Port Investments Are Strategically Reshaping the Indo-Pacific," C4ADS, 2018.

Asia but now encompassing projects around almost the entire globe. Based on recent evidence, this chapter aims to provide a wide-angle view of the initiative's form, purposes, and challenges and consider the implications for the United States and the international community.

At a macro level, BRI is more than a random assortment of Chinese infrastructure projects that share nothing but a common designator. As Nadège Rolland and others have argued, the initiative is strategic in nature, with infrastructure financing and assistance being employed in pursuit of long-range Chinese Communist Party (CCP) objectives.[3] The most direct evidence is that BRI is centrally coordinated. Xi Jinping himself is nominally in charge, but the real work of managing the initiative has fallen to a leading group under the National Development and Reform Commission, initially directed by Politburo Standing Committee member Zhang Gaoli (later replaced by Han Zheng) and composed of senior economic and diplomatic officials.[4] Christopher Johnson reports that China's National Security Commission staff also has been heavily involved in planning from a geopolitical perspective.[5] Moreover, while China's external propaganda has favored the benign word "initiative," authoritative Chinese sources refer to BRI domestically as a "strategy."[6] The best evidence for its strategic nature, however, is how BRI has actually unfolded in its first five years (2013–18), in terms of both the political theatrics surrounding it and identifiable projects.

This chapter argues that BRI is composed of not one but three distinct strategies, each with its own purposes, pursued in its own way, and facing its own challenges. As a political strategy, BRI is a way to enhance Xi's authority and the CCP's legitimacy, often through grandiose activities and dizzying statistics. Yet it faces mixed public opinion and skewed political incentives that could undermine the quality of projects and official data. As an economic strategy, BRI as a label is less important than its underlying economic features—investments and construction contracts—which help relieve China's industrial overcapacity and provide benefits for both

---

[3] Nadège Rolland, *China's Eurasian Century? Political and Strategic Implications of the Belt and Road Initiative* (Seattle: National Bureau of Asian Research [NBR], 2017).

[4] "China Sets Up Leading Team on Belt and Road Initiative," Xinhua, March 29, 2015, http://www.xinhuanet.com/english/2015-03/29/c_134107435.htm; and Xinyi Yang and David A. Parker, "Buckling Down: How Beijing Is Implementing Its 'One Belt, One Road' Vision," Center for Strategic and International Studies (CSIS), cogitASIA, May 7, 2015, https://www.cogitasia.com/buckling-down-how-beijing-is-implementing-its-one-belt-one-road-vision.

[5] Christopher K. Johnson, "President Xi Jinping's 'Belt and Road' Initiative: A Practical Assessment of the Chinese Communist Party's Roadmap for China's Global Resurgence," CSIS, CSIS Freeman Chair in China Studies, Report, March 2016, 19.

[6] See Liu Zhaoyong, "Zhudong rongru 'Yidai Yilu' zhanlüe, jiji dazao kongzhong sichou zhi lu" [Actively Integrate 'One Belt, One Road' Strategy and Positively Develop an Aerial Silk Road], *Qiushi*, no. 5 (2017), http://www.qstheory.cn/dukan/qs/2017-02/28/c_1120536650.htm. *Qiushi* is the official journal of the CCP Central Committee.

state-owned enterprises (SOEs) and underdeveloped Chinese provinces and cities. However, projects have been endangered by various economic, legal, and governance risks, which in some cases have resulted in delays or outright failures. As a geopolitical strategy, BRI helps China secure its frontiers, advance key diplomatic relationships, diversify energy sources, and compete more effectively with the United States. Challenges in this area include ideological constraints, hedging by recipients, and increasingly compelling foreign counter-narratives.

This chapter details these strategies in three successive sections. The conclusion then outlines several lessons that can be drawn from BRI about China's rise as a global power and argues that the emergence of an illiberal Sinocentric order based, in part, on the architecture of BRI is not a preordained outcome. China's own limitations, hedging by its partners, and alternative financing provided by other states and international organizations could all militate against the initiative in the opposite direction. Although the United States cannot compete symmetrically with BRI, it can instead leverage its own comparative advantages, such as its extensive network of regional alliances, to encourage regional balance, market access, and liberal values.

A Political Strategy

Announced less than a year after Xi Jinping emerged as party general secretary in November 2012, BRI complements other distinctive policies to strengthen his authority and the CCP's legitimacy, such as the "China dream," the "two centennials," the "community of shared destiny," and the "new type of great-power relations." All these ideas help distinguish Xi from other senior party officials, build his public reputation, and ultimately lay the groundwork for his political legacy. In these respects, Xi is no different from his two predecessors, Jiang Zemin and Hu Jintao, who likewise developed their own personal brands through signature formulas.[7]

Politically, BRI has allowed Xi to take credit for projects initiated by his predecessors. Chinese construction firms were involved in the global infrastructure development arena for more than two decades prior to his arrival.[8] Projects regarded as part of BRI that were actually conceived, pursued, or in some cases completed under Jiang and Hu include the Bangladesh-China-India-Myanmar economic corridor (1999), upgrades to the Karakoram Highway linking China and Pakistan (2006), discussions

---

[7] For instance, Jiang is best known for his "theory of the three represents," while Hu introduced the "scientific outlook on development."

[8] Rolland, *China's Eurasian Century?* 32–39.

on China's role in Pakistan's Gwadar port project (2006), parts of the China–Central Asia natural gas pipeline (2007–9), China's involvement in Greece's Piraeus port (2009), and construction of a China-Russia oil pipeline (2011). Yet Chinese official sources on BRI make no mention of either Jiang's or Hu's contributions.[9]

While building on those earlier achievements, BRI has been closely associated with Xi since its inception. He announced the initiative's two chief components—the Silk Road Economic Belt and the Maritime Silk Road—in the fall of 2013 and has personally inaugurated several high-profile projects, such as the Colombo Port City project in Sri Lanka in September 2014 and the arrival of a new Chinese freight train line in Warsaw in June 2016.[10] The highlight of his foreign policy calendar in 2017 was the Belt and Road Forum, which included participation by 29 heads of state or government. Most of the Chinese state media coverage of that event focused on Xi's remarks—including a lengthy applause segment evoking widespread appreciation for his leadership.[11] At the 19th Party Congress in October 2017, the initiative was included in the CCP constitution as a key element of "Xi Jinping Thought."[12]

To a certain extent, BRI also strengthens the legitimacy of the party itself. The CCP justifies its continued grip on power on the basis of its ability to achieve nationalist goals and deliver strong economic performance.[13] BRI is relevant to both of these rationales. First, it underscores the party's willingness to undertake bold foreign policies in support of China's strategic interests, shifting from the earlier dictum of "keeping a low profile" (*tao guang yang hui*) to a more activist posture. Domestic nationalists can take pride in China assuming a leading role in Asia's overall economic development and in more specific achievements such as the inauguration of China's first

---

[9] For instance, neither Jiang nor Hu is mentioned in two key official sources on BRI. See Information Office of the State Council of the People's Republic of China (PRC), "Action Plan on the Belt and Road Initiative," March 30, 2015, http://english.gov.cn/archive/publications/2015/03/30/content_281475080249035.htm; and Office of the Leading Group for the Belt and Road Initiative, *Building the Belt and Road: Concept, Practice, and China's Contribution* (Beijing: Foreign Languages Press, 2017), https://eng.yidaiyilu.gov.cn/zchj/qwfb/12731.htm.

[10] Wang Cong and Meng Na, "Xi's Belt and Road Vision Points the Way to Global Prosperity," Xinhua, May 13, 2017, http://www.xinhuanet.com/english/2017-05/13/c_136279798.htm.

[11] Igor Denisov, "China's Belt and Road Project: What's at Stake for Xi Jinping," Carnegie Moscow Center, May 29, 2017, https://carnegie.ru/commentary/70096.

[12] An Baijie, "Xi Jinping Thought Approved for Party Constitution," *China Daily*, October 24, 2017, http://www.chinadaily.com.cn/china/19thcpcnationalcongress/2017-10/24/content_33644524.htm.

[13] For further discussion, see Phillip P. Pan, *Out of Mao's Shadow: The Struggle for the Soul of a New China* (New York: Simon and Schuster, 2009), 323; and Erica S. Downs and Phillip C. Saunders, "Legitimacy and the Limits of Nationalism: China and the Diaoyu Islands," *International Security* 23, no. 3 (1991): 117–20. For an alternative view, see Heike Holbig and Bruce Gilley, "Reclaiming Legitimacy in China," *Politics and Policy* 38, no. 3 (2010): 395–422.

overseas military base in Djibouti. Second, as discussed below, BRI projects contribute to the economic vitality of several domestic groups, such as construction SOEs, as well as inland provinces and cities. In particular, as Christopher Johnson argues, BRI has focused on developing poorer interior regions as a corrective to complaints that Jiang had failed to "develop the west" and that Hu was unable to fully rehabilitate the northeastern rust belt during his term.[14]

Chinese officials and state media have worked in various other ways to maximize BRI's political value. News reports and official documents convey dizzying statistics, designed to impress both a domestic and international audience. Readers are often told that BRI partner countries account for 60% of the world's population and 30% of global GDP and that the initiative has "won support" from "more than 100 countries and international organizations."[15] BRI has also been stretched beyond its original focus on Eurasian infrastructure development to encompass new domains and far-flung regions. One often hears, for instance, about a "polar Silk Road," a "BRI space information corridor," a "digital Silk Road," and invitations for countries in multiple regions, including Africa, Latin America, and Oceania, to board this "express train" to prosperity.[16] All of this helps associate Xi, and the party as a whole, with the themes of grandiosity, magnanimity, and conquering new frontiers.

Conceiving of BRI as a political strategy also explains the initiative's fuzzy contours. Chinese officials have never provided a complete catalogue of projects or even a detailed map of key locations and routes.[17] Since 2015, Chinese sources have identified six "economic corridors" that form the core of the initiative's focus on regional connectivity (see **Figure 1**), but

---

[14] Johnson, "President Xi Jinping's 'Belt and Road' Initiative," 20.

[15] Cong and Na, "Xi's Belt and Road Vision"; and Office of the Leading Group for the Belt and Road Initiative, *Building the Belt and Road*, 7–8.

[16] Phillip Wen, "China Unveils Vision for 'Polar Silk Road' Across Arctic," Reuters, January 26, 2018, https://www.reuters.com/article/us-china-arctic/china-unveils-vision-for-polar-silk-road-across-arctic-idUSKBN1FF0J8; "China's 'One Belt, One Road' Takes to Space," *Wall Street Journal*, China Real Time Report, December 28, 2016, https://blogs.wsj.com/chinarealtime/2016/12/28/chinas-one-belt-one-road-takes-to-space; and Owen Fishwick, "China in the Fast Lane on Digital Silk Road," *China Daily*, December 4, 2017, http://www.chinadaily.com.cn/business/4thwic/2017-12/04/content_35201648.htm. For further discussion of China's outreach to new countries, see Fabian Cambero and Dave Sherwood, "China Invites Latin America to Take Part in One Belt, One Road," Reuters, January 22, 2018, https://www.reuters.com/article/us-chile-china/china-invites-latin-america-to-take-part-in-one-belt-one-road-idUSKBN1FB2CN; and Li Xiang, "China to Boost Ties, Advance Belt and Road Initiative in Africa," *China Daily*, March 8, 2018, http://www.chinadaily.com.cn/a/201803/08/WS5aa0d6b3a3106e7dcc140675.html.

[17] Xinhua has published a generic map with lines that depict the Silk Road Economic Corridor and the Maritime Silk Road, but this does not include specific project details. See "Chronology of China's Belt and Road Initiative," Xinhua, June 24, 2016, http://www.xinhuanet.com/english/2016-06/24/c_135464233.htm.

FIGURE 1 China's Silk Road Economic Belt, Maritime Silk Road, and economic corridors

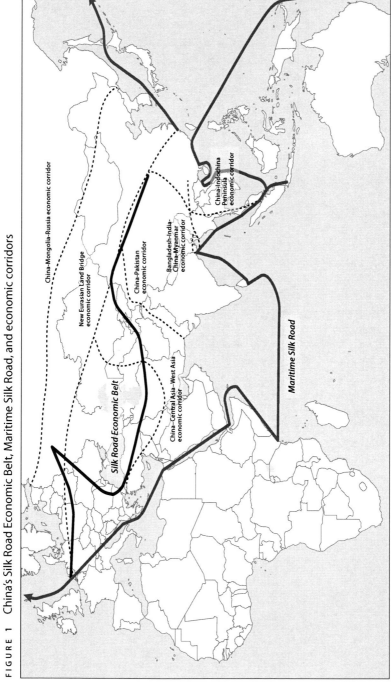

China-Mongolia-Russia economic corridor

New Eurasian Land Bridge economic corridor

China-Pakistan economic corridor

Bangladesh-India-China-Myanmar economic corridor

China-Indochina Peninsula economic corridor

China–Central Asia–West Asia economic corridor

Silk Road Economic Belt

Maritime Silk Road

SOURCE: Mercator Institute for China Studies; and Hong Kong Trade Development Council Head Office, "The Belt and Road Initiative," January 21, 2016.

these remain vague and aspirational.[18] The absence of comprehensive details is likely intended, at least in part, as a hedge against criticism. No one can demonstrate conclusively that BRI is losing momentum since no official benchmark has been provided in the first place. Ambiguity may also reflect the difficulties attendant in individual bureaucracies attempting to translate broad policy statements issued by the center into concrete, actionable terms.[19]

Nevertheless, the political stakes attached to BRI have created a series of challenges for Chinese policymakers. The first is sustaining domestic interest and enthusiasm for the initiative, year after year. Officials have attempted to keep public attention at a high level in a variety of ways, including endless media exposés, Xi's personal involvement, and documentation of concrete successes and firsts, such as the advent of train lines between Europe and China and the opening of ports, bridges, and energy facilities.[20] Authoritative media commentary also links BRI to related Xi-era themes such as the China dream. [21] Yet sustaining public interest has been difficult due to the competition for media and personal attention, the tendency of many observers to simply write off high-level political slogans, and the marginal impact that foreign infrastructure projects have on the lives of most ordinary Chinese citizens.[22]

A second challenge is justifying the massive government expenditures needed to finance overseas infrastructure projects on a large scale. The onus has been on the party to convince the public that the allocation of the equivalent of hundreds of billions of U.S. dollars for infrastructure loans to poorer states—some of which may be unrecoverable—is reasonable in light of China's slowing economic growth, incomplete social safety net, and continued problems of poverty and inequality. Anecdotal evidence

---

[18] Information Office of the State Council (PRC), "Action Plan on the Belt and Road Initiative." The exception is the China-Pakistan Economic Corridor, which does have an official website with a full project catalogue. However, this website is maintained by Pakistan rather than China. See "China-Pakistan Economic Corridor," Ministry of Planning, Development and Reform (Pakistan), http://cpec.gov.pk.

[19] The author thanks an anonymous reviewer for this insight.

[20] Cong and Na, "Xi's Belt and Road Vision."

[21] See Zhao Zhouxian and Liu Guangming, "Renmin ribao: 'Yidai, Yilu,' Zhongguo meng yu shijie meng de jiaohui qiaoliang" ["One Belt, One Road": The Bridge Between the China Dream and the World Dream], *People's Daily*, December 24, 2014, http://opinion.people.com.cn/n/2014/1224/c1003-26263405.html; and Ding Yifan, "Yidai Yilu' shi Zhonghua minzu weida fuxing de guangkuo zhi lü" ["One Belt, One Road" Is the Broad Road to the Great Rejuvenation of the Chinese People], 71.cn, March 20, 2017, http://www.71.cn/2017/0320/939834.shtml.

[22] One analyst notes, for instance, that BRI coverage in state media is increasingly "sharing the spotlight" with other domestic and foreign news. Johan van de Ven, "The Belt and Road Initiative: Is China Putting Its Money Where Its Mouth Is?" Jamestown Foundation, China Brief, March 26, 2018, https://jamestown.org/program/belt-road-initiative-china-putting-money-mouth.

suggests that residents in major cities, such as Shanghai, may also be less than enthusiastic about plans to shift regional transportation networks in ways that advantage poorer inland cities, such as Chongqing.[23] The government has used state media to explain how average citizens can benefit from these projects—such as through lower prices for cheap consumer goods produced in BRI countries and fewer travel restrictions—but doubts remain in some quarters.[24]

A third challenge is that BRI's political aims may be creating distorted incentives for the central and provincial bureaucrats, firms, and foreign leaders responsible for implementing it. Luo Jianbo, director of the China Foreign Policy Center at the Central Party School, writes that the political priority placed on the initiative has given rise to an "anxiousness of relevant departments to see an early harvest of results," citing especially the China-Pakistan Economic Corridor (CPEC), "without a consideration of costs."[25] A more insidious problem concerns how financial results are reported: companies may hide failures to stay in officials' good graces,[26] while Chinese and foreign officials may inflate statistics to appease Xi and those around him.[27] The extent of these problems is unknown and probably impossible to measure, though the incentives for false reporting could be reduced by tightening capital controls and keeping public statements vague (thus allowing officials to cherry-pick successes and gloss over failures).[28] However, because of the political stakes, it is doubtful that senior officials can have high confidence in the quality of data being supplied by those actively involved in BRI projects.

---

[23] Author's interviews in Shanghai, September 2018.

[24] See "Zhuyi la, 'Yidai Yilu' gei ni dai lai zhei ba da fuli!" [Pay Attention to the Eight Great Benefits That "One Belt, One Road" Will Bring You!], People's Daily, May 17, 2017, http://www.gov.cn/fuwu/2017-05/17/content_5194579.htm; and Qi Zhiming, "Dakai Yidai Yilu minsheng da libao" [Open Up the One Belt, One Road Livelihood Gift], People's Daily, August 17, 2018, http://world.people.com.cn/n1/2018/0817/c1002-30234538.html.

[25] "Zhongyang dangxiao jiaoshou: Zhongguo jiu shi xintai yao bu de" [Central Party School Professor: China Does Not Need a Savior Mentality], July 21, 2017, https://think.sina.cn/jujiao/doc--ifyihrit1109365.d.html.

[26] Derek Scissors, "China's Global Investment: Neither the U.S. nor the Belt and Road," American Enterprise Institute (AEI), July 11, 2018, 7.

[27] Thomas S. Eder and Jacob Mardell, "Belt and Road Reality Check: How to Assess China's Investment in Eastern Europe," Mercator Institute for China Studies, July 10, 2018, https://www.merics.org/de/blog/belt-and-road-reality-check-how-assess-chinas-investment-eastern-europe.

[28] Enoch Yiu, "Beijing's Strict Capital Controls Are Delaying Belt and Road Project Approvals," South China Morning Post, April 4, 2017, https://www.scmp.com/business/companies/article/2084738/beijings-strict-capital-controls-are-delaying-belt-and-road#add-comment.

An Economic Strategy

An Overview of BRI-Related Investment

In a second sense, BRI is a well-planned economic strategy intended to support China's internal development by strengthening regional connectivity, especially in the infrastructure arena. It is important, however, to keep the initiative's economic significance in perspective. In terms of FDI, Derek Scissors finds that BRI-linked projects accounted for less than 25% of Chinese outbound investments between 2013 and mid-2018.[29] The Economist Intelligence Unit similarly assesses that investments in BRI partner countries represented only 12% of China's total outward FDI in 2017.[30] Part of the reason is that private Chinese firms are reluctant to invest in BRI projects due to low profit potential and other complications (such as the fact that most investments are being made by SOEs, which act at the government's behest).[31] This conforms to statistical evidence showing that Chinese investors are focused primarily on large developed markets such as the United States, Japan, and the European Union.[32] Developing countries with abundant natural resources are also a target, but simply being labeled a BRI partner has no effect on investment flows.[33]

Moreover, from the perspective of domestic growth, BRI's contributions are relatively small. According to data from the American Enterprise Institute (AEI), the total value of BRI investments and construction contracts between January 2013 and June 2018 was a little over $420 billion, a tiny fraction of China's $11.2 trillion GDP in 2016 (though the actual impact on GDP could be larger due to multiplier effects).[34] The Chinese economy has been heavily oriented toward exports, but few of the 70 or so formal BRI partners rank among its major export markets. **Table 1** lists China's top export and BRI investment partners. Even if China manages to increase trade and investment with BRI partners, those gains will be overshadowed by its continued equities

---

[29] Scissors, "China's Global Investment."

[30] "Belt and Road Initiative Quarterly: Q1 2018," Economist Intelligence Unit, February 27, 2018, http://country.eiu.com/article.aspx?articleid=1306471714. See also Cheng King and Jane Du, "Could 'Belt and Road' Be the Last Step in China's Asian Economic Integration?" *Journal of Contemporary China*, July 12, 2018.

[31] Cecilia Joy-Perez and Derek Scissors, "The Chinese State Funds Belt and Road but Does Not Have Trillions to Spare," AEI, March 28, 2018.

[32] David Dollar, "Is China's Development Finance a Challenge to the International Order?" (paper presented at the Japan Center for Economic Research conference, Tokyo, October 2017), 7.

[33] Ibid.

[34] AEI and Heritage Foundation, "China Global Investment Tracker," http://www.aei.org/china-global-investment-tracker; and World Bank, China data, https://data.worldbank.org/country/china.

TABLE 1   China's top export markets and top BRI partners

Rank	Export market (2016)	Value (billion $)	Rank	Investments in BRI countries (2014–18)	Value (billion $)
1	United States	$436.0	1	Singapore	$24.3
2	Hong Kong	$250.0	2	Malaysia	$14.6
3	Japan	$149.0	3	Russia	$10.9
4	Germany	$99.0	4	Israel	$9.8
5	South Korea	$87.2	5	India	$9.0
6	Mexico	$63.7	6	Indonesia	$8.7
7	Vietnam	$60.0	7	South Korea	$8.5
8	United Kingdom	$59.8	8	Pakistan	$7.6
9	India	$58.9	9	United Arab Emirates	$5.6
10	Australia	$43.8	10	Vietnam	$4.3

SOURCE: Massachusetts Institute of Technology, Observatory of Economic Complexity, https://atlas.media.mit.edu/en/profile/country/chn/#Destinations; and AEI and Heritage Foundation, "China Global Investment Tracker," http://www.aei.org/china-global-investment-tracker.

in the major industrial economies and offset to a degree by its economic rebalancing toward domestic consumption.[35]

Nevertheless, BRI should not be dismissed as a mere economic sideshow. While Xi took credit for projects launched by his predecessors, he has also overseen a variety of new projects during his own tenure. Examples include CPEC, toward which he committed nearly $46 billion, and its constituent projects such as a second phase of the Karakorum Highway and a new section of the Peshawar-Karachi Motorway;[36] a second China-Russia oil pipeline, which began operations on January 1, 2018, and is expected to double Chinese imports of Russian oil;[37] a new line of the China–Central Asia

---

[35] "Future of Consumption in Fast-Growth Consumer Markets: China," World Economic Forum, Insight Report, January 2018, 8; and "Meet the 2020 Chinese Consumer," McKinsey and Company, March 2012.

[36] Mehreen Zahra-Malik, "China Commits $45.6 Billion for Economic Corridor with Pakistan," Reuters, November 21, 2014, https://www.reuters.com/article/us-pakistan-china/china-commits-45-6-billion-for-economic-corridor-with-pakistan-idUSKCN0J51C120141121. For project details, see "China-Pakistan Economic Corridor."

[37] "Russia Tightens Oil Grip with China's Second Pipeline," Bloomberg, January 1, 2018, https://www.bloomberg.com/news/articles/2018-01-01/second-chinese-crude-oil-pipeline-linked-to-russia-s-espo-opens.

natural gas pipeline; a high-speed rail linking Jakarta and Bandung; and new pan-Eurasian freight lines such as one between Changchun, in China's northeast, and Hamburg.

BRI-related investments have also spread far beyond the Eurasian heartland. The Maritime Silk Road stretches from East Asia through the Indian Ocean to the east coast of Africa, where major land-based infrastructure projects include the $3.2 billion Nairobi-Mombasa railway, which began operations in May 2017,[38] and the $4 billion Djibouti–Addis Ababa railway, which opened in January 2018.[39] In Eastern Europe, China has focused its investments in the Balkans, including a high-profile rail link connecting Serbia and Hungary, in addition to the aforementioned Piraeus port project.[40] In a sign of its ever-expanding geographic scope, BRI has also begun to subsume projects taking place in West African countries, such as Senegal, while a handful of Latin American and Caribbean countries have signed agreements as well.[41] **Figure 2** provides a map of ongoing BRI projects.

China's participation in these projects comes in two main forms: investments and direct involvement through construction contracts. While China's outward FDI in BRI countries is relatively small, lending provided by the two primary policy banks—China Development Bank and the Export-Import Bank of China—is significant. David Dollar notes that total lending by Chinese policy banks at the end of 2016 was $675 billion, more than double the size of the World Bank's portfolio.[42] Comparisons with U.S. and European institutions are more striking: in 2015 the U.S. Overseas Private Investment Corporation (OPIC) had a portfolio of only $20 billion (which rose to $60 billion in 2018), while European development finance institutions possessed around $45 billion.[43] The percentage of Chinese loans devoted to BRI projects is unclear because China does not report lending data at a

---

[38] Duncan Miriri, "Kenya Inaugurates Chinese-Built Railway Linking Port to Capital," Reuters, May 31, 2017, https://www.reuters.com/article/us-kenya-railways/kenya-inaugurates-chinese-built-railway-linking-port-to-capital-idUSKBN18R2TR.

[39] "Chinese-Built Ethiopia-Djibouti Railway Begins Commercial Operations," Xinhua, January 1, 2018, http://www.xinhuanet.com/english/2018-01/01/c_136865306.htm.

[40] Maesea McCalpin, "Belt & Road Is Back on the Rails in Eastern Europe," CSIS, Reconnecting Asia, December 12, 2017, https://reconnectingasia.csis.org/analysis/entries/belt-road-back-rails-eastern-europe.

[41] "With Senegal Deals, China's Belt and Road Reaches across Africa," *Asia Times*, July 24, 2018, http://www.atimes.com/article/with-senegal-deals-chinas-belt-and-road-reaches-across-africa; and Ricardo Barrios, "China's Belt and Road Lands in Latin America," China Dialogue, July 11, 2018, https://www.chinadialogue.net/article/show/single/en/10728-China-s-Belt-and-Road-lands-in-Latin-America.

[42] Dollar, "Is China's Development Finance a Challenge to the International Order?" 6–9.

[43] George Ingram, "Testimony on Modernizing Development Finance," testimony before the Senate Foreign Relations Committee, Washington, D.C., May 11, 2018, https://www.brookings.edu/testimonies/testimony-on-modernizing-development-finance/#footnote-3.

FIGURE 2 Existing and planned infrastructure in China's BRI

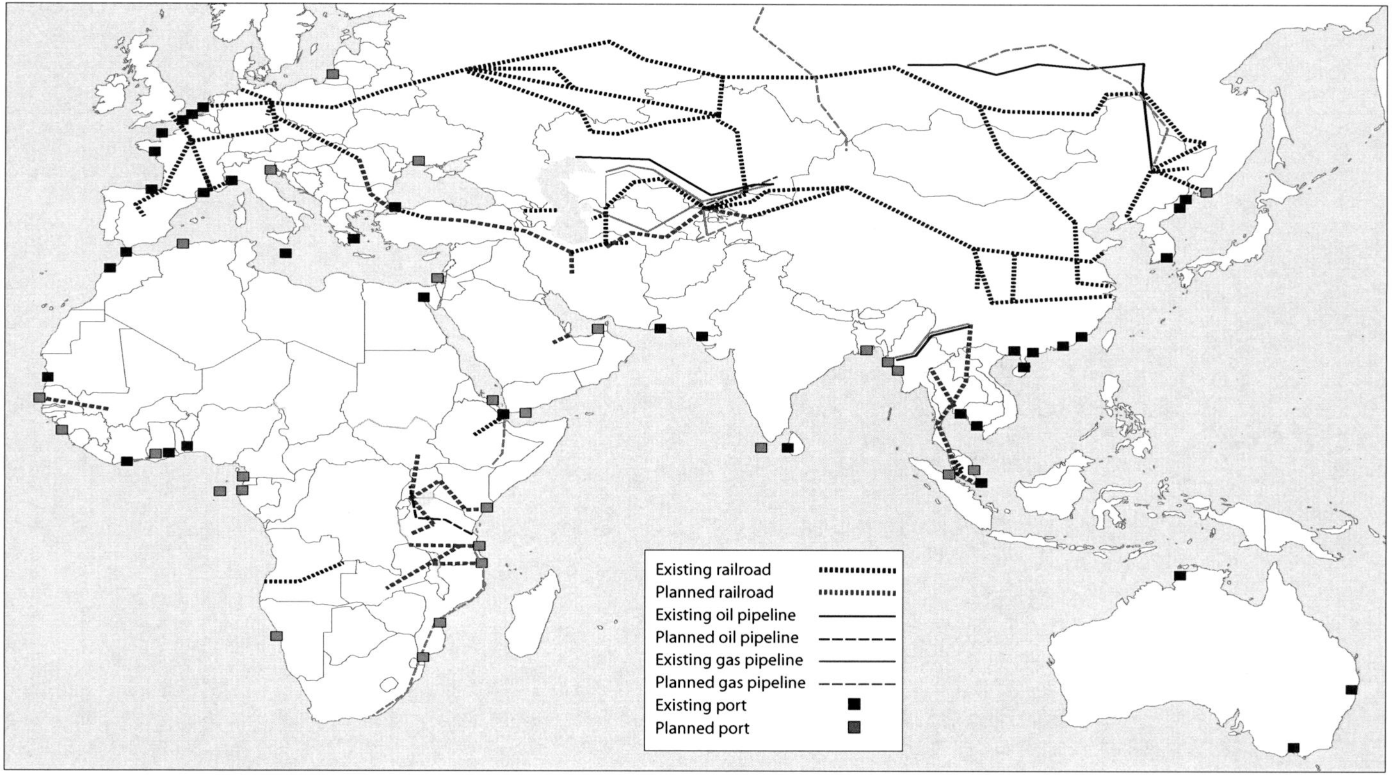

Legend:
- Existing railroad
- Planned railroad
- Existing oil pipeline
- Planned oil pipeline
- Existing gas pipeline
- Planned gas pipeline
- Existing port
- Planned port

SOURCE: Mercator Institute for China Studies.

granular level. However, Chinese sources assert that the two primary banks had a portfolio of $239 billion in BRI-related projects in 2016, accounting for 35% of total overseas lending.[44]

The scale of Chinese involvement in construction projects is also impressive. Data compiled by AEI suggests that Chinese firms signed construction contracts for BRI-related projects worth over $250 billion between 2013 and mid-2018, representing more than 60% of total overseas contracts.[45] This is consistent with claims by China's Ministry of Commerce that BRI contracts in 61 countries accounted for 54% of all Chinese overseas contracts between January and November 2017.[46] Most of these construction projects involve considerable demand for Chinese workers, materials (especially steel and concrete), and services that help maintain employment levels and boost the Chinese economy. The AEI dataset also offers a unique window into the focus of Chinese activities. By sector, most projects are being conducted in the energy, real estate, and transportation industries, with smaller participation in areas such as chemicals, metals, and utilities. By region, Chinese firms are primarily carrying out BRI-related work in East Asia, especially countries in the Association of Southeast Asian Nations (ASEAN), South and Central Asia, and the Middle East. This data is reported in **Figures 3** and **4**.

The lack of tangible results is a reason for skepticism about BRI's economic contributions, though this is partly a result of long time horizons for infrastructure projects. CPEC, for instance, has three time frames: short-term projects are due for completion in 2020, medium-term projects in 2025, and long-term projects in 2030.[47] A dataset from the Center for Strategic and International Studies confirms that a majority of BRI projects remain in the negotiation or construction phase as of mid-2018 (see **Figure 5**). The few completed projects were mostly pursued under Jiang and Hu but are now labeled as BRI projects. Moreover, a number of factors may lead to project delays or cancelations, as will be discussed in greater detail below. This means that the economic value of BRI projects may not be apparent until the 2020s or later.

---

[44] David Dollar, "Yes, China Is Investing Globally—But Not So Much in Its Belt and Road Initiative," Brookings Institution, Order from Chaos blog, May 8, 2017, https://www.brookings.edu/blog/order-from-chaos/2017/05/08/yes-china-is-investing-globally-but-not-so-much-in-its-belt-and-road-initiative.

[45] Scissors, "China's Global Investment."

[46] "Shangwu bu zhaokai liexing xinwen fabu hui" [Ministry of Commerce Holds Routine Press Conference], Ministry of Commerce (PRC), December 14, 2017, http://www.mofcom.gov.cn/article/ae/ah/diaocg/201712/20171202684925.shtml.

[47] "China-Pakistan Economic Corridor: Opportunities and Risks," International Crisis Group, Asia Report, no. 297, June 29, 2018, 10.

FIGURE 3 Chinese BRI construction contracts by sector (January 2013–June 2018)

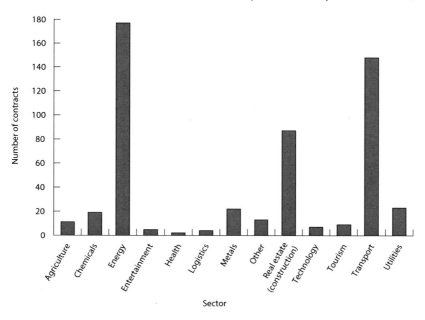

SOURCE: AEI and Heritage Foundation, "China Global Investment Tracker."

FIGURE 4 Chinese BRI construction contracts by region (January 2013–June 2018)

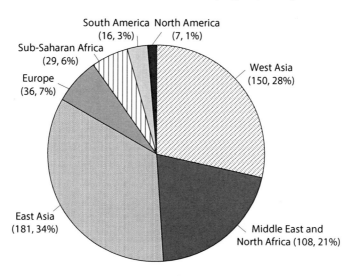

SOURCE: AEI and Heritage Foundation, "China Global Investment Tracker."

FIGURE 5   BRI project status as of July 2018

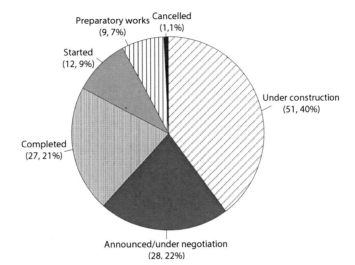

SOURCE: CSIS, Reconnecting Asia Project, https://reconnectingasia.csis.org.

The Economic Goals of BRI

As an economic strategy, BRI serves several interrelated goals. The first is increasing economic integration within Asia's subregions and between Asia and Europe, Africa, and beyond. This requires investment in both hard infrastructure, such as bridges, rail lines, and ports, and soft infrastructure, such as fiber-optic cable networks.[48] Those investments will contribute to Asia's prodigious need for additional infrastructure spending, which the Asian Development Bank (ADB) estimates at $1.7 trillion per year to maintain growth, reduce poverty, and prepare for the negative effects of climate change.[49] For China, infrastructure development also requires supporting policy coordination, bilateral and multilateral trade deals, new financing platforms such as the Asian Infrastructure Investment Bank (AIIB) and the Silk Road Fund (which provide modest funding for BRI infrastructure

---

[48] Information Office of the State Council (PRC), "Action Plan on the Belt and Road Initiative."

[49] "Meeting Asia's Infrastructure Needs," Asian Development Bank, Key Indicators for Asia and the Pacific, February 2017.

projects), and even enhanced cultural exchanges to improve the quality of people-to-people interactions.[50]

China's official explanation is that regional integration will allow partner countries to "tap market potential in this region, promote investment and consumption, create demands and job opportunities," and promote "harmony, peace, and prosperity."[51] Although this explanation is self-serving as a public relations message, economists often agree that regional integration can produce economic benefits for participants. For instance, a World Bank study found that long transportation times between Asia and Europe reduce the value of trade by 1% per day. Regional cooperation can help solve this problem by facilitating more rapid trade flows.[52] Investing in soft infrastructure may also help create more stable and secure data linkages between two continents.[53] Speaking at the Belt and Road Forum, World Bank president Jim Yong Kim stated that BRI will help "lower trade costs, increase competitiveness, improve infrastructure, and provide greater connectivity for Asia and its neighboring regions."[54] China would be a clear beneficiary of such outcomes as reflected in the fact that all six planned economic corridors radiate from China to surrounding regions.

The second goal is alleviating China's significant industrial overcapacity.[55] A result of China's attempt to stimulate the domestic economy following the 2008 global financial meltdown was excess capacity in construction materials such as steel, aluminum, concrete, and glass. Although Chinese officials have often downplayed any relationship between the initiative and the problem of alleviating industrial overcapacity,[56]

---

[50] The initial capitalizations of the AIIB and the Silk Road Fund were $100 billion and $40 billion, respectively. "Full Text of President Xi's Speech at Opening of Belt and Road Forum," Xinhua, May 14, 2017, http://www.xinhuanet.com/english/2017-05/14/c_136282982.htm.

[51] Information Office of the State Council (PRC), "Action Plan on the Belt and Road Initiative."

[52] Michele Ruta, "Three Opportunities and Three Risks of the Belt and Road Initiative," World Bank, Trade Post blog, May 4, 2018, http://blogs.worldbank.org/trade/three-opportunities-and-three-risks-belt-and-road-initiative.

[53] Chas W. Freeman Jr., "The Geoeconomic Implications of China's Belt and Road Initiative" (remarks at the Conference of the University of San Francisco's China Business Studies Initiative, San Francisco, February 8, 2017), https://chasfreeman.net/the-geoeconomic-implications-of-chinas-belt-and-road-initiative.

[54] Jim Yong Kim (remarks at the Belt and Road Forum for International Cooperation, Beijing, May 14, 2017), http://www.worldbank.org/en/news/speech/2017/05/14/remarks-of-world-bank-group-president-jim-yong-kim.

[55] Rolland, *China's Eurasian Century?* 100–101; Johnson, "President Xi Jinping's 'Belt and Road' Initiative," 20; and Hong Yu, "Motivation Behind China's 'One Belt, One Road' Initiatives and Establishment of the Asian Infrastructure Investment Bank," *Journal of Contemporary China* 26, no. 105 (2017): 358.

[56] Michael Lelyveld, "China Argues over "Belt and Road' Goals," Radio Free Asia, June 26, 2016, https://www.rfa.org/english/commentaries/energy_watch/china-argues-over-belt-and-road-goals-06262017105633.html.

sponsoring infrastructure development in emerging Eurasian economies that utilize Chinese construction firms and materials clearly serves this goal. In a 2014 editorial, then vice foreign minister He Yafei acknowledged that BRI could be an avenue for addressing Chinese overcapacity in iron, steel, chemicals, and shipbuilding (thus providing a service for the recipients of those products).[57] A February 2016 editorial by the State Council on steel overcapacity also identified BRI projects as one means of reducing China's steel overcapacity by 100–150 million tons over five years.[58]

A third goal is advantaging Chinese firms, especially SOEs. Common international complaints about BRI include that the bidding process is noncompetitive and designed to favor SOEs, that Chinese rather than local employees are used to complete projects,[59] and that the adoption of Chinese technical standards in areas such as construction, transportation, and communications places Chinese firms at a competitive advantage.[60] More complicated, however, is the issue of whether Beijing is using BRI to build "national champions," referring to globally competitive enterprises—usually SOEs—that benefit from preferential state policies. The long-term trend for China's SOEs is one of growth. In 2000 the Fortune 500 list included only 9 Chinese SOEs, whereas the 2017 version included 75, with Chinese construction firms accounting for 7 of the world's top 10.[61] Analysts argue that BRI could accelerate this trend by providing new opportunities for SOEs, both in the construction arena and in other sectors such as energy and communications.[62] Nevertheless, data compiled by the RWR Advisory Group suggests that Beijing is parceling out opportunities to many firms, both state-owned and private, rather than promoting a select few.[63]

---

[57] He Yafei, "China's Overcapacity Crisis Can Spur Growth through Overseas Expansion," *South China Morning Post*, January 7, 2014, https://www.scmp.com/comment/insight-opinion/article/1399681/chinas-overcapacity-crisis-can-spur-growth-through-overseas.

[58] "Guowuyuan guanyu gangtie hangye huajie guosheng channeng shixian tuokun fazhan de yijian" [State Council Opinion on Alleviating Overcapacity and Achieving Development in the Steel Industry], Information Office of the State Council (PRC), February 4, 2016, http://www.gov.cn/zhengce/content/2016-02/04/content_5039353.htm.

[59] One study found that China-funded transportation infrastructure projects in 34 Asian and European countries involved the use of Chinese workers in 89% of cases. James Kynge, "Chinese Contractors Grab Lion's Share of Silk Road Projects," *Financial Times*, January 24, 2018, https://www.ft.com/content/76b1be0c-0113-11e8-9650-9c0ad2d7c5b5.

[60] This is in fact an explicit BRI goal. The 13th Five-Year Plan pledges to "increase cohesion between the development plans and technological standards of China and those of other countries" along BRI routes. Central Committee of the Communist Party of China, *The 13th Five-Year Plan for Economic and Social Development of the People's Republic of China: 2016–2020* (Beijing, 2016), 147.

[61] Jonathan Hillman, "China's Belt and Road Initiative: Five Years Later," testimony before the U.S.-China Economic and Security Review Commission, Washington, D.C., January 25, 2018, 4.

[62] Rolland, *China's Eurasian Century?* 102–4.

[63] According to the data, no company has been awarded more than 4% of projects per year since 2016. Van de Ven, "The Belt and Road Initiative."

A fourth ambition is spurring growth in China's border provinces and second-tier cities through stronger trade and investment linkages with surrounding countries.[64] Clear winners include Xinjiang, which is the terminus of CPEC; Yunnan Province, where a planned high-speed rail network stretching into Southeast Asia is slated to end in the capital city of Kunming; and Fujian Province, which serves as the hub of the Maritime Silk Road.[65] The three northeastern provinces—Liaoning, Jilin, and Heilongjiang—could also see gains, especially in the energy sector, as part of the China-Russia-Mongolia economic corridor.[66] Overall, Nadège Rolland describes BRI as a "stimulus package in disguise" that could provide a boost at a time of slowing growth rates.[67]

Economic Risks

The most skeptical economic analysis is that BRI actually consists of an assemblage of low-quality projects, some of which may have been rejected by the World Bank or other national policy banks, and many of which are destined for failure. As mentioned earlier, international media reports tend to dwell on individual problem cases, such as Sri Lanka's Hambantota port. That project, often dismissed as a political boondoggle, resulted in barely used transportation infrastructure and substantial debt for the host nation.[68] Empirically, however, it appears that most BRI projects are not in immediate danger of failure. The China Global Investment Tracker database classifies only 45 of 785 BRI-related projects (6%) as troubled, encompassing problems such as multiyear operating losses or blocked transactions by Beijing or the host government.[69] Moreover, an analysis by RWR Advisory Group using a

---

[64] The Information Office of the State Council identifies sixteen provinces and four autonomous cities that will be integral to BRI, though this seems more like a message of inclusivity targeted at a domestic political audience than a concrete plan. See Information Office of the State Council (PRC), "Action Plan on the Belt and Road Initiative."

[65] Wu Chengliang, "China-Laos Railway Project Set to Be Complete by Late 2021," *People's Daily,* November 15, 2017, http://en.people.cn/n3/2017/1115/c90000-9293209.html; and "Fujian: A New Star on Ancient Maritime Silk Road," Xinhua, March 8, 2017, http://www.xinhuanet.com/english/2017-03/08/c_136112968.htm.

[66] Information Office of the State Council (PRC), "Action Plan on the Belt and Road Initiative."

[67] Rolland, *China's Eurasian Century?* 98–99. Rolland cites one Chinese study that claims that BRI could contribute up to 0.25% to China's economic growth rate.

[68] Jonathan Hillman, "The Hazards of China's Global Ambitions," *Washington Post,* February 5, 2018, https://www.washingtonpost.com/news/theworldpost/wp/2018/02/05/obor-china-asia/?noredirect=on&utm_term=.ac40a74f5f32.

[69] AEI and Heritage Foundation, "China Global Investment Tracker." For a discussion of troubled transactions, see Derek Scissors, "Chinese Investment Still Rising Globally; Tough Choices for the U.S.," testimony before the House Committee on Financial Services, Subcommittee on Monetary Policy and Trade, Washington, D.C., January 9, 2018, 8.

separate dataset found that only 234 of 1,674 China-funded infrastructure projects (14%) in 66 BRI countries have met with trouble.[70]

While perhaps not widespread, the notable failures illustrate the economic, legal, and governance constraints facing Chinese investments and construction activities in BRI countries. In a broad sense, China has finite resources that it can use to invest in overseas infrastructure projects. The total amount that the Chinese government plans on spending on BRI is a matter of much speculation and debate, with estimates ranging from the equivalent of several hundred billion to several trillion U.S. dollars.[71] An AEI study estimates that $1 trillion is possible by the mid-2020s, but rejects higher figures for two reasons. First, China's foreign currency reserves, which in 2018 stood at around $3 trillion, are vast but not endless and must serve multiple purposes. Second, private Chinese companies have shown limited appetite for investing in BRI countries.[72] Li Ruogu, former chairman of the Export-Import Bank of China, explains that private investors are wary of the complications of dealing with foreign tax systems, labor laws, customs-clearance processes, and the currencies of most BRI nations.[73]

Credit risks associated with overleveraged target countries could also pose problems for Chinese investments. Li acknowledges that few BRI countries have credit ratings above the BB level (defined as noninvestment grade speculative) and concludes that the "investment risks are relatively large."[74] Moody's similarly assesses that "large funding from [Chinese] policy banks to countries rated with high implementation risks could lead to asset quality erosion at the banks and increase contingent liabilities."[75] On the other hand, Liu Yong, chief economist of the China Development Bank, claims that the credit ratings of partner countries are "carefully and jointly evaluated." He concedes that problems of nonperforming assets exist but argues that they are "within our tolerance range."[76] This assessment is supported with evidence

---

[70] James Kynge, "China's Belt and Road Difficulties Are Proliferating Across the World," *Financial Times*, July 9, 2018, https://www.ft.com/content/fa3ca8ce-835c-11e8-a29d-73e3d454535d.

[71] The figure of $4–$8 trillion that has been cited in some media reports appears to have resulted from an ADB estimate of infrastructure investment requirements rather than Chinese spending plans.

[72] Joy-Perez and Scissors, "The Chinese State Funds Belt and Road," 2.

[73] He Huifeng, "Is China's Belt and Road Infrastructure Development Plan about to Run Out of Money?" *South China Morning Post*, April 14, 2018, https://www.scmp.com/news/china/economy/article/2141739/chinas-belt-and-road-infrastructure-development-plan-about-run.

[74] Li Liuxi and Fran Wang, "Veteran China Banker Warns of 'Belt and Road' Risks," Caixin, April 13, 2018, https://www.caixinglobal.com/2018-04-13/veteran-china-banker-warns-of-belt-and-road-risks-101234218.html.

[75] "Moody's Rates Belt and Road Initiative 'Overall Credit Positive' but Warns China of Risks," Silk Road Briefing, September 21, 2017, https://www.silkroadbriefing.com/news/2017/09/21/moodys-rates-belt-road-initiative-overall-credit-positive-warns-china-risks.

[76] Huifeng, "Is China's Belt and Road Infrastructure Development Plan about to Run Out of Money?"

that review times for BRI projects are increasing, both to control for credit risk and to prevent companies from using projects to store funds overseas as a hedge against loss of valuation of the renminbi.[77]

Another challenge is that Chinese firms may not be familiar with foreign legal systems and could be ill-equipped to utilize international arbitration processes based on Western common law and the English language. Legal disputes have resulted in complications and losses. For example, in 2016, Sinopec lost $478 million when Saudi Arabia changed the terms of a contract.[78] Chinese firms have attempted to reduce these risks by hiring international legal consultants to conduct due diligence and litigate disputes. Beijing has also stepped in by establishing three new international commercial courts under the Supreme People's Court to handle BRI cases and promoting new arbitration mechanisms "based on China's existing judicial, arbitration, and mediation institutions."[79] The presumption is that smaller partners may be forced to accept Chinese arbitration as a contractual term.

Compounding these problems is the issue of political risk. Poor governance—ranging from bureaucratic red tape to rent-seeking and corruption—degrades what Alexander Cooley calls the necessary political "software" behind successful infrastructure projects.[80] One example is the Bandung-Jakarta high-speed railway, one of Indonesia's two BRI projects. That project has been complicated by the failure of the host government to disburse funding, difficulties in acquiring the necessary permits, and the inability to secure the necessary land.[81] More broadly, a World Bank analysis suggests that corrupt officials may divert funding to offshore bank accounts and opaque companies, resulting in BRI taking "several detours off course."[82]

Democratic politics may also exacerbate political risks in some cases. Politicians may seek to manipulate various aspects of infrastructure projects

---

[77] Enoch Yiu, "Beijing's Strict Capital Controls Are Delaying Belt and Road Project Approvals," *South China Morning Post*, April 4, 2017, https://www.scmp.com/business/companies/article/2084738/beijings-strict-capital-controls-are-delaying-belt-and-road#add-comment.

[78] Laurie Chen, "Rewards Outweigh Risks for Chinese Firms Involved in Belt and Road Projects, Say Legal Experts," *South China Morning Post*, April 16, 2018, https://www.scmp.com/business/global-economy/article/2141791/rewards-outweigh-risks-chinese-firms-involved-belt-and-road.

[79] Sabena Siddiqui, "Beijing Plans New Mechanism for Belt and Road Arbitration," *Asia Times*, February 7, 2018, http://www.atimes.com/belt-road-arbitration-new-mechanism; and Willa Wu, He Shusi, and Deng Yanzi, "HK Role Vital in B&R Arbitration Solution: Experts," *China Daily*, January 25, 2018, http://www.chinadaily.com.cn/a/201801/25/WS5a6929bea3106e7dcc1366ce.html.

[80] Alexander Cooley, "China's Changing Role in Central Asia and Implications for U.S. Policy: From Trading Partner to Collective Goods Provider," testimony before the U.S.-China Economic and Security Review Commission, Washington, D.C., March 18, 2018, 4.

[81] Go Yamada and Stefania Palma, "Is China's Belt and Road Working? A Progress Report from Eight Countries," *Nikkei Asian Review*, March 28, 2018, https://asia.nikkei.com/Spotlight/Cover-Story/Is-China-s-Belt-and-Road-working-A-progress-report-from-eight-countries.

[82] Ruta, "Three Opportunities and Three Risks for the Belt and Road Initiative."

for electoral gain, with one example being the Sharif government's rerouting of CPEC projects in Pakistan to pass through territory controlled by the ruling party.[83] Another case is the Hambantota port, which was located in the home district of former president Mahinda Rajapaksa despite little local economic activity or transportation infrastructure to justify such an investment.[84] The election of new officials can also pose hurdles, such as occurred when Malaysian prime minister Mahathir Mohamad froze the China-funded East Coast Rail Link and other projects in order to investigate his predecessor's alleged corruption.[85] There are no easy solutions to these problems. Although Beijing can try to exert pressure to keep projects on course, Chinese investors may simply seek to avoid politically turbulent areas in the first place.

A Geopolitical Strategy

Geopolitical Objectives

In a third sense, BRI is a geopolitical strategy to stabilize China's frontier regions and strengthen its diplomatic influence in Eurasia (including the subregions of Central, South, and Southeast Asia) as well as in the Middle East, Africa, Eastern Europe, and Latin America. Chinese officials tend to downplay such motivations, but they do connect BRI with foreign policy goals in broad terms. Building hard and soft infrastructure along China's periphery and beyond is an integral part of developing a "community of shared destiny," a Xi-era diplomatic concept that implies a more robust whole-of-government effort to maintain a favorable international context for the country's economic development.[86] Within this overall approach, Beijing appears to be pursuing at least four specific geopolitical objectives.

The first is stabilizing China's border regions. Chinese analysts argue that promoting regional economic growth can ameliorate the underlying social and political conditions that precipitate terrorism and other transnational maladies, and which ultimately threaten China's

---

[83] "China-Pakistan Economic Corridor: Opportunities and Risks," 14.

[84] Iain Marlow, "China's Belt-and-Road Billions Come with a Cost," Bloomberg, May 2, 2018, https://www.bloomberg.com/news/articles/2018-05-02/costly-lessons-for-leaders-eyeing-china-s-belt-and-road-billions.

[85] "Malaysia Halts Work on Major Belt and Road Rail Project," Nikkei Asian Review, July 5, 2018, https://asia.nikkei.com/Politics/Malaysia-in-transition/Malaysia-halts-work-on-major-Belt-and-Road-rail-project.

[86] For further discussion, see Denghua Zhang, "The Concept of 'Community of Common Destiny' in China's Diplomacy: Meaning, Motives, and Implications," Asia and the Pacific Policy Studies 5, no. 2 (2018): 196–207.

internal security.[87] A specific focus is on countering Uighur separatism by supporting the development of states such as Kazakhstan and Kyrgyzstan, which have large Uighur diasporas, and by positioning Xinjiang as a regional logistics hub.[88] BRI agreements also complement law-enforcement cooperation between China and its neighbors and in multilateral forums such as the Shanghai Cooperation Organisation.[89] Some Chinese analysts even describe joint infrastructure projects in countries such as Vietnam and the Philippines as ways to promote mutual trust and ultimately resolve territorial conflicts along China's maritime periphery.[90]

A second geopolitical objective is facilitating greater energy diversification. For years, China has sought to reduce its reliance on vulnerable energy shipment routes. Hu Jintao famously referred to this problem as the "Malacca dilemma," given the amount of Chinese oil and natural gas imports that traverse the Malacca Strait and other maritime routes that are susceptible to piracy and even interdiction by the U.S. military during a crisis. Efforts to alleviate this problem have focused on the need for additional port development in and beyond the Indian Ocean and new continental pipelines.[91] BRI projects contribute to both goals as new ports, such as Gwadar, are developed and new overland pipelines, such as a planned China-Pakistan natural gas pipeline connecting Gwadar with Xinjiang and a new addition to the China–Central Asia natural gas pipeline, come online.

Third is expanding Chinese influence in a range of developing countries. BRI agreements are an extension of China's bilateral diplomacy, complementing high-level visits, trade deals, scientific and technical cooperation, arms sales, military exchanges, and other efforts.[92] Infrastructure development assistance and financing, which are usually based on bilateral accords, can help strengthen strategic partnerships with states such as Kazakhstan and Indonesia, where Xi announced the land- and sea-based components of BRI, respectively. CPEC, for its part, is an outgrowth of China's

---

[87] Joel Wuthnow, "Chinese Perspectives on the Belt and Road Initiative: Strategic Rationales, Risks, and Implications," Institute for National Strategic Studies, China Strategic Perspectives, no. 12, October 2017, 9–10.

[88] Michael Clarke, "The Belt and Road Initiative: Exploring Beijing's Motivations and Challenges for Its New Silk Road," *Strategic Analysis* 42, no. 2 (2018): 84–102.

[89] Wuthnow, "Chinese Perspectives on the Belt and Road Initiative," 9–10.

[90] Ibid.

[91] Theresa Sabonis-Helf, "Infrastructure and the Political Economies of Central Asia," in *Central Asia in the Era of Sovereignty*, ed. Daniel L. Burghart and Theresa Sabonis-Helf (Lanham: Lexington Books, 2018), 228.

[92] See, for example, "Joint Declaration on New Stage of Comprehensive Strategic Partnership between the People's Republic of China and the Republic of Kazakhstan," August 31, 2015, http://www.fmprc. gov.cn/mfa_eng/wjdt_665385/2649_665393/t1293114.shtml.

long-term efforts to cultivate Pakistan as an "all-weather" partner in South Asia and a counterweight to a rising India.[93] Indeed, data from the RWR Advisory Group suggests that while most BRI recipients initiated fewer new projects after 2016, those that saw greater activity were most likely to be ascending partners. These include Iran, where sanctions relief, followed by the United States' withdrawal from the multilateral nuclear deal in May 2018, contributed to major new Chinese-funded infrastructure projects, and Egypt, where China has become a key investor in the strategic Suez Canal corridor and other projects.[94]

While many BRI partners are financially sound, China has appeared to use debt obligations associated with infrastructure financing to solidify its diplomatic influence in a number of smaller, more economically vulnerable states. In extreme cases, excessive debt could shackle partners and allow China to gain preferential access to their ports and other infrastructure (which may be used for military purposes) as well as natural resources.[95] For example, China's navy may be able to rely on access to BRI-funded ports, such as the deep-sea port at Kyaukpyu in Myanmar, Colombo harbor in Sri Lanka, or Gwadar in Pakistan, to facilitate resupply and replenishment. Beijing may also seek to extract concessions from BRI partners to build overseas bases, although financial and operational challenges may limit this approach.[96] China's inaugural base in debt-distressed Djibouti, for instance, can be used to monitor regional maritime shipping and naval traffic and conduct surveillance on U.S. military assets in the region.[97]

A study by the Center for Global Development found that eight countries, including Djibouti, Kyrgyzstan, Laos, Maldives, Mongolia, Montenegro, Pakistan, and Tajikistan, were at serious risk of debt distress (referring to a high level of public debt that could severely damage economic growth).

---

[93] See Jeremy Garlick, "Deconstructing the China-Pakistan Economic Corridor: Pipe Dreams Versus Geopolitical Realities," *Journal of Contemporary China* 27, no. 112 (2018): 519–33.

[94] Van de Ven, "The Belt and Road Initiative." On Iran, see Roie Yellinek, "A Reappraisal of China-Iran Ties after U.S. JCPOA Withdrawal," Jamestown Foundation, China Brief, August 10, 2018, https://jamestown.org/program/a-reappraisal-of-china-iran-ties-after-us-jcpoa-withdrawal.

[95] Brahma Chellaney, "China's Creditor Imperialism," Project Syndicate, December 20, 2017, https://www.project-syndicate.org/commentary/china-sri-lanka-hambantota-port-debt-by-brahma-chellaney-2017-12?barrier=accesspaylog.

[96] Joel Wuthnow, "China's Overseas Basing: Will the PLA Follow the Renminbi?" *National Interest*, February 17, 2018, https://nationalinterest.org/feature/chinas-overseas-basing-will-the-pla-follow-the-renminbi-24551.

[97] For further analysis, see Erica Downs, Jeffrey Becker, and Patrick deGategno, "China's Military Support Facility in Djibouti: The Economic and Security Dimensions of China's First Overseas Base," CNA, July 2017.

Several other countries are at lesser risk.[98] The most notable of these cases from a strategic perspective are Sri Lanka, which had to grant China a 99-year lease on the Hambantota port after running into financial trouble, and Djibouti, which sits alongside critical sea lanes linking the Red Sea with the Gulf of Aden.[99] The case of Maldives, which occupies a key geographic position in the heart of the Indian Ocean, has also caused concern among both domestic and foreign analysts. In September 2018 an opposition candidate won the country's presidential election on a platform highlighting the Chinese "debt trap."[100]

A fourth objective is more effectively competing with the United States. Analysts such as Rolland portray BRI as a response to the Obama administration's rebalancing strategy, which sought to shift U.S. economic and military resources to Asia following a decade of focus on the Middle East.[101] Some Chinese sources, especially hawkish ones, help substantiate this argument. For example, Qiao Liang, a professor at the PLA National Defense University, referred to increased economic cooperation with countries along China's western periphery as a "very clever and nonconfrontational type of strategic hedging" against the United States.[102] BRI, in this sense, is the embodiment of Mao's military axiom: "Where the enemy advances, we retreat. Where the enemy retreats, we pursue."[103]

In terms of competition with the United States, BRI has benefited China in several ways. First, it has allowed China to solidify relations with

---

[98] John Hurley, Scott Morris, and Gaiylyn Portelance, "Examining the Debt Implications of the Belt and Road Initiative from a Policy Perspective," Center for Global Development, Policy Paper, no. 21, March 2018. David Dollar notes that most recipients of Chinese infrastructure financing are fiscally sound, with only a few having taken on excessive debt. See Dollar, "Is China's Development Finance a Challenge to the International Order?" 12.

[99] For example, Panos Mourdoukoutas, "China Is Doing the Same Things to Sri Lanka That Great Britain Did to China after the Opium Wars," *Forbes*, June 28, 2018, https://www.forbes.com/sites/panosmourdoukoutas/2018/06/28/china-is-doing-the-same-to-sri-lanka-great-britain-did-to-china-after-the-opium-wars/#2c43330f7446; and Jon Connars, "Djibouti the Latest to Fall Victim to China's 'Debt Trap Diplomacy,'" *Asia Times*, March 27, 2018, http://www.atimes.com/djibouti-latest-fall-victim-chinas-debt-trap-diplomacy.

[100] Iain Marlow, "Maldives Boots Out Pro-China President in Election Surprise," Bloomberg, September 24, 2018, https://www.bloomberg.com/news/articles/2018-09-24/tiny-maldives-boots-out-pro-china-president-in-election-surprise.

[101] Rolland, *China's Eurasian Century?* 116–19. In the context of the AIIB, see Lai-Ha Chan, "Soft Balancing Against the U.S. 'Pivot to Asia': China's Geostrategic Rationale for Establishing the Asian Infrastructure Investment Bank," *Australian Journal of International Affairs* 71, no. 6 (2017): 568–90.

[102] Qiao Liang, "Meiguo de zhanlüe dongyi yu Zhongguo de zhanlüe xijin" [The U.S. Strategic Eastward Shift and China's Strategic March West], *High End Talk*, 2015, 24. See also Wang Haiyun, "Geostrategic Thinking of Belt and Road Initiative," *International Strategic Studies*, no. 3 (2015): 13–23.

[103] Yun Sun, "March West: China's Response to the U.S. Rebalancing," Brookings Institution, January 31, 2013, https://www.brookings.edu/blog/up-front/2013/01/31/march-west-chinas-response-to-the-u-s-rebalancing.

traditional partners, such as Russia, Pakistan, and Iran, just as the United States was reinforcing its regional alliances and partnerships. Those states are useful sources of support on regional issues, such as territorial disputes, as well as in global institutions such as the UN Security Council and other UN institutions such as the Human Rights Council. Second, China has used the prospect of expanded economic cooperation to entice U.S. allies and partners, most notably the Philippines but also to a lesser degree South Korea and New Zealand, which have expressed support for BRI. Even Japan has explored joint cooperation as a way to improve relations with Beijing.[104] Third, energy diversification has helped mitigate the risks to China's energy imports posed by the stronger U.S. military presence in Asia and new operational concepts that envision imposing blockades on Chinese oil imports during a major conflict.[105]

Geopolitical Challenges

Despite the benefits that China has reaped from BRI thus far, it faces a variety of challenges in converting BRI projects into geopolitical advantages. The first are ideological constraints. China may be strengthening its network of strategic partners, but there is little evidence that it is prepared to upgrade those relations to security alliances that include firm guarantees. Instead, it frequently derides such arrangements as Cold War relics.[106] That attitude limits the prospects that a China-led order will compete with or replace the U.S. hub-and-spoke alliance system. The principle of noninterference may also limit China's influence over its partners, no matter how dependent they may become, since it is unlikely to use overt military force to enforce its preferences. Nevertheless, this constraint should not be overstated: China's adherence to this principle has waned in recent years,

---

[104] See Gaku Shimida, "Japan and China Take First Step toward Joint Infrastructure Abroad," *Nikkei Asian Review*, September 4, 2018, https://asia.nikkei.com/Politics/International-Relations/Japan-and-China-take-first-step-toward-joint-infrastructure-abroad.

[105] In this vein, the most eye-catching proposal from a Chinese perspective was "offshore control," which suggested that China's oil imports could be cut off. See T.X. Hammes, "Offshore Control: A Proposed Strategy for an Unlikely Conflict," Institute for National Strategic Studies, Strategic Forum, no. 278, June 2012. For an alternative analysis, see Gabriel Collins, "A Maritime Oil Blockade against China—Tactically Tempting but Strategically Flawed," *Naval War College Review* 71, no. 2 (2018): 49–78.

[106] Tsinghua University professor Yan Xuetong has been a notable outlier in calling for China to consider military alliances. See Chen Weihua, "Is It Time for China to Start Looking for Strategic Allies?" *China Daily*, November 30, 2015, http://usa.chinadaily.com.cn/opinion/2015-11/30/content_22528521.htm.

as demonstrated by its quiet outreach to opposition parties and insurgents in partner countries.[107]

The second challenge is resistance among recipient states to being drawn into China's strategic orbit. In recent years, many smaller Asian states have hedged against an overreliance on China as an economic benefactor by establishing and maintaining positive economic, diplomatic, and security relations with the United States, Japan, India, and other major powers.[108] In the context of infrastructure financing, states may simply avoid projects that would create excessive debt (helping explain the absence of serious debt problems in many cases) or seek assistance from a variety of other lenders, such as the World Bank, Japan, or the European Union. Jonathan Hillman notes that in 2016 every new ASEAN leader held discussions on infrastructure projects with both China and Japan.[109] Some Chinese analyses acknowledge that hedging by partners will reduce Beijing's ability to convert economic relationships into political influence and also may let partners obtain better terms from both China and other lenders.[110]

Third, China has faced a barrage of criticism about the geopolitical objectives motivating parts of BRI. One prominent critique is that Xi's initiative is essentially a 21st-century version of the Marshall Plan (i.e., designed to counter geopolitical rivals through massive foreign development spending).[111] At a press conference in March 2015, Chinese foreign minister Wang Yi forcefully rebuked this notion by calling the comparison one of "apples and oranges" and saying that BRI should "not be viewed with an outdated

---

[107] Chen Zheng, "China Debates the Non-interference Principle," Chinese Journal of International Politics 9, no. 3 (2016): 349–74. Examples of China's interference include support for insurgent groups in Myanmar and direct contacts with insurgents in Pakistan's Baluchistan Province. See, respectively, Henrik Hallgren and Richard Ghiasy, "Security and Economy on the Belt and Road: Three Country Case Studies," Stockholm International Peace Research Institute (SIPRI), SIPRI Insights on Peace and Security, no. 2017/4, December 2017, 7; and Farhan Bokhari and Kiran Stacey, "China Woos Pakistan Militants to Secure Belt and Road Projects," Financial Times, February 19, 2018, https://www.ft.com/content/063ce350-1099-11e8-8cb6-b9ccc4c4dbbb.

[108] Evelyn Goh, "Great Powers and Hierarchical Order in Southeast Asia: Analyzing Regional Security Strategies," International Security 32, no. 3 (2007/08): 113–57; and G. John Ikenberry, "Between the Eagle and the Dragon: America, China, and Middle State Strategies in East Asia," Political Science Quarterly 131, no. 1 (2016): 9–43.

[109] Hillman, "China's Belt and Road Initiative: Five Years Later."

[110] For instance, Zhang Jie, a scholar in the Institute of Asia-Pacific and Global Strategy at the Chinese Academy of Social Sciences, describes the Joko Widodo government's balancing of economic relationships between China and Japan and argues that hedging allowed Indonesia to avoid adopting China's position on a South China Sea legal ruling. Zhang Jie, "'Yidai Yilu' yu 'quanqiu haiyang zhidian': Zhongguo yu Yini de zhanlüe duijie ji qi tiaozhan" ["One Belt, One Road" and "Global Maritime Fulcrum": China and Indonesia Strategic Abutment and Challenges], Contemporary World, no. 8 (2015): 40.

[111] See Enda Curran, "China's Marshall Plan," Bloomberg, August 7, 2016, https://www.bloomberg.com/news/articles/2016-08-07/china-s-marshall-plan; and Theresa Fallon, "The New Silk Road: Xi Jinping's Grand Strategy for Eurasia," American Foreign Policy Interests 37, no. 3 (2015): 142.

Cold War mentality."[112] Chinese officials have also been on the defensive about international complaints over the country's "debt trap diplomacy," going so far as to condemn foreign media reporting on Sri Lanka's debt—which resulted in China gaining ownership in the Hambantota port—as "fake news."[113]

Fourth, while BRI may be envisioned in part to create a more stable periphery, it has also created more demanding security requirements.[114] At the Belt and Road Forum, Xi acknowledged that the initiative encompasses regions that are "often associated with conflict, turbulence, crisis and challenge."[115] Risks to overseas Chinese nationals have been apparent for years, but the large influx of personnel and investments associated with BRI is drawing new attention to the problems of protecting those assets.[116] Perhaps the most serious case is Pakistan, where 30,000 Chinese workers contributing to CPEC projects are subject to the threats of kidnappings and terrorist attacks, especially in insurgency-prone regions such as Baluchistan.[117] Those risks are heightened by local resentment over CPEC's close association with the central government, heavy use of Chinese (rather than local) workers, and contracts that disadvantage local economies.[118]

Ameliorating these security risks has been a key priority for Beijing, which wants to protect overseas assets and avoid the negative publicity that attacks on BRI projects would entail.[119] One focus has been on improving cooperation with partner countries, as illustrated by the creation of a new China-Pakistan-Afghanistan-Tajikistan security mechanism focused on addressing counterterrorism challenges.[120] In the context of CPEC, China has also relied on significant support from Pakistan, which has allocated more than fifteen thousand soldiers to guard Chinese workers.[121] In the absence of effective local support, Chinese firms have hired Chinese and foreign private

---

[112] "Foreign Minister Wang Yi Meets the Press," Ministry of Foreign Affairs (PRC), March 8, 2015, http://www.fmprc.gov.cn/mfa_eng/zxxx_662805/t1243662.shtml.

[113] "China Refutes So-Called 'Debt Trap' over Sri Lanka's Hambantota Port Project," Xinhua, July 3, 2018, http://www.chinadaily.com.cn/a/201807/03/WS5b3b8a3da3103349141e07a0.html.

[114] For a discussion, see Wuthnow, "Chinese Perspectives on the Belt and Road Initiative," 13–17.

[115] Xi, "Work Together to Build the Silk Road Economic Belt."

[116] For a discussion, see Jonas Parello-Plesner and Mathieu Duchâtel, *China's Strong Arm: Protecting Citizens and Assets Abroad* (London: Routledge, 2015).

[117] "China-Pakistan Economic Corridor: Opportunities and Risks," 7.

[118] For instance, over 90% of profits from the Gwadar port project will be given to China, with the remainder due to the central government; no profits will be remunerated to the local Baluchistan government. Ibid., 21.

[119] Wuthnow, "Chinese Perspectives on the Belt and Road Initiative," 22–24.

[120] Michael Martina, "China Joins Afghanistan, Pakistan, Tajikistan in Security Alliance," Reuters, August 4, 2016, https://www.reuters.com/article/us-china-security-idUSKCN10F1A6.

[121] "China-Pakistan Economic Corridor: Opportunities and Risks," 7–8.

security companies to provide risk assessments, training, and security.[122] To prepare for worst-case scenarios, Beijing has also considered how best to prepare for the evacuation of Chinese citizens using a mix of civilian and military assets. Part of the rationale for the new facility in Djibouti is to facilitate noncombatant evacuations, and the PLA may develop additional logistics hubs in states such as Pakistan to meet similar objectives.[123]

Conclusion: Implications and Strategic Options

Implications

BRI comprises three distinct strategies (outlined in **Table 2**), each with its own goals, tools, and constraints. Politically, the initiative burnishes Xi's, and the CCP's, image through grandiose rhetoric and statistics, though it faces challenges such as mixed public opinion and distorted bureaucratic incentives. Economically, foreign infrastructure investments and construction contracts help alleviate China's industrial overcapacity and provide new opportunities for Chinese regions and firms. Projects, however, have been hindered by economic, legal, and governance problems. Geopolitically, BRI aims to stabilize China's frontier regions, enhance relations with strategic partners, diversify energy sources, and promote more effective competition with the United States. Yet those goals have been constrained by partner hedging and international counter-narratives that highlight China's purported ulterior motives and predatory behavior.

Given the publicity—and even hype—surrounding BRI, it is not difficult to overstate its significance relative to other major party objectives. In political terms, the initiative supports a positive image for Xi and the party, but its contributions as a source of legitimacy are minor compared with China's domestic economic reforms and progress on key nationalist missions such as Taiwan's unification with the "motherland." As ballast for the Chinese economy, foreign infrastructure spending is significant for particular Chinese regions and sectors but contributes only marginally to overall growth. More important is the shift toward domestic consumption and high-end manufacturing and the preservation of stable relations with the major industrial economies. With respect to the United States, BRI is but one component of a larger strategic rivalry, the diplomatic, intelligence, military, and economic contours of which are only beginning to become apparent. However, because of its relevance

---

[122] Charles Clover, "Chinese Private Security Companies Go Global," *Financial Times*, February 26, 2017, https://www.ft.com/content/2a1ce1c8-fa7c-11e6-9516-2d969e0d3b65.

[123] This is not a new challenge. In 2011, China had to repatriate more than 30,000 Chinese workers during the Libyan civil war. That crisis arguably led to greater consideration of how personnel might be evacuated.

TABLE 2   Summary of the three BRI strategies

	Political	Economic	Geopolitical
Ends	Solidification of Xi's reputation and CCP legitimacy	Improved regional integration, reduced cost of overcapacity, and aid for SOEs and provinces	Increased frontier security, strengthened partnerships, and improved energy security; challenge to the United States
Ways and means	Domestic messaging, association with Xi, and lack of data for objective assessment	Financing, contracts, Chinese standards, Chinese courts	Links with border regions; prioritization of strategic partners, pipelines, and LNG ports; debt-to-equity contracts
Challenges	Possible public apathy or skepticism and distorted incentives	Economic, legal, and political risks	Host-country hedging and hostile foreign narratives

across the political, economic, and geopolitical arenas, BRI will remain an important element of the party's long-term agenda, and its outcomes will be integral to Xi's ability to claim progress in fulfilling the China dream.

The unfolding of BRI over its first half decade reveals several lessons about how China is pursuing its global interests and what constraints and challenges it faces as a newly minted global power. First, the initiative represents China's emphasis on flexibility in carrying out major strategic endeavors. Beijing has been careful to maintain only the vaguest criteria for involvement as a BRI partner state, never publicizing a specific list of criteria and taking pains not to exclude any country or region, despite the original focus on the Asian continent. This flexibility allows China to shift its diplomatic and economic resources to utilize emerging opportunities while retaining the possibility of renewed cooperation when relationships sour. The same flexibility is evident in China's approach to international negotiations—for instance, Beijing often refrains from taking positions in the UN Security Council until the last possible moment—and in its dynamic relations with states such as the United States and Russia.

The second lesson is the significance of economic statecraft in China's diplomatic toolbox.[124] In the context of BRI, the Chinese state has been able to leverage control over policy banks and SOEs to direct investments in countries with poor credit ratings, legal or governance challenges, and other dilemmas that deter private investors. China has also demonstrated its ability to utilize economic tools to pursue diplomatic goals in ways that would be difficult, if not completely unfeasible, for other countries to undertake. Examples include incentives such as massive debt relief as well as more coercive efforts to reduce trade, promote domestic boycotts, and suspend tourism in order to prod countries to adopt positions in line with Beijing's preferences.[125] Such economic manipulation represents a comparative strategic advantage for China, helping offset relative weaknesses such as its lack of formal alliances and military constraints. The latter include China's inability to sustain combat operations far from its immediate periphery.

Third, China's conversion of economic resources into diplomatic influence is contingent, to a degree, on the policies of its interlocutors. For instance, its ability to translate infrastructure assistance into diplomatic leverage in BRI countries has been shaped by the domestic political climate in those countries, including the willingness of elites to accept financing with diplomatic strings attached and countervailing nationalistic currents that militate in the opposite direction, as recently witnessed in Malaysia and Maldives. As discussed further below, China is also somewhat limited in this respect insofar as other actors, including major powers and international financial institutions, can provide alternative financing. Similar dynamics are at play outside BRI: North Korea, for instance, has prioritized economic self-reliance over integration with China, while Taiwan has tried—albeit with limited success—to avoid overreliance on China by cultivating relations with Southeast Asian states.[126]

Fourth, important aspects of China's behavior on the world stage represent the influence, and in some cases the primacy, of domestic political and economic calculations. While it may be tempting to reduce BRI to the apparent goal of countering U.S. influence, the shaping and execution of the initiative has arguably been just as much a result of imperatives to establish Xi's personal authority and cater to the needs of domestic stakeholders such as provincial governments and SOEs. Domestic objectives are also apparent

---

[124] For an overview, see William J. Norris, *Chinese Economic Statecraft* (Ithaca: Cornell University Press, 2016).

[125] For a good discussion, see Peter Harrell, Elizabeth Rosenberg, and Edoardo Saravalle, "China's Use of Coercive Economic Measures," Center for a New American Security (CNAS), June 2018.

[126] David Green, "Taiwan's Economic Charm Offensive Hits Chinese Walls," *Foreign Policy*, August 24, 2017, https://foreignpolicy.com/2017/08/24/taiwans-economic-charm-offensive-hits-chinese-walls.

in other foreign policy contexts. For example, China's more assertive approach to the territorial disputes in the South China Sea over the past decade has arguably been driven as much by nationalism and the promotion of local and national economic interests as by a desire to expand China's strategic influence at the expense of other countries.[127]

Fifth, while direct evidence is scant, Chinese bureaucracies and other interest groups may be working at cross purposes in designing and implementing foreign economic and diplomatic policies.[128] For example, bureaucrats engaged in development finance may value the need to approve high-quality projects that meet strict lending criteria, avoid problems of unrecoverable debt, and provide real assistance for countries in need, while those in strategic circles may advocate lending to vulnerable but geopolitically important countries, such as Djibouti and Sri Lanka, irrespective of the potential economic drawbacks. Similar intra-bureaucratic conflict can be found in many complex policy arenas, such as China's management of its major-power relations and decisions on how assertively to prosecute maritime territorial claims. To manage those tensions, China is likely to continue relying on interagency coordination mechanisms such as leading small groups and the National Security Commission, with Xi himself serving as the ultimate arbiter.

As a manifestation of China's rise as a global power, what can be said about BRI's impact on recipient countries as well other major powers? If left unchecked, Chinese financing of infrastructure and a host of supporting activities could contribute to a general restructuring of the balance of power in Central Asia, Southeast Asia, and to a degree South Asia, the Middle East, and beyond—in a way that provides long-term benefits to China and disadvantages the United States and others. China may not only acquire new forms of diplomatic leverage based on its partners' financial obligations but also lock these states into more exclusive economic relations due to physical and soft infrastructure (built to Chinese standards) connecting them to China and greater use of the renminbi to settle accounts. China may also expand its soft power by promoting its own preferred norms, such as an ideological pluralism that discounts Western-style democracy, and by

---

[127] "Stirring Up the South China Sea (I)," International Crisis Group, Asia Report, no. 223, April 23, 2012, 19–28.

[128] For an overview of influential foreign policy actors, see Linda Jakobson and Dean Knox, "New Foreign Policy Actors in China," SIPRI, Policy Paper, no. 26, September 2010. For a recent analysis of the role of Chinese provinces in setting foreign policy goals, see Audrye Wong, "More than Peripheral: How Provinces Influence China's Foreign Policy," China Quarterly, no. 235 (2018): 735–57.

increasing people-to-people exchanges, including efforts to cultivate support from foreign elites through training programs.[129]

BRI could also produce a more substantial Chinese security presence outside the country's borders. While analysts have paid particular attention to the prospects for additional Chinese naval bases, which may eventually play a role in supporting deterrence or combat operations, the more likely outcome, at least in the near term, is an expansion of security partnerships.[130] Milestones of evolving partnerships might include formal agreements on the use of Chinese private security companies to patrol BRI sites and personnel, agreements whereby host nations would provide security for Chinese laborers, closer law-enforcement cooperation in areas such as counterterrorism and drug trafficking, more regular military exchanges, expanded arms sales, and even the provision of Chinese surveillance technology to authoritarian states.[131] These activities would result in more robust and tangible security partnerships between China and many states without the necessity of offering reciprocal security guarantees.

A more Sinocentric order, based on such arrangements, would have deleterious effects on both smaller states and major countries. The former could lose autonomy over their economic and foreign policy decisions, and potentially their transportation infrastructure (if, as in the case of Sri Lanka, debts are transferred to Chinese ownership stakes), while vulnerable populations could be exposed to risks if authoritarian leaders are strengthened. Major powers, including countries such as Japan, India, the United States, and even Russia, could see their influence in critical and secondary regions decline. For instance, it is plausible that states drifting into China's strategic orbit could fail to support U.S. positions in international forums, deny access to U.S. firms, or refuse to join a U.S.-led coalition in a future military campaign. Asia's subregions, in a general sense, could become less "free and open," to borrow from the language employed by the United States and several allies and partners to describe the preferred Indo-Pacific order.

The reality, however, is likely to be complicated by a number of competing factors. The first, as discussed above, is China's own limitations.

---

[129] See He Huifeng, "China Is Training Foreign Officials to Spread Its Political Model, Including How to 'Guide Public Opinion' Online," *South China Morning Post*, July 15, 2018, https://www.businessinsider.com/china-training-asean-officials-2018-7.

[130] See David Brewster, "China's New Network of Indian Ocean Bases," Lowy Institute, Lowy Interpreter, January 30, 2018; Joel Wuthnow, "China's Overseas Basing"; and Timothy R. Heath, *China's Pursuit of Overseas Security* (Santa Monica: RAND Corporation, 2018).

[131] Daniel Benaim and Hollie Russon Gilman, "China's Aggressive Surveillance Technology Will Spread Beyond Its Borders," *Slate*, August 9, 2018, https://slate.com/technology/2018/08/chinas-export-of-cutting-edge-surveillance-and-facial-recognition-technology-will-empower-authoritarians-worldwide.html.

Beijing does not have unlimited resources to devote to foreign infrastructure financing and may have to make hard choices about where to invest as domestic economic growth slows and the Chinese public becomes warier of the costs of underwriting the development needs of other countries. Second, while analysts write about the possibility of a new regional order in general terms, the actual nature of Chinese influence will vary by state. Poorer, more authoritarian, and more isolated countries may find it hard to resist China's economic overtures, but those with stronger domestic governance, sounder finances, and more intricate relations with other major powers will be more likely to avoid overreliance on China. Third, outcomes will depend in part on the behavior of other major states and international organizations: having more choices means fewer incentives for countries to rely on China.

Options for the United States

For the United States, there are two basic strategic options to preserve regional balance, market access, and liberal values in light of the challenges posed by BRI. The first is a symmetrical response. Under this approach, Washington would strengthen its own lending in the infrastructure arena and encourage private U.S. investors to more proactively compete for projects. The Trump administration has already followed this approach by proposing reforms to the United States' development finance institution, OPIC, under which the contingent liability ceiling would be raised from $30 billion to $60 billion, in part to stimulate private investment in emerging markets.[132] A symmetrical policy might also involve greater U.S. contributions to alternate funding sources, such as the International Monetary Fund and the ADB; support for other countries' regional connectivity programs, such as the Asia-Africa Growth Corridor created by Japan and India;[133] and promotion of traditional lending norms that correlate with U.S. interests and values, such as sustainability, the creation of local jobs, and environmental protection. In the latter case, the United States could highlight instances in which BRI projects fail to meet such standards.[134]

---

[132] Glenn Thrush, "Trump Embraces Foreign Aid to Counter China's Global Influence," *New York Times*, October 14, 2018, https://www.nytimes.com/2018/10/14/world/asia/donald-trump-foreign-aid-bill.html.

[133] Wade Shepard, "India and Japan Join Forces to Counter China and Build Their Own New Silk Road," *Forbes*, July 31, 2017, https://www.forbes.com/sites/wadeshepard/2017/07/31/india-and-japan-join-forces-to-counter-china-and-build-their-own-new-silk-road/#29aff0db4982.

[134] See Daniel Kliman and Abigail Grace, "Power Play: Addressing China's Belt and Road Strategy," CNAS, September 30, 2018.

While some aspects of this approach are feasible, and additional funding sources, either unilaterally or in concert with others, may allow states to hedge their bets against China in some cases, there are notable limits. First, the United States cannot begin to match the resources that China has already devoted to BRI: the $60 billion allocated for OPIC pales in comparison with the half trillion or so dollars that Beijing has spent on BRI projects and the hundreds of billions yet to come. Second, there does not appear to be a political appetite in the United States to increase funding for developmental agencies that would complement such an approach, including USAID and the ADB, both of which have been targeted for cuts in recent U.S. budgets. Third, as with Chinese private investors, U.S. private firms have limited interest in funding infrastructure in countries challenged by economic, legal, and political deficits, and it will be difficult for U.S. government agencies such as OPIC to change those calculations. Fourth, enforcing strict lending guidelines means that the United States, and in many cases its partners and other international financial institutions, will not be willing to participate in some projects, such as those that threaten debt distress on the part of recipients or pose environmental hazards. This means that China will retain advantages in certain circumstances (even though it may have its own incentives to avoid such projects on economic grounds and to sidestep international opprobrium).

The second option for the United States is an asymmetrical strategy that would play to U.S. strengths. Instead of competing with Chinese lending, the United States could position itself as a reliable partner in other areas. This would include solidifying its global alliance network, which requires care and attention at every level of government, but especially at the presidential level; regaining leadership in the trade and investment arena, such as by advocating a renegotiated Trans-Pacific Partnership; supporting a "free and open" Indo-Pacific in tangible ways, such as by enhancing cooperation with Southeast Asian states in maritime capacity-building; nurturing links with other democracies, such as India and Japan, both bilaterally and in multilateral formats such as the Quadrilateral Security Dialogue; and continuing to promote universal political and civil rights while emphasizing areas of contrast between the United States and China.

This approach would acknowledge U.S. financial and political limitations and grant that, barring some unforeseen turn of events, China will remain the dominant state actor in infrastructure financing. Instead, the United States would draw on its traditional comparative advantages in the security, economic, and ideological arenas, thus providing smaller states confidence in maintaining their own sovereignty in light of any efforts by China to translate its infrastructure financing into diplomatic demands.

The linchpin of such an approach, of course, is the United States continuing to recognize that its own fortunes are bound up in unfettered access to foreign markets, regional balances of power, and a stable and open international order across the Indo-Pacific and beyond. Anything less will increase the chances that something akin to a Sinocentric order, with all that it implies, could one day emerge.

EXECUTIVE SUMMARY

This chapter argues that China's maritime power projection will occur along a continuum of national interests and capabilities that diminish dramatically with distance and could be subject to slowing, setbacks, or even outright reversal.

MAIN ARGUMENT

Under Xi Jinping's ambitious emphasis on national rejuvenation, China is growing in all dimensions of national power, acquiring increasingly far-flung interests overseas. It is facing mounting domestic and international pressure to address them with unprecedented capabilities, particularly with its rapidly developing navy, and is allocating increasing resources with which to do so. Yet approaching and sustaining the remarkable U.S. constellation of global support capabilities that allow the U.S. to engage in combat operations against another major military worldwide seems unrealistic for China—even looking out over decades—given both the uniquely favorable opportunities that the U.S. has enjoyed and China's geographic liabilities. Moreover, in its fourth decade of sustained growth in national power, China faces increasing headwinds that will likely slow its future progress overseas, as well as internal risks that may even draw it inward. Even if China becomes convulsed by internal problems, its very disarray could subject its immediate neighbors lacking significant sea buffers to tremendous challenges.

POLICY IMPLICATIONS

- To counter China's expanding maritime presence, the U.S. should carefully cultivate its global network of alliances and partnerships, which is a unique strength offering unparalleled influence, access, and power projection.

- Particularly for worst-case scenarios, U.S. decision-makers must consider how to leverage China's strong power-distance gradient to shape its behavior across a full spectrum of contingencies.

- U.S. planners must address enduring technological imbalances and invest accordingly in capabilities to counter China's military counterintervention approaches while targeting its vulnerabilities.

Power vs. Distance:
China's Global Maritime Interests and Investments in the Far Seas

Andrew S. Erickson

One of the great transformations of the 21st century is the increasingly global activities of the People's Republic of China (PRC), particularly at sea. Beijing's domestic exigencies, growing overseas interests, and increasing capability to advance and defend those interests are combining to produce unprecedented ambitions that in turn are driving resource allocations and efforts. Already China has achieved a status and confidence unseen in nearly two centuries and a presence never before seen in geographic scope and sophistication. It is going, literally and figuratively, where elements of Chinese state power have not gone before. The People's Liberation Army (PLA) naval force that underwrites these historic breakthroughs is increasingly able to project power in new and influential ways. Indeed, the extent to which China can project power sustainably over growing distances to further its burgeoning interests is one of the key questions of 21st-century geopolitics. It has major consequences for China's role and footprint in the world, as well as for the interests of the United States and its allies. In coming years, Beijing may well make considerably great strides in the global arena and be able to deploy a force with truly global influence and reach. But it could also

Andrew S. Erickson is a Professor of Strategy in the China Maritime Studies Institute at the U.S. Naval War College. He can be reached at <andrew.erickson@usnwc.edu>.

The views expressed here are those of the author alone. They do not represent the policies or estimates of the U.S. Navy or any other organization of the U.S. government. He thanks Walter Berbrick, Daniel Caldwell, Christopher Carlson, Gabriel Collins, Suzanne Freeman, Conor Kennedy, Ryan Martinson, Michael Petersen, Rebecca Pincus, and multiple anonymous reviewers for invaluable input.

face significant challenges in doing so, and might even have to shift its focus inward to address challenges closer to home.

This chapter examines potential future PLA Navy (PLAN) activities, basing, and other Chinese investments in the maritime realm that could extend far beyond East Asia, and even the Indian Ocean and East African littoral. The first section explains how China's national priorities and interests are radiating outward, but that projecting power to defend them grows increasingly difficult with distance. The next section surveys China's maritime strategy, doctrine, and missions in the Indo-Pacific and beyond. The third section outlines progressive benchmarks for Chinese naval power projection, what is required to reach them, and what China can achieve when it does so. The penultimate section considers three possible alternative futures for Chinese naval power projection. The conclusion suggests implications for the region and the United States.

Going Global: Priorities, the Power-Distance Gradient, and Proliferating Drivers

This section describes Beijing's grand strategy and outlines factors affecting the execution of that strategy. Xi Jinping has articulated, and is working to bring to fruition, a comprehensive "China dream" of "national rejuvenation" to achieve global power and influence on a par with the United States by 2049. He calls for completing China's defense modernization to meet related goals in 2020, 2035, and 2050. This fits with growing assumptions that within 10 to 25 years the global order will witness a "return to bipolarity," this time between the United States and China.

This ambitious effort draws on tremendous advantages and resources, but its outcome will be shaped by the following Chinese characteristics and challenges. First, Xi's China is politically centralized but potentially brittle. Beijing can rally tremendous resources to rapidly further top national goals such as sea-power development, but this is contingent on concerted guidance and prioritization. Such impressive focus may dissipate quickly if some of China's many potential sources of instability rise to the fore.

Second, geography matters, and cannot be fully re-engineered. Within the bounds of the possible, China has indeed made impressive efforts to alter geography in its favor. Its South China Sea "island" construction and fortification, as well as its integrating Eurasia more deeply through Belt and Road Initiative (BRI) investment and infrastructure, represent the maximum of what can be done to recast geography. But even under the most favorable domestic and overseas development scenarios, China simply cannot make its geographic situation as advantageous as that of the United States, a natural maritime power with the most favorably situated homeland of any great power. As a hybrid land-sea power that operates on both interior and exterior lines, China faces both opportunities and unavoidable challenges, as well as tremendous opportunity costs.

Third, based on the two abovementioned factors, PRC foreign policy and defense strategy have long centered on the principal goal of regime survival via continued economic development, maintenance of a peaceful regional and international security environment, territorial integrity and sovereignty, and prestige. China's traditional military policy has focused on a strict hierarchy of security interests that attenuate rapidly with distance from China's shores. Throughout its history, regime continuity has come first, followed by domestic legitimacy and stability in core Han-dominated areas. In different periods, homeland defense has included more broadly various assortments of Han-minority or -plurality borderlands and national borders. Since the end of the Cold War, success in the aforementioned areas has enabled an additional layer of focus: Taiwan and other unresolved island and maritime claims in the "near seas" (the Yellow, East China, and South China Seas). Meeting the aforementioned goals has fostered a relatively narrow foreign policy agenda, which permitted China to maintain a low profile internationally and focus on domestic development. Now China is beginning to operate in new areas beyond the near seas in unprecedented ways. Its history offers no forecast for its future outward progress but could nevertheless be instructive if setbacks redirect its focus inward.

The radiating ranges of China's weapons systems and their delivery platforms overlap strikingly with this geography of national security priorities. Like the operating areas, sensor range coverage, and potential kinetic reach of China's weapons, the intensity of national security priorities and future military and geostrategic prospects diminish progressively with distance. Rather than operate freely on exterior lines like geographically advantaged sea powers such as the United States, the United Kingdom, and Japan, China must radiate maritime power from interior lines in a way that currently prioritizes the assertion of increasing control over its disputed sovereignty claims in the near seas while seeking growing influence across the Indo-Pacific and nascent global access and presence.

Increasingly, however, Beijing also faces numerous diverse challenges and threats to its interests as a result of its growing overseas presence, resource reliance, and the need for logistical and resupply points. Today, in the maritime dimension and beyond, China's hierarchy of national security priorities is best mapped as radiating geographic layers of progressively diminishing focus and capability from the near seas to the far seas and far oceans. Xi has further emphasized the opportunity and possibilities for force multiplication in "new strategic frontiers" (*zhanlüe xin jiangyu*)—the *res nullius* areas of the poles, deep seabed, and outer space,[1] which "are the new strategic territories where China will draw the resources to become a global power."[2] As the authoritative doctrinal text *The Science of Military Strategy* (2013) explains, in an era in which China's national interests have "surpassed the traditional [territorial land], territorial sea, and territorial airspace scope to continuously expand toward the periphery and the world, continuously extending towards the ocean, space, and electromagnetic space," and in which "the main war threat has switched from the traditional inland direction towards the ocean direction," the PLA "must expand its military strategic view and provide strong and powerful strategic support within a greater spatial scope to maintain national interests."[3] A key variable is the extent to which China can progress along this geographic continuum, and by when.

Beyond the abovementioned drivers, additional factors are pushing China in a global direction. Its overseas citizens, businesses, assets, and investments are proliferating, particularly in unstable areas. Resource access abroad is essential to fueling the Chinese economy, which remains energy-intensive and manufacturing-focused. China is already the world's second-largest oil consumer, and by 2035 is projected to import 80% of its oil and 46% of its natural gas.[4] The majority will come by sea, given that no feasible level of overland pipeline construction can alleviate this dependency. These factors may force Beijing to become involved in complex regional issues that it previously could avoid as a free rider on U.S. security provision.

Incremental and stopgap measures have only worked so far. These include new types of overseas operations such as noncombatant evacuation operations from Libya and Yemen, UN peacekeeping operations, over 30 antipiracy patrols to protect sea lines of communication (SLOCs), hospital ship activities, humanitarian assistance and disaster relief, and more than

---

[1] Cyber is also sometimes included in this concept of *res nullius* but is beyond the scope of this chapter. See "Guofang keda juban yantao hui jujiao taikong wangluo deng zhanlüe xinjiang yu" [The National Defense University of Science and Technology Held a Seminar to Focus on Strategic New Domains Such as Space and the Internet], "'Zhanlüe xinjiang yu yu guojia anquan' xueshu yantao hui jujiao taikong wangluo" [Academic Seminar on "New Strategic Domains and National Security" Focuses on Space and the Internet], China Military Network, December 4, 2015, http://www.cac.gov.cn/2015-12/04/m_1117354623.htm.

[2] Anne-Marie Brady, "China's Undeclared Foreign Policy at the Poles," Lowy Institute, Interpreter, May 30, 2017, https://www.lowyinstitute.org/the-interpreter/china-undeclared-foreign-policy-poles.

[3] Academy of Military Sciences of the People's Liberation Army of China, *The Science of Military Strategy* (Beijing, 2013), 105–6.

[4] Gabriel Collins, "China's Evolving Oil Demand," Baker Institute for Public Policy, Working Paper, 2016, http://www.bakerinstitute.org/research/chinas-evolving-oil-demand; and U.S. Department of Defense, *Annual Report to Congress: Military and Security Developments Involving the People's Republic of China 2018* (Washington, D.C., 2018), 54.

75 multinational security patrols on the Mekong River. Over time, however, China seeks to increase influence, deterrence, and actual combat capabilities beyond its borders as well. Recent years have witnessed a positive feedback loop: Beijing has burgeoning interests and the ability to address them. Citizens' expectations of their government's ability to uphold the national interests and status it trumpets in patriotic messaging are rising apace. In pursuing these imperatives, Chinese people, assets, and forces overseas encounter new challenges and opposition. Increasing resources and confidence propel the cycle onward and outward, with no major setbacks thus far.

Maritime Missions: Projecting Power Across the Indo-Pacific and Beyond

China's global drive has pressured the country to become more involved, reach out to more partners, and develop the ability to project force to protect its interests.[5] This has gradually eroded previous obstacles, including a long-standing, if unevenly applied, noninterference policy, lack of experience, and limited capabilities. China is radiating ripples of capability and activity to promote its expanding overseas interests. Its grand strategy encompasses diplomatic, economic, and military means in service of safeguarding such interests as energy supply security. In parallel, Chinese naval doctrine encompasses progressively less intense arcs of control, influence, and reach.[6] Xi's efforts to develop and operationalize China's naval doctrine represent the latest stage in a longer-term plan by further pursuing the four "new historic missions" (*xin de lishi shiming*) articulated by Hu Jintao in 2004 and adding as a fifth mission the realization of his own centenary goals.[7] These objectives

---

[5] This section draws on Andrew S. Erickson, "Doctrinal Sea Change, Making Real Waves: Examining the Naval Dimension of Strategy," in *China's Evolving Military Strategy*, ed. Joe McReynolds (Washington, D.C.: Jamestown Foundation, 2016), 102–40.

[6] Peter A. Dutton, "Three Disputes and Three Objectives: China and the South China Sea," *Naval War College Review* 64, no. 4 (2011): 42–67.

[7] At an expanded Central Military Commission conference in December 2004, Hu introduced new military policy that defined four "new historic missions" for the PLA: first, to serve as an "important source of strength" for the Chinese Communist Party to "consolidate its ruling position"; second, to "provide a solid security guarantee for sustaining the important period of strategic opportunity for national development"; third, to "provide a strong strategic support for safeguarding national interests"; and fourth, to "play an important role in maintaining world peace and promoting common development." The latter two missions were unprecedented. "Earnestly Step Up Ability Building within CPC Organizations of Armed Forces," *Liberation Army Daily*, December 13, 2004; and "Sange tigong, yige fahui" [Three Provides and One Bring into Play], Sina, September 29, 2005, http://news.sina.com.cn/c/2005-09-29/08517064683s.shtml. The fifth mission was enshrined in China's latest defense white paper as "strive to provide a strong guarantee for completing the building of a moderately prosperous society in all respects and achieving the great rejuvenation of the Chinese nation." Information Office of the State Council of the People's Republic of China (PRC), *China's Military Strategy* (Beijing, May 2015), http://www.xinhuanet.com/english/china/2015-05/26/c_134271001_2.htm.

helped justify China's subsequent Gulf of Aden and Mekong interventions.[8] Also in 2004, China's Ministry of Foreign Affairs adopted the guideline of "diplomacy serving the people," making protecting PRC citizens abroad a national priority.[9] The unprecedentedly robust maritime content in the 13th Five-Year Plan (2016–20) passed by the National People's Congress and released on March 17, 2016, declares that China will, among other things, build itself into a "maritime power," create a highly effective system for protecting overseas interests and safeguarding the legitimate overseas rights and interests of Chinese citizens and legal persons, and actively promote the construction of strategic strong points (*zhanlüe zhidian*) for the 21st Century Maritime Silk Road.[10]

Indo-Pacific Focus

Moving forward, Chinese naval strategists envision a very significant further radiating outward of China's maritime interests, capabilities, and forces. This relates to a formulation appearing increasingly in Chinese sources: "using the land to control the sea, and using the seas to control the oceans" (*yi lu zhi hai, yi hai zhi yang*).[11] Building on a general call for the protection of strategic capabilities radiating across coasts, seas, and oceans from China's continental core, the concept of "forward edge defense" articulated in *The Science of Military Strategy* has clear maritime implications, calling specifically for the establishment of a Chinese "arc-shaped strategic zone that covers the western Pacific Ocean and northern Indian Ocean."[12] Termed the "two oceans region/area" (*liang yang diqu*),[13] it is described as "mainly" including "the Pacific Ocean, Indian Ocean, as well as the littoral regions of neighboring Asia, Africa, Oceania, North America, South America, and Antarctica, etc., with a total area spanning over 50% of the globe; within which the

---

[8] Andrew S. Erickson and Austin M. Strange, "Ripples of Change in Chinese Foreign Policy? Evidence from Recent Approaches to Nontraditional Waterborne Security," *Asia Policy*, no. 17 (2014): 93–126.

[9] Mathieu Duchâtel, Oliver Bräuner, and Zhou Hang, *Protecting China's Overseas Interests: The Slow Shift Away from Non-interference*, SIPRI Policy Paper, no. 41 (Stockholm: SIPRI, 2014), 58.

[10] Su Xiangdong, ed., "Zhongguo guomin jingji he shehui fazhan di shisange wu nian guihua gangyao (quanwen)" [China's Five-Year Plan for Social and Economic Development (Full Text)], Xinhua, March 17, 2016.

[11] Academy of Military Sciences, *The Science of Military Strategy*, 102, 109.

[12] Ibid., 106.

[13] Most Chinese sources to date, including Xiao Tianliang, ed., *Zhanlüe xue* [The Science of Military Strategy] (Beijing: National Defense University Press, 2015), use the term "far-seas protection" [yuanhai huwei] rather than "two-oceans area." Yet Chinese strategists are clearly most focused on the western Pacific and the northern Indian Ocean, and other concepts rarely reveal geographically specific priorities. "Two oceans" is therefore used here for purposes of geographic clarity.

Two Oceans have a total area of 254.6 million square meters, occupying 71% of the global ocean area."[14]

The Science of Military Strategy deems the two-oceans region extremely important to Chinese security interests. It represents "a crucial area in influencing" China's "strategic development and security in the future" as well as "the intermediate zone of our entrance into the Atlantic Ocean region, Mediterranean Sea region, and Arctic Ocean region." In accordance with the globalizing nature of China's activities, its "national interests will surpass in an extremely large manner the traditional territorial land, territorial sea, and territorial air scope, while the Two Oceans region will become the most important platform and medium." On this basis, Chinese actors "will create conditions to establish ourselves in the Two Oceans region, participate in resource extraction and space utilization of the oceans, and boost development in the two polar regions." To be sure, the authors of this doctrinal publication allow that new challenges and "security threats" of both a traditional and a nontraditional nature should be expected to accompany this sweeping geostrategic expansion, "especially [from] the oceanic direction." These interrelated factors, in turn, offer a rationale for further security development in a manner that is likely to provide a continued rationale for concerted qualitative and quantitative development of the PLAN for years to come:

> Because our at-sea sovereignty and interests have frequently come under intrusions, while intensification in the crises may very possibly ignite conflicts or war, we need to form into a powerful and strong Two Oceans layout in order to face the crises that may possibly erupt. Therefore, we should focus on maintaining expansion in the national interests, defend the at-sea interests, and rely upon the home territory to reasonably and appropriately expand the strategic space toward the Two Oceans region.[15]

Emerging Far-Seas Missions

Accordingly, China is enacting a maritime theater concept that provides a focus for the PLAN extending across the Indo-Pacific and beyond. Relevant missions include the following.

Protecting overseas interests and the rights and interests of Chinese nationals. The massive "going out" abroad of PRC passport holders in recent years to pursue resources and wealth on land and sea creates new interests and vulnerabilities, particularly in the form of growing risks to their life and property. Overseas PLAN rescue missions assumed "a new precedent" with the service's limited role in the 2010 Libya evacuation. *The Science of Military Strategy* holds that "protecting national overseas interests and the rights of

---

[14] Academy of Military Sciences, *The Science of Military Strategy*, 247.

[15] Ibid., 246–47.

citizens and expatriates will become a regular strategic mission of the navy." The 2015 defense white paper places unprecedented emphasis on having the PLA "safeguard the security of China's overseas interests" and the PLAN engage in "far seas protection."[16]

Protecting maritime transportation security. This reflects an outer layer of Chinese maritime interests and effort ranging far beyond the near seas. Sea lanes are regarded as "the 'lifeline' of China's economic and social development." Since December 2008, threats from nonstate actors such as pirates have been addressed effectively by the PLAN's continuous Gulf of Aden escort task forces, but the additional concern that "once a maritime crisis or war occurs, China's sea transport lanes could be cut off " is much harder to address. Accordingly, the authors predict, "the navy's future missions in protecting SLOCs and ensuring the safety of maritime transportation will be very arduous."[17]

Protecting the security of international sea space. In fulfilling the goal promulgated in a report from the 18th Chinese Communist Party (CCP) National Congress to "build China into a maritime power," the PLAN is also charged with safeguarding "international sea security" in increasingly numerous and diverse ways under the rubric of "harmonious oceans." This will help China not only ensure its own specific security interests but also further assert itself more generally as "a major power with global influence" that is credited with "fulfilling its international responsibilities."[18] On a related note, the PLAN is charged with multifarious military operations other than war, whose missions must reflect the diversity of the threats they are designed to address. In particular, the authors of *The Science of Military Strategy* close their navy-specific section by stressing that "China should fully use the international platform provided by the multinational far seas escort and joint rescue missions to continuously expand and deepen maritime security cooperation." Doing so "will gradually improve China's voice and influence in international maritime security affairs."[19] This relates to a larger emphasis in the 2015 defense white paper in wording echoing repeated statements by Xi: "The national security issues facing China encompass far more subjects, extend over a greater range, and cover a longer time span that at any time in the country's history." Accordingly, the PLA must embrace a "holistic view of national security" encompassing both traditional and nontraditional security and be prepared for full-spectrum operations, including peacetime probing

---

[16] Information Office of the State Council (PRC), *China's Military Strategy.*

[17] Academy of Military Sciences, *The Science of Military Strategy*, 210.

[18] Ibid., 209–12.

[19] Ibid., 215, 217–18.

and pressure, as well as "comprehensively manag[ing] crises" in addition to full-fledged combat readiness.[20]

To support these emerging missions, China is altering its naval force structure and deployment concepts. Carrier battle groups are envisioned to be at the core of the PLAN's future fleet, as "a strategic 'fist' for mobile operations at sea."[21] A progressive radiating of capabilities outward, and particularly southward, from mainland China, together with their consolidation and integration, will be underpinned by "strengthen[ing] construction of large and medium-sized ports and core airports focusing on strategic home ports to fulfill the stationing, mooring, and supply needs of carriers, strategic nuclear submarines, and heavy destroyer-escort formations." These "strategic prepositioning" efforts are clearly underway in the form of Chinese port development in the greater Indian Ocean region, particularly with China's establishment of its first overseas naval support facility in Djibouti.

New Chinese Waves

As China moves farther into the two oceans, even the next layer of ripples—throughout maritime Southeast Asia, across the Indian Ocean, into the Red Sea, and down Africa's east coast—overlaps geographically with the seven imperially sponsored voyages of Admiral Zheng He (conducted in 1405–33) and enduring Chinese interests.[22] The Mongols and later the Ming intervened militarily in places like Java and Sri Lanka. The show of naval force to get Malacca to trade could also be seen today as a form of gunboat diplomacy.[23] "Today's global and regional trading networks and China's gravitational pull on world trade are very much akin to the late Ming," Andrew Wilson notes, which suggests that "maritime China in the twenty-first century will look much more like China in the sixteenth century than China of the recent past.... [T]here is ample historical precedent for China as a major sea power, an innovator in nautical technology, and a significant player in East and Southeast Asia as well as in the Indian Ocean."[24]

---

[20] Information Office of the State Council (PRC), *China's Military Strategy*.

[21] Academy of Military Sciences, *The Science of Military Strategy*, 213–15.

[22] Edward L. Dreyer, *Zheng He: China and the Oceans in the Early Ming Dynasty, 1405–1433* (London: Pearson, 2006).

[23] Yuan-kang Wang, *Harmony and War: Confucian Culture and Chinese Power Politics* (New York: Columbia University Press, 2010); Geoffrey Wade, ed., *China and Southeast Asia*, vols. 1–6 (New York: Routledge, 2009); and Geoffrey Wade, "The Zheng He Voyages: A Reassessment," *Journal of the Malaysian Branch of the Royal Asiatic Society* 78, no. 1 (2005): 37–58.

[24] Andrew R. Wilson, "The Maritime Transformation of Ming China," in *China Goes to Sea: Maritime Transformation in Comparative Historical Perspective*, ed. Andrew S. Erickson, Lyle J. Goldstein, and Carnes Lord (Annapolis: Naval Institute Press, 2009), 242.

In the foreign policy, geoeconomic, and geostrategic realms, operationalizing Xi's grand strategy involves making China great again abroad while supporting its internal development. The vision for these ambitions is encapsulated by his signature BRI project, which is focused primarily on infrastructure development to encourage greater regional integration and connectivity in Eurasia. In a sign that the international and domestic pieces of Xi's grand strategy are linked, BRI is arguably at least as much (if not more) about supporting domestic growth and stabilizing border regions as it is about gaining influence in distant places. Nevertheless, the initiative has global economic, political, and security implications. BRI encompasses most of the world, albeit in different layers of prioritization and functionality: (1) a Silk Road Economic Belt from China through Eurasia to Europe, (2) a 21st Century Maritime Silk Road through Southeast Asia and the Indian Ocean to Africa, the Middle East, and beyond; and (3) a "Polar Silk Road."[25]

Poor in people but rich in resources, the polar regions merit particular attention. China seeks to join the United States as the only other nation capable of comprehensive presence, activities, and influence in both the Arctic and Antarctic.[26] In keeping with Xi's grand strategy, China has a timetable for polar development that corresponds to his two centenary rubric. In the Arctic, China seeks maximum access and influence as an outside actor. Primarily a maritime domain, the Arctic will increasingly offer a shortened summer shipping SLOC, helping China reduce reliance on such potential chokepoints as the Malacca Strait. "By 2030," the U.S. National Intelligence Council projects, "it will be possible to transit both the Northern and Northwest Passage for about 110 days per year, with about 45 days easily navigable."[27] Eager to increase access and influence, China is investing heavily across the Arctic. It may already lead Arctic FDI, and its FDI constitutes 5.7% of Iceland's GDP and 11.6% of Greenland's GDP.[28] It is becoming a major partner for smaller, sparsely populated Arctic nations, where its funding, training of host nation officials, and supply of foreign labor could have tremendous impact. With a population of only 56,000, limited infrastructure but tremendous resources, the U.S. Armed Forces' northernmost installation at Thule Air Base, and aspirations for independence, Greenland is particularly

---

[25] Joel Wuthnow, *Chinese Perspectives on the Belt and Road Initiative: Strategic Rationales, Risks, and Implications*, China Strategic Perspectives, no. 12 (Washington, D.C.: National Defense University Press, 2017); and Zhang Yunbi and Zhang Yue, "Xi Backs Building of Polar Silk Road," *China Daily*, November 2, 2017, http://www.chinadaily.com.cn/world/cn_eu/2017-11/02/content_34007511.htm.

[26] Russia is a first-rank power in the Arctic but not in the Antarctic.

[27] *Global Trends 2030: Alternative Worlds* (Washington, D.C.: National Intelligence Council, 2012), 68.

[28] Mark E. Rosen and Cara B. Thuringer, "Unconstrained Foreign Direct Investment: An Emerging Challenge to Arctic Security," CNA, November 2017, 33, 54–55, https://www.cna.org/cna_files/pdf/COP-2017-U-015944-1Rev.pdf.

susceptible to Chinese incentives.[29] China's extensive investments in Arctic port infrastructure enhance its influence and could facilitate PLAN access.[30] In 2016, China established its first overseas facility to receive remote-sensing satellite data in Kiruna, Sweden. This "North Pole" ground station is a key component of its global surveillance network.[31] Beijing depicts its burgeoning polar activities selectively and ambiguously, heretofore attracting little notice outside specialized professional communities that interact minimally.

Nevertheless, China's development as a polar great power is now enshrined in the country's first-ever Arctic white paper as a critical maritime component of Xi's grand strategy and will critically shape the emerging new geopolitical order and the way it is governed.[32] Beijing regards the polar regions—Antarctica in particular—as vital domains important for fishing and replete with energy and minerals and as a permissive zone for the expansion of Chinese influence and creation of norms. Unencumbered by national borders in Antarctica, China is rapidly enhancing its presence and has established five base sites. The majority are arrayed synergistically in a pie-wedge-shaped "east Antarctica sector" that "looks remarkably like the triangle-shaped territorial claims of the claimant states in Antarctica."[33] They include the continent's highest point, Dome Argus, which could support flexible aircraft flight paths as well as long-distance communications and surveillance. To end reliance on foreign airports in Antarctica, China is developing its own facility to serve its first polar plane, the Xueying 601.[34] It thus appears to be staking out a position that facilitates science and communications now and greater geopolitical influence over time.

Overseas Power Projection: Power Lags Distance

This section examines the specific benchmarks and implications for Chinese naval power projection to support China's growing interests overseas via the missions discussed in the previous section. Historically, the country

---

[29] Rebecca Pincus and Walter A. Berbrick, "Gray Zones in a Blue Arctic: Grappling with China's Growing Influence," War on the Rocks, October 24, 2018, https://warontherocks.com/2018/10/gray-zones-in-a-blue-arctic-grappling-with-chinas-growing-influence.

[30] Thus far, aspirations have lagged reality: some prospective deals have been blocked by national authorities in various Arctic nations, while others have fallen through.

[31] "China's 1st Ground Satellite Receiving Station Overseas Starts Trials," Xinhua, December 15, 2016, http://www.xinhuanet.com/english/2016-12/15/c_135908732.htm.

[32] Information Office of the State Council (PRC), China's Arctic Policy (Beijing, January 2018), https://www.chinadailyasia.com/articles/188/159/234/1516941033919.html.

[33] Anne-Marie Brady, China as a Polar Great Power (Cambridge: Cambridge University Press, 2017), 159.

[34] "China to Build Its First Antarctic Airport in November," People's Daily, October 29, 2018, http://en.people.cn/n3/2018/1029/c90000-9512711.html.

has never enjoyed a sustained overseas presence, yet the specific drivers of change outlined in the first section are already motivating unprecedented extroversion on China's part. Beijing is increasingly seeking to develop a PLA that can deploy not only in China's immediate periphery but also throughout the Indo-Pacific and around the globe.

The PLA's foremost power-projection capabilities belong to the PLA Air Force and PLAN Aviation. Now that the force structure to support near-seas objectives has largely been achieved and China's shipbuilding and aviation industries have demonstrated the capability to consistently produce advanced products in most respects, an effort is underway to gradually increase the numbers of some of the more successful platforms that could be useful for far-seas operations.[35] These include area-air-defense destroyers and frigates, replenishment vessels, and fighter aircraft.

China's future force posture is likely to advance along a predefined path that focuses on the ability to sustain high-intensity combat under increasingly contested and uncertain conditions at ever-greater distances from mainland China. To realize Xi's vision overseas, the PLAN and its sister services must master, successively, what I and others have termed "extended blue water counterintervention, limited expeditionary, and global expeditionary" operations.[36] Accordingly, the PLA must effect a broader transformation from traditional "active defense" to a more comprehensive maneuver warfare based on "integrated system of systems operations," akin to the United States' pursuit of network-centric warfare to support blue water operations.[37] Aircraft carriers are envisioned to "form maritime operations systems" (*xingcheng haishang zuozhan tixi*) to fill strategic space as part of a move toward a joint, integrated, networked concept to support "information systems-based systems operations" (*jiyu xinxi xitong de tixi zuozhan*).[38] While Western strategists would view such developments—to the extent that they

---

[35] For an overview of China's burgeoning naval shipbuilding capabilities, see Gabe Collins and Eric Anderson, "Resources for China's State Shipbuilders: Now Including Global Capital Markets," in *Chinese Naval Shipbuilding: An Ambitious and Uncertain Course*, ed. Andrew S. Erickson (Annapolis: Naval Institute Press, 2016).

[36] Ely Ratner et al., "More Willing and Able: Charting China's International Security Activism," Center for a New American Security, May 2015, 37, https://s3.amazonaws.com/files.cnas.org/documents/ CNAS_ChinaMoreWillingAndAble_Final.pdf; and Andrew S. Erickson, "China's Strategic Objectives at Sea," in *Asia-Pacific Regional Security Assessment 2017: Key Developments and Trends*, ed. Tim Huxley and William Choong (London: International Institute for Strategic Studies, 2017), 37–50.

[37] Nan Li, "China's Evolving Naval Strategy and Capabilities in the Hu Jintao Era," in *Assessing the People's Liberation Army in the Hu Jintao Era*, ed. Roy Kamphausen, David Lai, and Travis Tanner (Carlisle: U.S. Army War College Press, 2014), 257–300.

[38] See, for example, Lin Dong, "Jiyu xinxi xitong de junshi liliang tixi de fazhan linian" [Development Concepts on Information Systems-Based Military Force Systems], *China Military Science* 1 (2011): 22; and Li Dapeng, Tan Lezu, and Yang Genyuan, "Yujingji zhiyuan xia jianting biandui wangluo hua xietong fan dao yanjiu" [Warship Formation Network-Centric Cooperative Antimissile under Early Warning Aircraft Support], *Modern Defense Technology* 41, no. 1 (2013): 9–14.

prove successful in practice—as simply what the United States and other advanced navies have long pursued, this would represent a difficult, expensive, long-term effort for the PLAN.[39]

Two postures represent the low-end and high-end versions of a regional blue water defensive and offensive navy and accompanying air forces. Extended blue water counterintervention implies the ability to deny access by holding opposing forces at risk up to a distance of over one thousand nautical miles from China's territorial waters and airspace. By contrast, going beyond counterintervention to proactively conduct high-level opposed noncombatant contingency and evacuation operations, as well as possibly some form of maritime interdiction operations, in or above far seas (the western Pacific and the Indian Ocean) would require a limited expeditionary posture with all the aforementioned capabilities. At a minimum, such a force would be capable of distant low-intensity conflict, freedom of navigation operations, carrier operations, and far-seas anti-submarine, anti-surface, and anti-air warfare. The capabilities needed to support air-power operations include aerial refueling, over-water flight, extended-duration maritime patrol and intelligence collection, anti-ship missile strike, and strategic bombing.[40] Given sufficient Chinese prioritization, acquiring these capabilities before 2030 should be feasible.

Developing the capabilities for a global expeditionary or "global blue-water type" posture, as Chinese planners categorize today's U.S. Navy, and corresponding air operations will be far more demanding. Beyond the previously listed capabilities, a blue water expeditionary posture would require some form of limited-intensity global presence and the ability to surge combat-ready forces in or above core strategic far-seas areas (e.g., the Persian Gulf). A full global expeditionary posture, maximal in scope and intensity, would require both this and the robust presence of combat-ready naval or air forces in all major strategic regions of the world. The ability to engage in major combat operations would confer the comprehensive capability to contest for maritime supremacy and engage in distant joint forcible-entry operations and amphibious assault. Moving from denial to control requires a much broader range of capabilities, even for operations within the same geographic area.

At present, the PLA remains incapable of conducting most aspects of far-seas operations against a capable opponent, including force projection, sustainment, capacity, coordination, defense, and opposed intervention.

---

[39] For a Chinese study of best-practice examples in the history of U.S. carrier operations, see Zhao Guangzhi and Li Daguang, "Hangmu zhandou qun de bian cheng yu yunyong" [The Formation and Use of Carrier Battle Groups], *Defense Science and Technology Industry* 10 (2012): 20–22.

[40] Phillip C. Saunders and Erik Quam, "Future Force Structure of the Chinese Air Force," in *Right-Sizing the People's Liberation Army: Exploring the Contours of China's Military*, ed. Roy Kamphausen and Andrew Scobell (Carlisle: U.S. Army War College, 2007), 381.

Although it is learning from the trails blazed by other major sea powers,[41] emulating the most capable sea powers involves demanding dynamics in which resource requirements increase with distance in exponential fashion.

Force Projection, Sustainment, and Port Access

One major challenge to projecting power is the "tyranny of distance."[42] To cover greater geographic areas while fulfilling existing missions, China must increase production of major ships. Steadily increasing force deployment to distant areas is slowly raising familiarity and readiness. To project air power across far greater ocean spaces, the PLAN is gradually developing deck aviation, with increased helicopter use and every large modern surface combatant capable of embarking at least one helicopter.[43] To enhance long-range air power, China is developing aircraft to operate off carriers and possibly eventually overseas land bases, aerial refueling capabilities, and related doctrine and training programs.

Building a successful carrier-centric navy capable of long-distance power projection is extremely demanding and expensive, however. For long-distance deployments, a total of three to four carriers (together with their accompanying coterie of protective submarines, surface ships, and aircraft and supportive replenishment ships) will be necessary for every carrier presence equivalent that China wishes to maintain in a given region. In other words, the farther out the PLAN goes, the more the ratio of total to deployed carrier groups will increase. Specifically, PLAN analysts commonly cite the need to possess three carrier groups overall to maintain one consistently conducting missions at sea. Yet the U.S. Navy has learned an even more demanding rule of thumb through unparalleled experience: four carrier groups in total for every one conducting missions at sea. Even this gold-standard force confronts tough choices and has long gapped its Mediterranean presence in order to meet more pressing requirements in the Central Command and Indo-Pacific Command areas of operations.[44]

---

[41] Christopher D. Yung et al., *China's Out of Area Naval Operations: Case Studies, Trajectories, Obstacles, and Potential Solutions*, China Strategic Perspective, no. 3 (Washington, D.C.: National Defense University Press, 2010), 2, http://ndupress.ndu.edu/Portals/68/Documents/stratperspective/china/ChinaPerspectives-3.pdf.

[42] Unless otherwise specified, this and the next several paragraphs draw on ibid., 19–21, 32, 40–46.

[43] Andrew S. Erickson, "A Work in Progress: China's Development of Carrier Strike," *Jane's Navy International*, June 19, 2014.

[44] Roland J. Yardley et al., *A Methodology for Estimating the Effect of Aircraft Carrier Operational Cycles on the Maintenance Industrial Base* (Santa Monica: RAND Corporation, 2007); Roland J. Yardley et al., *Increasing Aircraft Carrier Forward Presence: Changing the Length of the Maintenance Cycle* (Santa Monica: RAND Corporation, 2008); and U.S. Government Accountability Office, "Navy Aircraft Carriers: Cost-Effectiveness of Conventionally and Nuclear-Powered Carriers," August 1998.

A related difficulty is sustaining extended-duration missions. As the PLAN ventures farther out, it must bring a greater logistics train with it. Driven in part by naval operations in the Gulf of Aden, China is already pursuing several enablers of long-duration operations. Its capacity to supply and replenish vessels at sea has increased rapidly since the first antipiracy task force in late 2008. A network of China Ocean Shipping Company suppliers and husbanding agents enables resupply in foreign ports. The PLAN also has made great progress in managing stocks, preserving perishables, and generating potable water. Yet supporting more than limited long-range operations would require additional, improved replenishment ships. China's shipbuilding industry has already started to build such vessels and has the capacity to build them far more rapidly, if requested. A sprawling global infrastructure supported by dozens of negotiated agreements allows the U.S. military to move parts globally. China would presumably require the same network to support similar operations. Access to neutral repair facilities is not politically controversial—Pakistan, for example, has already offered such services in Karachi—but developing high-caliber maintenance capabilities far from home will be expensive. China is pursuing access to neutral ports for supplying the PLAN but not yet to neutral airfields.

The establishment of overseas military bases is another option for equipping, servicing, and other support beyond replenishment, albeit one with lingering political costs and risk of operational vulnerability. Access to overseas facilities is already being realized to a modest extent in practice. The PLAN utilizes a network of access points, including its first overseas naval supply facility in Djibouti. The nature, scope, and configuration of the emerging architecture of China's access to overseas facilities will offer particularly important indications of its intentions with regard to far-seas operations. This architecture will be foreshadowed, in turn, by the PLAN's operational patterns and port calls; for instance, numerous port calls presaged China's establishment of a permanent facility in Djibouti. **Appendix 1** details potential ports of interest, with a particular focus on the Indian Ocean region where the PLAN has called extensively and for which substantial open source data is readily available.

Appendix 2 places China's evolving port network in an international historical context. As with force-projection capabilities, China has a continuum of progressively robust and demanding options for overseas port infrastructure and access.

Already, the PLAN has extensive experience calling on ports around the world, which enables a basic level of global presence in unchallenged peacetime conditions. Additionally, it may benefit from a global network of PRC-funded commercial shipping and ports infrastructure with a scope and dynamism with some historical similarities with the Dutch East India Company.[45] This state-owned and state-funded juggernaut has engulfed such locations of potential strategic relevance as Piraeus, Greece, and is impressive in many respects. But even these strong commercial alliances and sinews do not translate directly into reliable great-power naval capabilities in the far seas; their influence may prove unreliable precisely when it is needed most.

To truly enable reliable PLAN operations in contested or wartime conditions, China must supplement transshipment points and entrepôts with militarily-capable facilities that it is fully capable of supplying—either through local resources and contracts, from robust regional hubs, or from farther afield—and defending. Moreover, an undefended carrier group would be lost in a maritime conflict without the protection of submarines, which are only sustainable with a forward base. With respect to these requirements, China's first overseas base in Djibouti represents the bare minimum, and it is unclear how Beijing would defend it from serious supply disruption or high-intensity attack. The base's isolation may explain why the Pentagon anticipates that "China may establish additional logistics facilities over the next decade" that could "further extend and sustain regional and global operations."[46] The Pentagon specifically projects that "China will seek to establish additional military bases in countries with which it has a longstanding friendly relationship and similar strategic interests, such as Pakistan, and in which there is a precedent for hosting foreign militaries."[47]

Yet such efforts, groundbreaking for Beijing as they would be, would remain far from the naval port network that major sea powers have needed to establish to ensure their ability to project major naval power under all conditions. Given favorable conditions and sufficient effort, China could reach such a status by its 2035 milestone, but the costs and challenges would be formidable. Soviet-style establishment and maintenance of key nodes would be still more time-consuming and difficult. While Beijing could hope to fund such an expensive system more sustainably than Moscow did, it is starting significantly farther behind the ally curve and would be very hard-pressed to create the reliable network of alliances and access that the Soviet Navy enjoyed, let alone that which the United Kingdom and France have developed through their colonial history and the United States has achieved through decades of intensive engagement and investment. The Pentagon emphasizes that "China's overseas military basing will be constrained by the willingness

---

[45] Christopher Odea, "Ships of State?" *Naval War College Review* 72, no. 1 (2019).

[46] U.S. Department of Defense, *Annual Report to Congress*, 67, 70.

[47] Ibid., 112.

of potential host countries to support a PLA presence."[48] Absent a major new constellation of bases that require strong host-nation partnerships and tremendous investment, it would be very difficult for the PLAN to achieve a permanent large-scale presence beyond the western Pacific, Indian Ocean, and Persian Gulf. Under such limitations, the PLAN could make excursions into the Mediterranean Sea and polar regions, but it would likely lack the logistics train to maintain a constant presence in those far seas.

As for the possibility of China someday acquiring a global network of bases on a par with that of the United States, this scenario is worth considering theoretically but is unrealistic. Besides being constrained by its unshakable geographic liabilities, China does not benefit from the diverse array of reliable treaty allies that permitted Washington to amass, and thus far sustain, such a remarkable constellation of global support. During the Cold War, for instance, the United States operated from submarine bases in Holy Loch (Scotland), La Maddalena (Italy), and Guam and also enjoyed ad hoc access to additional bases such as Faslane (United Kingdom).

Coordination

To detect, report, and direct activities over the two oceans and beyond, China is developing an increasingly complete and integrated command, control, communication, computers, intelligence, surveillance, and reconnaissance (C4ISR) network. Ground-based (radar, electronic surveillance, and AIS stations) and sea-based ISR systems can provide persistent, accurate surveillance with massive data transmission to around one hundred nautical miles from shore. Farther afield, however, patrol ships and air- and space-based systems are required despite their intermittent coverage. Even with ongoing improvements, C4ISR—particularly the critical architecture coordination and data fusion components—is likely to remain one of the lagging enablers for China's far-seas operations.

Space systems are often tailored for specific signals transmission, area coverage, and operational parameters. Both space-based capabilities and ground-based counterspace systems are currently optimized to support near-seas counterintervention. Satellites with expanded geographic coverage are especially important to support expeditionary operations farther afield for which fewer alternatives are available. China is rapidly developing a constellation of remote-sensing, communications, and data-relay satellites second only to that of the United States in aggregate scope and capability. Its Beidou (Compass) positioning, navigation, and timing satellite constellation achieved regional coverage in 2013 and is on track to become

---

[48] U.S. Department of Defense, *Annual Report to Congress*, 112.

only the third network to provide global coverage by 2020. As part of its Digital Earth initiative, one of sixteen national strategic technological megaprojects under the State Council–sponsored Medium- and Long-Term Plan for the Development of Science and Technology (2006–20), Beijing plans to significantly enhance its land- and space-based remote-sensing architecture to include polar facilities. Currently having only four overseas ground stations, China plans to establish "network nodes" at the North and South Poles and in Brazil as part of a "Digital Earth scientific platform" by 2030.[49] Meanwhile, it continues to maintain the world's second-largest fleet of intelligence-gathering, surveying, and space-event support ships. Survey vessels, which typically precede naval operations, are studying relevant routes in the South Pacific and Indian Ocean.[50] Yuanwang-class space-event support ships, which have operated far from China since 1980, facilitate a wide range of space-based operations and occasionally engage in naval diplomacy. They may also gather intelligence and could conceivably facilitate a range of far-seas operations.[51]

Defense

Deploying increasing numbers of assets farther away creates new vulnerabilities for China. To have deterrence or operational value in a crisis or wartime situation, assets must be defendable. To address this challenge, China will need to develop its extremely limited open-ocean antisubmarine warfare (ASW) capabilities by adding quiet long-range nuclear submarines, maritime patrol aircraft, and helicopters. Constructing nuclear-attack submarines and deployment of additional units of these and other platforms with significant demonstrated ASW capabilities, such as helicopters and fixed-wing aircraft, can help greatly. Just as manifold factors optimize diesel submarines for littoral operations, the speed and range (and relative stealth within these demanding performance parameters) of nuclear submarines, together with their ability to shoot formidable anti-ship weapons, make them especially useful for defense of blue water SLOCs. However, their cost and need for highly trained crews and sophisticated maintenance facilities make nuclear submarines worth acquiring in substantial numbers only if China prioritizes SLOC defense,

---

[49] Huadong Guo and Ji Wu, eds., *Space Science and Technology in China: A Roadmap to 2050* (Beijing: Science Press, 2010), 76.

[50] Ryan D. Martinson and Peter A. Dutton, "China's Distant-Ocean Survey Activities: Implications for U.S. National Security," Naval War College, China Maritime Studies Institute, China Maritime Report, no. 3, November 2018.

[51] Andrew Erickson and Amy Chang, "China's Navigation in Space: What New Approaches Will China's Space Tracking Take?" *Proceedings*, April 2012, 42–47.

an extremely demanding task that requires a credible capability to destroy military and commercial shipping.

Opposed Intervention

Operating in a hostile environment remains one of the most sensitive and difficult areas for China. Even at the low end, such operations bring complex questions of sovereignty and the risk of civilian casualties and other political vulnerabilities. Moreover, the capabilities to conduct combat air patrol and establish air superiority from carrier aircraft that are required for high-intensity operations will likely take years to develop. China also has not invested substantial resources or effort in developing out-of-area ASW capabilities and cannot easily use closer-in compensators such as sound surveillance systems.

For all these reasons, there is currently no immediately visible pathway for China to conduct joint forcible-entry operations or amphibious assault in scenarios outside of the Taiwan Strait or parts of the South China Sea. There is also currently no apparent or foreseeable strategic or operational rationale for Chinese forces to conduct such missions outside of a near-seas context. Even assuming a very robust "going out" by China into the world in all areas of the capabilities spectrum (diplomacy, information, military, and economic), employment of military platforms in force projection will trail behind actual capabilities. Much of the country's overseas activities and presence will be "lower end" in nature. However, China may derive additional power from the perception that it could soon have the capability and intention to do more, if it does not already.

Alternative Futures

As discussed in the first section, China's priorities in the maritime sphere can be mapped as radiating geographic layers of progressively diminishing focus extending from the near seas to the far seas to the far oceans. There is still considerable uncertainty, however, as to how China will attempt to realize its maritime goals over the next several decades. Assessing its prospects for developing distant bases, for example, requires a multi-decade outlook.

The Indian Ocean region is likely to be an area of development for quite some time to come. In that area alone, there are many uncertainties about speed, scope, and even potential setbacks. A study by the National Defense University emphasizes the challenges in predicting China's long-term trajectory:

> First, even if some national leaders plan beyond a few years, that information is not readily available to outside observers. Second, it is extremely difficult to

forecast the security environment in which that trajectory will occur in the upcoming years. Third, China is entering uncharted territory with regard to out of area operations, so its future direction (long-term trajectory) is somewhat unpredictable. The best guide to possible future Chinese directions is to study the experiences of other countries as they began to conduct more ambitious out of area operations.[52]

Thus, it is helpful to consider multiple scenarios. This section employs the alternative scenarios methodology used in many U.S. government studies to consider three force postures looking out five, ten, and twenty years: high-end, low-end, and retrenchment.

High-End Scenario

Under a high-end scenario, specific potential new naval dynamics might well include the following. China rapidly pursues comprehensive efforts to defend its burgeoning overseas interests, with no insuperable obstacles. The PLAN would have sophisticated platforms and well-trained personnel. Supporting them would be technologies developed through disruptive innovation, particularly in the space, missile, and defense electronics sectors, as well as in specific frontier technologies where the United States and other established economies have had less history of leadership (e.g., hypersonics, nanotechnology, and additive manufacturing). China would have the world's largest civilian and military shipbuilding industry by tonnage, capable of building sophisticated vessels of all types. Its aviation industry would finally be able to develop and deploy the most advanced systems, including aeroengines. Such advances, in turn, could support robust arms sales networks and growing influence to help forge stronger partnerships, including with such pivotal states as Turkey and Saudi Arabia.

Fielding new systems thus derived could enable the PLA to hold at risk U.S. land-, sea-, and air-based forces not only in the western Pacific but also in Hawaii and manifold overseas locations. Chinese platforms would be able to engage in regular high-intensity intelligence gathering even as far away as just off the U.S. west coast. While Washington accepts such activities as a matter of policy, their intensification would entail a significant shift in bilateral military activities, which have heretofore been concentrated near China.

China would rapidly advance its geostrategic objectives closer to home and become a great maritime power on a par with the United States with global commercial networks and robust military presence and capabilities. BRI would continue to succeed, reordering key areas in Eurasia and beyond both economically and geostrategically and commanding the PLAN's

---

[52] Yung et al., *China's Out of Area Naval Operations*, 6.

comprehensive protection. In addition to Djibouti, China might develop robust overseas basing capacity in the Indo-Pacific, the Mediterranean Sea, and the polar regions (in the last case, with a focus on C4ISR, presence, and specialized protection of resource extraction and transportation). It is impossible to predict exactly where China would establish naval bases, but a desired geographic distribution might include such regions as the central Indian Ocean (e.g., Maldives or Sri Lanka) and the South Pacific (e.g., Vanuatu or Fiji). In addition, it could establish a land base in Central or Southwest Asia (e.g., Afghanistan). Beijing might also increase its influence in the Indo-Pacific by covertly funding protest movements in Okinawa, Guam, and Hawaii or by using aid and presence operations to complicate the renewal of the Compact of Free Association, an international agreement between the United States and three Pacific Island nations (the Federated States of Micronesia, the Marshall Islands, and Palau) currently scheduled to expire in 2023.[53] Assuming progress in these areas, China might then pursue enhanced access or basing in Greece (with Piraeus as a key anchor point for BRI), Pacific South America (e.g., Ecuador or perhaps Peru), Scandinavia (e.g., Iceland or perhaps a more autonomous Greenland), and Antarctica.

China could advance tremendously in "new strategic frontiers," where it enjoys particular room for maneuver as rival powers struggle to expend the resources required for competition in a relatively new, unestablished arena. China would achieve a more comprehensive, active presence around the world, including in areas of special strategic importance, such as the deepwater or seabed areas, outer space, and the Arctic and Antarctic. It might well become a great polar power with a Scandinavian base to support tracking and communications as well as commercial shipping in increasingly navigable Arctic sea lanes. Likewise, China could use a strategically positioned network of Antarctic bases for covert military tracking, communications, and presence as well as for geopolitical leverage as it strives to renegotiate the 1991 Protocol on Environmental Protection to the Antarctic Treaty when it comes up for renewal in 2048 in order to open Antarctica to large-scale energy and mineral exploitation.[54] It is not entirely far-fetched to imagine Beijing offering Greenland finances for greater autonomy or independence from Denmark in exchange for enabling Chinese resource access. China would also develop a robust network of space-based assets and global ground-based tracking stations. The country would thus greatly reduce its dependence on its fleet of space-event support ships, even as it increased its deepwater presence and seabed exploitation capabilities.

---

[53] Thomas R. Matelski, "America's Micronesia Problem," *Diplomat*, February 19, 2016, https://thediplomat.com./2016/02/americas-micronesia-problem..

[54] For more information on reviewing the treaty, see Brady, *China as a Polar Great Power*, 29.

Low-End Scenario

In a low-end scenario, by contrast, Beijing would struggle to further its geostrategic objectives closer to home and to succeed with BRI abroad. Mounting resource constraints, financial and otherwise, could impose challenges as China's growth rate in economic and overall national power slowed in an S-curved trajectory. BRI might prove unprofitable and unaffordable, leaving port infrastructure saddled with unsustainable debt. China would limit overseas military power projection and would not develop robust dedicated basing access beyond Djibouti. Instead, it would continue to rely heavily on its fleet of space-event support ships.[55] Its activities in new frontier domains would be focused more narrowly on supporting specific military and economic objectives.

Retrenchment Scenario

Finally, a retrenchment scenario would entail an outright reversal of China's power-distance gradient to prioritize core interests close to home or even domestic issues. At present, the CCP has significant resources at its disposal, achievements with which to secure popular legitimacy, and narratives to exploit should it feel pressured to shore up support. In a worst-case scenario, however, the CCP's survival might be severely threatened, a situation that in the party's view would justify the mobilization of all available resources in its defense. Beyond the personal risks to Xi that have accrued from his consolidation of power at the expense of many rival elites, China is ruled by a Leninist party that has linked its legitimacy to the continued delivery of exceptional economic and nationalistic achievements. As the CCP itself fears greatly, policy failure or opposition close to home could rapidly undermine the party's rule. It therefore dedicates tremendous resources to domestic surveillance, security, and propaganda, a trend that will likely accelerate with future problems.

Besides these domestic economic and political challenges, Taiwan's status, the territorial dispute with Japan, and possibly other disputed sovereignty claims could challenge the party's nationalist credentials and motivate it to order military action. However, there are no core interests beyond China's immediate periphery that could readily force the CCP to choose between distant overseas concerns and the overwhelming prioritization of domestic stability and security close to home. If something had to give, therefore, it would likely be overseas force posture and operations.

---

[55] Erickson and Chang, "China's Navigation in Space."

Implications for the Region and the United States

The previous section considered multiple scenarios for China's projection of capabilities and influence along a power-distance gradient with sharply diminishing returns. In the high-end scenario, a growing network of overseas bases, facilities, and access points would underwrite Chinese maritime power and influence. Particularly if Washington fails to get its finances and focus in order, China might even challenge the United States for naval hegemony in the Indo-Pacific. The National Intelligence Council observes that "as global economic power has shifted to Asia, the Indo-Pacific is emerging as the dominant international waterway of the 21st century." It warns that "U.S. naval hegemony over the world's key sea lanes, in this and other oceans, will fade as China's blue water navy strengthens. This could beg the question of which power is best-positioned to construct maritime coalitions to police the commons and secure universal freedom of passage."[56]

Whatever Beijing's actions in coming decades, they will almost certainly be informed by a foreign policy calculus that is far more multidimensional and flexible in practice than its deftly diversified approaches to date. Such evolution could entail increased security support to the UN and increased Chinese organization of bilateral and multilateral security arrangements and exercises. This concluding section considers the implications of China's pursuit of its maritime interests for the region and the United States.

Implications for the Region

There is a geographic gradient to the challenges China may pose to the United States and its regional allies and partners. The United States would be most threatened by an increasingly powerful and assertive China, whereas immediate neighbors—particularly those lacking significant sea buffers—would face tremendous challenges whether China remains highly centralized or suffers internal disarray. Regardless of the scenario that ultimately plays out, host and nearby nations and regions are likely to be affected considerably by relative power differentials: thriving autonomously on China's periphery is no easy task. A China whose growth slowed significantly and which decreased emphasis on overseas power projection would still be a large and powerful neighbor with nationalism likely sustaining sovereignty disputes along its periphery. Even a China convulsed by internal problems to the point of no longer being a potent unitary actor could still pose tremendous challenges to nearby nations, in part through its very lack of centralized control. If, on the other hand, a

---

[56] *Global Trends 2030*, 80.

stable China continues to achieve both rapid economic and military growth, it could attempt to increase its already significant economic partnerships and leverage with its neighbors while undermining the alliances and partnerships that they have long prioritized with the United States.

To undercut U.S. military capabilities and presence in the region, China would likely penetrate, surround, or further undermine key U.S. basing and access locations, starting along the first and second island chains running through Japan and Guam, respectively, as well as possibly extending to what some term a third island chain running through Hawaii. This is likely to include close monitoring of, and possible interference with, the Ronald Reagan Ballistic Missile Defense Test Site (formerly Kwajalein Missile Range) in the Marshall Islands. Beijing may go so far as making concerted attempts at eroding local support for basing in Okinawa, Guam, and Diego Garcia. If not countered effectively, such Chinese efforts could cause a geostrategic shift in which the island chains transition from being barriers to Chinese expansion to being barriers to U.S. access to support East Asian allies in military contingencies.

To the extent that it continues to focus farther afield, China is likely to develop close partners or quasi-allies that rely closely on it to further their (usually authoritarian) leaders' key goals. Nations of limited resources or geostrategic position such as Maldives, Sri Lanka, Vanuatu, Fiji, Greenland, Ecuador, Bolivia, or even Greece could become deeply beholden to Beijing and hence perceived as reliable—if demanding—supplicants.

Implications for the United States

To counter Chinese efforts to undermine the U.S. maritime presence in the Indo-Pacific, the United States and its regional allies and partners are likely to support nearby partners who allow access to counter Chinese activities and balance China's quasi-allies. While potential options are limited, in selected cases the United States could pursue enhanced or alternative basing and access. Possibilities include new basing or access in French Indian Ocean region territories to supplement or replace Diego Garcia and Bahrain should political developments compromise U.S. military access, new basing or access in Micronesia and the South Pacific to supplement Guam, and even enhanced polar capabilities based in Alaska or Antarctica.

Although China may significantly increase its geostrategic position, even under the most favorable scenario it will not achieve a "convergence of constraints" vis-à-vis the United States overall. Whatever its progress, for example, China will not succeed in fully escaping its geography. The United States as a maritime power operating on exterior lines generally faces the greatest challenges in Asia the more China focuses on its home region while operating on interior lines; on the other hand, the farther Beijing focuses outward overseas, the greater the U.S. opportunities. Moreover, China's centralized, brittle political system embodies risks that decentralized American democracy does not. Finally, the United States is poised to retain significant advantages in such areas as demographics and the environment.

In several significant areas, however, China may converge increasingly with the United States. Most importantly, based on the spate of development and deployment that has already given China the world's largest conventional ballistic missile force and is positioning it as a leader in the emerging field of hypersonics, within roughly a decade both China and the United States will likely be able to target each other's homelands with conventional long-range precision-strike weapons, thereby eliminating previous areas of sanctuary. This has significant implications for their deterrence relationship.

Moreover, for the first time since the Cold War, Washington must seriously consider possible setbacks to its own power-distance gradient—whether self-inflicted, systemic, or deliberately engineered by Beijing—and how to counter them. To mitigate this risk, Washington should tend to its alliances and partnerships, a unique strength and source of unparalleled influence and access required for global power projection. This network has long-standing affinities that Beijing would struggle to replicate and sustain with its more transactional approach to foreign policy. Additionally, particularly in worst-case scenarios, U.S. decision-makers must consider how to target Beijing's strong power-distance gradient to shape its behavior across a full spectrum of contingencies. To do so, planners must consider enduring technological imbalances and invest efficiently in capabilities to counter China's military counterintervention approaches while targeting its vulnerabilities. For the foreseeable future, it will generally be easier to attack with missiles than to defend against them, so the U.S. Navy should continue to rectify the relatively low, short-range anti-ship cruise missile loadouts on its vessels. The United States also should continue to build on its formidable advantages in undersea warfare, which remains an extremely difficult and expensive discipline to master.[57] Finally, its withdrawal from the 1987 Intermediate-Range Nuclear Forces Treaty opens up options for U.S. development and peacetime and wartime forward deployment of new types of ground-based missiles with ranges between 500 and 5,500 kilometers, heretofore a loophole that China exploited unilaterally. Measures such as these can help the United States recalibrate the power-distance gradient vis-à-vis China in its favor.

---

[57] Andrew S. Erickson, "China's Naval Modernization: Implications and Recommendations," testimony before the House Armed Services Committee Seapower and Projection Forces Subcommittee, Washington, D.C., December 11, 2013.

APPENDIX 1   Selected Indian Ocean region ports and PLAN access

Country	Port	Maximum draft (meters)	Level of replenishment/ repair facilities	Development/significance	Most frequent nature of visits
Bangladesh	Chittagong	9.2	Longshore, ship repairs (limited), marine railroad (small), dry dock (medium)	Private repair yards available; dry dock available for vessels up to 16,500 deadweight tonnage (DWT); home to Bangladesh Navy's largest base and most of its fleet, including submarines	Replenish, overhaul, joint drills
Djibouti	Djibouti	18.0	Mobile cranes, floating cranes, longshore, electrical repair, navigation equipment, ship repairs (limited), marine railroad (medium), garbage disposal	Multiple foreign naval/military bases, including China's naval support facility; small repairs possible; container terminal phase-one construction completed; with the new Doraleh multipurpose port, plus the older Doraleh container terminal, the port can berth at least four container ships; major repair and replenishment facilities are expected soon	Replenish, overhaul
Maldives	Malé	19.2	Mechanical and electrical repairs, roll-on/roll-off facility, fresh water and marine diesel/gas/oil available	Three sub-ports; breakbulk, liquid, and multipurpose facilities; no dry dock or LNG facilities	Show of presence during a constitutional crisis
Myanmar	Kyaukpyu	4.8	Longshore, ship repairs (extremely limited)	Kyaukpyu deep-sea port on Maday Island by Than Zit River mouth; initiated in 2009, project will produce 91 berths and accommodate 300,000-ton oil tankers; shallow draft, problematic currents, rocky obstacles; navy facility for Myanmar's Danyawadi Naval Regional Command can host up to frigate-size vessels, has floating dry dock for smaller vessels	N/A

Appendix 1 continued

Country	Port	Maximum draft (meters)	Level of replenishment/ repair facilities	Development/significance	Most frequent nature of visits
Myanmar	Yangon	9.0	Repairs at dry dock, engineering works, roll-on/ roll-off facilities, bunkering by barge, fresh water at quay, garbage disposal	PLAN visits the 9-meter-deep Thilawa outer harbor downstream, not 8-meter-deep inner harbor by city	Friendly visits
Oman	Salalah	17.5	Longshore, electrical repair, navigation equipment, ship repairs (limited), marine railroad size (small), garbage disposal	Focus on transshipment container traffic; 800-meter turning basin	Replenish, overhaul
Pakistan	Gwadar	13.8	Control tower (footprint only), maintenance workshop (general), multiuse quay wall, vehicle servicing garage, laydown yard, bunkering fuel	Acquired by China Overseas Port Holdings Ltd. in 2013; hazardous cargo storage yard; desalination plant can supply 100,000 gallons/day to visiting ships; can berth at least two container ships; still being dredged, should accommodate around 20-meter draft once complete; yard and cranes could be used for loading weapons	N/A
	Karachi	13.0	Naval servicing and repair capabilities, including for nuclear submarines; dry dock facilities	PLAN's preferred Indian Ocean repair facility on the territory of close strategic partner; Karachi Shipyard and Engineering Works onsite; two dry docks available: 18,000/25,000 DWT; deepwater container terminal and other expansion underway	Friendly visits, joint drills, visits of conventional and nuclear submarines with tenders

Appendix 1 continued

Country	Port	Maximum draft (meters)	Level of replenishment/repair facilities	Development/significance	Most frequent nature of visits
Seychelles	Port Victoria	11.5	Longshore, electrical, ship repairs (limited), marine railroad (small), garbage disposal	Seychelles foreign minister invited China to establish antipiracy base; divers and underwater welding equipment available; dry-dock shipways available for vessels greater than 300 gross tonnage	Friendly visits
Singapore	Singapore	16.7	Electrical repair, ship repairs (major), dry dock (large), dirty ballast	World-class complex: one terminal, nine subports; military ports	Replenish, overhaul, friendly visits
	Colombo	16.0	Longshore, ship repairs (major), marine railroad (medium), dry dock (small)	Multiple afloat repair berths; dry docks to 120,000 DWT; deepwater port opened in 2012; Colombo South Harbor Development project will increase depth to 18 meters and then 23 meters; reported $500 million Chinese investment; base for Sri Lanka Navy Western Fleet	Friendly visits, visit of conventional submarine and tender
Sri Lanka	Hambantota	17.0	Laydown yards, several multiuse and roll-on/roll-off berths, multiuse quay walls, adjoins Mattala Rajapaksa International Airport	Ship-serving capabilities planned; port to be constructed in three stages over fifteen years; phase one accommodated first vessel in 2010; general cargo berth of 610 meters; handles vessels up to 100,000 DWT; phase two initiated; recent presence of survey ship suggests near-term progress; 85% leased to China Merchant Ports Holding for 99 years in controversial debt-for-equity swap; Sri Lanka reportedly to locate naval base there	Friendly visits

Appendix 1 continued

Country	Port	Maximum draft (meters)	Level of replenishment/ repair facilities	Development/significance	Most frequent nature of visits
Sri Lanka	Trincomalee	12.5	Longshore, ship repairs (limited), marine railroad (very small), dirty ballast	Slipways for commercial and naval vessels	Friendly visits
Tanzania	Bagamoyo	To be dredged	Under development	Construction commenced in 2018 in association with China Merchants Holdings International Co. Ltd. and State General Reserve of Oman; $10 billion in Chinese investment projected; will include special economic zone, road, and rail links; envisioned to be East Africa's largest port and leading shipping/logistics center when completed	N/A
Yemen	Aden	14.7	N/A	National dockyard company offers range of limited facilities and services: two floating docks, in-water repair services, repair shops and other workshops, large lathes, electrical, casting, and refrigeration	Replenish/overhaul, noncombatant evacuation operations in 2015, civil war suspended usage

SOURCE: Data obtained from IHS Maritime Sea-web and individual port websites, as well as input from Colonel Vinayak Bhat, Indian Army (ret.); Conor Kennedy; Collin Koh; Terence Nicholas; Vice Admiral Arun Kumar Singh, Indian Navy (ret.); and Austin Strange.

APPENDIX 2 Military basing spectrum and China's potential place

	Port calls	Basic access	Civil-military	Naval port network	Key nodes	Gold standard
Nature	Commercial ports	Commerce-centric permanent access	Dual-use	Develop and build on commercial port infrastructure	Concentrate capabilities and supplies in key ports	Comprehensive support for military operations
Example	Russia, India today	Dutch East India Company, imperial Germany, imperial France	Logistics Group, Western Pacific (U.S. today)	France today; imagined "string of pearls"	United Kingdom (interwar period), Soviet Union (Cold War)	United States
Services	Refueling, provisioning, electricity, waste disposal	Basic services, commercially based	Dedicated medical, communications, housing, rest, training, medical facilities; refrigerated storage; limited ship and equipment repair; replenishment and resupply through distribution networks, extensive use of husbanding agents	Covert capabilities, resources	–	Complete, albeit with some distribution among facilities
Legal or diplomatic basis	Local law	Political backing, commercial contracts	Memoranda of agreement/status of forces agreements (SOFA)	SOFA (infrastructure development = aid)	SOFA + subsidies	SOFA + major subsidies
Footprint	Small, transient	Dual-use	Low profile, several hundred personnel	More personnel, some covert?	Significant facilities and personnel	Major facilities and personnel

Appendix 2 continued

	Port calls	Basic access	Civil-military places	Naval port network	Key nodes	Gold standard
Pros	Politically easiest, benefits local economy	Economic logic, aligns with China's preferences and strengths, unprovocative	Balanced economic and political costs	Leverage foreign investment	Cost-effective, limits allies' approval required, effective defense and offense	Maximizes capability and capacity
Cons	Limited support and slots, standards not guaranteed, Chinese military and civilians skeptical, high cost-capacity ratio	Historically checkered, unreliable in conflict	Modest capability and capacity	Less familiar places for PLAN, politically sensitive with instability and risk	Expensive, concentrated targets	High political and resource costs
Status	Approach widely used by China since 2000	China is pursuing such an approach by funding and managing global shipping and port networks	China already has such facilities in Djibouti, and may soon develop others elsewhere in Indo-Pacific	Conceivable by 2035, would require tremendous resources and effort	Unlikely before 2035, achievable by 2050 under favorable conditions	Likely unachievable before 2030, achievable by 2050 under favorable conditions

SOURCE: Christopher D. Yung et al., *China's Out of Area Naval Operations: Case Studies, Trajectories, Obstacles, and Potential Solutions*, China Strategic Perspective, no. 3 (Washington, D.C.: National Defense University Press, 2010), 6, 12–47; and Andrew S. Erickson, Lyle J. Goldstein, and Carnes Lord, eds., *China Goes to Sea: Maritime Transformation in Comparative Historical Perspective* (Annapolis: Naval Institute Press, 2009).

EXECUTIVE SUMMARY

This chapter explores how China's efforts to reshape the international financial architecture fit within a larger grand strategy to blunt U.S. financial power and build constraining financial leverage over China's neighbors.

MAIN ARGUMENT

The rise of China marks the first time in centuries that the world's largest economy will not be English-speaking, Western, democratic, liberal, or market-driven. The country's security anxieties as a rising power—one that faces both the risk of confrontation with the U.S. hegemon and the risk of encirclement by wary neighbors—will shape its international economic and financial strategies. To deal with the U.S., China has pursued blunting strategies against U.S. financial power. It has supported monetary diversification and the creation of parallel payment and credit rating institutions to reduce its vulnerability to U.S. financial sanctions. To deal with its neighbors, China has pursued building strategies to enhance its financial leverage over them. It has promoted a renminbi zone, new financial institutions, and infrastructure investment that together foster asymmetric interdependence.

POLICY IMPLICATIONS

- In the short term, China's efforts to build constraining leverage over its neighbors could lay the foundation for a sphere of influence unless the U.S. both re-engages regional multilateral economic processes and multilateralizes some of China's own bilateral efforts such as the Belt and Road Initiative.

- Over the medium term, China's efforts to duplicate the substructure of the international financial system may provide sanctioned states an opportunity to escape U.S. financial pressure while reducing Chinese vulnerability to U.S. financial sanctions.

- Over the long term, China's effort to promote monetary diversification, bypass the dollar, and promote its own currency and payments systems also could reduce its vulnerability to U.S. financial sanctions.

China's Role in Reshaping the International Financial Architecture: Blunting U.S. Power and Building Regional Order

Rush Doshi

Four decades ago, Deng Xiaoping boldly integrated China into the U.S.-led economic system after observing that it was hardly a coincidence that the United States' friends had grown rich and its enemies poor. Deng's decision catapulted China into the ranks of great powers and may yet produce a bipolar order by the end of the next decade. But it has also raised an important question: what will become of the order that enabled China's rise now that the country has almost finished rising?

China's emergence presents a notable departure from past precedent. Indeed, for the first time in centuries, the world's largest economy will not be English-speaking, Western, democratic, liberal, or market-driven.[1] The period in which the global economic order shaped China is already giving way to a new period in which China will shape the global economic order. For now, this transition is occurring peacefully. While many scholars have studied wartime transitions, which often reveal the stark passing of hegemony from one power to another and make clear the critical juncture between the old economic order and the new one that replaces it, peacetime transitions have received less attention and have fewer historical reference points.

Rush Doshi is the Brookings-Yale Postdoctoral Research Fellow at the Brookings Institution. He can be reached at <rdoshi@brookings.edu>.

---

[1] This is a point that former Australian prime minister Kevin Rudd frequently makes. See, for example, Kevin Rudd, "Viewpoint: China and the World," BBC News, November 9, 2012, https://www.bbc.com/news/world-asia-china-20217333.

Because the existing system that serves so many so well is unlikely to be swept away through measures short of war, it may be that the emerging Chinese order will increasingly run parallel to the U.S. order in some places (especially those related to international finance) and layer over it in others (such as within the Indo-Pacific).

This chapter argues that, while difficult to determine *ex ante*, China's impact on the global economic order, and in particular the global financial order, is likely to be shaped by its long-standing security-related concerns. Indeed, even as the country has grown stronger, its structural security environment continues to present enduring challenges that date back to the end of the Cold War. China is a rising power that, on the one hand, faces a confrontational external hegemon in the United States and, on the other hand, must cope with the possibility—especially given its geographic position—that its wary neighbors may jointly form a balancing coalition encircling it in concert with the United States or other great powers. This chapter argues that financial instruments in particular are one part of China's broader grand strategy to break out of this challenging security environment. This approach has involved China first blunting U.S. power by minimizing U.S. economic leverage and then building a China-led regional order both by acquiring economic leverage over its neighbors and by gaining legitimacy through public goods provision and institutional leadership.

This chapter discusses economic instruments broadly before delving into a more focused discussion of China's use of financial instruments to achieve its strategic goals. Accordingly, in the succeeding sections, this chapter first explains in theoretical terms how a wide range of economic instruments fit into grand strategy. The second section briefly surveys China's use of these instruments, while the third section outlines China's efforts to blunt U.S. financial power through monetary diversification as well as through alternative payment mechanisms and indigenous credit rating agencies that constitute a parallel substructure to the global economy. The fourth section then explores China's efforts to build a China-led order in Asia through the creation of a renminbi zone, trade promotion, and infrastructure investment that layer over the existing U.S. order.

The chapter concludes that, in the period ahead, China may intensify this approach. Beijing is likely to more overtly weaken the financial pillars of U.S. power while strengthening the financial pillars that support China's own order-building in Asia. Together, these tools will take their place alongside other economic instruments that constrain China's neighbors and lay the foundation for regional hegemony.

The Economic Instruments in Grand Strategy

Grand strategy is a state's theory of how it can achieve security for itself that is coordinated and implemented across military, economic, and political means of statecraft. Too often, studies of a state's grand strategy focus on military means because these have the clearest link to security matters. Comparatively less attention is directed toward understanding the role of economic instruments in grand strategy.

Part of this oversight is understandable. Many believe that economic policymaking is primarily driven by economic motivations, which span from national welfare and development at the broadest level to the parochial preferences of interest groups at the narrowest level. While these two drivers explain a considerable amount of economic activity, many consequential economic decisions are also made for strategic reasons. Indeed, economic instruments have long been part of states' grand strategies. Great Britain developed plans for economic warfare against Germany in World War I, Nazi Germany made its neighbors dependent on the German economy to reduce their freedom of maneuver, and the United States absorbed the exports of Europe and Japan to bolster their economies and prevent their turn to Communism. These were not simply tactical applications of economic power but parts of larger, sustained grand strategies intended to create security and outcompete rival great powers through the use of economic statecraft.

What exactly does it mean to use economic means for political ends? Economics is a vast, interconnected, and dynamic domain of activity that includes diverse forms of leverage such as "sanctions, taxation, embargoes, trade agreements, asset freezing, engagement policies, currency manipulation, subsidies, tariffs, trade agreements," and more—all of which could conceivably be used in myriad ways to affect international politics or security.[2] Despite this complexity, it is possible to fit most forms of economic leverage into three broad categories: (1) bilateral leverage, (2) structural leverage, and (3) domestic-political leverage. Across these categories, states can pursue blunting strategies to enhance their autonomy from others and building strategies to enhance their influence over others.[3]

Bilateral leverage. State-to-state relationships of asymmetric interdependence constitute the basic unit on which more systemic or regional forms of leverage are based. Such bilateral leverage involves the manipulation of dependencies to actively coerce or passively induce a state to

---

[2] William J. Norris, *Chinese Economic Statecraft: Commercial Actors, Grand Strategy, and State Control* (Ithaca: Cornell University Press, 2016), 14.

[3] This approach is adapted from Susan Strange's two-dimensional approach to economic power. See Susan Strange, *States and Markets*, 2nd ed. (New York: Pinter Publishers, 1994), 24–29.

change its behavior. China and the United States enjoyed economic ties in the 1990s, but China was more dependent on the United States than the United States was on China, which afforded Washington bilateral leverage. Blunting strategies, like China's successful pursuit of permanent normal trade relations, limit Washington's ability to exercise bilateral leverage. Building strategies, like China's willingness to "absorb" exports from Taiwan by dropping trade barriers and purchasing exports (e.g., agricultural products) at generous prices, enhance China's leverage over Taipei.

Structural leverage. This refers to the ability of a state to wield its role in the global economic structure—whether atop the economic hierarchy, in command of economic institutions, or as a node in economic exchanges—to shape the framework in which economic activity takes place and thereby change another state's behavior. For example, the dollar's centrality to global finance allows Washington to turn foreign banks into instruments of U.S. policy and cut off Iran and North Korea from the global financial system, even though Washington has limited bilateral economic ties with both countries. Similarly, U.S. influence over global payments, sovereign credit ratings, arbitral bodies, and other institutions may constitute structural leverage. Blunting strategies might involve Chinese efforts to reduce the centrality of the U.S. dollar or to build institutions that bypass U.S. economic infrastructure; building strategies might include efforts to promote a country's own currency or payment system. In structural leverage, there is sometimes overlap between blunting and building strategies because bypassing another state's leverage might involve creating competing institutions.

Domestic-political leverage. Not all economic power exists in bilateral flows between states or in the foundations of global economic structures. One of the most important forms involves the economic instruments of one state being used to reshape the domestic politics of another state, alter its conception of its own interests, and thereby change its behavior. Blunting involves protecting a country's political system from such economic influence through anticorruption laws and the registration of foreign agents; building, by contrast, involves developing economic ties with politically influential groups, such as China's targeted inducements to farmers in Taiwan during the debates over a bilateral free trade agreement or to political elites in Maldives.

Together, these three forms of leverage account for most of the major ways that economic instruments are directed for political purposes, and blunting and building strategies encompass the primary means by which economic leverage may translate into great-power competition. Many Chinese economic initiatives cut against China's own economic interests, which strongly suggests that strategic motivations are behind them.

Three Phases of Chinese Economic Statecraft

China's international economic policymaking is at times driven by strategic considerations—that is, by an appreciation of the use of economic power or statecraft to force changes in state behavior. This is not to say that strategic motivations are the exclusive driver of Chinese policymaking, but that in many prominent cases strategic logics explain the variation in China's behavior at least as well as, and often significantly better than, economic logics. Even in those few cases where they do not, China's economic behavior nonetheless has important implications for U.S. strategy and the exercise of power.

China's approach to economic instruments in its grand strategy has evolved over three broad phases. In the first phase, which runs from reform and opening into the late 1980s, China was fairly ambivalent about the use of economic power and its vulnerability to Western economic leverage and focused far more on economic development. This ambivalence stemmed from the fact that the United States and China largely worked cooperatively to balance the Soviet Union throughout the decade, despite occasional disputes over Taiwan and despite China's claim to be pursuing formal equidistance between the superpowers in the late 1980s. Indeed, as Deng Xiaoping argued in an enlarged Central Military Commission meeting in 1985, "In view of the threat of Soviet hegemonism, over the years we formed a strategic 'line' of defense—a 'line' stretching from Japan to Europe to the United States."[4] Because China considered the West its partner in resisting Soviet hegemonism, it could more confidently turn away from Maoist autarky and allow itself to grow increasingly dependent on Western technology, investment, managerial experience, and global economic institutions without fear that the resulting bilateral, structural, and domestic-political vulnerability would be exploited.[5] Indeed, during this period, China did not appear to ameliorate these vulnerabilities in any comprehensive way.

The second phase began after the traumatic trifecta of the Tiananmen Square massacre, the Gulf War, and the collapse of the Soviet Union increased China's perception of the United States as a threat and raised new concerns about Beijing's vulnerability to economic coercion. These fears concentrated on U.S. bilateral economic power over China and the possibility that the United States could manipulate asymmetric interdependence by effectively revoking most-favored-nation (MFN) status, which would have more than doubled the price of many Chinese exports. Indeed, the U.S. Congress voted

---

[4] *Deng Xiaoping wenxuan* [Deng Xiaoping Selected Works], vol. 3 (Beijing: People's Press, 1993), 127–28.

[5] Harold K. Jacobson and Michel Oksenberg, *China's Participation in the IMF, the World Bank, and GATT* (Ann Arbor: University of Michigan Press, 1990).

to revoke MFN status in 1992 but was stopped by a presidential veto. The next president, Bill Clinton, was initially willing to effectively revoke MFN status by tying it to progress on human rights.[6] Chinese leaders understood that securing MFN status would not free China from dependence on the United States, but it would blunt the discretionary exercise of U.S. power over bilateral economic exchanges. This goal therefore became the focus of much of China's economic policymaking as well as bilateral negotiations with the United States and multilateral negotiations involving the Asia-Pacific Economic Cooperation (APEC) and the World Trade Organization. As He Xin, a prominent if controversial foreign policy adviser to Deng Xiaoping, Jiang Zemin, and Li Peng, asserted in 1993, "The issue of MFN status between China and the United States is a central issue that will determine the rotation of world history."[7] Premier Li stated that securing MFN would ensure that "China has more room for maneuver on the international stage."[8] China was eventually successful, and all the while, it continued to increase its stake in Western economic institutions while attempting to reduce its vulnerability to unilateral exercises of U.S. economic power.

The third phase of China's efforts to shape the global economic architecture began after the 2008 global financial crisis, which led Beijing to revise downward its estimation of U.S. power and to grow more confident about its own ability to set the terms of global economic statecraft. In this third phrase, China has shifted away from the second phase's narrower concern with blunting the United States' bilateral economic leverage. Beijing now feels emboldened to expand its blunting behavior to include U.S. structural power in international finance (often considered the backbone of U.S. hegemony) as well as to build alternative financial arrangements and accumulate constraining leverage over its neighbors in Asia. China's alternative arrangements in international finance run parallel to U.S. architecture; meanwhile, its efforts in Asia layer over elements of the existing U.S. order. Admittedly, some of these arrangements also serve economic purposes, but many seem redundant and defy clear economic rationales. In both cases, regardless of the murky intentions behind these institutions, they nonetheless have clear implications for China's ability to resist U.S. economic power and project its own economic power—whether bilateral, structural,

---

[6] Jim Mann, "Senate Fails to Override China Policy Veto," *Los Angeles Times*, March 19, 1992, http://articles.latimes.com/1992-03-19/news/mn-5919_1_china-policy.

[7] *He Xin zhengzhi jingji lunwen ji* [Selected Works of Hexin on Political Economy] (Beijing: Heilongjiang Jiaoyu Chubanshe), 17.

[8] Li Peng, *Shichang yu tiaokong: Li Peng jingji riji* [Market and Regulation: Li Peng's Economic Diary] (Beijing: Xinhua Chubanshe, 2007), 3:1546.

or domestic-political—over neighboring countries and perhaps eventually around much of the world.

The remainder of this chapter discusses this third phase of economic statecraft, especially its focus on blunting and building financial architecture.

Blunting U.S. Financial Power

The 2008 global financial crisis precipitated a coordinated effort by China to gradually reduce its vulnerability to U.S. financial power, which China was previously too weak to bypass. The decline in the prestige of the United States' economic model was perceived to have created an opening for Beijing to question elements of the existing system and to target the substructure of U.S. financial power with alternative institutions. Beijing's efforts in (1) diversifying the monetary system, (2) building alternatives to SWIFT (Society for Worldwide Interbank Financial Telecommunication), and (3) sponsoring alternative credit rating agencies together targeted three important elements of U.S. (and in the case of SWIFT, European) structural power. Indeed, structural power is often difficult to counter unless a country either leaves the economic system, which would be economic suicide, or alternatively builds parallel infrastructure. China has naturally chosen the latter option. While progress remains slow and the possibility of success remains somewhat distant, China's preferences are clear and its efforts remain coordinated and purposeful: as its power grows, Beijing will seek to shape the international economic architecture to reduce the importance of the U.S. dollar, thereby weakening U.S. hegemony and enhancing Chinese autonomy.

Diversifying the Monetary System

After the 2008 global financial crisis, China's leadership increasingly called into question the dollar's reserve currency status. Of course, various Chinese officials have for decades criticized the international economic order as unfair and called for its reform, and leading central bank officials have at times been critical of the "irrational" monetary system and urged greater monetary surveillance of advanced economies.[9] Even so, the 2008 global financial crisis marked a shift less in China's preferences and more in its confidence that the country could reshape the international economic architecture around it. Accordingly, as Gregory Chin notes, after the crisis

---

[9] Gregory Chin, "China's Rising Monetary Power," in *The Great Wall of Money: Power and Politics in China's International Monetary Relations*, ed. Eric Helleiner and Jonathan Kirshner (Ithaca: Cornell University Press, 2014), 190–92. See also Hongying Wang, "China and the International Monetary System: Does Beijing Really Want to Challenge the Dollar?" *Foreign Affairs*, December 19, 2017, https://www.foreignaffairs.com/articles/asia/2017-12-19/china-and-international-monetary-system.

"China's leaders elevated financial and monetary policy, and monetary diplomacy, to a top priority."[10] The same year the crisis broke out, China's Central Economic Work Conference set a Chinese Communist Party (CCP) line on monetary policy and promptly concluded that "international monetary diversification will advance, but the status of the U.S. dollar as the main international currency has not fundamentally changed."[11] In other words, it would take concerted effort to promote diversification.

An important symbol and proponent of this effort was President Hu Jintao, who quickly "became the lead spokesperson on China's global monetary thinking." This marked a shift from the pre-crisis decade when China's monetary statecraft was largely "the preserve of senior technocrats from the central bank, and to a lesser extent, the finance ministry."[12] At the G-20 meeting in 2008, the first one called to coordinate a response to the crisis, Hu asked the leaders of each country to "improve the international currency system and steadily promote the diversification of the international monetary system."[13]

These views were expressed in a far more operational form in a 2009 essay by the then governor of the People's Bank of China, Zhou Xiaochuan, who specifically advocated for special drawing rights (SDR) as an alternative to the dollar-based system.[14] In a provocative essay entitled "Reform the International Monetary System" and timed for impact just before the 2009 London G-20 summit, Zhou argued that the use of the U.S. dollar as the reserve currency "is a rare special case in history" and that "the crisis again calls for creative reform of the existing international monetary system."[15]

Although Zhou only implicitly referenced the dollar, Hu was far more direct about his intentions to diversify away from it at the Central Economic Work Conference held shortly after Zhou's essay was published: "Since the international financial crisis, the international community has generally recognized a major reason for the imbalance in the world economy and for the international financial crisis is the inherent drawback associated with a U.S. dollar–dominated international monetary and financial system."[16] For that

---

[10] Chin, "China's Rising Monetary Power," 192.

[11] Hu Jintao, *Hu Jintao wenxuan* [Hu Jintao Selected Works], vol. 3 (Beijing: People's Press, 2016), 280.

[12] Chin, "China's Rising Monetary Power," 192.

[13] Hu, *Hu Jintao wenxuan*, 139.

[14] An SDR is a unit of account created by the International Monetary Fund (IMF) and based on a basket of major world currencies. It represents a claim that member countries of the IMF have on the currencies within the basket, and for that reason, it is not quite the same as an international currency.

[15] Zhou Xiaochuan, "Reform the International Monetary System," March 23, 2009, http://www.china-un.org/eng/zt/g20_london_summit/t554938.htm.

[16] Hu, *Hu Jintao wenxuan*, 281.

reason, "promoting the diversification and rationalization of the international monetary system" was essential to reform. Hu was explicit that weakening the centrality of the dollar was a key goal, but that it would not be quick. "At the same time," Hu continued, "we must see that the dominant position of the U.S. dollar is determined by U.S. economic strength and comprehensive national power, and for a long period of time it would be relatively difficult to fundamentally change it." China's strategy would be prolonged: "We must adhere to the principles of comprehensiveness, balance, gradualism, and effectiveness in promoting the reform of the international monetary system."[17]

For the next several years, at major multilateral economic gatherings—including most G-20 summits, BRICS (Brazil, Russia, India, China, and South Africa) summits, and the G-8 + G-5 summit—Hu or other high-level Chinese officials continued to call for reserve diversification, the SDR, and monetary reform.[18] Many G-7 countries, including the United Kingdom, Canada, and Japan, all defended the dollar and questioned the "appropriateness" of China's focus on it.[19] But China continued to push, in part because, as the president of China's Export-Import Bank Li Ruogu noted, the dollar's power was dangerous to China: "the U.S. used this method [manipulation of the dollar] to topple Japan's economy, and it wants to use this method to curb China's development."[20] Chinese leaders believed that they needed to blunt and bypass this U.S. power, and Li asserted that "only by eliminating the U.S. dollar's monopolistic position" would it be possible to reform the international monetary system.[21]

China's support for a diversified international monetary system with a reduced role for the dollar and a greater role for the SDR cannot be explained in terms of its "economic interest," as Hongying Wang argues.[22] A decline in the value of the dollar would damage China's export-driven economy and reduce the value of its enormous holdings of dollar-denominated assets. Although Wang contends that national identity concerns explain China's policy, Hu's explicit call for a reduced role for the dollar in internal CCP documents is not accompanied by any chest-beating nationalist rhetoric about China's status, nor are his statements at the G-20. Indeed, the call for diversification is made separately from any discussion of renminbi internationalization. Instead, the best explanation is that China recognizes the dollar as an enduring source

[17] Hu, *Hu Jintao wenxuan*, 281–82.

[18] Ibid., 218; and Chin, "China's Rising Monetary Power," 196–98.

[19] Chin, "China's Rising Monetary Power," 195.

[20] Jonathan Kirshner, "Regional Hegemony and an Emerging RMB Zone," in Helleiner and Kirshner, *The Great Wall of Money*, 223.

[21] Quoted in ibid., 223.

[22] Wang, "China and the International Monetary System."

of U.S. structural power and wishes to weaken it. Even so, after four years of intense diplomatic effort and lobbying by Hu, it was clear that efforts to put forward the SDR as an alternative to the U.S. dollar, or to promote reserve diversification away from the dollar, would not succeed in the short term. Despite failing to advance the SDR, China was able to gain approval from the International Monetary Fund (IMF) for the renminbi to join the fund's SDR basket in 2016, though this particular move was largely symbolic and had little direct economic impact.[23] Nevertheless, despite China's shortcomings in promoting financial diversification, its actions reveal intense and long-standing hopes for an international economic architecture in which the dollar is only one among many reserve currencies. As we will see, Beijing has increasingly turned to renminbi internationalization as an instrument to not only hasten diversification but also build the foundation for China's own structural power across Asia.

Developing SWIFT Alternatives

SWIFT is a standard-setting and messaging institution with a network that makes cross-border financial payments possible, thereby constituting the substructure of global finance. The organization, known as the Society for World Interbank Financial Telecommunication, was founded in 1973 when 239 banks from fifteen different countries created unified messaging standards, a messaging platform, and a network to route messages.[24] It replaced Telex, a slow and error-prone patchwork manual system with conflicting standards that effectively required banks to work in several contradictory formats to make payments. Today SWIFT spans two hundred countries and more than ten thousand institutions, facilitates fifteen million messages daily, and is the essential infrastructure that makes international payments possible. Although SWIFT is a messaging service and does not engage in clearing and settling, if a bank is cut off from the network, it is essentially cut off from the global financial system and from much of the clearing and settling infrastructure that exists. In this way, control over SWIFT offers considerable structural power.

That structural power has already been wielded against countries. While the organization sees itself as apolitical, it is nonetheless required to comply with the laws of Belgium, the European Union, and—through the threat of secondary sanctions—the United States as well. In 2012 the United States and Europe used their influence over the organization to force it to delink Iranian banks from SWIFT networks, which marked the first

---

[23] For example, the SDR currently determines the mix of currencies countries receive when requesting IMF support.

[24] "SWIFT History," SWIFT, 2018, https://www.swift.com/about-us/history.

time in its history that the institution had cut off an entire country from access to the company's network.[25] Iran had relied on SWIFT for two million cross-border payments annually—a volume that could not be replaced by another messaging network—and loss of access made payment for Iranian oil impossible, devastated the country's economy, and prevented the government from accessing substantial amounts of its own foreign reserves that it had invested abroad.[26] A few years later, in 2017, SWIFT access was also denied to North Korean banks.[27]

SWIFT's structural power has even been threatened against great powers like Russia after its invasion of Crimea. The threat was concerning enough that Prime Minister Dmitri Medvedev discussed it publicly and threatened that Russia's "reaction will be without limit."[28] Russian Central Bank governor Elvira Nabiullina then began preparing a Russian alternative to SWIFT as early as 2014. In a meeting with Putin, she stated that "there were threats that we can be disconnected from SWIFT. We have finished working on our own payment system, and if something happens, all operations in SWIFT format will work inside the country. We have created an alternative."[29] Russia has sought to popularize this alternative system within the Eurasian Union and discussed it with Iran. Though imperfect, the system demonstrates that great powers are actively searching for ways to bypass U.S. influence over SWIFT for strategic reasons.[30]

The United States has threatened to wield SWIFT against China. Washington already sanctioned at least one Chinese bank involved in trade with North Korea, and Treasury Secretary Steven Mnuchin threatened that "if China doesn't follow these sanctions [on North Korea], we will put additional

---

[25] Philip Blenkinsop and Rachel Younglai, "Banking's SWIFT Says Ready to Block Iran Transactions," Reuters, February 17, 2012, https://www.reuters.com/article/us-iran-sanctions-swift/bankings-swift-says-ready-to-block-iran-transactions-idUSTRE81G26820120217.

[26] "Payments System SWIFT to Cut Off Iranian Banks," Reuters, March 15, 2012, https://www.reuters.com/article/us-eu-iran-sanctions/payments-system-swift-to-cut-off-iranian-banks-idUSBRE82E0VR20120315.

[27] Jeremy Wagstaff and Tom Bergin, "SWIFT Messaging System Bans North Korean Banks Blacklisted by UN," Reuters, March 8, 2017, https://www.reuters.com/article/us-northkorea-banks-swift/swift-messaging-system-bans-north-korean-banks-blacklisted-by-u-n-idUSKBN16F0NI.

[28] Henry Farrell, "Russia Is Hinting at a New Cold War over SWIFT. So What's SWIFT?" *Washington Post*, January 28, 2015, https://www.washingtonpost.com/news/monkey-cage/wp/2015/01/28/russia-is-hinting-at-a-new-cold-war-over-swift-so-whats-swift/?noredirect=on&utm_term=.29c15baefc36.

[29] "Russia's Banking System Has SWIFT Alternative Ready," RT, March 23, 2017, https://www.rt.com/business/382017-russia-swift-central-bank.

[30] Leonid Bershidsky, "How Europe Can Keep Money Flowing to Iran," Bloomberg, May 18, 2018, https://www.bloomberg.com/view/articles/2018-05-18/how-europe-can-keep-money-flowing-to-iran. See also Natasha Turak, "Russia's Central Bank Governor Touts Moscow Alternative to SWIFT Transfer System as Protection from U.S. Sanctions," CNBC, May 23, 2018, https://www.cnbc.com/2018/05/23/russias-central-bank-governor-touts-moscow-alternative-to-swift-transfer-system-as-protection-from-us-sanctions.html.

sanctions on them and prevent them from accessing the U.S. and international dollar system." Similarly, members of Congress suggested cutting off some of China's largest banks from the global financial system.[31] China indeed has reasons to fear these threats, and like Russia it appears to be acting on them.

The People's Bank of China—with approval from the Chinese government—began developing its own alternative to SWIFT for financial messaging and interbank payments as early as 2013, roughly one year after the West cut off Iran, and it went live around two years later.[32] This system, known as the China International Payment System (CIPS), not only insulates China from financial pressure but also increases its autonomy, giving the country sovereign control over all information that passes through its network, the power to help others bypass sanctions, and the ability to one day cut others off from this system. Moreover, the ambition for CIPS exceeds that for SWIFT: the former will not only be a messaging service like SWIFT but also provide clearance and settlement—that is, full integration of the payment process. Unlike Russian elites, Chinese elites have been far less obvious in telegraphing their system's possibility as a rival to SWIFT; nevertheless, its strategic potential is real, if still somewhat distant.

Skeptics of these strategic motivations point out that China's pursuit of CIPS has some genuine economic motivations as well. First, CIPS is an improvement on the previous system of cross-border renminbi payments. Before CIPS, China's domestic interbank clearing and settlement system, the China National Advanced Payment System (CNAPS), could not support international payments; instead, cross-border transactions took place through designated offshore yuan-clearing banks or correspondent banks in China. Moreover, CIPS for the moment is primarily concerned with clearing and settling. Indeed, CIPS signed a 2016 agreement that provides it access to the SWIFT messaging system. From that perspective, a charitable observer might conclude that the system does not appear to be an alternative to SWIFT financial infrastructure but a complementary appendage.

Neither of these arguments dismisses the strategic logic underlying CIPS. First, if China had purely economic and technical motivations for launching CIPS, it may have been more economical to simply reform the existing CNAPS system so it could communicate with SWIFT. Other countries with domestic interbank payment systems that similarly do not communicate with SWIFT have often modified those systems to allow communication.

[31] Zhenhua Lu, "U.S. House Committee Targets Major Chinese Banks' Lifeline to North Korea," *South China Morning Post*, September 13, 2017, https://www.scmp.com/news/china/policies-politics/article/2110914/us-house-committee-targets-major-chinese-banks-lifeline.

[32] Michelle Chen and Koh Gui Qing, "China's International Payments System Ready, Could Launch by End-2015," Reuters, March 9, 2015, http://www.reuters.com/article/2015/03/09/us-china-yuan-payments-exclusive-idUSKBN0M50BV20150309.

This suggests that economic motivations may not have been the leading factors in the establishment of CIPS.

Second, the fact that CIPS has signed an agreement for access to the SWIFT network and uses SWIFT messaging standards does not reduce its viability as a strategic alternative because CIPS is building the capability to process messages outside the SWIFT network. Indeed, just as SWIFT requires banks to purchase costly technology connecting them to the network, so does CIPS, which allows it to exist in parallel to SWIFT's technology.[33] As CIPS continues to develop, the goal is in many ways to operate independently from SWIFT. As an individual with knowledge of the People's Bank of China's plans for CIPS told the *Financial Times*, "In the future CIPS will move in the direction of using its own dedicated [communications] line. At that point it can totally replace SWIFT" for interbank messaging involving renminbi.[34] Indeed, as Eswar Prasad argues:

> CIPS has been designed as a system that could eventually also serve as a conduit for interbank communications concerning international RMB transactions that operates independently of SWIFT. This would make it not only a funds transfer system, but also a communication system, reducing the SWIFT's grip on interbank communications related to cross-border financial flows. China's government is astute enough not to challenge SWIFT until the CIPS has matured, but no doubt one day the challenge will come.[35]

The collaboration between SWIFT and CIPS helps the latter mature, providing China with market share and expertise as it builds a parallel system. It also gives SWIFT continued relevance, and indeed employees at the company have been concerned that "Chinese authorities were considering replacing SWIFT with an indigenous network built to rival, if not exceed, SWIFT's own."[36] Its China head, Daphne Wang, apparently tried to persuade CIPS not to invest in alternative messaging but to focus on clearance: "We do not do clearing, as in CIPS's case. When we talked to CIPS, we said: 'Why build your highway [i.e., messaging platform] if the highway exists already? As of now it's as if you are selling a car [i.e., clearance and settling] but nobody can drive it on the

---

[33] Don Weinland, "China's Global Payment System CIPs Too Costly for Most Banks—For Now," *South China Morning Post*, October 17, 2015, https://www.scmp.com/business/banking-finance/article/1868749/chinas-global-payment-system-cips-too-costly-most-banks-now.

[34] Gabriel Wildau, "China Launch of Renminbi Payments System Reflects SWIFT Spying Concerns," *Financial Times*, October 8, 2015, https://www.ft.com/content/84241292-66a1-11e5-a155-02b6f8af6a62.

[35] Eswar S. Prasad, *Gaining Currency: The Rise of the Renminbi* (Oxford: Oxford University Press, 2017), 116.

[36] *China and the Age of Strategic Rivalry* (Ottawa: Canadian Security Intelligence Services, 2018), 113–22.

highway that's already built.'"[37] Despite SWIFT's attempt to disincentivize the creation of an alternative highway, China's desire remains to develop one. As one person involved with CIPS noted, the system was launched without all these features but there was "ambition" for more: "[CIPS] doesn't include a lot of things [yet], but there is pressure for delivery."[38] Eventually, the system is intended to "allow offshore banks to participate, enabling offshore-to-offshore renminbi payments as well as those in and out of China."[39] This would make CIPS a wholly independent financial infrastructure and provide any two parties anywhere in the world a method for messaging, clearance, and settlement entirely free from U.S. review, which would seriously undermine the United States' financial power worldwide.

Third, even when CIPS does not act in parallel to SWIFT, its connection to and through SWIFT still provides useful influence. Before CIPS, SWIFT had already operated in China for more than 30 years and was connected to four hundred Chinese financial institutions and corporate treasuries.[40] Now, all SWIFT messages to China must be routed through CIPS. As one payment expert notes, "CIPS is trying to be the middleman between SWIFT and CNAPS," which would give China's central bank an ability to determine who has access to the country's financial system.[41] This provides a central control point over transactions in renminbi and boosts China's structural power.

For now, CIPS is not a meaningful alternative to SWIFT. It may bolster China's structural power by making it much easier for China to cut off other institutions or countries from its financial system, but CIPS is not yet ready to serve as an alternative messaging system for cross-border payments outside China. Even so, that day will come, and this makes CIPS one of the most promising initiatives for the country's hopes of diversifying the international monetary system. Other great powers like Russia are already investing in such systems, and China—which also faces the threat of Western financial sanctions—has ample reason to continue developing CIPS into an alternative that can bypass U.S. structural power over international payments in the coming decade. As one columnist has observed, "A return to a pre-SWIFT world, in which banks were forced to send and accept transaction information in a multitude of formats, isn't unimaginable," and this demonstrates how

---

[37] Stefania Palma, "SWIFT Dips into China with CIPS," Banker, July 1, 2016, https://www.thebanker.com/Global-Transaction-Banking/Swift-dips-into-China-with-CIPS.

[38] "Beijing's International Payments System Scaled Back for Launch," South China Morning Post, July 13, 2015, https://www.scmp.com/business/money/article/1838428/beijings-international-payments-system-scaled-back-launch.

[39] Wildau, "China Launch of Renminbi Payments System Reflects SWIFT Spying Concerns."

[40] China and the Age of Strategic Rivalry, 113–22.

[41] Wildau, "China Launch of Renminbi Payments System Reflects SWIFT Spying Concerns."

China's strategic anxieties will intertwine with its rise to fragment the substructure of global finance.[42]

Alternative Credit Rating

Credit rating agencies help provide investors information on the risks of various kinds of debt, and their ratings can significantly alter the fortunes of companies and countries. The market for international credit ratings is largely dominated by the "big three" U.S. firms—Standard and Poor's, Moody's, and Fitch Group—which together have a global market share of more than 90%. The dominance of these three firms is in part a function of the United States' structural power, including the centrality of the dollar, the importance of New York financial institutions, and the ability of the Securities and Exchange Commission to determine who can issue ratings.

After the 2008 global financial crisis, the big three were seen as vulnerable, given their mistaken appraisal of the assets that set off the crisis. Many European leaders blamed them as biased and political for having touched off and then intensified the eurozone debt crisis, especially following their downgrade of Greek debt to junk status in 2010, and some leaders encouraged (unsuccessfully) the creation of an alternative European credit rating agency.[43] The fact that even U.S. allies sought alternatives to the influence of the big three, which have retained more than 76% market share within Europe even after the crisis, should make it relatively uncontroversial that China might act according to similar motivations.[44]

As with Europe, China's interest in alternative agencies was precipitated by the global financial crisis that tarnished the big three firms while also revealing their ability to shape capital flows. Although Washington lacks the ability to directly control these credit raters or manipulate their ratings, China views them as tools of direct or indirect U.S. power corrupted by political bias. At the 2010 G-20 summit in Toronto, President Hu Jintao called for the countries to "develop an objective, fair, reasonable, and uniformed method and standard for sovereign credit rating," demonstrating that the issue had received top-level political attention. Only a month later, seemingly in coordination with Hu's call, Dagong Global Credit Rating—China's largest credit rating agency—launched its own sovereign credit ratings for the first time. For years following the crisis, China's government has continued to

[42] Bershidsky, "How Europe Can Keep Money Flowing to Iran."

[43] "EU Criticizes Role of U.S. Credit Rating Agencies in Debt Crisis," Deutsche Welle, July 11, 2011, https://www.dw.com/en/eu-criticizes-role-of-us-credit-rating-agencies-in-debt-crisis/a-15225330.

[44] Huw Jones and Marc Jones, "EU Watchdog Tightens Grip over Use of Foreign Credit Ratings," Reuters, November 17, 2017, https://www.reuters.com/article/us-britain-eu-creditratingagencies/eu-watchdog-tightens-grip-over-use-of-foreign-credit-ratings-idUSKBN1DH1J1.

formally attack the credit rating agencies. Finance Minister Lou Jiwei declared that "there's bias" in the ratings of the "big three," while the Finance Ministry issued a statement calling a Moody's downgrade of China's credit "the wrong decision" in 2017.[45]

Dagong is the lead instrument in China's effort to influence the global ratings system. The company's public documents, as well as the statements by its CEO and founder Guan Jianzhong—essentially the face of credit rating in China—indicate a view both that credit ratings are strategic instruments and that the United States' domination of them is harmful to China's political interests. As Guan wrote in 2012, "U.S. dominated ratings serve the global strategy of the United States" and "the existing international rating pattern will restrict the rise of China." Guan and others argue that rating agencies exercise "rating discourse power" that enables them to shape the global economy. If the United States controls this "rating discourse power," then China "will lose financial sovereignty." Worst, the "rating discourse power can be manipulated…in an effort to erode the social basis of the ruling party." In contrast, the 2008 global financial crisis offered "a great historical opportunity for China to strive for international rating discourse power."[46] China's ratings, even if they do not gain overwhelming market share, could nonetheless pressure the big three to adjust their ratings and "converge" toward China's, an outcome Guan welcomes.[47]

Accordingly, in the midst of the global financial crisis in 2008, Dagong began to float proposals for the Universal Credit Rating Group (UCRG), which was finally launched in June 2013 when Dagong partnered with a Russian firm and smaller U.S. rater. The new initiative's mission was to compete with the big three, and it purported to be a private, collaborative, and apolitical venture. These claims proved false when the CEO of that initiative, Richard Hainsworth, stepped down and later admitted that the effort was essentially financed and supported by the Chinese government.[48] Hainsworth claimed that the Russian and U.S. partners provided little capital, that the venture was primarily controlled by Dagong, that virtually every major

---

[45] "China's Finance Minister Accuses Credit Rating Agencies of Bias," *South China Morning Post*, April 16, 2016, https://www.scmp.com/news/china/economy/article/1936614/chinas-finance-minister-accuses-credit-rating-agencies-bias; and Joe McDonald, "China Criticizes S&P Rating Cut as 'Wrong Decision,'" Associated Press, September 22, 2017, https://apnews.com/743f86862f5a4b85844dcc10f96e3f8c.

[46] Guan Jianzhong, "The Strategic Choice of Chinese Credit Rating System," Dagong Global, 2012, http://www.dagonghk.com/upload/rating/1374474970800.pdf.

[47] Guan Jianzhong, "It Takes Innovative Thinking to Reform the International Credit Rating System," Dagong Global, September 7, 2012, available at https://web.archive.org/web/20160805123457/http://en.dagongcredit.com/content/details58_6632.html.

[48] "Man in the Middle," *South China Morning Post*, April 26, 2014, https://www.scmp.com/business/china-business/article/1497241/man-middle.

expenditure was subject to a vote by Dagong's board, and that the Chinese government was likely bankrolling not only UCRG but even Dagong. In this light, Dagong's collaboration with foreign raters appeared to be a fig leaf to boost the legitimacy of its revisionist undertaking. Hainsworth further argued that UCRG's true purpose appeared political rather than commercial—both to reduce the legitimacy of Western ratings and to put forward a Chinese alternative, though spending on the latter objective was inadequate. Dagong hired a number of senior Western officials on behalf of UCRG to criticize U.S. ratings, including former French prime minister Dominique de Villepin, who traveled the world attacking Western agencies in ideological terms and drew a "straight line from the Opium Wars, the British Raj, and the European colonial powers' grab for Africa to current forms of Western privilege, including its control of credit ratings."[49] Eventually, despite its ideological bent and alleged Chinese-backing, UCRG sputtered and was shut down.

The failure of UCRG did not mark the end of China's ambition to reshape global credit ratings. Instead, the country appears to have increased its support for Dagong to go global. The firm has opened up offices around the world and overtly stated its interest in competing with the big three. Dagong is clearly carrying on the mission that UCRG was to have undertaken and has retained many of the same international advisers to give it legitimacy.[50] Although Dagong claims to be fully private, Hainsworth suggested that the company was funded by Beijing; moreover, Guan Jianzhong was a government official immediately before he launched Dagong. Not only did he apparently continue to be employed by China's State Council for years while running Dagong, his firm so directly affects the interests of SOEs that it is genuinely hard to believe it is free from state influence.[51] Even so, Beijing clearly seeks to maintain some plausible distance from Dagong to enhance its legitimacy. Indeed, Chinese officials have privately opposed efforts to create a BRICS credit rating agency precisely because they believe that "a government-backed credit rating agency will not have any credibility" in challenging the big three.[52] Despite the fact that Dagong is formally a private and apolitical entity, its rankings have also given rise to claims of political bias. Dagong raised eyebrows when it rated

---

[49] "Man in the Middle."

[50] Liz Mak, "China's Dagong Global Credit Mounts Challenge to 'Big Three' Rating Agencies," *South China Morning Post*, August 7, 2016, https://www.scmp.com/business/banking-finance/article/2000489/chinas-dagong-global-credit-mounts-challenge-big-three.

[51] Reports of Guan's government ties are discussed in Christopher Ricking, "U.S. Rating Agencies Face Chinese Challenge," Deutsche Welle, November 19, 2012, https://www.dw.com/en/us-ratings-agencies-face-chinese-challenge/a-16389497; and Guan, "The Strategic Choice of Chinese Credit Rating System."

[52] Asit Ranjan Mishra, "China Not in Favor of Proposed Brics Credit Rating Agency," Livemint, October 14, 2014, https://www.livemint.com/Politics/btAFFggl1LoKBNZK0a45fJ/China-not-in-favour-of-proposed-Brics-credit-rating-agency.html.

the Chinese Railways Ministry's debt higher than China's sovereign debt, as well as when it rated Russia's and Botswana's debt higher than U.S. debt. In a discussion of its methodology, Dagong includes ideological CCP phrases and claims to use "dialectical materialism" as part of its evaluative approach.[53] The firm is usually eager to downgrade the United States. Its own website boasts that "Dagong is the first agency in the world to study American credit rating theories and methodologies and reveal their shortcomings. It is also the first agency to downgrade the U.S. credit rating."[54]

Nonetheless, China's efforts to influence global credit ratings remain relatively modest. Its goal appears to be to gradually gain market share rather than to displace the big three, especially given that a higher market share may be sufficient to bring about convergence. Moreover, China has allowed the big three into the country, a policy ostensibly intended to help promote foreign investment as the Chinese government pursues deleveraging. This is a positive step, though one possibly consistent with the goal of influencing global credit ratings: as U.S. credit rating agencies gain access to China's lucrative domestic market, they may find it more challenging to negatively rate politically sensitive Chinese entities or the government's sovereign debt.

Together, China's focus on monetary diversification and construction of both an alternative payment substructure through CIPS and an alternative credit rating agency through Dagong reveal a long-standing interest in weakening and bypassing the U.S. dollar's constraining effects on China. For the most part, these efforts have not yet been successful in dislodging the United States' financial dominance, but they do represent a clear Chinese desire to transform the global economic architecture into one of financial multipolarity. At some point in the future, if concerns grow about the dollar and China offers an alternative financial architecture and a more open capital account, Chinese leaders could conceivably begin that process.

Building Chinese Structural Power

China has also sought to expand its use of financial instruments to gain constraining leverage over neighboring countries, provide them public goods, and claim leadership and legitimacy. Many of these initiatives explicitly fall under China's conceptual framework of a "community of common destiny" in Asia. These efforts, which operate at the multilateral and bilateral levels, require too much effort and planning to be improvisational and should be

---

[53] "Corporate Culture," Dagong Global, 2016, https://web.archive.org/web/20160704062906/http://en.dagongcredit.com:80/about/culture.html.

[54] "About Us," Dagong Global, 2016, https://web.archive.org/web/20160326131607/http://en.dagongcredit.com/about/aboutDagong.html.

seen as part of a longer-term effort to enhance China's structural power within Asia propelled by the country's confidence following the global financial crisis. Some of these initiatives also cut against China's economic interests, making strategic motivations likely.

Building a Renminbi Zone

China's efforts on international currency can be divided into two broad initiatives. On the one hand, Beijing has sought to promote international monetary diversification through its quixotic quest for SDR adoption and through informal agreements on central bank reserve diversification away from dollars and into other currencies. This aspect of its approach largely targets U.S. structural power by gradually eroding the dollar's central position in the global economy. On the other hand, China has also sought to carefully promote and internationalize its currency, especially with Asia and its commodity suppliers. This second aspect of its strategy indeed partly targets the dollar, but it more fundamentally reflects China's desire to build structural power by increasing the use of the renminbi in international transactions. As Jonathan Kirshner argues, "States that pursue leadership of regional (or global) monetary orders are almost always motivated by political concerns—in particular, the desire to gain enhanced influence over other states."[55] He notes that France sought to establish a franc area to exclude Germany in the 1860s, that Nazi Germany and imperial Japan extended their currencies in the twentieth century to gain structural power, and that the United States did this as well following World War II.

Like so many of China's efforts to reshape the global economic order, the promotion of the renminbi began after the 2008 global financial crisis. Conventional wisdom holds that a currency's role in the international system depends on the capital account convertibility of the country issuing it, the currency's usage in denominating and settling cross-border trade and financial transactions, and the currency's proportion in central bank reserves. China increased its efforts in all three areas after 2008 to varying degrees.[56] It has taken extremely modest steps toward capital account convertibility and attempted to promote the renminbi as a reserve currency.

Ultimately, however, where China has been most active is in promoting the renminbi's use in international trade, especially through signing several dozen swap agreements of different varieties that facilitate the use of its currency overseas. By 2015, trade settlement in renminbi reached

---

[55] Kirshner, "Regional Hegemony and an Emerging RMB Zone," 215.

[56] Prasad, *Gaining Currency*.

$1.1 trillion—30% of China's total trade—up from virtually zero in 2000.[57] If this percentage increases, it partly reduces China's vulnerability to U.S. structural power because the country will increasingly be able to settle trade in its own currency. At the same time, however, the development should not be overstated. The fact that China uses renminbi in settling its own trade does not mean that the currency is becoming a widely accepted medium for international transactions, which limits China's own ability to exercise structural power over others. Data from SWIFT suggests that the renminbi only accounts for between 1% and 2% of all international payments. While SWIFT data is not reflective of all transactions worldwide (especially those denominated in renminbi), it nonetheless provides a useful estimate.[58]

Although the renminbi has so far failed to gain a global position, it may still achieve a regional one. By 2015, the renminbi constituted 30% of all transactions between China and an Asian state, which made it the main currency in regional trade with China, outstripping the dollar, the yen, and the euro.[59] If that proportion continues to rise over the next decade, China may enjoy a renminbi zone within Asia that allows it to wield structural power over its neighbors. Indeed, as Kirshner argues, the renminbi is not likely to overtake the dollar globally in the near future, but China's centrality to Asia's economy and supply chains makes it likely that the renminbi will eventually become the dominant currency in the region.[60] He further argues that China may be taking a different path to regional internationalization, one that involves creating infrastructure for the renminbi, promoting its use in transactions, and encouraging central banks to hold it as a reserve currency—all while retaining some capital controls and regulation.[61] China's swap agreements help advance this goal, as does its promotion of renminbi-denominated bonds that can be purchased by foreign central banks.

For the most part, the promotion of the renminbi in Asian payments has generated little concern within Asia. Moreover, several Asian states have signed swap agreements with China for economic reasons, including Australia, Indonesia, Japan, Malaysia, Mongolia, Nepal, New Zealand, Pakistan, Singapore, South Korea, Sri Lanka, and Thailand, among others.

---

[57] Prasad, *Gaining Currency*, 103.

[58] Huileng Tan, "China's Currency Is Still Nowhere Near Overtaking the Dollar for Global Payments," CNBC, February 2, 2018, https://www.cnbc.com/2018/02/02/china-currency-yuan-the-rmb-isnt-near-overtaking-the-us-dollar.html.

[59] James Kynge, "Renminbi Tops Currency Usage Table for China's Trade with Asia," *Financial Times*, May 27, 2015, https://www.ft.com/content/1e44915c-048d-11e5-adaf-00144feabdc0.

[60] Kirshner, "Regional Hegemony and an Emerging RMB Zone," 214.

[61] See ibid., 236–37.

These swaps enable settling trade in renminbi, and indeed it continues to be the major currency for Asian trade within China.

However, if much of Asia becomes an effective renminbi zone in the next decade or more, then China could wield some of the instruments of U.S. financial power against its neighbors. Those neighbors would need access to the renminbi system, payment infrastructure like CIPS and CNAPS, and Chinese banks—all of which China can control. An era of Chinese financial statecraft and sanctions within Asia, though perhaps not globally, may not be so distant, and may in turn lay the foundation for a regional sphere of influence. In this way, a Chinese financial zone in Asia could be layered over the U.S. financial order worldwide.

Infrastructure Investment

Infrastructure investment not only facilitates trade and connectivity but also offers the opportunity to practice economic power projection—and through it, an opportunity to reshape the strategic geography of great-power competition. In the first half of the twentieth century, a rising Germany pursued the Berlin-Baghdad railway to bypass British naval supremacy and create an outlet into Asia and the wider Indian Ocean. During the same period, Japan considered a canal on the Isthmus of Kra to bypass the British advantage over the Malacca Strait. Like these past great powers, China has used infrastructure investment not only for economic purposes but also as a tool to enhance its great-power competitiveness. The foremost example is of course the Belt and Road Initiative (BRI) and the financial institutions that support it. Because BRI is discussed in greater detail in Joel Wuthnow's chapter in this volume, the following discussion will focus only on the forms of economic leverage that the initiative may offer.

Some believe that BRI is primarily an economic initiative or a status-driven project for President Xi Jinping and is not at all aimed at acquiring economic leverage. Those who view it in purely economic terms are generally unable to explain why Beijing has invested vast funds in projects that are not only loss-making, but could not absorb much of China's surplus capacity, even if they were all funded and successfully completed.[62] Those who view BRI in status terms may be right, but they generally overlook the fact that the initiative as a practical matter did not begin with Xi. Many of the projects, especially in the Indian Ocean and Southeast Asia, not only preceded him but also were explicitly described in strategic terms in

[62] David Dollar, "The AIIB and the 'One Belt, One Road,'" Brookings Institution, 2015, https://www.brookings.edu/opinions/the-aiib-and-the-one-belt-one-road; and Devin Thorne and Ben Spevack, "Harbored Ambitions: How China's Port Investments Are Strategically Reshaping the Indo-Pacific," C4ADS, 2017.

Chinese government discourses. A number of critics argue that BRI has been overhyped and that if everything China does is now folded under it by the government—from a polar belt to even a space road—then the term means nothing. This criticism is entirely warranted, but BRI is taken here to mean "core BRI"—that is, the infrastructure projects located in the original geographic focus of the initiative (the Indo-Pacific) that may have been initiated before or after BRI was formally announced. Even if BRI is an empty concept, the infrastructure is very real.

Understood in these narrower terms, BRI is at least as much a strategic initiative as an economic or domestic-political one. First, it creates multiple channels of bilateral leverage for China over regional states. It creates financial leverage over those that accept Chinese loans, such as Sri Lanka and Maldives, the latter of which pays 20% of its budget to Beijing in interest.[63] It creates asymmetric interdependence with respect to trade, especially as greater connectivity effectively increases bilateral trade between China and its neighbors. It also creates leverage over maintenance. Several Chinese projects will require Chinese engineers for upkeep, especially given that Chinese state firms dominate many of these markets, ranging from hydroelectric power to high-speed rail.

Second, with respect to structural leverage, the program allows Beijing to create connectivity that essentially excludes other countries. Commercial ports in some ways constitute the new chokepoints of maritime trade and coexist along with more traditional focuses on sea lines of communication and geographic chokepoints. A growing number of critical ports are operated or leased by Chinese state companies. Finally, the possibility that Beijing will export its engineering standards not only for traditional infrastructure like rail lines but also for high-tech infrastructure supporting the internet and 5G networks could create considerable leverage. One can imagine, for example, that future U.S.-made autonomous vehicles could be unable to connect to Chinese wireless networks in BRI countries.[64]

Third, with respect to domestic-political leverage, BRI creates clear opportunities to bribe powerful constituencies in recipient countries, altering their politics. Chinese SOEs have been implicated in payoffs to politicians in Sri Lanka and Malaysia, among other countries.[65] Favorable business terms,

---

[63] Robert A. Manning and Bharath Gopalaswamy, "Is Abdulla Yameen Handing Over the Maldives to China?" *Foreign Policy*, March 21, 2018, https://foreignpolicy.com/2018/03/21/is-abdulla-yameen-handing-over-the-maldives-to-china.

[64] The author thanks Tarun Chhabra for suggesting this point.

[65] Maria Abi-Habib, "How China Got Sri Lanka to Cough Up a Port," *New York Times*, June 25, 2018, https://www.nytimes.com/2018/06/25/world/asia/china-sri-lanka-port.html; and Michael Bristow, "The 'Great-Grandmother of all Scandals' Comes to China," BBC, July 16, 2018, https://www.bbc.com/news/business-44813753.

consulting contracts, and direct payments could reshape the incentives of some politicians and generate policies more favorable to Beijing. Behind BRI stands a variety of financial institutions that enhance China's structural power. These include the New Development Bank launched by the BRICS, the Silk Road Fund, and the Asian Infrastructure Investment Bank (AIIB). However, the financial power of most of these initiatives is still miniscule compared to preexisting domestic institutions in China, such as the China Development Bank and the Export-Import Bank of China, which together have in some years engaged in more lending to developing countries than the World Bank.[66]

Of all these institutions, the AIIB is the most intriguing because it offers a roadmap to leadership and legitimacy rather than just power. The AIIB is neither a naked instrument of economic statecraft nor a benign multilateral bank with Western best practices. China's initial negotiating preferences for a 50% stake with a powerful Chinese veto make clear that Beijing wanted the bank to be a tool that it could dominate. The AIIB clearly had a political purpose as well, with Xi marketing it explicitly as a companion to BRI, despite later attempts to distance the bank from that initiative. Such a nakedly political bank, however, would not be viewed as legitimate by China's own neighbors. Instead, the result was a kind of hegemonic grand bargain—much like the United States' own postwar institutions—that reflects a liberal compromise between the AIIB's founder and its client states that tempers, but does not eliminate, the bank's potential use as a political tool. China accepted diminished direct political control and greater institutionalization in exchange for legitimacy; Asian and European states in turn offered legitimacy in exchange for institutionalization, checks on direct Chinese political influence, and economic public goods. Although the bank is a not a complete political tool, it nonetheless can be directed by Beijing to act politically. Indeed, development banks like the Inter-American Development Bank and Asian Development Bank have occasionally served the political aims of their founders, even if such use was tempered by inclusive institutionalization. Ultimately, the AIIB's true influence lies in its ability to signal the legitimacy of Chinese leadership; set norms and even technical standards through reports, indices, conditionality, and other bank functions; and perhaps even occasionally coerce states through the denial of loans. In any case, the bank offers a unique template for future efforts by China to institutionalize its power within Asia.

Despite the success of the AIIB, the region's reaction to Chinese infrastructure financing has been mixed. Many Asian states have responded warmly to institutionalized Chinese power, such as that exercised through the

---

[66] Alex He, "China in the International Financial System: A Study of the NDB and the AIIB," Centre for International Governance Innovation (CIGI), CIGI Papers, no. 106, June 2016, 4–5.

AIIB and the New Development Bank. But in contrast to these multilateral institutions, the more unilateral Belt and Road Initiative has provoked growing concern and backlash. Skepticism in the region was first concentrated in Japan and India, which tentatively put forward their own alternative concepts. But suspicions about the purpose of Chinese investments, the difficulty of repaying loans, concerns over procurement requirements from Chinese companies, and frustration with the extensive use of Chinese labor have filtered down to a wide range of Asian states, including Thailand, Myanmar, and Malaysia, among others. Even China's "all-weather friend" Pakistan has pushed to review all BRI agreements signed with China.[67]

Conclusion

As China collides with the international economic architecture, it is likely to create a parallel substructure in international finance at the global level while accumulating financial leverage over its neighbors at the regional level. The former threatens U.S. structural power, whereas the latter creates Chinese bilateral, structural, and domestic-political power over Asian states. These trends generate important implications for China, the United States, and the region.

Implications for China

In the decade since the global financial crisis, China has sought to blunt elements of the United States' financial power while building the foundations of its own. Its efforts have partly been defensive, with Chinese leaders hoping that their attempts to promote monetary diversification, bypass the dollar, and promote China's own currency and payment systems could eventually reduce the country's vulnerability to U.S. financial sanctions. Beijing's aspirations to build financial power, both through promoting the renminbi in regional transactions and through the use of financial instruments in BRI, have seen advances in some areas and setbacks in others.

With respect to blunting U.S. financial power, China has largely failed to diversify the international monetary system. Alternative currencies such as the euro, pound, yen, and renminbi all have limitations, and the world's

---

[67] For more on these trends, see Andrew Small, "The Backlash to the Belt and Road: A South Asian Battle over Chinese Economic Power," *Foreign Affairs*, February 16, 2018, https://www.foreignaffairs.com/articles/china/2018-02-16/backlash-belt-and-road; Christopher Balding, "Why Democracies Are Turning Against Belt and Road," *Foreign Affairs*, October 24, 2018, https://www.foreignaffairs.com/articles/china/2018-10-24/why-democracies-are-turning-against-belt-and-road; and Hiroyuki Akita, "Backlash Builds Against China as Belt and Road Ties Fray," *Nikkei Asian Review*, September 2, 2018, https://asia.nikkei.com/Spotlight/Comment/Backlash-builds-against-China-as-Belt-and-Road-ties-fray.

major economies tend to be U.S. allies skeptical of Chinese initiatives for diversification. Yet the fact that China has not dislodged the dollar does not mean it has failed to blunt U.S. financial leverage. Chinese efforts to enmesh U.S. financial institutions in China are not only an attempt at attracting capital but, at least according to some Chinese financial officials, also an attempt at mitigating asymmetric dependence.[68] Moreover, while its alternative credit rating agencies have yet to gain international traction, China's decision to open its market to them, as well as its efforts to win support from others for alternative rating standards, could both complicate the independence of major rating agencies and promote some convergence on standards. Taken together, these efforts could render the country less vulnerable to Western ratings. Most importantly, China's efforts at duplicating SWIFT's messaging system will eventually produce a parallel financial architecture that will allow messaging, clearance, and settling outside the U.S. financial system. This effort to recreate the substructure of the international financial system, especially through an alternative payments system, may offer U.S. adversaries or nonstate actors that China supports an opportunity to escape U.S. financial pressure, which could seriously undermine Washington's financial power worldwide, even if China fails to fully internationalize the renminbi. It also would reduce the potency of U.S. financial sanctions over China.

With respect to building financial power, China's hesitancy to pursue full capital account liberalization for fear that doing so could bring economic and political instability reduces the ability of the renminbi to rise as a share of global transactions. Even so, China's success in promoting its currency in regional transactions involving China has indeed created structural power that will likely grow in the future. The fact that the renminbi may remain a small portion of international transactions does not prevent China from accumulating leverage if the renminbi becomes the major currency for regional transactions—even if only for those involving China. Such status would allow Beijing to exercise financial leverage it has not previously enjoyed.

Meanwhile, China's efforts to use financial instruments to boost connectivity with its own economy through BRI have provoked a wave of backlash. A more concessionary approach—one that lowers interest rates, prevents debt traps, uses more local labor, and eschews the kinds of bribes that alienate local populations and embolden opponents—could well emerge and be quite successful. The fact that China is struggling now with BRI does not mean that it cannot adapt its approach.

---

[68] Author's interviews.

Implications for the United States

The dollar's status as reserve currency is the backbone of U.S. hegemony, allowing the United States to spend beyond its means, monitor international transactions, cut states and individuals from the global financial system, and finance its military advantage. As the preceding discussion makes clear, China's efforts to weaken the United States' financial power have had mixed success so far. Ultimately, they will be far more successful if the U.S. system loses its luster. Indeed, the global financial crisis raised concerns about the role of the dollar and credit rating agencies, while Washington's renewed willingness to sanction allies over Iran has already raised serious concerns about payment systems and U.S. financial power more broadly. Although U.S. financial power is strong, the United States' position is nonetheless most vulnerable when the hegemon overuses the privileges of its dominant currency.

Accordingly, Washington needs to elevate the maintenance of financial power into a national security priority. This of course has both domestic and international components. First, at the domestic level, the United States needs to prudently manage its fiscal deficits to reduce the risk that allies, who previously raised concerns over the dollar's role after the financial crisis, do not feel that the dollar is being misused and work with competitors like China on robust diversification efforts. Indeed, the fact that many U.S. allies previously blanched at China's SDR proposals should not be taken for granted.

Second, financial regulation should be seen not merely in economic terms but also in strategic ones. A balance needs to be struck that maintains the competitiveness of U.S. financial institutions and their nodal position in global finance while also reducing the risk of another financial crisis that could erode their legitimacy.

Third, the United States must not overuse financial sanctions. The current re-imposition of sanctions on Iran is driving U.S. allies to look for ways to bypass the U.S. financial architecture. European initiatives, such as the "special purpose vehicle" backed by France, Germany, and the United Kingdom, are now eagerly embraced by China and Russia. This unprecedented vehicle would serve as a barter exchange disconnected from the dollar-based financial system. It would allow Iranian exporters to acquire "credits" they could use to purchase products from European firms on the exchange. Despite lingering skepticism about whether such an approach would work, whether it would protect companies from U.S. secondary sanctions, and whether any state is willing to host the exchange, the fact that U.S. allies are working to create a mechanism to bypass the dollar is a serious development that threatens the foundations of U.S. financial leverage even if it fails to threaten the dollar's nodal position.

Finally, engagement with countries that are "global swing states" on financial issues, such as India and Brazil, is necessary. These states often share China's objections to U.S. financial power and have at various times supported its calls for diversification. Efforts to engage these states, address their concerns on financial matters, and integrate them into financial institutions could complicate Chinese coalition-building. In short, even if the dollar remains dominant, the United States must attend to the foundations of its financial power. In many ways, its financial power has political roots in the acquiescence of allies that the United States is now alienating.

At the regional level, China's financial power, as well as its growing economic influence, requires U.S. attention. If the United States does not re-engage the region's multilateral economic processes, then China's attempts to build constraining leverage over its neighbors will be likelier to succeed and could eventually form the foundation for an enduring sphere of influence. A more active U.S. policy could exploit certain openings that are materializing as Chinese order-building stokes nationalist opposition in Asian states.

Specifically, preventing Chinese regional hegemony requires strengthening the autonomy of Asian states vis-à-vis China where possible. This could be accomplished in a number of ways. First, Washington could join China's economic initiatives (e.g., the AIIB) and influence, repurpose, or stall them from within. Even if Congress proves unable to authorize funding for a U.S. contribution, especially as trade tensions with China continue, the Trump administration could propose an advisory or observer role for the United States as part of a U.S.-China deal on some other issue. The legitimacy benefit China gains from U.S. participation is outweighed by the possible voice opportunities the United States would gain within the system, especially because they could provide support for Asian states and bring transparency to Chinese practices. Relatedly, U.S. financial partnerships with BRI projects would shine a light on Chinese practices while simultaneously reducing dependence on Chinese financing. Second, Washington could create parallel trade, investment, and even financial alternatives of its own with its allies and partners—taking a page from China's book—and thereby reduce the dependence of Asian countries on China. The current BUILD (Better Utilization of Investments Leading to Development) Act marks a step in the right direction. Third, Washington could strengthen and engage existing multilateral bodies, including the World Bank and the Asian Development Bank, to ensure that they play a higher-profile role in Asia's financial future. Efforts to strengthen regional multilateral bodies, including Association of Southeast Asian Nation (ASEAN) forums and the East Asia Summit, reduce the likelihood that Chinese-led alternatives become focal.

Implications for the Region

China's efforts to build financial power could reshape Asian politics. The promotion of the renminbi and Chinese financing creates bilateral, structural, and domestic-political leverage that could seriously constrain the autonomy of Asian states.

China's trade ties within the region provide a window into how the country may convert its financial leverage into political power, as well as insight into how the region might productively respond. Especially after the 2008 global financial crisis, China has been increasingly willing to wield its leverage in trade, including against Japan over the East China Sea, Norway over the Nobel Prize, Taiwan over its elections, the Philippines over the South China Sea, Mongolia over a Dalai Lama visit, and South Korea over Terminal High Altitude Area Defense.[69] These efforts have accompanied a change in China's domestic discourse on the appropriateness of economic coercion that also followed the crisis.[70] The country's willingness to use instruments of trade coercively suggests the possibility that financial instruments would be similarly employed.

The case of trade also shows that in many instances China has run into obstacles when its agenda is multilateralized. For example, China has long seen the Regional Comprehensive Economic Partnership (RCEP)—a multilateral economic agreement that would cover sixteen countries, nearly half of the world's population, and roughly one-third of its GDP—as an important vehicle for regional leadership. In a 2014 statement by the Ministry of Commerce, China made clear that "the smooth establishment of the RCEP is of great importance to China's fighting for the initiative [in] the new round [over the] reconstruction of international economic and trade rules."[71] After the United States' withdrawal from the Trans-Pacific Partnership (TPP), China's Foreign Ministry initially elevated these efforts. The head of the ministry's Department of International Economic Affairs declared, "If China has taken up a leadership role, it is because the front runners have stepped back, leaving that place to China. If China is required to play that leadership role then China will assume its responsibilities."[72]

---

[69] Peter Harrell, Elizabeth Rosenberg, and Eduardo Saravalle, "China's Use of Coercive Economic Measures," Center for a New American Security, June 2018.

[70] James Reilly, "China's Unilateral Sanctions," *Washington Quarterly* 35, no. 4 (2012): 121–33.

[71] "Give Play of China's Important Role and Accelerate RCEP Negotiations," Ministry of Commerce of the People's Republic of China, September 1, 2014, http://english.mofcom.gov.cn/article/newsrelease/significantnews/201409/20140900720384.shtml.

[72] "Diplomat Says China Would Assume World Leadership if Needed," Reuters, January 23, 2017, https://www.reuters.com/article/us-china-usa-politics-idUSKBN1570ZZ.

These lofty leadership ambitions, however, encountered obstacles from regional states—especially Australia, India, and Japan. China's desire to enshrine its preferences on issues relating to cross-border data flows and intellectual property face Japanese and Australian opposition; meanwhile, India is extremely reluctant to extend to China the same low tariffs it offers ASEAN, given the enormous Sino-Indian goods deficit, especially in manufactures. Under Japanese instigation, Asian states even managed to resurrect the TPP as RCEP floundered. At least for now, RCEP remains an example both of Chinese order-building ambitions and of Asian resistance, as well as a keen demonstration of how China's agenda can stall when it is multilateralized.

In financial matters, China's efforts to internationalize its currency within the region have largely been welcomed for the economic benefits and convenience they bring, especially amid concerns about U.S. protectionism. Japanese prime minister Shinzo Abe, for example, pushed forward a $30 billion three-year swap agreement with China in 2018, and nearly half of all Chinese swap agreements are in Asia. But concerns over Chinese investment in infrastructure have engendered a stronger response featuring a wide mix of strategies—some more successful than others.

Some states like India have pursued hardline strategies and largely boycotted BRI. This approach avoids offering legitimacy to the initiative but reduces the possibility of influencing its investments. Other states, particularly recipient states like Malaysia, Myanmar, Pakistan, and Thailand, have revisited, scaled back, or canceled some Chinese infrastructure investments while continuing others. This approach may provide an opportunity for recipient countries to push China to adjust its practice, thereby putting recipients on stronger and more independent financial footing. Finally, some donor states like Japan have objected to BRI while at the same time pushing to work with China on some infrastructure projects. This more participatory and multilateral approach could bring greater transparency to BRI projects, effectively reducing their political component and the leverage that they can generate. Indeed, the transformation of the AIIB from China's initial proposal to the institution that was subsequently launched demonstrates the power of such approaches. While BRI projects are largely bilateral, efforts to multilateralize them attenuate China's influence.

Indeed, just as the multilateral structure of RCEP provided Asian states more options than a strictly bilateral structure, so too would attempting to multilateralize some elements of Chinese financial power. Ultimately, regional states do want Chinese funding for infrastructure, but they want it on terms that are less politically and financially problematic. By supporting them, and where possible partnering with Chinese entities, donors like the United States could enhance the leverage of these smaller states and, in so doing, reduce the risk of asymmetric dependencies.

For these reasons, the United States should re-engage regional multilateral economic processes and endeavor to multilateralize some of China's own bilateral efforts, such as its BRI investments. Doing so can make it easier for Asian states to resist or repurpose China's financial statecraft and would also bring greater transparency to its efforts to harness such instruments for political purposes. In contrast, U.S. disengagement promotes bilateral approaches between China and its Asian neighbors and only hastens the arrival of a Chinese sphere of influence.

EXECUTIVE SUMMARY

This chapter quantifies how Beijing wields its official finance abroad to advance its national interests and discusses the implications for recipient countries, the U.S., and U.S. allies.

MAIN ARGUMENT

China's opaque official finance fuels a narrative that the country is a rogue donor that partners with corrupt regimes, entices countries to borrow beyond their capacity, and extracts security or economic concessions from recipient governments. Leaders in capital-hungry economies counter that China is one of the few partners willing to finance infrastructure projects. This chapter argues that Chinese official finance has evolved in four phases driven by both economic and geostrategic interests. Some evidence suggests that Beijing's efforts are paying off in more favorable popular perceptions in recipient countries, inroads with foreign leaders, and discrete economic and security concessions. However, Beijing's "power of the purse" does not always garner influence in the ways that might be expected and even provokes backlash under specific conditions.

POLICY IMPLICATIONS

- If China continues to deploy its vast foreign currency reserves to invest in infrastructure around the world, then it will likely further consolidate its influence with foreign leaders and citizens.

- If China demonstrates that it can follow through on its financial promises and mitigate negative local spillovers from its projects, it will be difficult for other countries to usurp China's clout.

- If the U.S. and other Western powers were to choose to increase the supply of capital for infrastructure projects on more generous terms, China's dominance as the lender of choice could be mitigated or displaced.

China's Global Development Spending Spree: Winning the World One Yuan at a Time?

Samantha Custer and Michael J. Tierney

China has an estimated $3 trillion in surplus foreign currency reserves that it can deploy to pursue its interests.[1] Since 1999, Beijing has explicitly sought overseas investment opportunities for its excess capital with its "going global" strategy.[2] However, China is opaque about how it employs its official finance—a basket of outright grants, concessional loans, nonconcessional lending, and equity investments in private companies all directed by the Chinese government—to win friends and allies around the world.[3] Beijing does not consistently disclose which countries receive its assistance, nor does

Samantha Custer is Director of Policy Analysis at AidData, a research lab at the College of William & Mary. She can be reached at <scuster@aiddata.wm.edu>.

Michael J. Tierney is the George and Mary Hylton Professor of Government and International Relations at the College of William & Mary. He can be reached at <mjtier@wm.edu>.

The authors would like to acknowledge several individuals who contributed to the underlying data collection and analysis that made this chapter possible, including Mengfan Cheng, Harsh Desai, Matthew DiLorenzo, Sid Ghose, Taka Masaki, Brad Parks, Brooke Russell, Tanya Sethi, Jacob Sims, and Jennifer Turner. John Custer provided graphic design support for the conception of the figures. They also thank an anonymous reviewer for making suggestions that improved the quality of this chapter.

[1] Salvatore Babones, "China Is Sitting on $3 Trillion in Currency Reserves, but Is That Enough?" *Forbes*, May 24, 2018.

[2] Hongying Wang, "A Deeper Look at China's 'Going Out' Policy," Centre for International Governance Innovation, March 2016, https://www.cigionline.org/publications/deeper-look-chinas-going-out-policy; and David Dollar, "China's Rise as a Regional and Global Power: The AIIB and the 'One Belt One Road,'" Brookings Institution, July 15, 2015.

[3] See Organisation for Economic Co-operation and Development (OECD), "Glossary of Statistical Terms," https://stats.oecd.org/glossary/detail.asp?ID=1893.

it provide any systematic project-level details on the nature of these loans, grants, and investments.

Limited transparency around China's official finance exacerbates the prevailing narrative among its critics that Beijing is a "rogue donor" willing to partner with corrupt regimes, entice countries to borrow more than they are able to repay, and strategically position itself to extract security or economic concessions.[4] Leaders of capital-hungry countries respond that China is one of few development partners willing to make large loans to support infrastructure investments, and they thus welcome Beijing's largesse in the absence of credible alternatives.[5] Moreover, they argue that China is not unique in its desire to garner economic or security dividends from its official finance, as other donors often impose conditions on their lending in order to advance their own interests.[6]

Nonetheless, Sri Lanka and Cambodia serve as cautionary tales of borrowers becoming indebted to China, particularly in light of its extensive use of less concessional loans. The Sri Lankan government relinquished control of its Hambantota port "to Chinese interests on a 99-year lease in exchange for a billion dollars of debt relief."[7] Some speculate that China, knowing Sri Lanka would be unable to service this debt, entered into a series of loans in order to secure a strategic transportation hub.[8] Meanwhile, the Cambodian government has recently put itself in similar jeopardy, having accumulated $4.3 billion in debt to Beijing, equivalent to 20% of its GDP.[9]

In this chapter, we leverage the best available evidence to quantify how China wields the "power of its purse" to advance its national interests, assess the downstream effects of these overtures on popular perceptions and the behavior of foreign leaders, and discuss the implications for the United States and other countries. Given the global wave of populism that is pushing the

---

[4] See Moises Naim, "Rogue Aid," *Foreign Policy*, October 15, 2009. For an alternative view drawing on project-level data, see "Why China Is Not a Rogue Donor," *Foreign Affairs*, October 15, 2015.

[5] During the 1980s and 1990s, traditional Western donors shifted away from providing infrastructure funding and refocused development aid and lending on the social, health, environmental, governance, and financial sectors. Michael J. Tierney et al., "More Dollars Than Sense: Refining Our Knowledge of Development Finance Using AidData," *World Development* 39, no. 11 (2011): 1891–906.

[6] For canonical theoretical and empirical illustrations of this point, see Hans Morgenthau, "A Political Theory of Foreign Aid," *American Political Science Review* 56, no. 2 (1962): 301–9; and Axel Dreher and James Vreeland, *The Political Economy of the United Nations Security Council: Money and Influence* (New York: Cambridge University Press, 2014).

[7] Darren J. Lim and Rohan Mukherjee, "Does Debt Pay? China and the Politics of Investment in Sri Lanka," *Diplomat*, January 20, 2018.

[8] Maria Ali-Habib, "How China Got Sri Lanka to Cough Up a Port," *New York Times*, June 25, 2018.

[9] John Hurley, Scott Morris, and Gailyn Portelance, "Examining the Debt Implications of the Belt and Road Initiative from a Policy Perspective," Center for Global Development, Policy Paper, no. 121, March 2018, https://www.cgdev.org/publication/examining-debt-implications-belt-and-road-initiative-a-policy-perspective.

United States and Europe to turn inward and reduce their foreign aid budgets, it is tempting (for voters and elected leaders) to forgo the immediate costs paid by taxpayers to fund foreign aid budgets in light of uncertain future benefits. One thing becomes clear from the analysis in this chapter: if Western powers scale back their global aid, China has the means (e.g., a vast arsenal of surplus reserves) and the mandate (e.g., high-level political support to use official finance to advance its interests) to step into the breach and cement its role as the preferred lender to the developing world.

There is some evidence, which we discuss later in this chapter, that Beijing's "charm offensive" is paying off in more favorable popular perceptions, inroads with foreign leaders, and discrete economic and security concessions.[10] However, China's ability to sustain these gains depends on several factors. The country must follow through in translating financial promises into completed projects that deliver sustainable benefits. It must continue to convince foreign leaders (and their citizens) that accepting Chinese grants, loans, and/or equity investments is a net positive for their countries. Finally, Beijing's ability to "run the table"—to secure a dominant position as the lender of choice for low- and middle-income countries—is vulnerable to a renewed effort from the United States and other powers to increase the supply of available capital on more generous terms.[11] Our specific analysis of Chinese development finance as a tool of foreign policy fits into broader discussions about the future of the liberal order, the possibility that China could lead an alternative order, and the nature and utility of soft power in international politics.[12]

---

[10] Joshua Kurlantzick, *Charm Offensive: How China's Soft Power Is Transforming the World* (New Haven: Yale University Press, 2007); and Samantha Custer et al., "Ties That Bind: Quantifying China's Public Diplomacy and Its 'Good Neighbor' Effect," AidData, College of William & Mary, June 2018, http://docs.aiddata.org/ad4/pdfs/Ties_That_Bind--Full_Report.pdf.

[11] Ben Zimmer, "Running the Table: From Pool to Politics," *New York Times*, March 4, 2016. The Better Utilization of Investment Leading to Development (BUILD) Act, passed by the U.S. Congress and signed into law in October 2018, doubles the size of the Overseas Private Investment Corporation's budget and creates a new U.S. agency, the U.S. International Development Finance Corporation, which has the authority to take equity positions in development projects. The stated purpose of this new organization is to allow the United States to compete with China and other sovereign donors and investors in developing countries. See Patricia Zengerle, "Congress, Eying China, Votes to Overhaul Development Finance," Reuters, October 3, 2018.

[12] Allan Bentley, Srdjan Vucetic, and Ted Hopf, "The Distribution of Identity and the Future of International Order: China's Hegemonic Prospects," *International Organization* 72, no. 4 (2018): 839–69; David Shambaugh, "China's Soft-Power Push," *Foreign Affairs*, July/August 2015; and Joseph S. Nye, "China and Soft Power," *South African Journal of International Affairs* 19, no. 2 (2012): 151–55. Yet others argue that China's approach is not necessarily practicing soft power but "sharp power" in attempting to displace the interests of its competitors through coercion and limited transparency. See, for example, Christopher Walker and Jessica Ludwig, "Sharp Power: Rising Authoritarian Influence," International Forum for Democratic Studies, December 2017, https://www.ned.org/wp-content/uploads/ 2017/12/Sharp-Power; and Joseph S. Nye Jr., "How Sharp Power Threatens Soft Power," *Foreign Affairs*, January 24, 2018.

The remainder of this chapter is organized in five sections. The first section describes the guiding principles and the manner in which Beijing has used development finance over the past 60 years. The second section quantifies the scope, distribution, and composition of China's official finance to other countries over a fourteen-year period, while the third section explores three possible motives for China's official financing. The fourth section then considers the downstream perceptions of Beijing's overtures among foreign leaders and citizens in the East Asia and Pacific region, both from a regional perspective as well as via three country case studies. The chapter concludes with a discussion of the implications of these trends for China, recipient governments, the United States, and other powers.

History: How Has Beijing's Approach to Official Finance Evolved over Time?

China classifies the details of its foreign aid and official investment programs as state secrets, and thus its financial statecraft has been a virtual black box.[13] However, in recent years, new data collection methods have made it easier to quantify China's official finance to developing countries. This section defines official finance and then examines how Beijing's use of this foreign policy tool has evolved through four distinct phases in response to emerging opportunities and threats.

Most Western governments ascribe to the view of the Organisation for Economic Co-operation and Development (OECD) that foreign aid is limited to official development assistance (ODA).[14] Primarily intended for development and highly concessional in its terms, these flows must include a grant element of more than 25%.[15] But this notion of concessional aid does not fit the approach of emerging donors like China and discounts other official flows (OOF) that are less concessional or multipurpose in advancing development along with commercial or diplomatic ends.[16] Counting ODA alone would dramatically underestimate China's financial footprint in other

---

[13] Deborah Brautigam, *The Dragon's Gift: The Real Story of China in Africa* (Oxford: Oxford University Press, 2009).

[14] See OECD, "Glossary of Statistical Terms."

[15] OECD, "Glossary of Statistical Terms." For a detailed discussion, see OECD, "What Is ODA?" 2018, http://www.oecd.org/dac/stats/What-is-ODA.pdf. For a detailed description of how AidData researchers estimate development intent and concessionality of any given Chinese project in the dataset, see Austin M. Strange et al., "AidData TUFF Coder Instructions," Version 1.3, AidData, 2017.

[16] Charles Wolf Jr., Xiao Wang, and Eric Warner, *China's Foreign Aid and Government-Sponsored Investment Activities: Scale, Content, Destinations, and Implications* (Santa Monica: RAND Corporation, 2013), https://www.rand.org/content/dam/rand/pubs/research_reports/RR100/RR118/RAND_RR118.pdf.

countries. This chapter includes, and distinguishes between, both concessional and less concessional Chinese official finance that does not always fit the strict ODA definition of aid.

China uses a range of official finance instruments to advance its interests—from grants and zero- or low-interest concessional loans to export credits and higher-interest loans at competitive market rates.[17] The differences between these financial instruments are not superficial, as the terms can vary substantially in whether and how long countries have to repay loans and at what rate of interest. Beijing often bundles different financial instruments together when negotiating an assistance package with its partner countries.[18]

China has long served as a provider of concessional aid to the rest of the world. The Chinese government cites its provision of "material assistance to the Democratic People's Republic of Korea and Vietnam" as the first concrete examples, followed by aid to several African countries dating back to 1956.[19] The country's use of less concessional official finance is a more contemporary phenomenon, with the earliest examples arising in the mid-1990s.[20] Its official finance efforts have evolved over time in four phases, as dictated by political philosophy, national priorities, and level of currency reserves.

Predominantly directed toward countries in Asia, the first phase of Chinese official finance (1950–74) came in the form of concessional aid and was conceived as a vehicle both to facilitate the "export" of Marxist values and to curb the influence of the United States and its allies.[21] Following a high point in 1973, China's enthusiasm for supplying aid to other countries waned in the second phase (1974–90), characterized as a period of "adjustment and transformation" where Deng Xiaoping and other economic reformers adopted a "hide and bide" approach.[22]

With burgeoning current account surpluses and an economy hungry for natural resources, Beijing's interest in supplying concessional aid surged under

---

[17] Wolf et al., *China's Foreign Aid and Government-Sponsored Investment Activities*; and Deborah Brautigam, "Aid with Chinese Characteristics: Chinese Foreign Aid and Development Finance Meet the OECD-DAC Aid Regime," *Journal of International Development* 23, no. 5 (2011): 752–64. For a detailed discussion of the differences between Chinese ODA and OOF and for empirical evidence showing that China employs these different financial instruments for different reasons, see Axel Dreher et al., "Apples and Dragon Fruits: The Determinants of Aid and Other Forms of State Financing from China to Africa," *International Studies Quarterly* 62, no. 1 (2018): 182–94.

[18] Brautigam, "Aid with Chinese Characteristics."

[19] Information Office of the State Council of the People's Republic of China (PRC), *China's Foreign Aid* (Beijing, April 2011), 1–2.

[20] Brautigam, "Aid with Chinese Characteristics"; John F. Copper, *China's Foreign Aid and Investment Diplomacy* (Basingstoke: Palgrave-MacMillan, 2016); and Hong Zhou and Hou Xiong, eds., *China's Foreign Aid: 60 Years in Retrospect* (Singapore: Springer, 2017).

[21] Li Xiaoyun, "China's Foreign Aid to Africa: Overview," unpublished manuscript.

[22] Ibid.

the leadership of Jiang Zemin and Hu Jintao in the post–Cold War period.[23] This third phase (1991–2007) witnessed a shift toward aid as solidarity or "mutual reciprocity and mutual benefit." This period also witnessed a substantial increase in the volume of assistance and the number of countries receiving support from Beijing as compared to the previous period.[24]

With the establishment of the Forum on China-Africa Cooperation in 2000, Africa surpassed Asia as the largest recipient of Beijing's foreign aid.[25] During this third phase, China also started to employ less concessional forms of official financing. "Reorganizing its state banking system" in 1994, the Chinese government established "two sources of official bank finance" that could be deployed to advance its national interests: export credits from the Export-Import Bank of China and the China-Africa Development Fund via the China Development Bank.[26]

We may now be experiencing a fourth phase of Chinese official finance that began with the 2008 global financial crisis during Hu's second term in office and has been shaped by President Xi Jinping's embrace of a more active foreign policy since 2013.[27] While scholars and journalists often point to the Xi administration as an inflection point in China's engagement with other countries, there were clear indications in Hu's public speeches and his administration's growing official finance portfolio that as early as 2008 China was laying the groundwork for the strategic deployment of its financial reserves as a tool of public diplomacy.[28] The articulated aim was to change

---

[23] Li, "China's Foreign Aid and Aid to Africa"; and Wolf et al., *China's Foreign Aid and Government-Sponsored Investment Activities*. See also Copper, *China's Foreign Aid and Investment Diplomacy in Retrospect*.

[24] Li, "China's Foreign Aid and Aid to Africa." For a quantitative measure of this increase in volume and in the number of countries receiving Chinese official finance, see Austin M. Strange et al., "Tracking Underreported Financial Flows: China's Development Finance and the Aid-Conflict Nexus Revisited," *Journal of Conflict Resolution* 61, no. 5 (2017): 935–63.

[25] Brautigam, "Aid with Chinese Characteristics."

[26] Ibid. See also Henry Sanderson and Michael Forsythe, *China's Superbank: Debt, Oil and Influence—How China Development Bank Is Rewriting the Rules of Finance* (Singapore: Wiley, 2012).

[27] For a description of how the Belt and Road Initiative and the allocation of official finance reflect a growing consensus among the Chinese foreign policy community regarding the need to shift from a "low profile" stance toward active engagement with other countries, see Mingjiang Li, "China's 'One Belt, One Road' Initiative: New Round of Opening Up," S. Rajaratnam School of International Studies (RSIS), RSIS Commentaries, March 11, 2015; Wenjuan Nie, "Xi Jinping's Foreign Policy Dilemma: One Belt, One Road or the South China Sea," *Contemporary Southeast Asia* 38, no. 3 (2016): 422–44; Yan Xuetong, "From Keeping a Low Profile to Striving for Achievement," *Chinese Journal of International Politics* 7, no. 2 (2014): 153–84; and Peter Cai, "Understanding China's Belt and Road Initiative," Lowy Institute, March 2017.

[28] For deeper insight into how both Hu and Xi view the role of various foreign policy tools to strengthen China's soft power with other countries and counter negative images of China in the international media, see Xin Liu, "Look Beyond and Beneath the Soft Power: An Alternative Analytical Framework for China's Cultural Diplomacy," *Cambridge Journal of China Studies* 12, no. 4 (2017); and Peter Ferdinand, "Westward Ho—The China Dream and 'One Belt, One Road': Chinese Foreign Policy under Xi Jinping," *International Affairs* 92, no. 4 (2016): 941–57.

the international media narrative from the "China threat" to a story of the country's "peaceful rise."[29]

China is often portrayed in Western media and policy circles as a strategic unitary actor that rationally weighs costs and benefits in pursuit of its geopolitical interests, but the reality is more complex. In fact, Beijing's management of its official finance has historically been fragmented across myriad bureaucratic and provincial actors that have expanded their roles over time, often without a clear coordinating direction from the State Council. As the government created various forms of official finance, different actors either asserted authority or were delegated authority over those tools. The Ministry of Foreign Affairs, Ministry of Finance, and Ministry of Commerce play important roles when it comes to ODA-like flows, while most nonconcessional lending runs through the Export-Import Bank or the China Development Bank.

As a result, official finance is allocated in a way that is consistent with the policy goals of the particular ministries or agencies charged with those tasks. Ministries that oversee ODA-like flows view these funds as cementing geopolitical alliances and winning coalitions within international organizations.[30] Conversely, the Export-Import Bank and China Development Bank select projects based upon the recipient country's ability to repay loans or the bank's ability to realize good returns on equity investments. Provincial governments, meanwhile, often take the lead on the planning, funding, and implementation of projects in particular sectors in a way that would be unrecognizable in other federal systems such as the United States, Canada, or Australia.

This state of affairs prompts some scholars of Chinese public policy to label Beijing's approach as "incoherent," in that multiple ministries may be implementing projects in a single developing country simultaneously, without being aware of what each is doing.[31] In this respect, Xi's April 2018 announcement of a new international development cooperation agency may be viewed as an attempt to remedy this organizational incoherence.

---

[29] Ferdinand, "Westward Ho."

[30] Statistical results show that Chinese ODA and grant allocation are strongly associated with voting with China at the United Nations, whereas the less concessionary flows controlled by the Chinese policy banks are not correlated with the positions of the Chinese government in international organizations and instead appear to be driven by the ability to repay loans and the expected economic return on investment. See Dreher et al., "Apples and Dragon Fruits," 187–89.

[31] Denghua Zhang and Graeme Smith, "China's Foreign Aid System: Structure, Agencies, and Identities," *Third World Quarterly* 38, no. 10 (2017): 2330–46; and Chih-shian Liou, "Bureaucratic Politics and Overseas Investment by Chinese State-Owned Oil Companies: Illusory Champions," *Asian Survey* 49, no. 4 (2009): 670–90. Our own experiences doing field research in China and speaking with government officials have reinforced the conclusion that Chinese ministries often do not agree on whether or how to track and coordinate their own investments. Authors' interviews with an official from the Ministry of Health (PRC), Beijing, November 2016.

Specifically, the creation of this agency signals that China may be taking steps toward greater centralization and coordination of its efforts, at least with regard to the flows commonly categorized as ODA.

Money: How Do We Quantify China's Global Development Spending Spree?

This section provides a detailed quantitative description of the scope, distribution, and composition of Beijing's outward-focused official finance from 2000 to 2014. Using project-level data from AidData, a research lab at the College of William & Mary, we quantify Chinese global official finance investments, including both concessional ODA and other less concessional official flows. Triangulating information from multiple data sources—media reports, academic papers, government ministry and embassy websites, and field research—the global dataset captures $354 billion in official finance investments made by China to support 4,300 discrete projects in countries around the world between 2000 and 2014.[32] With this dataset, we can begin to separate myth from fact to quantify how much money Beijing is spending, on what terms, with whom, and to what end.

If we were to look at ODA alone, the United States dwarfs China's foreign aid program, contributing $366 billion in concessional aid between 2000 and 2014 compared to a modest $81 billion from China. By contrast, if we broaden the aperture to take into account a country's total official finance portfolio of concessional and less concessional lending, China and the United States have similarly sized overall official finance portfolios. In the same fourteen-year period, China committed $354 billion in official finance to low- and middle-income countries compared to $395 billion by the United States.

While both portfolios are allocated at the direction of their respective governments, the majority (77%) of Beijing's expenditures between 2000 and 2014 do not meet the level of concessionality to be considered "aid" by OECD standards.[33] Nonetheless, Beijing's official finance is often still more attractive to recipient countries because it is given without the behavioral or institutional conditions favored by Western donors (e.g., favorable regulatory environments for business, political competition, human rights,

---

[32] Axel Dreher et al., "Aid, China, and Growth: Evidence from a New Global Development Finance Dataset," Working Paper, no. 46, 2017. To access the data and for more information on the methodology, see AidData, Chinese Global Official Finance Dataset, Version 1.0, 2000–2014, http://aiddata.org/data/chinese-global-official-finance-dataset.

[33] By comparison, the United States had a much smaller proportion of its overall official finance (7%) classified as less concessional OOF between 2000 and 2014.

and environmental safeguards). That said, Chinese financing may come with different conditions, such as requiring recipient countries to use Chinese labor or take positions favorable to China in international organizations.

Politicians, journalists, and academics have long argued that Chinese overseas investments have grown in both volume and sophistication in recent years. Our official financing estimates support this view: globally, China has been steadily increasing its overall official financing in other countries, exceeding the United States since 2009 (**Figures 1** and **2**). The marked uptick in Chinese global official finance lends further credence to a growing consensus that Beijing is more assertively using official finance to position itself favorably vis-à-vis other powers on a global stage.[34]

Seven of the top ten recipients of Chinese ODA between 2000 and 2014 were in Africa (**Table 1**). By contrast, Beijing weighted its less

FIGURE 1   Chinese and U.S. official finance over time, all flows, 2000–2014

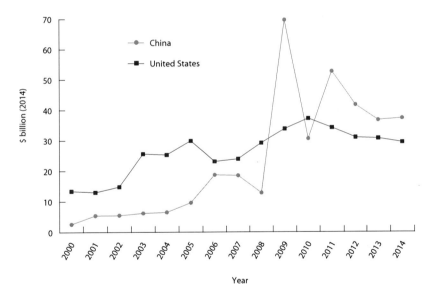

SOURCE: AidData, 2017.

---

[34] For further discussion of China's desire to leverage its economic power to win admiration for its development model and compete with the West for influence, see Leonard K. Cheng, "Three Questions on China's 'Belt and Road Initiative,'" *China Economic Review* 40 (2016): 309–13; William Overholt, "One Belt, One Road, One Pivot," *Global Asia* 10, no. 3 (2015); Francis Fukuyama, "Exporting the Chinese Model," Project Syndicate, December 1, 2016; and Michael D. Swaine, "Chinese Views and Commentary on the 'One Belt, One Road' Initiative," Hoover Institute, China Leadership Monitor, no. 47, July 2015.

FIGURE 2   Chinese official finance over time by flows type, 2000–2014

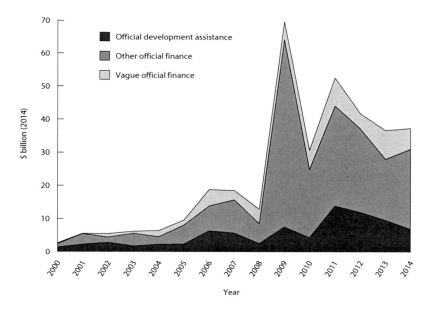

SOURCE: AidData, 2017.

TABLE 1   Top ten recipients of Chinese ODA and OOF, 2000–2014

Top ten recipients of Chinese ODA		Top ten recipients of Chinese OOF	
1.	Cuba ($6.7 billion)	1.	Russia ($36.6 billion)
2.	Cote d'Ivoire ($4.0 billion)	2.	Pakistan ($16.3 billion)
3.	Ethiopia ($3.7 billion)	3.	Angola ($13.4 billion)
4.	Zimbabwe ($3.6 billion)	4.	Laos ($11.0 billion)
5.	Cameroon ($3.4 billion)	5.	Venezuela ($10.8 billion)
6.	Nigeria ($3.1 billion)	6.	Turkmenistan ($10.1 billion)
7.	Tanzania ($3.0 billion)	7.	Ecuador ($9.7 billion)
8.	Cambodia ($3.0 billion)	8.	Brazil ($8.5 billion)
9.	Sri Lanka ($2.8 billion)	9.	Sri Lanka ($8.2 billion)
10.	Ghana ($2.5 billion)	10.	Kazakhstan ($6.7 billion)

SOURCE: AidData, 2017.

concessional flows toward its Asian neighbors, which accounted for six of the ten top recipients. Consistent with its efforts to set up the Asian Infrastructure Investment Bank (AIIB), China is making big bets with its official finance in the infrastructure sector. The lion's share of its global spending between 2000 and 2014 was on energy ($134.1 billion), transportation and storage ($88.8 billion), mining, construction, and industry ($30.3 billion), and telecommunications projects ($16.9 billion).

Motives: What Drives China's Allocation Choices?

China has taken decisive steps in recent years to use its official finance as a central tool in its engagement strategy with other countries—from championing the AIIB and announcing the Belt and Road Initiative (BRI) in 2013 to creating a new bilateral international development cooperation agency in March 2018.[35] But what motivates China to deploy its official finance abroad rather than at home, and what does Beijing hope to get in return for these investments? This section considers three possible motives for Beijing's global spending spree—money, security, and reputation—and assesses the merits of these factors in light of the available evidence.

Economic opportunity is a compelling explanation for China's allocation of official finance, particularly for less concessional loans with profitable repayment terms. Beijing has an absorption problem: "falling capital productivity" and "low consumption" at home juxtaposed with surplus foreign capital reserves mean that China increasingly must look beyond its own borders to find profitable uses for its capital.[36] Chinese leaders have articulated a clear and explicit mandate for the country's official finance to promote business and investment opportunities outside China as part of its "going global" strategy since 1999.[37]

---

[35] For more in-depth discussion of the centrality of the AIIB and BRI to Beijing's foreign policy strategy, see Hong Yu, "Motivation behind China's 'One Belt, One Road' Initiatives and Establishment of the Asian Infrastructure Investment Bank," *Journal of Contemporary China* 26, no. 105 (2016): 353–68; and William A. Callahan, "China's 'Asia Dream': The Belt Road Initiative and the New Regional Order," *Asia Journal of Comparative Politics* 1, no. 3 (2016): 226–43. While the AIIB is a multilateral institution, rather than a bilateral development finance organization, China has significant influence on the broad policy of the AIIB and on specific allocation decisions. Just as the United States uses its formal voting power and informal influence at the World Bank to pursue its own geopolitical interests, the political economy literature suggests China is now in a good position to do the same thing within the AIIB, given its voting shares on the board and the stated purpose of the bank as reflected in its articles of agreement. See Randall Stone, "Informal Governance in International Organizations," *Review of International Organizations* 8, no. 2 (2013): 121–36.

[36] In macro terms, China is in a position that is similar to the United Kingdom in the nineteenth century or the United States after World War II. See Dollar, "China's Rise as a Regional and Global Power."

[37] Wang, "A Deeper Look at China's 'Going Out' Policy."

The potential economic returns from these opportunities include new export markets for Chinese firms, goods, and services, as well as revenues from the interest payments that other countries make on their loans. For foreign leaders, Beijing offers the promise of unrestricted funding without the traditional good governance strings attached by Western donors or multilateral organizations like the World Bank. If the economic opportunity argument drives Chinese allocations, we would expect to see Beijing channeling more of its assistance toward countries with high-value market opportunities.[38] In fact, there are several indications that it aims to maximize likely economic returns in determining how to allocate its overseas official finance. Past research has shown that less concessional financing was allocated disproportionately to countries with greater capacity to repay Chinese loans, larger natural resource endowments, and more trade with China.[39] Other studies have recently shown that economic opportunity alone cannot explain the allocation of Beijing's official finance. More concessional foreign aid was allocated disproportionately toward lower-income countries, which are a riskier bet for Beijing as they are more liable to default on their loans and are less likely to provide long-term investment opportunities or markets for Chinese exports.[40] Similarly, countries rich in natural resources were no more likely than those with relatively meager resource endowments to receive Chinese aid on generous terms during the same period.[41]

Purchasing security concessions through access to capital as a *quid pro quo* for aligning with Chinese foreign policy interests is another possible explanation for China's increased use of the power of its purse. According to this view, China desires acquiescence to its territorial claims in its "greater periphery," while farther afield it cultivates the allegiance of foreign governments to support its positions in international forums.[42] By this logic, China's official finance aims to buy the loyalty of allies, or at least the acquiescence of potential opponents, in support of its foreign policy interests.

Leaders in capital-hungry countries, particularly those with few alternative financial partners, may be willing to grant security concessions in return for access to aid or investment capital. If the quid pro quo narrative

---

[38] Custer et al., "Ties That Bind." To access the data and for more information on the data collection methodology, see "China's Public Diplomacy in East Asia and Pacific," Version 1.0, AidData, June 2018, https://www.aiddata.org/data/chinas-public-diplomacy-in-east-asia-and-pacific.

[39] Dreher et al., "Aid, China, and Growth."

[40] Dreher et al., "Apples and Dragon Fruits."

[41] Ibid.

[42] Denghua Zhang, "Why Cooperate with Others? Demystifying China's Trilateral Aid Cooperation," *Pacific Review* 30, no. 5 (2017): 750–68. See also Georg Strüver, "What Friends Are Made of: Bilateral Linkages and Domestic Drivers of Foreign Policy Alignment with China," *Foreign Policy Analysis* 12, no. 2 (2016): 170–91.

holds, we would expect to see Beijing rewarding countries that are willing to back its positions and withholding access to capital for countries that are more distant from its interests. China also might be expected to focus its overtures on countries with authoritarian institutions or higher levels of corruption, given that leaders of such regimes may be more insulated from public criticism from an organized opposition for violating norms against selling favors.

The evidence on this point is mixed. On the one hand, Chinese ODA appears to be regime agnostic—between 2000 and 2014, Beijing did not target aid funds disproportionately toward authoritarian or corrupt regimes.[43] On the other hand, there is strong support for the argument that China is trading access to financing on favorable terms in return for votes in the UN General Assembly and statements of support in regional membership bodies. No matter how countries govern themselves, China is willing to assist those governments that support it in international forums. For example, when African countries voted with China in the General Assembly an extra 10% of the time, they, on average, received an 86% bump in Chinese ODA between 2000 and 2014.[44]

While ODA data provides evidence that China may trade official flows for geopolitical alignment, qualitative evidence from specific cases is also plentiful. One much-cited example of this type of quid pro quo is how Beijing allegedly uses promises of financing to cajole member countries of the Association of Southeast Asian Nations (ASEAN) such as Cambodia and the Philippines to influence the outcomes of regional meetings, particularly the language included in joint statements, such that they omit or soft-pedal politically contentious issues. Scholars and journalists have asserted that the announcement of a $90 million debt-forgiveness package in tandem with Cambodia's ASEAN chairmanship in 2016 indicates Beijing's willingness to use debt relief to reward leaders for acting in line with its interests.[45]

---

[43] Dreher et al., "Apples and Dragon Fruits."

[44] Ibid. See also "Diplomacy and Aid in Africa," *Economist*, April 14, 2016.

[45] For further discussion of this highly contentious debt-forgiveness package and the perceived relationship to Cambodia's role in ASEAN, see Sovinda Po, "The Limits of China's Influence in Cambodia: A Soft Power Perspective," University of Cambodia, Occasional Paper, 61–75, September 2017; Ananth Baliga and Vong Sokheng, "Cambodia Again Blocks ASEAN Statement on South China Sea," *Phnom Penh Post*, July 25, 2016; and Ith Sothoeuth, "China Inks Deals with Cambodia, Erasing $90m Debt," Voice of America Cambodia, October 17, 2016.

Similar claims have been made regarding Cambodia's previous ASEAN chairmanship in 2012 and that of the Philippines in 2017.[46]

While there is a clear logic to the arguments focused on seizing economic opportunity and purchasing security concessions, the public statements of Chinese leaders point to a longer-term ambition to "rejuvenate" China's image and reclaim the world's admiration for its civilization.[47] In this respect, Beijing may view official finance as a means of painting a positive picture of Chinese generosity and the success of the country's development model in ushering in prosperity. There is certainly a public relations component to China's official financing activities, from the prominent placement of "China Aid" placards on overseas investments to the pursuit of media coverage to promote new deals that signal China's interest in securing a reputational boost for its investments in other countries.[48] Further, China typically deploys its official finance alongside other forms of public diplomacy—cultural and exchange programs, as well as official visits by civilian and military leaders—which reinforces the notion that its financial tools of statecraft are integrated into an overall strategy for winning hearts and minds.[49]

Power: How Is China Using Its Financial Statecraft to Advance Its National Interests in East Asia and the Pacific?

China's ability to achieve its objectives—whether economic, security, or reputational—depends on the extent to which it can effectively convert official finance into greater influence. This section examines whether China's use of official finance helps it generate a "good neighbor" dividend with recipient countries in the form of more favorable popular perceptions and greater

---

[46] For a detailed account of Cambodia's decision as 2012 ASEAN chair to not sign on to a joint statement repudiating Chinese actions in the South China Sea, see Ernest Z. Bower, "China Reveals Its Hand on ASEAN in Phnom Penh," Center for Strategic and International Studies (CSIS), July 20, 2012. Philippine foreign policy scholars Richard Heydarian and Jay Batongbacal have argued that when President Rodrigo Duterte assumed the ASEAN chairmanship in 2017, subsequent statements released by the regional body took a "softer stance" toward China on issues such as its reclamation activities in the contested waters or the ruling by the Permanent Court of Arbitration at The Hague in favor of the Philippines' territorial claims. See Pia Ranada, "Assessing Duterte's ASEAN Chairmanship," Rappler, November 16, 2017.

[47] Liu, "Look Beyond and Beneath the Soft Power"; and Cheng, "Three Questions on China's 'Belt and Road Initiative.'"

[48] Custer et al., "Ties That Bind."

[49] For a discussion of cultural and exchange programs, see Liu, "Look Beyond and Beneath the Soft Power." For a description of the scope and purpose of official visits by civilian and military leaders, see David Shambaugh, "The Illusion of Chinese Power," Brookings Institution, June 25, 2014; and Kurlantzick, *Charm Offensive*.

willingness of foreign leaders to align with its national interests.[50] To shed light on this question, we triangulate insights from Chinese official finance outlays between 2000 and 2016,[51] public attitude surveys,[52] interviews with foreign leaders,[53] and the voting records of countries in the UN General Assembly,[54] all in one geographic context: the East Asia and Pacific region.

Whether this charm offensive is effective in helping China realize its goals is a point of vigorous debate among scholars and practitioners. On the one hand, several high-profile examples suggest that some countries accommodate Beijing on major issues of concern (e.g., territorial disputes and the "one China" policy) in order to open access to export markets or investment dollars. On the other hand, Chinese official finance has provoked substantial domestic criticism in many countries concerned about ceding ground to Beijing on security issues, the specter of debt default, and the proliferation of infrastructure projects that may not in fact be needed.

For the purpose of our analysis, we hypothesize that China is strategic in how it wields its official finance, directing a disproportionate amount of its spending toward countries with the highest potential returns in the form of economic, security, or reputational gains. Moreover, if we accept the underlying logic that money buys influence with (or at least the acquiescence of) foreign leaders and publics, then we would expect to see countries that receive a higher share of official finance as having more favorable views of China, as well as being more willing to grant valuable economic or security concessions.

---

[50] It is important to acknowledge that, due to data limitations, this analysis only looks at correlations and apparent relationships, rather than attempting to identify causality.

[51] Custer et al., "Ties That Bind."

[52] This chapter draws on analysis of perceptions data from waves three and four of the Asian Barometer, a respected public attitudes survey, as presented in Custer et al., "Ties That Bind." Asian Barometer, "Asian Barometer Survey Data Waves 3 and 4," Center for East Asia Democratic Studies, National Taiwan University, 2012 and 2016. Data analyzed in this article was collected by the Asian Barometer Project in 2010–12 and 2013–16, which was co-directed by Fu Hu and Yun-han Chu and received major funding from Taiwan's Ministry of Education, Academia Sinica, and National Taiwan University. The Asian Barometer Project Office is solely responsible for the data distribution. We appreciate the assistance from the institutes and individuals mentioned above in providing the data. The views expressed herein are our own.

[53] This discussion draws on interviews conducted by Samantha Custer and other AidData researchers with 76 individuals in three countries—the Philippines, Malaysia, and Fiji—during January–March 2018. Interviewees come from one of four audience segments: (1) academics, journalists, and think tank experts, (2) current or former government officials from the executive and legislative branches, (3) business, social, or cultural organization representatives, and (4) representatives from foreign embassies that interact with officials from both the sending country (e.g., China) and the receiving country. For the purpose of getting the most candid responses possible on a sensitive topic, we do not directly name or give attribution for quotes to individual interviewees, but rather use their combined responses to provide insight into elite perceptions of China.

[54] For this analysis we use data on the voting patterns of China and a given East Asia and Pacific country in the UN General Assembly during 2000–2016. More information on this data and approach is contained in Custer et al., "Ties That Bind."

The Regional View

In the sixteen-year period between 2000 and 2016, China directed $48 billion of its official finance toward countries within the East Asia and Pacific region—95% of which was squarely focused on the infrastructure sector (**Figures 3, 4, 5,** and **6**).[55] Notably, there was a huge spike in China's official financing in this region in 2016, which coincides with the implementation of BRI—Beijing's signature infrastructure initiative to develop a pan-Asian transportation and telecommunications network worth an estimated $1 trillion. Consistent with what we saw in the global view, China's spending in the East Asia and Pacific region reveals a preference for less concessional flows.[56]

Beijing awarded a greater share of its official finance to countries that were large markets for Chinese imports, such as the fast-growing and populous economies of Southeast Asia, which claimed a whopping 89% of these outlays between 2000 and 2016.[57] Meanwhile, East Asia and Pacific countries that were less willing to vote with China in the UN General Assembly tended to attract less official financing. This result holds for both ODA and less concessional official finance.[58] In other words, the data supports the hypothesis that Beijing aims to maximize the returns on its official finance through doubling down on its spending in countries that offer high-value market opportunities and in those that can be relied on to align with its positions in international voting bodies.

A good barometer of whether Beijing is able to convert official finance into reputational gains with foreign publics would be to approximate whether countries that receive a greater share of this largesse perceive China more favorably than those that receive less.[59] We define favorability as the proportion of respondents from a given country who viewed China as exercising the most

---

[55] Custer et al., "Ties That Bind." Notably, infrastructure receives the vast majority of Chinese official finance, regardless of flow type. In other words, China has doubled down on its infrastructure financing on both more and less generous terms.

[56] Globally, China gave the preponderance of its official finance using less concessional terms for the period of 2000–2014. This narrative largely holds true in the East Asia and Pacific region. There is one important exception to this rule—a spike in concessional aid funding from China to Malaysia in 2016 that was primarily driven by a single large infrastructure project under BRI. Notably, this high volume of concessional financing in 2016 runs counter to what we have seen in past years. However, since this is largely driven by a single project, it is too early to say whether this signals that China is pivoting to more generous terms with its lending or if this is more an anomaly in its giving patterns.

[57] When we restrict the analysis to just Asia-Pacific countries, the Southeast Asian nations of Malaysia, Cambodia, Indonesia, Laos, Vietnam, Myanmar, and the Philippines received approximately $42.8 billion of the total $48 billion that China invested between 2000 and 2016. Custer et al., "Ties That Bind."

[58] Ibid.

[59] The following analysis leverages three perception-based measures of favorability drawn from the Asian Barometer Survey.

FIGURE 3   Distribution of Chinese official finance in East Asia and the Pacific, 2000–2016

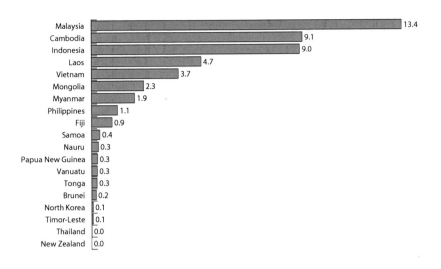

SOURCE: AidData, 2018.

NOTE: Countries not receiving official finance: Australia, Japan, Micronesia, and South Korea.

FIGURE 4   Chinese official investment by project completion status in East Asia and the Pacific, 2000–2016

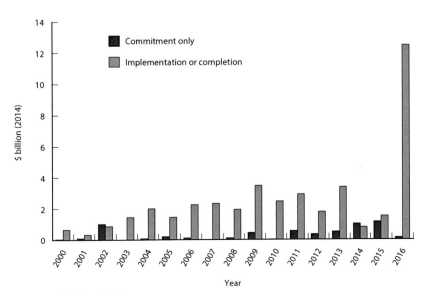

SOURCE: AidData, 2018.

FIGURE 5 Chinese official investment by flow type in East Asia and the Pacific, 2000–2016

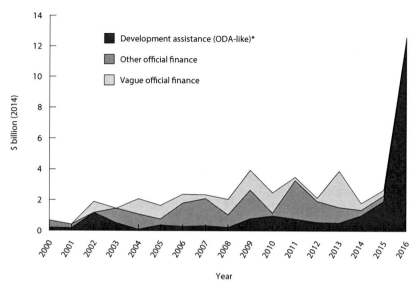

SOURCE: AidData, 2018.

NOTE: Asterisk indicates this funding includes at least a 25% grant element, which is the standard set by the OECD's Development Assistance Committee (DAC) for Official Development Assistance. Since China is not a DAC donor, AidData classifies these funds as "ODA-like."

FIGURE 6 Chinese official investment by sector, 2000–2016 ($ billion, 2014)

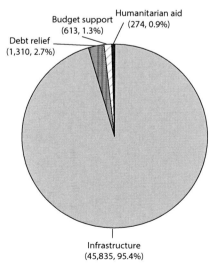

SOURCE: AidData, 2018.

influence in the region, having a net positive influence in their own country, and offering a development model to which they aspire.[60]

As expected, individuals from countries that received more Chinese official finance between 2000 and 2016 were more likely to view Beijing's influence favorably (on all three measures). In this respect, there is some evidence to support the idea that China is effectively converting the power of its purse into reputational gains with foreign publics. Interestingly, despite growing anecdotal concerns regarding the dangers of indebtedness to Beijing, individuals living in countries that received a greater share of less concessional lending were more likely to view China positively than those who received generous handouts (i.e., ODA).[61] This is good news for Beijing, given that the preponderance of its official finance does not meet the level of concessionality to be considered ODA. It remains to be seen whether this public enthusiasm for higher-interest loans is sustained in future years as East Asian countries confront repayment and see their neighbors struggling to service growing debt burdens.

Nonetheless, notable exceptions exist, indicating that there are limitations to the goodwill Beijing can buy with official finance, at least when it comes to popular perceptions. Less than 30% of citizens in Mongolia and the Philippines view China's influence as a positive trend, despite these countries receiving moderately large infusions of Chinese official finance at an estimated $2.3 and $1.1 billion, respectively, between 2000 and 2016. Even in a country like Myanmar that rated China as highly influential, citizens did not necessarily see this as a net positive for their country despite sizeable contributions from Beijing ($1.9 billion). Thailand received comparatively little in official finance commitments ($14.4 million) between 2000 and 2016,[62] and yet it is home to a relatively pro-China population: 93% of Thai citizens surveyed consider China's influence to be a net positive.

Greater favorability in the eyes of foreign publics may be one indication that Beijing is achieving its reputational goals, but when it comes to winning economic and security concessions, policymakers are the gatekeepers. There is good reason to believe the popular narrative that opportunistic leaders and bureaucrats, in the face of Beijing's checkbook diplomacy, will be tempted to compartmentalize—trading concessions on more distant concerns in exchange for proximate financial rewards.

---

[60] For our measures of China's favorability, we primarily draw on responses to three questions in the Asian Barometer Survey: (1) "Which country has the most influence in [Asia]?" (2) "Generally speaking, the influence China has on our country is...?" and (3) "Which country should be a model for our own country's development?" The surveys for waves three and four were conducted in 2010–11 and 2014–15 in fourteen countries.

[61] Custer et al., "Ties That Bind," 45.

[62] Custer et al., "Ties That Bind."

In the East Asia and Pacific region, we examine the relationship between receipt of Chinese official finance and foreign policy concessions by looking at UN General Assembly voting behavior in 25 countries. We also analyze qualitative interviews with 76 leaders in 3 countries (Malaysia, the Philippines, and Fiji) to shed light on domestic concessions that might be related to economic or security policy.[63] If the quid pro quo narrative holds true, leaders from countries that receive a greater share of Chinese official finance can be expected to be more willing to fall in line with Beijing in their domestic and foreign policy decisions.

At a regional level, voting behavior of 25 East Asia and Pacific countries between 2000 and 2016 shows there is indeed cause for concern. Governments were more likely to vote with Beijing when they received a greater share of concessional lending from China and financing for infrastructure projects that were less visible to the public, "ostensibly the pet projects of leaders."[64] These findings lend credence to our hypothesis that leaders from countries that receive more Chinese official finance are vulnerable to pressure from Beijing to back its foreign policy positions in order to maintain access to this important source of capital. Drawing on in-depth interviews with leaders in three East Asia and Pacific countries, we see very similar patterns and concrete examples of the types of concessions Beijing has been able to extract.

The Country View

In Malaysia, one of the largest recipients of Chinese official finance in the East Asia and Pacific region ($13.4 billion between 2000 and 2016),[65] interviewees explained that the administration of former prime minister Najib Razak was willing to "sell out to China" for two reasons: (1) Beijing's help in bailing out a troubled development fund owned by the government[66] and

---

[63] Five candidate countries were initially selected for the case studies (Cambodia, Myanmar, the Philippines, Malaysia, and Fiji) using the following criteria: size of Chinese financial and public diplomacy investments in the country, strategic importance to China, accessibility to relevant interviewees, and representativeness of China's broader engagements in the East Asia and Pacific region. All five candidate countries met these criteria as they are all large recipients of Chinese official finance and are good examples of countries where China has sought to leverage financial and nonfinancial tools in service of broader geopolitical strategies. Since AidData had budget available for conducting field research in only three countries, Samantha Custer and her team of researchers selected the three final case study countries based on feasibility of implementation.

[64] Custer et al., "Ties That Bind," 50.

[65] Infrastructure investments constitute over 99% of China's official finance dollars to Malaysia during this period, primarily driven by visible transportation infrastructure such as ports, railways, and bridges. In addition to infrastructure projects, Beijing twice aided Malaysian victims of flooding and tsunamis.

[66] The government-owned development fund in question was 1Malaysia Development Berhad (1MDB). Custer et al., "Ties That Bind," 29. See also "China to Help 1MDB Settle Multi-billion Dollar Legal Dispute with Abu Dhabi: Financial Times," *Straits Times*, December 7, 2016.

(2) access to finance for infrastructure projects on generally "favorable terms."[67] When asked about tangible wins for China, interviewees most frequently cited its clout in gaining an unfair advantage in economic deals—eschewing local content targets, evading labor regulations, and creating monopolies for Chinese businesses—and the Najib administration's failure to push back against Chinese aggression in Malaysia's exclusive economic zone.[68]

However, the Malaysia case is equally illustrative of the limitations of Beijing's strategy of courting political elites with official finance dollars, particularly in the face of leadership transitions and electoral pushback if China becomes too associated with any one party or administration. The surprise election of Mahathir Mohamad as prime minister in May 2018 was viewed by many as a public referendum on the previous administration's dealings with China and a sign of growing unease about the Najib administration's lack of transparency.[69] In this respect, it is unsurprising that the Mahathir administration decided to cancel (or delay indefinitely) three Chinese-backed projects worth an estimated $22 billion in August 2018 only a few months into its term. The rationale given by Prime Minister Mahathir that Malaysia would defer these projects until such a time when it could afford them indicates a growing wariness on the part of the region's leaders regarding the risk of becoming overly indebted to Beijing.[70]

Fiji receives a relatively small share of Chinese official finance in absolute dollar terms ($903 million between 2000 and 2016), but Beijing spends more per capita there ($1,005 per person) than it does in Malaysia ($430 per person).[71] Notably, Beijing gave 30% of its financing to Fiji in the form of budget support—unearmarked funding that is highly prized by governments because they have greater control over where and how to

---

[67] For example, the East Coast Rail Link (ECRL) project is financed "with a 20-year soft loan at a 3.25 percent interest rate and no payments due for the first seven years." Custer et al., "Ties That Bind," 30. See also Ganeshwaran Kana and Gurmeet Kaur, "The Real Economics of ECRL," *Star* (Malaysia), August 12, 2017. Nonetheless, for a growing number of Malaysians, Chinese official finance is worrisome because of its opaque terms, the prospect of mounting debt burden, and a suspicion that these investments were unnecessary for the country's growth. Investments to expand or build new deepwater ports, such as the Melaka Gateway port and the Kuantan port expansion, are particularly suspect because Malaysia's current ports are undersubscribed relative to their capacity.

[68] Interviewees often "complained that there was one set of rules for China and another for everyone else." Custer et al., "Ties That Bind," 32.

[69] Ibid., 29.

[70] "Burdened with Debt, Malaysia Cancels China-Backed Projects for Now," *Express Tribune* (Pakistan), August, 21, 2018, https://tribune.com.pk/story/1786033/2-burdened-debt-malaysia-cancels-china-backed-projects-now.

[71] Fiji was also notable in terms of the number of recorded projects investments it received from Beijing—26, including those committed, implemented, and/or completed—which far exceeds projects in Malaysia (9). Population numbers were sourced from UN Department of Economic and Social Affairs, "World Population Prospects: 2017 Revision," June 2017.

spend these funds.[72] China's willingness to bankroll large-scale infrastructure projects has endeared it to Fiji's leaders, who view this assistance as essential to realizing the country's vision of becoming an economic hub for the Pacific.[73] Interviewees gave several examples of how Beijing has wielded this economic clout to secure discrete foreign policy concessions on the part of Fiji's government. These include signing on to the one-China policy, closure of the Trade and Tourism Representative Office in Taipei, extradition of Chinese nationals back to China, and a prevailing perception that Fiji's state-controlled media publicizes Chinese development projects to a higher degree than those of similar size funded by other development partners.[74]

Nevertheless, the persuasive power of Beijing's official finance also has limitations in Fiji. Interviewees pointed to instances where the government has not fallen in line with China, despite considerable pressure. For example, Fiji has taken no position, as yet, on the South China Sea disputes. According to several interviewees, officials reportedly seek to play foreign powers off each other in search of "more favorable terms than might otherwise be on offer." Finally, there was widespread agreement among interviewees that Beijing's heavy-handedness in pushing the use of Chinese labor and materials in the projects it backs was unpopular with citizens and leaders alike.[75]

Between 2000 and 2016, the Philippines accounted for a mere 2% ($1.13 billion) of Beijing's official finance portfolio, but there were dramatic fluctuations in the annual amounts between administrations, largely driven by the personality of the chief executive.[76] China has become President Rodrigo Duterte's indispensable partner since 2016 by promising a seemingly limitless

---

[72] Custer et al., "Ties That Bind," 14.

[73] Nonetheless, Fiji receives a much larger proportion of its overall Chinese official finance in the form of less concessional loans than Malaysia does. These less generous terms do not diminish Beijing's enthusiasm for publicity, however, and interviewees noted that China often announced these new official finance packages with prominent launch events with local media in attendance and branding in the form of shiny "China Aid" signs on Chinese-backed infrastructure projects as a visible public reminder of their contribution. Ibid., 35.

[74] Ibid., 35–36.

[75] Custer et al., "Ties That Bind."

[76] Interestingly, unlike Fiji, once population is taken into account, China's contributions in the Philippines were even smaller (a mere $11.03 per person). UN Department of Economic and Social Affairs, "World Population Prospects." The composition of project investments also varied greatly, as inbound Chinese official finance investments under the Aquino administration were almost exclusively in the form of small donations to aid in relief and reconstruction following Typhoon Haiyan (2013) and Typhoon Yolanda (2015). This stands in stark contrast to the heavy infrastructure focus of 99% of China's investments overall in the Philippines during this period. Interviewees emphasized the rollercoaster relationship between the two countries "from the 'golden age' of relations under Gloria Macapagal Arroyo to the 'icy' interactions with Benigno Aquino, and subsequent 'thawing' with Rodrigo Duterte…who seeks to strengthen ties." Beijing bankrolled projects under the Arroyo administration (2001–10) to the tune of $1.1 billion, but Chinese official finance plummeted during the administration of Aquino (2010–16) to a low of $1.7 million. Meanwhile, there was an uptick in 2016 after the election of the more sympathetic Duterte, with investments worth over $17 million in that year alone. Ibid., 25.

supply of ready capital to finance his "build, build, build" agenda, as well as opening up access to export markets and tourism dollars.[77]

Interviewees argued that, in his enthusiasm to curry favor with Beijing to keep this source of capital flowing, Duterte has traded for short-term gains at the expense of the Philippines' long-term security and economic interests. Three anecdotal examples appear to validate this view: (1) Duterte's unwillingness to insist on the enforcement of the ruling in favor of the Philippines' territorial claims vis-à-vis China by the Permanent Court of Arbitration at The Hague, (2) his spurning of the long-standing military alliance with the United States, and (3) his strong support for inviting China Telecom to become the country's third telecommunications provider.[78]

Is its official finance opening doors for China to secure reputational, economic, and security gains with other countries? In this section, we have presented the results of statistical analysis of public attitudes and leader behavior in 25 countries in the East Asia and Pacific region, along with qualitative evidence to provide additional context in three country studies. Data limitations preclude us from definitively concluding that people view China more favorably or that leaders align with its foreign policy interests because their countries receive Chinese official finance. Nevertheless, we do see a relationship between the volume and type of financing a country receives and how its citizens view China and whether its leaders vote with China in international forums. Moreover, in three country studies, Chinese official finance loomed large in the minds of those we interviewed who felt that Beijing was effectively wielding the power of its purse to gain favor with foreign publics and win concessions from leaders. The concluding section discusses the implications of these findings for China, the recipients of Chinese official finance, and the United States and its allies.

Implications: What Does the Future Hold for Chinese Official Finance in the Era of BRI?

Journalists, politicians, and scholars have long argued that China adroitly uses its excess foreign currency reserves to win friends and allies in the pursuit of national interests. To what extent does this rhetoric match reality, and if so, what are the implications for the recipients of China's largesse, for other foreign powers like the United States that may be displaced by Beijing's growing influence, and for China itself? This concluding section examines what China's past actions, as well as the

---

[77] Custer et al., "Ties That Bind," 25.

[78] Ibid., 27–28.

responses of foreign leaders and publics to these overtures, might tell us about its ability to convert the power of its purse into future economic, security, and reputational gains with other countries.

This chapter has looked retrospectively at the scope, distribution, and influence of Chinese official finance to examine what this evidence tells us about whether China is truly "winning the world one yuan at a time." There is one point on which the data is unambiguously clear—China has dramatically increased its outbound official finance to other countries since 2000, with 2009 and 2016 as important inflection points. Moreover, our analysis of how, where, and when China deployed its official finance supports the view that Beijing is strategic in seeking to maximize economic, security, and reputational benefits.

However, Beijing's ability to convert its official financing into improved popular perceptions of China, as well as discrete economic and security concessions from foreign leaders, is neither straightforward nor permanent. There is some evidence that citizens from countries exposed to a higher volume of official finance tend to view China more favorably and their leaders have a greater likelihood of aligning their voting in the UN General Assembly with Beijing. However, there are important exceptions to this general rule. Popular perceptions of China did not always break in the way we would expect: some larger recipients of official finance remained skeptical of Beijing's motives (e.g., the Philippines), while other countries exhibited quite pro-China attitudes despite relatively modest outlays from China (e.g., Thailand). Meanwhile, China's ability to make inroads with foreign leaders appears to be tempered by cyclical changes (e.g., electoral cycles and administration turnover), which can bring about a decisive and rapid change in Beijing's influence and access to leaders (e.g., the Philippines and Malaysia).

Turning from this retrospective view of official finance to consider what the future holds for China's economic statecraft, it is clear that this question of what return Beijing can expect to collect from its generosity will continue to be extremely relevant. Notably, Xi Jinping appears to have doubled down on this strategy to leverage China's economic clout to advance its interests even in the face of criticism of its "debt diplomacy" abroad and growing murmurs of discontent at home.[79] His September 2018 pledge of $60 billion in new loans to Africa is a case in point. The remainder of this section lays out the implications of Beijing's future economic statecraft for various groups depending on their different vantage points.

---

[79] Lucy Hornby and Tom Hancock, "China Pledge of $60bn Loans to Africa Sparks Anger at Home," *Financial Times*, September 4, 2018.

Recipient Countries

What should recipients of Chinese official finance make of Beijing's overtures? In many capital-hungry countries, foreign leaders view Beijing as a willing partner to bankroll their infrastructure plans in the face of limited alternatives. Meanwhile, evidence from a recent research study on the Chinese infrastructure investments worldwide between 2000 and 2014 shows that these projects generate desirable economic spillovers that reduce inequality between administrative regions within countries.[80] Nonetheless, the lack of transparency on the terms and costs of these deals also creates substantial risks for recipient countries, some of which are beginning to play out on a global stage amid intense public scrutiny.

Rising debt-to-GDP ratios and the forfeiture of state assets as governments struggle to repay Chinese loans have sparked public outcry in many countries regarding the dangers of indebtedness to Beijing and fueled debates around costly infrastructure investments in the face of uncertain domestic demand. With BRI poised to pump trillions of dollars in new infrastructure financing to low- and middle-income countries worldwide, concerns over debt distress will likely grow rather than wane in future years.[81] This dynamic presents two implications for recipient countries. First, they will need to ensure that politicians are held accountable by their legislatures and citizens to appropriately weigh future costs of new official finance agreements in addition to current benefits. Second, this dynamic presents an opportunity for leaders to turn Beijing's desire to avoid a public loss of face from criticism of its debt diplomacy into leverage to negotiate better terms.

China is not alone in utilizing official finance as an instrument to cultivate relationships with other countries. But Chinese official finance is somewhat unique compared to other bilateral providers in three respects: the sheer volume of flows, the lower level of concessionality on average of those flows, and the relative opacity of the terms of those flows to the public. Taken together, these distinct features create higher risks of capture and moral hazard for politicians in recipient countries who view themselves as being able to gain access to lucrative benefits today (e.g., monetary and non-monetary perks or the ability to claim credit with constituencies for new public goods) in exchange for the distant costs of repaying expensive loans that will likely be borne by their successors. If recipient countries are to mitigate these risks, which may compound as Beijing ramps up the volume of its outbound official finance associated with BRI, they will need to put in place better checks and

---

[80] Richard Bluhm et al., "Connective Financing: Chinese Infrastructure Projects and the Diffusion of Economic Activity in Developing Countries," AidData, Working Paper, no. 64, September 2018.

[81] For a more fulsome discussion on forecasting debt distress in low- and middle-income countries from BRI loans, see Hurley et al., "Examining the Debt Implications of the Belt and Road Initiative."

balances to align the incentives of executive branch officials to appropriately weigh the future costs of new financing deals. One important step forward in this regard would be for recipient governments to mandate the public disclosure of the amounts and terms of Chinese official finance projects in their countries such that citizens, watchdog agencies, and legislatures have the opportunity to view and contest these agreements.

If one of Beijing's motives for its outbound official finance is to burnish its reputation and stature on a global stage, as we argue earlier in this chapter, then it stands to reason that Chinese officials want to minimize embarrassing setbacks in the form of public protests, media attacks, and censure from other leaders. For countries that are already recipients of fairly large outlays of Chinese official finance, growing international criticism of Beijing's debt diplomacy may give leaders leverage with their Chinese counterparts to negotiate better terms such as longer repayment periods or lower interest rates on loans. Similarly, for countries entering into the early stage of talks regarding new projects to be backed by Chinese official finance, government leaders can use Beijing's fear of reputation loss to their advantage to argue for a package of grants and more concessional loans with generous terms.

Implications for the United States and Other Western Powers

If China is indeed flexing its economic muscle to strengthen its geostrategic position with foreign leaders and citizens, this has two important implications for other powers whose influence could be displaced in the process. First, if Western powers give in to populist pressures at home to scale back their global footprint, China has the means (namely, a vast arsenal of surplus reserves) and the mandate (namely, high-level political support to use official finance to advance its interests) to step into the breach and cement its role as a preferred lender to the developing world. This could result in these other foreign powers inadvertently ceding ground to China's national interests when they run counter to their own. Second, China's ability to get the desired return from its official finance overtures in other countries (e.g., economic, security, and reputational gains) is partly dictated by the relative absence or presence of alternative sources of capital for infrastructure-hungry economies, making its influence conditional rather than deterministic. It is possible that other foreign powers, seeing the influence that China is able to garner via its official finance, may be provoked to take action to raise their own game.

As we have described in this chapter, under the leadership of Hu Jintao and Xi Jinping, China has adopted a more active foreign policy stance as it seeks to win the admiration of other countries for its culture and claim a prominent role for itself on the global stage. Official finance is not the only tool that China has at its disposal to win friends and allies in pursuit of national interests, but it is clearly a very important and influential one. This has not gone unnoticed in Western media and policy circles where debates have ensued about whether China's growing confidence and influence should be viewed as a threat (i.e., a zero-sum attempt to displace the current global order) or as a peaceful rise (i.e., a positive-sum attempt to take its place alongside other major powers). Although the debate over the merits of, and evidence for, these two views is beyond the scope of this chapter, it is important to acknowledge that there are likely instances where China's interests diverge from those of the United States and its allies. In these instances, official finance gives Beijing a powerful tool to coerce (or entice) foreign leaders to back its interests by making economic and security concessions that favor China over other actors, as well as supporting its positions in international forums. In this respect, the growing dependence of low- and middle-income countries on Chinese official finance increases the likelihood that Western powers could be ceding ground to Beijing's interests when these interests diverge from their own.

Yet China's ability to secure a dominant position as the lender of choice for low- and middle-income countries is also vulnerable to the willingness of United States and other powers to increase the supply of available capital with more generous terms.[82] There was a palpable sense in Malaysia, Fiji, and the Philippines that leaders were in part so enthusiastic about Chinese official finance investments because they viewed Beijing as the only willing investment partner. If Western powers were to ramp up their concessional lending for infrastructure in other countries with minimal strings attached, Beijing's dominance as the lender of choice could be displaced by donors that are more positively perceived by most leaders and their publics.

In the BRI era, China's exuberance to wield the power of its purse could provoke a backlash from other powers that feel threatened by its growing economic clout. The October 2018 passage of the BUILD Act in the United States is one such example of a response by a major power to counter, or at least contain, China's influence from its outbound official finance. The legislation doubled the budget of the U.S. Overseas Private Investment Corporation (OPIC) and created a new agency (the U.S. International Development Finance Corporation), which has the authority to take equity positions in development projects.[83] Notably, this is an abrupt about-face for the Trump administration, which originally deemed OPIC to be "one of

---

[82] Zimmer, "Running the Table."

[83] See Zengerle, "Congress, Eying China, Votes to Overhaul Development Finance."

62 agencies slated for elimination."[84] Public speeches by President Donald Trump and Secretary of State Mike Pompeo point to the major reason that the administration changed its stance—to enable the United States to compete with China and other sovereign donors and investors in developing countries by providing a clear alternative for capital-hungry economies.[85] If China continues its highly publicized official finance overtures, we anticipate that the United States and other powers will continue to look for ways to counter Beijing's gains from these overtures.

Implications for China

Where does all of this leave China? As mentioned previously, the enthusiasm of political leaders to send China's excess foreign currency reserves abroad via official finance projects is not equally felt by the general public. In fact, Chinese scholars and citizens have become increasingly restive and vocal in raising questions regarding why their government is exporting money to other countries when there are poor people and underdeveloped regions at home.[86] This raises two important implications for China in the BRI era: Beijing will be under increasing pressure in the coming years to demonstrate clear and compelling returns from its official finance investments abroad; at the same time, it will face greater difficulty in sustaining such gains in the face of growing opposition within recipient countries and competition from other powers.

If Chinese leaders are to quell discontent at home, Beijing must be able to show that its "going out" policy is bringing back tangible benefits, particularly in the form of jobs (i.e., opening up opportunities for Chinese firms and investment), finances to support public services (i.e., from interest rates on loans), and progress on issues important to national pride (e.g., concessions in territorial disputes). Beijing's ability to convert its official finance outlays into such gains likely depends on two factors that are only somewhat within its control: (1) the continued willingness of recipient countries to borrow from China at closer to market rates (i.e., less concessional OOF as opposed to concessional ODA) and (2) the relative dependence of recipient countries on Chinese capital as opposed to alternatives.

If Chinese leaders succumb to pressures at home, this may put Beijing at a disadvantage abroad with countries worried about indebtedness to China, especially in the face of competition from Western powers like

---

[84] Daniel F. Runde and Romina Bandura, "The BUILD Act Has Passed: What's Next?" CSIS, October 12, 2018, https://www.csis.org/analysis/build-act-has-passed-whats-next.

[85] Ibid.

[86] Hornby and Hancock, "China Pledge of $60bn Loans to Africa Sparks Anger at Home."

the United States that are incentivized to contain Chinese influence. There are three things that China must do to cement its position as the preferred lender of choice for foreign leaders. First, it must demonstrate follow-through—the ability to translate the fanfare of its financial commitments into projects delivered on the ground—or foreign leaders will see through its empty promises. Second, Chinese official finance must continue to be responsive to demands by leaders for access to ready capital for infrastructure investments. This has proved to be a comparative advantage for Beijing because what China typically prefers to pay for also happens to be what foreign leaders are demanding, particularly in the absence of credible alternative sources. Third, Beijing must be proactive in convincing foreign leaders (and their citizens) that accepting Chinese investment is a net positive for their countries. Many countries have become concerned as they watch their neighbors struggle to repay debts to China and increasingly question China for flouting local content requirements or labor regulations. To sustain its influence, China needs to mitigate the visible negative spillover effects from its investments.

EXECUTIVE SUMMARY

This chapter examines China's global values and argues that China neither promotes nor rejects wholesale existing global values and international law but rather reinterprets them according to its interests.

MAIN ARGUMENT

China has moved over time from a global alliance with the Soviet Union, followed by a short-lived revolutionary stance, to a path of integration with most international institutions and rules. But that course has abated as the country has gained wealth and power. With Xi Jinping's ascent, China has set aside its long-standing reservations and defensive stance and begun to directly contest the liberal world order through the promotion of Chinese alternatives presented as "complementary," with a strong preference for bilateral deals with other nation-states. China is more interested in hollowing out the international order than in a revisionist upheaval, and it also rides the trend of self-doubt and isolationism in several democracies. Mutual interest is the operative factor, often coinciding with the lure of financial gains for partners. China's approach remains pragmatic, emphasizing diversified participation in multilateral institutions. What China seeks is a nonintrusive, low-cost international order built on two very contrasting pillars: national sovereignty as an absolute principle, and the free flow of goods and services for as long as China's exceptional status as a nominal developing economy is maintained.

POLICY IMPLICATIONS

- Western democracies must work to check China's lobbying capacity, which is unprecedentedly wide for an authoritarian regime and seeks to erode democratic values.

- Western democracies should require financial and management transparency for China's outgoing enterprises and joint implementation of international rules and norms for cooperation.

- It is important to upgrade participation in the UN system and coalition building in these organizations by emerging and developing members.

China's Promotion of New Global Values

François Godement

The greatest question about China's attitude toward global values and institutions is the following: how much does China's language match with the reality of its practices? The question has become even more acute under President Xi Jinping's watch. From his 2015 statements that "China does not intend to pursue militarization" of the South China Sea and instead wants "to forge a new partnership of win-win cooperation" and "a community of shared future for mankind," to his January 2017 speech at Davos embracing multilateralism or his November 2018 pledge for "openness, innovation and inclusiveness" at the Shanghai World Import Fair, there is ample room for doubt about the reality of these commitments.[1] Global messaging has often been a function of domestic priorities. The People's Republic of China (PRC) has always been a great minter of concepts, language, and slogans showcasing its policies, if only to its own captive audience, but with vastly increased projection capacities abroad in the last decades.

One challenge is to distinguish how much the Xi-era expression of policies differs from that of his predecessors—and how much the gap

---

François Godement is Senior Adviser, Asia, at Institut Montaigne in Paris. He can be reached at <fgodement@institutmontaigne.org>.

---

[1] "Remarks by President Obama and President Xi of the People's Republic of China in Joint Press Conference," White House, September 25, 2015, https://obamawhitehouse.archives.gov/the-press-office/2015/09/25/remarks-president-obama-and-president-xi-peoples-republic-china-joint; Xi Jinping, "Working Together to Forge a New Partnership of Win-Win Cooperation and Create a Community of Shared Future for Mankind" (statement at the 70th Session of the UN General Assembly, New York, September 28, 2015), https://gadebate.un.org/sites/default/files/gastatements/70/70_ZH_en.pdf; and Xi Jinping, "Work Together for an Open Global Economy That Is Innovative and Inclusive" (keynote speech at the opening ceremony of the China International Import Expo, Shanghai, November 4, 2018), http://www.xinhuanet.com/english/2018-11/05/c_137583815.htm.

between language and reality has decreased or increased. How much Xi's language departs from preceding usage and how original it really is also matter. This chapter argues that the content of the words matters less than the call to follow China, or at least not to contradict its interests. China's expression of global values is vague enough to allow for compliance without much formal conflict with other values. It is the fast-expanding economic interests and the acceptance of strongly binding mutual ties with China's partners that are important.

There is also a need to distinguish between China's own assertion of a model, including alternative views of international relations, and its attempts simply to exploit the opportunities presented by the crises in many democracies and the discord among democratic allies. Anti-globalization movements and a pullback from international commitments and institutions have allowed China to appropriate language and values that were foundational in the post–World War II international order. The gap between its theory and its practice matters less if former Western bearers of these values and norms turn away from them. In international institutions, China appears increasingly as a source of support, starting from budget considerations. This allows for better processing of Chinese initiatives and ideas through these institutions. China is moving from defensive stands to positive proposals—and therefore promoting its worldview or practices. Should it become more competent and successful at this game, there will be no need to discuss whether the PRC is revisionist because values and rules are reinterpreted within the due process of international institutions rather than openly negated.

Global values are inseparable from their promotion. Lately, China's channels of influence abroad have received much more attention, as its capacity for lobbying, and indeed for capturing friends with access to positions of power, has been demonstrated around the world. This is a sharp departure from the Maoist era cultivation of small coteries of ideological followers. Is China approaching the will and capacity to manipulate democratic life that has become a hallmark of Russia's "sharp power"? This appears to be true of close neighbors and increasingly dependent economies. Taiwan obviously stands out as an example, but Australia has also become a target, and the recruitment or coercion of overseas Chinese as compatriots is disquieting. The farther one moves away from China, the more one finds that it is much less concerned with election results than with influencing the winners, whoever they may be, and with exercising influence over business, media, and academic elites as well as local politicians. To achieve this goal, China must project a successful but soft image of itself. Despite very large financial means and capabilities for public diplomacy, it is deeply hampered by contradictory facts emerging from the reality of domestic policies. "They should not hold a 'flashlight' in hand doing nothing but to check out on the weakness of others and not on their own," argues Xi of China's foreign partners.[2] This is a belated recognition of China's remaining weakness in the area of soft power.

China's drive inside international institutions is both impressive and a testimony to these ambiguities. It is a layered engagement, where China increases its stakes in some domains, uses its new leverage to prevent action in areas it dislikes, and pushes forward its interests. Positive participation focuses on the World Trade Organization (WTO) and sectoral institutions useful to China's economic outreach abroad. The Belt and Road Initiative (BRI) is distilled in those institutions that deal with development. China has long abstained from humanitarian contributions, although this policy has begun changing very recently. Its focus has been on reinterpreting human rights in ways that the regime can live with—and this is a distinctly revisionist perspective on founding values of the United Nations. But China also promises contributions to peacekeeping operations and some funds for select actions. In short, it promotes a low-cost and largely valueless international order, revolving around the country's self-interest. This is not a revolutionary or even revisionist stand, except for the fact that China's increasing influence is in practice a deterrent against the principled interpretation of existing global values. Yet the PRC does not challenge these values but instead works to erode them through ever more active presence in international organizations.

Engagement, Followed by Disengagement

China's engagement abroad has waxed and waned under the PRC. Strikingly, the rise to world power in the fourth decade of reform and opening up has not translated into global responsibility but into an assertive, decidedly interest-based and nationalist approach to global issues.

Since 1949, the PRC's international stance and slogans have largely been derived from domestic goals. "Resist America, aid Korea" coincided with a mass mobilization movement inside China. The Great Leap Forward, although it was also promoted abroad, was directed at domestic goals, such as to "overtake Britain" in steel production. Freed from the Soviet alliance, the Cultural Revolution's slogans could have a dual use: the Great Proletarian Cultural Revolution included an international ambition, with a drive to seize the leadership of the worldwide progressive camp from the Soviet Union. These slogans featured a struggle against the hegemonism of the two superpowers—the United States and the Soviet Union. This posited China as

---

[2] Xi, "Work Together for an Open Global Economy That Is Innovative and Inclusive."

a leader of the Third World and an influencer of the less remembered "Second World"—for the most part, Europe.

Deng Xiaoping's China inherited the latter concepts, but it largely did away with international messaging from the PRC. There is actually no accurate Deng quote for the celebrated 24-character maxim usually attributed to him, and summed up by an injunction usually translated as "keep a low profile" (*taoguang yanghui*). But there is also no question that under his watch, China's foreign policy focused on a series of choices about where to adapt to international rules and where to turn down these rules—but not whether to overturn them or to champion an alternate view of the world order.[3] It is no surprise then that this period coincided with a wave of engagement policies from the West. However, the Western promoters of these policies may mistake the cause with the consequence if they think that it was their open door to China that triggered the country's opening.

Deng's successor Jiang Zemin amplified Deng's adjustments to global rules—as shown, for example, in a series of accessions to international treaties, including on arms control. Altogether, between 1989 (when Jiang became party secretary) and 2002 (when he retired from the top position), China signed or ratified numerous international agreements, including the Nuclear Non-Proliferation Treaty and the United Nations Convention on the Law of the Sea (UNCLOS), and also joined the WTO.[4] This record is unmatched before or since.

Hu Jintao's rule over the following ten years, an apex of collective leadership, halted those trends without reversing them. But it is also under Hu that the debate about the merits and demerits of keeping a low profile began. Increasingly, China's "peaceful rise" (*heping jueqi*, though "jueqi" is better translated "surge") overshadowed the earlier *taoguang yanghui* maxim, even if it was never fully recognized officially. Liberals—including the chief promoter of *heping jueqi*, Zheng Bijian, fallen leader Hu Yaobang's former private secretary, was certainly among them—may have intended the formula to encourage China's participation in common rules of the road. Part of this was about China undertaking international responsibilities, answering the Western call to become a "responsible stakeholder," a phrase coined by

---

[3] Alastair Iain Johnston, "Learning Versus Adaptation: Explaining Change in Chinese Arms Control Policy in the 1980s and 1990s," *China Journal*, no. 35 (1996): 27–61.

[4] Other international agreements include the Convention on the Rights of the Child; the UN Framework Convention on Climate Change; the Chemical Weapons Convention; the International Covenant on Economic, Social and Cultural Rights; the Comprehensive Nuclear-Test-Ban Treaty (not ratified); and the International Covenant on Civil and Political Rights (not ratified).

Robert Zoellick in 2005.[5] Instead, China became a "reluctant stakeholder," as Zoellick later acknowledged in 2011.[6] The term "peaceful rise" was finally not retained. In China's official language, what has prevailed to this day is *heping fazhan*, or peaceful development, which focused instead on China's growth and self-interest and skirted controversial debates on its rise. On the question of participation in the world order, China has leaned toward another segment of the old maxim attributed to Deng, *yousuo zuowei*, loosely translated as "make contributions where there is a case." At its extreme, some would advocate a Chinese form of liberal internationalism, with China becoming a provider of international public goods on the model of the European Union.[7] But the debate also inadvertently opened the way for increased activism abroad and for moving from nonintervention to rewarding—or punishing—partner countries, if not creating alliances.[8] That was the other option, pushed with gusto by Yan Xuetong, the Tsinghua University don.[9] During the troubled period of 2009–12 that immediately preceded Xi's ascent to the top position, these ideas clashed quite openly. Mostly, a defiant version of patriotism, the increased prominence of army-related developments in education and the media, won the day: the giant People's Liberation Army (PLA) parade for the PRC's anniversary in 2009, a strong anti-Japanese campaign, and rapid development of China's military presence throughout the South China Sea were components.

It is in that changing context that Xi won—and consolidated beyond the predictions of almost all observers—his leadership over both the Chinese Communist Party (CCP) and China. Except in some calculated confidences about his personal and family history, his ideology had remained much harder to decrypt than that of other prospective leaders, such as the fallen Bo Xilai, who had campaigned openly on patriotism, the "mass line," and "red" nostalgia, or Wang Yang, the Guangdong party leader who had championed some societal opening before 2012 and has kept a discreet footprint inside the party leadership ever since. There is simply no way to tell whether it is

---

[5] Robert Zoellick, "Whither China: From Membership to Responsibility?" (remarks to the National Committee on U.S.-China Relations, New York, September 21, 2005), https://2001-2009.state.gov/s/d/former/zoellick/rem/53682.htm.

[6] Will McCallum, "Robert Zoellick: China 'Reluctant Stakeholder' in World Economic Woes," Asia Society, August 14, 2011,

[7] See, for example, Wang Yizhou, *Creative Involvement: The Evolution of China's Global Role* (Beijing: Peking University Press, 2013).

[8] Degang Sun, "Lun xinshiqi Zhongguo de zhun jiemeng waijiao" [On China's Semi-Alliance Diplomacy in a New Era], *Shijie jingji yu zhengzhi* 3 (2012): 57–158.

[9] Yan's advocacy remains anchored in realism: "China should have more allies than the U.S., but unfortunately at this moment, we fall far short." "Yan Xuetong on Chinese Realism, the Tsinghua School of International Relations, and the Impossibility of Harmony," Theory Talks, no. 51, November 28, 2012, http://www.theory-talks.org/2012/11/theory-talk-51.html.

nationalism and the rise of China's global ambitions that lifted up Xi, or whether he has been a major factor in the uplift for these ambitions.

Xi Jinping's Rebranding of China's Messaging

Xi Jinping's increasing grasp on power and its personalization coincide with far greater claims for China's influence and with a drive to assert China's interpretation of global values—or its own definition of these values. Yet before the Belt and Road theme started gaining international prominence, "win-win" was the most common theme from China in international relations, common enough to become the butt of jokes as to its interpretation, such as "China wins twice." Yet win-win is a child of free-trade rhetoric under the Clinton administration. What is uniquely Chinese is the ubiquitous use of the phrase in public diplomacy, and what is most telling is that China turned the table, using a Western-derived slogan to defend its status and interests within the world trading system.

Similarly, Xi has created or inherited keywords that are in themselves quite bland and certainly not unique. The "China dream" itself is of course borrowed from the American dream. "Creating a community of common destiny," as Hu Jintao was the first to express to China's neighbors, and "build[ing] a community of shared future for mankind," as Xi amplified in his January 2017 UN speech in Geneva,[10] are similar to Japanese mottos from an earlier era, such as *hakko ichiu* (eight corners under one roof), the slogan of the Co-prosperity Sphere. There is some recognition in China of this Asian linkage.[11]

Some will point out that the United States has claimed Manifest Destiny and that the EU seeks to attract partners on the basis of the values it upholds.[12] Xi is largely drawing from the repertoire of global values that is associated with post-1945 international institutions: Japan did so with the League of Nations in the 1920s. But he is also reclaiming the imperial legacy of the "great harmony under heaven" (*tianxia datong*) for BRI, claiming that the initiative will "stand on the international high ground of morality and justice"(*zhanjule*

---

[10] Xi Jinping, "Work Together to Build a Community of Shared Future for Mankind" (speech at the UN Office, Geneva, January 18, 2017), http://www.xinhuanet.com/english/2017-01/19/c_135994707.htm.

[11] See, for example, Feng Zhongping and Huang Jing, "China's Strategic Partnership Diplomacy: Engaging with a Changing World," European Strategic Partnerships Observatory, Working Paper, no. 8, June 2014, 17.

[12] For a robust comparison with Manifest Destiny, see Yuen Foong Khong, "The American Tributary System," *Chinese Journal of International Politics* 6, no. 1 (2013): 1–47, https://doi.org/10.1093/cjip/pot002.

guoji daoyi zhigaodian).[13] In this regard, Xi hovers at the border of a more fundamental claim for Chinese values, echoing Yan Xuetong's praise for "humane authority" (*wangdao*), as opposed to hegemonism (*badao*), from the period of the Warring States onward.[14] This, however, happens within a speech aimed at Chinese audiences. The same ambiguity exists over the issue of a "Chinese model" for the economy, even if official pronouncements avoid the term. The concept's leading exponent, Fudan University's Zhang Weiwei, has recently produced a ten-part documentary titled "The Chinese Way" on the China Global Television Network (CGTN).[15] Liberal Chinese economists have denounced the temptation, insisting on China's integration with the global economy. Peking University's Zhang Weiying, for example, published two pieces in 2018 arguing that the notion of a Chinese model leads to conflict with the West.[16] This debate suggests tensions behind Xi's holistic approach.

Similarly, the theme of "common but differentiated responsibilities" has become a hallmark of China's stand on development and environmental issues. But it is far from original, having evolved from decades of international negotiation on natural resources and environment issues.[17] What matters is not the "Chineseness" or "un-Chineseness" of these concepts, but China's ability to project them, if only through ceaseless repetition and a drive to promote the concepts' language.

Often, the concepts are not only far from original but also vague or ambiguous. Xi's well-known Davos speech of January 2017 does cite or refer to four Chinese proverbs.[18] Yet it also refers to five foreign personalities, ranging from Charles Dickens to Christine Lagarde. The speech salutes multilateralism and multilateral institutions, certainly an opportune choice

---

[13] Han Zheng, "Xi Jinping: Tuidong gong jian 'Yidai Yilu' zou shen zou shi zaofu renmin" [Xi Jinping: Promoting the Common Construction of the "Belt and Road" for the Deep and Sincere Benefit of the People], August 27, 2018, http://cpc.people.com.cn/n1/2018/0827/c64094-30254137.html.

[14] Yan Xuetong, "Chinese Values vs. Liberalism: What Ideology Will Shape the International Normative Order?" *Chinese Journal of International Politics* 11, no. 1 (2018): 1–22.

[15] Zhang Weiwei, "What Is the Unique Model Behind China's Rapid Rise?" China Global Television Network, March 26, 2018, https://news.cgtn.com/news/78497a4d7a6b7a6333566d54/share_p.html.

[16] Zhang Weiying, "Weilai shijie de geju, qujue yu Zhongguo zenme zuo" [The Future World Order Depends on How China Acts] (speech at the Symposium on Sino-U.S. Relations at the Institute of World Politics and Economics of the Chinese Academy of Social Sciences, Beijing, June 26, 2018), available in a version revised by the author at http://finance.qq.com/original/caijingzhiku/zhangweiying.html. A second article appearing on Peking University's website in October 2018 has been censored.

[17] For a genealogy of the terms, see "The Principle of Common but Differentiated Responsibilities: Origins and Scope," Centre for International Sustainable Development Law, Legal Brief, August 2002, http://cisdl.org/public/docs/news/brief_common.pdf.

[18] For the full text, see Xi Jinping (speech at World Economic Forum, Davos-Klosters, January 17, 2017), https://www.weforum.org/agenda/2017/01/full-text-of-xi-jinping-keynote-at-the-world-economic-forum.

after the 2016 U.S. presidential election, and reads like an effort to mesh China's concerns with existing global values. Only in its conclusion does the speech land squarely on its feet, with a direct reminder in the first person of BRI and its international reception. At this point, we have left the domain of values to enter that of policy; we are also witnessing the rare case of a Chinese top leader directly promoting himself.

More than the content of the message, the repetition and the methods of influence or coercion—depending on the targeted audience—are what create its power. It is not that "Chinese can't think," including experts and diplomats, to borrow from the title of a famous book.[19] But in a system that combines Leninism and a high degree of personal power and personality cult, it is safer to repeat party lines. There is of course a similarity with the domestic sloganeering—what Simon Leys called the *langue de bois* (wooden language) inherited from Maoism. One can also surmise the unexpected influence of Confucianism with its insistence on *zhengming* (correcting names). The rectification of names, as this practice is also called, has often been seen as an empty ritual form. But modern language theory teaches us that language is indeed a form of reality—the person who controls the words controls far more. China does not want to direct behavior, it wants to condition it: "correct thinking will lead to correct behavior."[20] Xi has continued, after Hu, to encourage a form of civic Confucianism that was also practiced in Taiwan under Chiang Kai-shek and by South Korea's Park Chung-hee.[21] The latter's *yushin* (revitalizing) constitution is echoed by Xi's "national rejuvenation" (*minzu fuxing*) theme. In Xi's words, "don't forget your original sentiment" (*buwang chuxin*).[22] The spread all over the world of Confucius Institutes managed by an official Chinese state agency also attests to the quest for legitimacy from China's cultural heritage.

The drive for dominance through language applies to many domains of foreign relations. One need just go back to the promotion of the one-China principle, which is now accepted and enshrined in bilateral communiqués with nearly every nation (even if some manage to finesse the issue). The drive to create "strategic partnerships," some of them "all around" (Germany and Brazil), one described as "all weather" (Pakistan), and another as

---

[19] Kishore Mahbubani, *Can Asians Think? Understanding the Divide between East and West* (Singapore: Times Books, 1998).

[20] Bilahari Kausikan, "Manipulation, Chinese Style," *Nikkei Asian Review*, August 22, 2018, https://asia.nikkei.com/Opinion/Manipulation-Chinese-style.

[21] Hamh Chaibong, "China's Future Is South Korea's Present," *Foreign Affairs*, September/October 2018, https://www.foreignaffairs.com/articles/asia/2018-08-13/chinas-future-south-koreas-present.

[22] From Xi Jinping's report to the 19th CCP Congress, where expression is translated as "never forget why you started." The Chinese-language text is available at http://www.xinhuanet.com/english/download/Xi_Jinping's_report_at_19th_CPC_National_Congress.pdf.

"comprehensive" (Russia), has become a charade with its bewildering variety of very similar terms.[23] The key term "comprehensive strategic partnership," often described as reserved for Russia, has also been used with regional groupings: first, the Association of Southeast Asian Nations (ASEAN) and second with the EU, which is a group of nations that have notorious divergences with the PRC on many major issues. Still, at times, it is the relationship with the United States that has been officially described as "the most important" relationship of all. More recently, regional agreements with the EU and ASEAN have also been framed with exactly the same language: three pillars of cooperation—political and security issues, economic and sustainable development, and social, cultural, and people-to-people exchanges.

The one-China principle is a key tenet for China, and it has been advanced worldwide. But this is now done through the language of interest, not that of values. One need only to look at the recent speech made by El Salvador's President Sanchez Ceren on the occasion of breaking ties with Taiwan and establishing diplomatic relations with the PRC: "This decision will allow for great benefits to the country and will bring extraordinary benefits to every one of us."[24] Foreign Minister Wang Yi salutes a decision to recognize one-China "without any precondition," but also holds out the prospect of tangible benefits for the country. There is nothing new, of course, in the money game played over the issue of recognizing or derecognizing Taiwan. What stands out today is that the game is out in the open, and in fact recognized as such by partner countries. The language chiefly used by China is that of pragmatism and self-interest, as these countries acknowledge. That perhaps trumps the value card.

The astonishing public success of the "One Belt, One Road" slogan with audiences all over the world also testifies to China's influence through public diplomacy. Partners have wanted to read so much into this grand design that it has had to be renamed an "initiative" for foreign consumption—emphasizing that there is no set strategy at work but rather a general offer of which others can avail themselves. Notwithstanding the huge number of conferences, think tanks, and academic institutions created in China around BRI, there has been more private skepticism about the initiative in China than abroad until recently. Like the Great Leap Forward—but with less ominous consequences, fortunately—BRI has met with a propaganda success that likely exceeds initial

---

[23] This has almost been acknowledged as such by reliable PRC experts. See, for example, Feng and Huang, "China's Strategic Partnership Diplomacy," 18–19.

[24] This statement was made in an August 21, 2018, television address, as translated from Spanish. The original statement is available at http://www.presidencia.gob.sv/mensaje-a-la-nacion-del-senor-presidente-de-la-republica-salvador-sanchez-ceren.

expectations. But this is not about "values," and perhaps not even about "policy," if one believes indeed the disclaimers from Beijing, which claims that the initiative has no set strategy. It is more about a promise of prosperity through massive projects and the money flowing around them.

China's promotion of values that it claims as its own, its de facto challenge to other values usually identified with a liberal international order, may be a part of its ascent toward the first rank of global powers—alone or *ex aequo* with the United States. But this could also be a marker of this ascent rather than a goal: what matters is less the values, or even the language, than compliance with China's interests and goals.

The contradiction between language and reality is a feature of advertising, which often chooses to hammer counterfactuals in order to hide weaknesses, as the tobacco industry has long practiced. Particularly striking is a recent CGTN advertisement displayed in airports and airline magazines. "'See the difference' is our motto. CGTN is a practitioner of objective and balanced reporting," reads a caption next to the photo of a stylish young Karl Marx–type armed with an old-fashioned film camera. In a similar vein, at a Huawei event in Rome attended by three thousand people, the company, now barred from public procurement in the United States and Australia, pledged to provide "an open, innovative and collaborative digital ecosystem" for Europe. "Open" is another buzzword used by Xi. Both cases are good examples of the "virtual politics" used by post-Leninist authoritarian regimes to counter criticism.[25] Such slogans are propagated by modern mass media and can be used indifferently by public or semiprivate actors.

A Mirror for Democracy's Self-Doubts

Because beauty is often in the eye of the beholder, how much does foreign acknowledgement of China's material successes in achieving wealth and power create a momentum toward recognition for Chinese policies and in turn an attraction to value systems associated with these policies? How much of these trends is driven by a Chinese strategy, with official policies and specific institutions, and how much are they the result of a contemporary cargo cult, facilitated by the growing divisions inside and among democratic societies? Is China superseding democratic and liberal value systems by design, or is it by happenstance well-placed to benefit from the hollowing out of these value systems?

---

[25] See Andrew Wilson, *Virtual Politics: Faking Democracy in the Post-Soviet World* (New Haven: Yale University Press, 2005).

These questions are very hard to answer. For one, a failure of the democracies to implement the values they claim does not per se invalidate these values. The accusations of Western "double standards" by defenders of China's politics and policies are sometimes deserved. Yet not living up to one's values is not the same as negating these values. Communism has rested on a much bigger lie, with the pretense to uphold values derived from the century of enlightenment, as exemplified by the Soviet Union's 1936 constitution. The recognition of these values is mirrored in China's 1956 text, written largely by the same authors as the most recent Constitution of 1982. Except during the Cultural Revolution, when "bourgeois rights" were reviled in the context of factional struggle, China has not rejected out of hand what liberal advocates would term as global values. Hypocrisy is a homage that vice pays to virtue. Whether this belated recognition has now ended is an important issue.

Second, even a cursory exploration of official Chinese ideology reveals an extraordinary gap between official political culture and the underlying society. Within China's political cycles, we are now in a phase of assertive self-confidence, promotion, and authoritarian extinction of voices that speak out for any competing value system or political path. But how much is this a defensive stance toward its own people by a leadership that was faced for several decades with the advance of democracy in Asia and the world at large? Indeed, the pushback started within the leadership in 1986, as it divided over political reform. Relations with Japan were the first casualty, and the pushback expanded to a nationalist backlash for the whole country after the 1989 Tiananmen Square protests. In simple terms, the turnaround on China's international vision started from within, sparked by fear of democratization.[26] Neo-authoritarian views, the renewed promotion of patriotism and nationalism, and the rehabilitation of some forms of Confucianism all started then. Remarkably, this was managed separately from China's economic reforms and opening up, which resumed in 1992.

The CCP's promotion of Chinese values has snowballed since, extending to claims of international superiority and increasing the negative propaganda on other competing political models. China does not claim the merits of illiberal democracy but simply the virtue of leadership by the CCP. There has also appeared an official determination of China as a "great power" and now occasionally as a "superpower." But this is also a reflection of the need to persuade Chinese citizens themselves that the world looks up to their leaders, policies, and political system. The 2008 Olympic Games, which occurred

---

[26] In the words of then PRC president Yang Shangkun answering Deng Xiaoping: "'Retreat, you tell me, to what point can we retreat?' I replied by saying, 'This is the last dike on the dam. If we retreat, the whole dam will collapse.'" "Internal Speech of Yang Shangkun (May 22, 1989)," *Chinese Law and Government* 23, no. 1 (1990): 70. Yang later championed the "go west" (*xibu kaifa*) policy stressing inland development and the Eurasian land bridge that prefigured BRI.

against the backdrop of strong international criticism of China's support for the murderous Sudan regime and repression in Tibet, highlighted these two sides of the coin: present an extraordinary face to the world and convince Chinese citizens that China indeed draws in the entire world. Again, these two goals are not original; they are probably in the line of sight of every country that organizes Olympic Games. It is the scale at which China accomplished them in 2008, or at the Shanghai World Expo one year later, that is so striking.

A founding motto of the PRC attributed to Mao was "we have friends all over the world" (*women de pengyou bian tianxia*), and managing foreigners has been a key goal for the CCP.[27] But in fact, there were very few "captive minds" abroad at the time—far fewer than what the Soviet promotion of Communism achieved.[28] China has become a success, and the material rewards for looking east have vastly increased. Its public diplomacy and propaganda have many more relays than was the case under Maoism. Money does talk indeed, but China's soft power and ability to convince others still lags behind its economic influence or military rise. There has in fact been a confusion between soft power and China's influence. The latter rests on commercial, financial, and classic diplomatic means as well as the anticipation of a further rise in the country's power. That is not the same thing as soft power, which relies on cultural attractiveness, the appeal of values, or historical ties. There is some overlap, but not much. When Joseph Nye first claimed the rise of China's soft power, one example he cited was Nobel prize winner Gao Xingjian.[29] In fact, Gao had been an exile in France since 1989, and he is not even recognized by the PRC as a prize recipient. Nye's second example was the acclaimed movie *Crouching Tiger, Hidden Dragon* (2000). But the movie's director, Ang Lee, is from Taiwan. Of the eight production companies for the movie, only two were PRC-based; two others were international, three were based in Hong Kong, and one was from Taiwan. There are of course many remarkable writers and movie directors in China, but those who are best known abroad often have strong overseas Chinese or international connections. Ai Weiwei—perhaps China's most talented cultural activist and the designer of Beijing's Olympic stadium known as "the bird's nest"—has a genuine international impact not only as an artist but also as a critic rather than a follower of official lines.

---

[27] Mao Zedong, "The Chinese People Have Stood Up!" (opening address at the first plenary session of the Chinese People's Political Consultative Conference, Beijing, September 21, 1949), available at https://china.usc.edu/Mao-declares-founding-of-peoples-republic-of-china-chinese-people-have-stood-up. As with Deng's *taoguang yanghui* maxim, the motto's veracity is debated, but it became a well-known song and a frequently used slogan. See Anne-Marie Brady, "Treat Insiders and Outsiders Differently: The Use and Control of Foreigners in the PRC," *China Quarterly*, no. 164 (2000): 961.

[28] Czeslaw Milosz, *The Captive Mind* (New York: Knopf, 1953).

[29] Joseph S. Nye Jr., "The Rise of China's Soft Power," *Wall Street Journal*, December 29, 2005, https://www.wsj.com/articles/SB113580867242333272.

Therefore, the popularity of the Chinese model, real or imaginary, and the increasing attraction of a global order that would reflect supposed Chinese values do not only originate from the Chinese effort to convince others of their merits. They also have to do with internal disappointment or disillusionment with the merits of liberal democracy, or with the rise of illiberal democracy as a political trend.

Sharp Power Is Not Soft Power

While soft power attracts and convinces, sharp power manipulates and coerces. China's public diplomacy falls in between soft and sharp power.[30] The PRC has made massive efforts at improving its public diplomacy by expanding programs for influence through audiovisual, semi-academic, and social media tools. Investment in CGTN offices abroad, including a satellite broadcast of its national and foreign-language channels, is now dwarfing other international media such as CNN and BBC. CGTN's channels focus very differently on public messaging. While the international channels carry uplifting and entertaining documentaries about China's economic prowess, the Chinese-language channels focus much more on presenting the image of a dangerous world, where war and militarization loom and Chinese citizens are at risk. Yet both will host foreigners on their talk shows, displaying a variety of opinions that is just not permitted to Chinese participants in these broadcasts. Semi-academic tools include the ubiquitous Confucius Institutes, which do testify to the attraction of learning Chinese today and may have the added advantage of early identification by the Chinese government of Chinese-language learners. Academic influence relies mainly on coveted exchange programs and degrees with Chinese universities. Large donations, in some cases by rich Hong Kong families rather than from the mainland, also play a role to influence China institutes, more embedded institutions than the Confucius institutes.

The role of social media is harder to assess beyond the Chinese-language sphere, where WeChat (Weixin) is said to have 900 million accounts, or 83% of all smartphone users.[31] Douban, the cultural web media, enjoys huge influence among Chinese student communities abroad, and it is censored as well. Perhaps for that same reason, foreign-language Chinese websites,

---

[30] For a realistic yet calm assessment of the issue, see Larry Diamond and Orville Schell, "Chinese Influence and American Interests: Promoting Constructive Vigilance," Hoover Institution, Report, November 29, 2018.

[31] Laurie Chen, "Why China's Tech-Savvy Millennials Are Quitting WeChat," *South China Morning Post*, July 22, 2018, https://www.scmp.com/news/china/society/article/2156297/how-growing-privacy-fears-china-are-driving-wechat-users-away.

including those of official media, are far less popular. The *Global Times*, a CCP newspaper, is an exception, mainly because of its calculated provocations that attract interest and stir controversy abroad. There is simply no comparison between the influence of key high-brow media from democracies and the slim audiences for Chinese media.[32] The very powerful and lively Chinese social media—which is the object of massive government surveillance and intervention—stop where the Chinese language ends, while their Western competitors are banned or disadvantaged in China. Thus, China's "great firewall" limiting access to information for ordinary Chinese has an unintended consequence abroad: the huge sphere of Chinese social media is largely self-contained. How can you create soft power if you hinder communications between societies?

The Chinese government has therefore resorted to buying foreign media, or more often buying space within the media, to convey official views abroad. Outright purchase usually takes place in smaller or less affluent countries, while buying space happens in large, developed markets, especially Europe. At the same time, visas for foreign correspondents in China are increasingly under pressure. The question here is whether this will lead to self-censorship by print media that need the resources from paid supplements or news organizations that want to keep a foothold in China.[33]

In fact, China is often admired for its performance, but it is not liked. This ambivalence is reflected in answers to questions from the Pew Research Center's Global Attitudes Project. In a spring 2017 survey of residents of 60 countries on their views of major countries, China ranked second only to the United States for favorable views.[34] But when residents in 38 countries were asked whether China's power and influence are a major threat, a minor threat, or no threat, the answers were split among the three answers. China's six neighbors all regard the country as a major threat.[35] In answers to both questions, residents of Latin America and the Middle East tend to rate China higher or to view it as posing little or no threat.

Marketplace attraction is an important feature of international influence, and this applies even more to developing or dependent societies. Only two decades ago, China was a producer of consumer goods without

---

[32] This judgment about the Chinese media's lack of appeal applies less in developing or middle-income societies, where it provides free entertainment, information, and reports on the wonders of Chinese infrastructure and industry.

[33] For further discussion, see François Godement and Abigaël Vasselier, "China at the Gates: A New Power Audit of EU-China Relations," European Council on Foreign Relations (ECFR), December 2017, 81, https://www.ecfr.eu/page/-/China_Power_Audit.pdf.

[34] Pew Research Center, Pew Global Attitudes and Trends Question Database, http://www.pewglobal.org/question-search/?qid=855&cntIDs=&stdIDs=.

[35] Ibid.

brand names. Today, Huawei, Haier, Xiaomi, Alibaba, and Tencent are spreading their wings throughout the global economy.

The skeptical views above do not apply to strategies to achieve overt or covert influence with key opinion leaders or decision-makers. The latter concern material rewards and lobbies rather than power appeal. From Australia to Europe and the United States, a number of investigative reports or studies have raised the alarm on China's growing influence games.[36] In almost all cases, money or the lure of money—whether it is for public interest or private gain —plays a major role. It is therefore all the more striking that the American Chamber of Commerce in China and the European Union Chamber of Commerce in China separately sound very similar notes: while their constituents are by nature the most vulnerable to local pressure, the business organizations are often very critical.

Yet self-doubts inside free societies, toned down for a while after the fall of the Soviet Union, again are playing a large role in enabling authoritarian messages, including China's. China plays the role of a countermodel to liberalism and individualism, strangely enough for a society that has become one of the most unequal in income. And unlike Putin's Russia, with its heavy accent on nostalgia, China is well-positioned to represent the future in marketable technological achievements that appeal to consumers. The branding for its message starts from verified successes, and thus blends ultraconservative values with the promise of quick riches for all. It therefore holds some allure for both sides of the political spectrum. Marxism claimed that ideas about society arise from the actual arrangements for production. Its more pedestrian exponent, Friedrich Engels, summed this up by declaring that the proof of the pudding was in the eating. There never was much pudding to be had in the Soviet Union. China is the first rich Leninist state, and it should therefore be no surprise that Xi Jinping attempts to reclaim Marxism, an ideology that had fallen in tatters. His official biography for the World Economic Forum starts with a reference to a "degree in Marxist theory and ideological and political education" from Tsinghua University.[37] Rather improbably, this happens as China advertises itself as a market economy.

Still, it is not the influence of the bearded prophet from Trier that strikes one most when arriving in China. Paris may have been the capital of the 19th century, and indeed remained long after a magnet for artistic and literary creation. New York was the capital of the 20th century, to which flocked the huddled masses of immigrants. It is on a physical scale that

---

[36] For Europe, see Godement and Vasselier, "China at the Gates"; and Thorsten Benner et al., "Authoritarian Advance, Responding to China's Influence in Europe," Global Public Policy Institute and Mercator Institute for China Studies, February 2018.

[37] See the World Economic Forum website, https://www.weforum.org/people/xi-jinping.

Shanghai is the capital of the 21st century, and that China has become the iconic factory of the world in a century of globalized trade. Foreign expatriates may disseminate the value of trading rules, as local *compradores* once did. But traders do not create values, and the soft power of China lags far behind its materialistic attraction.

China's Drive in International Institutions

International institutions are the clearest target of China's carefully crafted influence. Strong diplomatic presence, bilateral lobbying and cultivation of groupings of nations, and increasingly also budgetary and financial tools are applied. It may be hard to assess what new values are really being promoted. China's diplomacy is more on the initiative than in previous times. Its traditionally defensive approaches, based on sovereignty and noninterference, are completed by new interpretations of international norms, and in some cases by formal initiatives. Whether these imply more than language is often doubtful, but this clearly reinforces China's capacity to create and manage coalitions inside the UN General Assembly, while also dealing quietly with the other permanent members of the UN Security Council. At the United Nations, key phrases such as "win-win," "mutual respect," "global governance," and "multilateralism" increasingly turn up in resolutions and memoranda of understanding (MOUs). One can argue that several, if not all, of these terms were actually proposed to China by the West only two decades ago, before being appropriated by China. They also happen to be lifted from President Xi Jinping's speeches of the last few years, indicating that this is certainly a top-down drive, not a contagion of ideas. In several UN institutions such as the UN Development Programme, the UN Department of Economic and Social Affairs, and the UN High Commissioner for Refugees, China is meeting with at least a consensus not to oppose, and often a willingness to adopt, this language in resolutions, communiqués, and memoranda of agreement.

These are all being pushed on China's partners, including some EU member states, and they seem to have the function of legitimizing China's policies. They usually contain stereotyped language and no legally binding commitments, except disclaimers that have been required by the other signatories at the very end. It is the agreement on a common political vocabulary that seems to matter for China. In the words of one business law analyst, "the purpose of these non-legally binding MoUs is to influence, rather than direct—a subtlety that may be lost on some of the signatories."[38] China's aversion to legally binding agreements—and even more to their verification—is traditional. What is new is the appearance of claims to adjudicate international issues under Chinese law. This development was articulated by the Supreme People's Court in 2016, following the international arbitration on geographic criteria to adjudicate sovereignty in the South China Sea.[39] It is now spreading to international business arbitration, as evidenced by the creation of Chinese-based arbitration boards on BRI issues.[40] Here again, the change is qualitative rather than quantitative: foreign firms have always understood that recourse to arbitration in dealing with China is a death sentence for their future dealings with the country. But China is now crossing the line between informal avoidance of international law and the creation of its own jurisdictions. Extraterritorial justice is in general an internationally contested ground, as current debates on investor-state dispute settlement or the enforcement of international sanctions show. But China combines reluctance toward existing international arbitration with the creation of its own extraterritorial process. This happens in a context where the judiciary completely lacks independence, with no practical recourse to third-party arbitration for foreign companies.

As with its engagement in regional institutions, China's understanding of international institutions and multilateralism, which Xi Jinping has attempted to reclaim after Donald Trump's election, follows predictable patterns. China's approach on the multilateral or regional stage is to forge broad agreements, the substance of which is provided by traditional bilateral diplomacy. The Forum on China-Africa Cooperation, the Shanghai Cooperation Organisation, and the 16+1 meeting with sixteen Central and Eastern European countries run along these lines. While the formal meetings provide a stage, business is transacted separately from the meetings, and most often bilaterally. This is also true of China's relations with the EU, which Chinese officials persist in calling a "regional organization."[41] In spite of proclamations of support for European integration, the Chinese

---

[38] Chris Devonshire-Ellis, "Vassal States: Understanding China's Belt and Road MoU," Silk Road Briefing, February 8, 2018, https://www.silkroadbriefing.com/news/2018/02/08/vassal-states-understanding-chinas-belt-road-mou.

[39] "China's Supreme Court Clarifies Maritime Jurisdiction," Xinhua, August 2, 2016.

[40] China International Commercial Court, "Opinion Concerning the Establishment of the Belt and Road International Commercial Dispute Resolution Mechanism and Institutions," updated on June 27, 2018, http://cicc.court.gov.cn/html/1/219/208/210/819.html.

[41] "The EU is a regional organization composed of sovereign states, not a sovereign country itself," said Hua Chunying, spokesperson of the PRC's Ministry of Foreign Affairs. "Foreign Ministry Spokesperson Hua Chunying's Regular Press Conference on August 31, 2017," Ministry of Foreign Affairs (PRC), August 31, 2017, https://www.fmprc.gov.cn/mfa_eng/xwfw_665399/s2510_665401/2511_665403/t1488873.shtml.

government has often delayed or abstained from high-level dialogues on economics or human rights in recent years.

There is one area where China's integration with the liberal international order has been the subject of long debates: the internationalization of the Chinese currency. Yet the same pattern described above largely holds for China's currency policies. The renminbi entered the International Monetary Fund's reserve currency basket in 2016, thus gaining acceptance as a key global currency. The argument is often made that this is tantamount to liberalization of the renminbi.[42] Yet China has done so on its own terms. To this day, the renminbi is not freely tradable as the other reserve currencies are. The process of internationalizing the renminbi has often happened through swap agreements with other central banks and therefore is closely tied to trade with these countries. This is not liberal internationalization but a mercantilist approach that recalls the preferential trading zones of European powers in the 1930s. Of course, this places limitations on the actual role played by the renminbi in international finance, and as a result, the currency remains a very limited instrument of payment in global trade. At the end of 2017, China settled only 16% of its foreign trade in renminbi. Its share of international payments was only 1.3%, and 97% of renminbi trading is done against the U.S. dollar.[43] Ultimately, a country with an international currency is one that is a borrower and has a deep international debt market. Were the WTO agreement to tank, however, or other major currencies to resort again to capital control, China would be well-placed to fight in a postliberal world order.

China's layered understanding of the multilateral order allows it to pick and choose among international institutions and rules. Thus, the WTO is sanctified. This is because China's greatest success with international institutions is to have entered the trading system with the status of a developing economy in perpetuity. China has converged with other international actors on climate and environmental issues because the decisions involved no longer imply binding verification, and the legal obligations are vaguely defined: this does leave the option of bottom-up initiatives and voluntary contributions, or the half-full, half-empty glass. Conversely, China largely shuns the UN High Commissioner for Refugees and sabotages the UN Human Rights Council (UNHRC). For example, China worked with states like Sudan, Syria, and Venezuela to push a resolution through the UNHRC in March 2018 that

---

[42] For this thesis, see Barry Eichengreen and Guangtao Xia, "China and the SDR: Financial Liberalization through the Backdoor," Centre for International Governance Innovation, CIGI Paper, no. 170, April 2018, https://www.cigionline.org/sites/default/files/documents/Paper%20no.170_0.pdf.

[43] See the SWIFT RMB Tracker reports for January 2018 and September 2018, available at https://www.swift.com/our-solutions/compliance-and-shared-services/business-intelligence/renminbi/rmb-tracker/document-centre.

promotes human rights by way of a "mutually beneficial" or "constructive" cooperation.[44] This is sometimes presented as the start of an active role for China in redefining human rights, as opposed to defending its own case or opposing reviews of other countries. Watered down after a first attempt in 2017, the text was vague enough to warrant the abstention of EU and other countries, with only the United States opposing it. But the issue became clearer when some other countries, including Cuba, Syria, and Venezuela—without China—championed a more explicit measure at the next UNHRC session.[45] This new resolution confuses human rights with "a sense of community and international solidarity," repeatedly mentioning states but never the individual. Despite the opposition of fourteen countries (with Mexico abstaining), this resolution also passed, with China's support. China's ambiguity in a global setting is exactly captured here. Its own resolution of March 2018 is couched in language that does not negate individual rights but emphasizes interstate cooperation as a path. But when some states subsequently went further down the revisionist road by dropping the rights of the individual, China was happy to sign on the dotted line. This is a striking example of leading from behind, but also a sign that China does not want to go beyond a certain point in the promotion of different global values; instead, it will let others do so.

In all this, China does not fear contradicting itself. For instance, it hails local and grassroot initiatives on environmental issues but wages a war on civil society and NGOs speaking out on human rights, promoting instead its own government-organized nongovernmental organizations.

It should be reiterated that there are really no "new" values involved here. What is indeed novel is the degree of acceptance by other countries of China's excuses, either out of relief for many or out of embarrassment in regions that are internally divided, such as the EU.

China thus positions itself in a middle space of the international order. It embraces the post-1945 UN order that includes compromise among the five permanent members of the UN Security Council but freezes that number. It idealizes free trade under the special conditions it obtained in 2001. China participates in UN peacekeeping while restraining the scope of operations. But with the exception of trade, it rejects most of the features added to the international order after 1989, such as humanitarian intervention and the responsibility to protect, binding verification of agreements that intrude on sovereignty, and binding international arbitration in areas as essential as territorial boundaries. China is thus more involved in a conservative drive

---

[44] This resolution is available from the Office of the High Commissioner for Human Rights, https://ap.ohchr.org/documents/dpage_e.aspx?si=A/HRC/38/L.3.

[45] This resolution can be found at https://documents-dds-ny.un.org/doc/UNDOC/LTD/G18/066/67/PDF/G1806667.pdf.

for "old" values than in promoting new standards, and it is of course far from alone in this endeavor.

Promoting Language over Values

Under a liberal internationalist framework, foreign policy is the means to promote values internationally. Interest gains are a byproduct, even if the overall philosophy explains that interests are best achieved through the realization of these common values. In a realist framework, values reflect power and influence, and they are secondary to national interests. No state follows completely one or the other path; instead, states generally claim both interests and values, depending on the domestic or international audience. There are aspects of China's public diplomacy—themes borrowed from a large international repertory and tools of overt or covert influence—that do not deviate from the policies of previous great powers or even other nations. Selling China's achievements, promoting the Chinese language (even if this is hampered by an extraordinary level of censorship and self-censorship), looking for like-minded coalitions in international organizations, using rewards and punishment with international partners, employing lobbies: these all constitute the oldest game in the world for strong nation states, a game that is exacerbated by the new mushrooming of media and communications.

China's unicity is not there, even if one admits that quantity matters, as size does. And it does not lie either in an openly revisionist vision of the international order. As much as China's actions on occasion deviate from international law, often invoking historical rights in the process, they do not challenge international law and institutions but rather their interpretation and processes. Instead of looking either for signs of China's acceptance of and integration with global values[46] or for proof of a revisionist ambition to create a new global system and values, we should consider that China's ruling group regards values as playing the same role as operators in language grammar or lubrication in mechanics. They play a binding or facilitating function—in this case for the pragmatic and eventually changing interests of the party-state, which are equated with national interest. One recent attempt at defining this strategy terms it "portfolio diversification," a description borrowed from finance.[47] This captures well the apparent contradictions in China's international posture that often mystify observers. The Sino-Russian strategic partnership, resulting in mutual support in almost every UN vote,

---

[46] As discussed by Johnston, "Learning Versus Adaptation."

[47] Evan A. Feigenbaum, "China and the World: Dealing with a Reluctant Power," *Foreign Affairs*, January/February 2017, https://www.foreignaffairs.com/articles/china/2016-12-12/china-and-world.

can be described as a contribution to multilateralism: "China has been trying to combine its strategic partnerships with forms of multilateralism. So far, one of the few successful combinations of the two is Sino-Russian cooperation in the United Nations."[48]

China can be a supporter of the G-77 grouping (a loose coalition of developing and emerging nations) and philosophy, while quietly reaching compromises with the other four permanent members of the UN Security Council. It can claim developing economy status and at the same time reach for all the financial and legal leverage of a highly developed economy. China's attitude toward international institutions is highly variable. It claims one interpretation of maritime law while practicing another in different areas. If Japan created a full-set industry during its rise, China increasingly practices a full-set diplomacy with no holds barred. This explains why it borrows and reuses so much language from global values and rules. China has no more qualms about the reinterpretation of these values and rules than about its refusal to follow them in other circumstances.

But as much as this description fits China's current international behavior, it does not answer a fundamental question: how much will China's status as the second global power reshape the international system? Beyond portfolio diversification as a description of the country's pragmatic or contradictory international positioning, are we witnessing a return by China to a Darwinian vision of the world, where a valueless foreign policy fits its interests and serves its growing strength? Much of China's official history, including Xi Jinping's veiled admonition to "remember where we came from," emphasizes the past era of national humiliation.

Yet China's integration into many normative aspects of the international system remains. Its very insistence on gaining international legitimacy, its prickliness toward international criticism, its growing international networking in education, health, agricultural, and social projects show a mixed picture. China needs a benevolent or neutral international system, and its leaders understand that wealth and power must be supplemented by a usefulness to others, if only in the developing world.

This is a minimal understanding of China's insertion into the international order. The project involved appears far more pragmatic and opportunist than grand and strategic. There is no world revolution for China, no promotion of a detailed or even spelled out global agenda beyond the repetition of operative keywords that are often borrowed from the West's past repertoire. These mottos are abstract enough to be understood only in informal, but not legal, ways. China has no claim on what foreign governments and societies

---

[48] Feng and Huang, "China's Strategic Partnership Diplomacy," 17.

should do for themselves. In many areas, it is still following the old practice of borrowing models from outside—and that is also the ultimate cultural heritage that explains its prevalent theft of technology and business models. Filtering foreign influence and indigenization of the economy are also traditions. What is new is that China has acquired a capacity to influence from the inside international institutions and the interpretation of global values that were thought to be intangible. If China exhibits revisionism, it is in the reinterpretation—often with limitations that amount to hollowing out—of global institutions and values. This it does with one key objective: maintaining the state as the unquestionable agent of international relations. This strategy coincides with the interests of a party-state whose own legitimacy is in doubt, but it also attracts many coalition partners and even happens to coincide with the retreat from internationalism in some democracies. In fact, the chief argument of Chinese soft or sharp power is that it has no requirements for its partners, no goals beyond interdicting judgments and behavior directly detrimental to Chinese interests: China first.

It is in such abstention that one can perceive a valueless foreign policy at work. The lack of values becomes a value in itself. Aid, for example, is presented as nondiscriminatory, unconditional, and therefore much less demanding than Western and more recently Japanese foreign assistance, which hovers between conditionality, sanctions, and forgiveness over time.

Of course, as befits the cardinal principle of pragmatism, the regime's neutrality also varies according to circumstances. It does not apply equally to China's neighborhood, where some Chinese voices have begun to claim that the country is pursuing its own Monroe Doctrine (clearly not a new value either). Such neutrality also implies that China is not keen on making long-term bets that involve significant risks. Its equidistant positions in relation to many partners inside a Middle East and Near East on fire are revealing of a preference to avoid difficult choices. China will not move in the decisive fashion that Putin's Russia has adopted in Syria, with a forward diplomacy followed by military intervention. The contrast here between China's absolute geoeconomic superiority and Russia's remaining geopolitical edge is striking, and this alone casts a doubt on China's status as a truly revisionist power.

Instead, China's preference is for a low-cost international order. It prioritizes economic growth (described as development) and stability (hailed as peace) and downplays the political rights of the individual (a UN covenant that China has never ratified). China is also reluctant to agree to any extension of international legal constraints, adverse to or at least reluctant toward the forced implementation of international resolutions by a sanctions process, and almost entirely absent from humanitarian involvement through international institutions. Above all, it approaches the international order as a trading system where rules and norms apply, and where the goal of free trade remains accepted by others, while China can still claim its highly formal status as a developing economy to make exceptions. It is not very concerned by the lack of positive intervention or even implementation by the UN system in the area of peace and security. But China remains highly interested in the legal constraints on the use of force that this system carries. Even in its engagement with ASEAN, China has not appeared to be a risk taker and has remarkably calibrated its testing of red lines and controlled its occasional use of force.

Adapting and Competing with China's International Drive

China's global influence plays on partners' self-interest and acceptance of compliance rather than on ideology or faith. One need only recall the selfless dedication of former Soviet agents and fellow travelers, the contemporary will to manipulate democratic processes, or the will to sacrifice of many contemporary jihadists to understand that China plays on a limited keyboard and on non-messianic appeal. Patriotism applies to Chinese citizens and in a growing but limited extent to overseas Chinese. Economic outmigrants are more often ignored. Students and scientists are courted and influenced whenever possible, if only because reversing the country's brain drain is an essential goal of Chinese policy. Troublesome minorities—specifically Tibetans and Uighurs—are increasingly threatened and coerced wherever they may reside. Overall, this is still an inward-looking policy.

China of course still keeps an eye open for opportunities. Fractures are growing inside and among democratic societies, while authoritarian systems either reduce or repress them. But unlike with Russia or Turkey, where leaders are elected, however imperfectly, Chinese leaders do not feel the urge to influence democratic choices elsewhere. They are content with wavering or embattled democracies, which they believe are too preoccupied with themselves to intervene seriously in other regimes, after many failed cases. Frequent change through elections helps persuade Chinese leaders that chaos could be looming in the ballot box. The Chinese leadership can therefore afford to play a long game, that of a timeless self-reinforcement bequeathed from the late imperial era, while exploiting the risk-free openings that are available.

Responding to this strategy will require changes, large and small, in democracies, including some seeming trivial, yet difficult. Given its economic and financial means, China plays its game of influence by exploiting myriad cracks in Western legislative systems that allow for lobbying at various levels. Lobbyists for China do not act differently from others, but they do act on a wider front, reflecting the country's multiple interests, and answer to a better-coordinated authority than any previous case in history.

First, to check this development, democracies must check lobbyism itself in many forms. The obvious case to move forward is that China itself acts more and more strongly against all forms of foreign influence. The counterargument is that democracy itself rests on persuasion, political and interest-based coalitions, and advocacy. Liberal democracy with its corollary—the globalizing economy—has to contain adverse influences while preserving freedom of opinion. Although China has not become "more like us," we should not become "more like China." A particularly thorny case in point is that of communities of Chinese origin. They are being reclaimed today by the PRC's United Front organizations and methods, and there is a danger that they are also viewed as a "fifth column," as was the case in Southeast Asia during the 1950s and 1960s. Another area is the imbalance in news operations between what is permissible to foreign media in China and the free hand given to Chinese state media abroad.

A second larger issue is with the state economy in China that allows for its international mode of operation. The very foreign companies that operate there are prime targets for propagating influence, and they also become hostages at times of difficult relations, showing that interest, not proximity, is the primary issue. China's asymmetric economy has long generated surpluses that almost no Western economy can afford. This in fact has been the source of BRI projects, of outward investment, and of the increasing range of China's official and social media abroad. Changing this situation will not be easy: just defining which companies are really state enterprises, when there are many hybrid cases where ownership is doubtful and state subsidies or pricing policies in China address whole sectors, makes this an impossible task. Furthermore, those Chinese partners that are market economies and democracies remain wedded to the notion that China's private sector is the future agent of change, perhaps even at the political level. A blanket break of free trade and value chains with China would involve, for example, massive anti-dumping and custom penalties, justified by the existence of Chinese government subsidies. This can hardly be achieved within existing WTO rules. Reforming those rules requires consensus among trading nations. Breaking with the WTO may alienate many other trading partners. Similarly, placing strong obstacles against sensitive Chinese investment abroad and even more controls and limits on technology transfers to China also require full coordination with China's main trading partners. Consensus and coordination with allies and partners require dialogue and compromise. Should they be successful, this would surely precipitate a crisis in China. It is a gamble, as we do not know what the outcome might be from that crisis, which may well bring to the fore an even more nationalist hard line.

Third, China's stability and the acquiescence of its society to outward expansion rests on a precarious balance. A very individualistic society lives in a compromise with the state that is ensured by a growing economy and an increasing freedom to travel. At the expense of political freedom and the right to choose forms of government, this has been a win-win compromise for both sides: the CCP and the beneficiaries of China's unequal growth. A key component of this compromise is the ability to move money offshore, which requires at least tacit acceptance by the Chinese state and access to offshore financial centers. Paradoxically, it is under Xi Jinping's watch that some of this license is being taken away, as the regime fights domestic corruption. The regime is not well placed to turn down international requirements for transparency, whether for companies moving abroad or for individuals. In the case of BRI projects, both the EU and Japan are conditioning offers to cooperate with China in third countries with the acceptance of international standards (in the case of Japan) or through joint decisions on rules and norms (in the case of Europe). Parallel efforts are being made in the United States, Japan, and the EU to screen incoming investment, an effort that largely applies to China. Although most of the legislation in place or contemplated concerns the issues of high technology, emerging sectors, and critical infrastructures, a broader approach to the origins of funding, accounting, and ownership of the companies involved would be useful. Nobody can change China from the outside, but inasmuch as the Chinese economy expands broadly, the leverage on its norms and practices increases. This is the reverse of sanctions—a grading of possibilities open to Chinese actors according to their observance of international rules. The key to China's international posture has moved from the sheer defense of sovereignty to its interlocking economic interests with the global economy. Of course, one should recognize that any requirement related to financial transparency and norms applies equally to all: what Chinese actors have often done is exploit existing international loopholes.

Fourth, China's status as a developing economy is an important factor, if not the only one, in its phenomenal growth. Average income—not even adjusted by purchasing power parity—now surpasses that of the lowest income country inside the EU.[49] The Chinese government is right to argue from the remaining pockets of poverty and the need to protect socially exposed sectors to retain some exceptionality. Other developed economies have long retained subsidies that are in fact allowed by the WTO, as well as

---

[49] Figures for China and Bulgaria, as shown by International Monetary Fund (IMF), "GDP Per Capita, Current Prices," IMF DataMapper, October 2018, https://www.imf.org/external/datamapper/ NGDPDPC@WEO/OEMDC/ADVEC/WEOWORLD?year=2018.

special rules that are the subjects of negotiation or quarrels. But the overall asymmetry must end. China's advantageous run of four decades must now be checked, lest we see the disadvantaged inside democracies blame globalization for their ills. Reciprocity—admittedly a difficult goal to implement—must be recognized in principle by China. This in itself will make changes necessary that are bound to limit China's temptations to claim a uniquely successful model and rules.

Fifth, the world's democracies are undermining their future when they disregard existing international institutions and rules. Coordination and cohesion are the essential resources that give bargaining strength to the EU. The attractiveness of the United States is tied to its support for a rules-based environment and to its own acceptance of arbitration and treaties. Preserving the international system requires making more room for rising participants, not debasing rules and goals. This applies to the leaders of international organizations themselves. In their drive to gain China's active participation and offset diminishing support from the United States, the six international institutions involved in "6 + 1" roundtables with China go very far in the direction of a blanket approval of China's policies.[50]

Sixth, a key issue for future global values remains the fate of the UN system. China's participation in the United Nations has become the anchor of its international pronouncements, both for purposes of international legitimacy and as a channel of global influence. China is both supporting and undermining the system: it is becoming an indispensable funder and beginning to use voluntary contributions to shape UN actions, including by hollowing out the terms of action in key areas such as human rights, peacekeeping, and humanitarian intervention. On a case-by-case basis, China finds many willing coalition partners for these measures, and sometimes acquiescence by default from one of the other four permanent members of the Security Council, which have shown a reluctance for international engagement or action through international institutions. This is a defeat in practice for global values, and from there it is only a short step to treating the international system as another League of Nations. Realism is not about ignoring the constraining value of global rules and institutions. Active investment and diplomatic involvement with other participants in the UN system are the only answer to the intractable problem of both recognizing a larger role for a rising China and checking its attempts to erode the system from within.

---

[50] "Joint Press Release of the Third '6 + 1' Roundtable," World Bank, November 8, 2018, https://www.worldbank.org/en/news/press-release/2018/11/08/joint-press-release-of-the-third-16-roundtable. The six institutions involved are the Word Bank, International Monetary Fund, WTO, Organisation for Economic Co-operation and Development, Financial Stability Board, and International Labour Organization.

About the Contributors

David Brewster is a Senior Research Fellow with the National Security College at Australian National University, where he specializes in maritime security in the Indian Ocean and the Indo-Pacific. Dr. Brewster's books include *India's Ocean: The Story of India's Bid for Regional Leadership* (2014), which examines India's strategic ambitions in the Indian Ocean. His latest edited volume is *India and China at Sea: Competition for Naval Dominance in the Indian Ocean*, which addresses Indian and Chinese perspectives about their roles in the Indian Ocean and their evolving naval strategies toward each other. Dr. Brewster is also the author of a forthcoming report, "Australia's Second Sea: Facing Our Multipolar Future in the Indian Ocean," which proposes a new roadmap for Australia's strategic engagement in the Indian Ocean.

Michael S. Chase is a Senior Political Scientist at the RAND Corporation and an Adjunct Professor in the China Studies and Strategic Studies Departments at the Johns Hopkins University's Paul H. Nitze School of Advanced International Studies (SAIS) in Washington, D.C. A specialist in China and Asia-Pacific security issues, he was previously an associate professor at the U.S. Naval War College, where he served as director of the strategic deterrence group in the Warfare Analysis and Research Department and taught in the Strategy and Policy Department. Prior to joining the faculty at the Naval War College, he was a research analyst at Defense Group Inc. and an associate international policy analyst at RAND. Dr. Chase is the author of the book *Taiwan's Security Policy* and numerous chapters and articles on China and Asia-Pacific security issues. His work has appeared in journals such as *Asia Policy, Asian Security, China Brief, Survival*, and the *Journal of Strategic Studies*. His current research focuses on Chinese military modernization, China's nuclear policy and strategy, and Taiwan's defense policy. Dr. Chase holds a PhD in international affairs and an MA in China studies from SAIS. In addition, he studied Chinese at the Hopkins-Nanjing Center in China.

Ja Ian Chong is Associate Professor of Political Science at the National University of Singapore. He previously worked at the Center for Strategic and International Studies in Washington, D.C., and the Institute of Defence and Strategic Studies in Singapore, and was a Princeton-Harvard China and the World Program Fellow. Dr. Chong's work crosses the fields of international relations, comparative politics, and political sociology, with a focus on security issues relating to Asia, China, and the United States. He has particular interest in security cooperation and major-power rivalry. Additionally, Dr. Chong follows the interplay of social movements, politics, and foreign policy in Asia closely. His research has received support from the East-West Center, Hong Kong Research Grants Council, Sasakawa Peace Foundation, Singapore Ministry of Education, Social Science Research Council, and Woodrow Wilson Circle of Fellows. His work has appeared in a number of journals, edited volumes, and newspapers, including *Asian Security*, *China Quarterly*, *European Journal of International Relations*, *International Security*, and *Security Studies*. Dr. Chong is the author of *External Intervention and the Politics of State Formation: China, Thailand, Indonesia, 1893–1952* (2012), which received the 2013–14 Best Book Award from the International Security Studies Section of the International Studies Association.

Samantha Custer is Director of Policy Analysis at AidData, a research lab at the College of William & Mary. She leads a multidisciplinary group of researchers who produce data, tools, and analysis that governments and organizations use to increase the effectiveness of their development cooperation efforts. Ms. Custer leads AidData's efforts to track China's official financing worldwide and co-authored "Ties That Bind," a research report funded by the U.S. Department of State to quantify the scope, distribution, and effectiveness of Beijing's public diplomacy in the East Asia and Pacific region. She directs AidData's efforts to analyze how China is perceived by leaders in 126 low- and middle-income countries. Ms. Custer has previously published research studies in partnership with the Asia Society Policy Institute, the Brookings Institution, the Center for Strategic and International Studies, the World Bank, and the governments of Denmark, Germany, and the United States, among others.

Rush Doshi is the Brookings-Yale Postdoctoral Research Fellow at the Brookings Institution. He is also Special Advisor to the CEO of the Asia Group, Research Director for the McCain Institute's Kissinger Fellowship Series on U.S.-China Relations, and an Adjunct Fellow at the Center for a New American Security. Previously, Dr. Doshi was a member of the Asia Policy Working Group for Hillary Clinton's 2016 presidential campaign, an analyst at the Long Term Strategy Group and Rock Creek Global Advisors, an Arthur Liman Fellow at the Department of State, and a Fulbright Fellow in China. His research has appeared in the *Wall Street Journal, Foreign Affairs*, the *Washington Post*, and the *Washington Quarterly*, among other publications. Dr. Doshi received his PhD from Harvard University, where he wrote his dissertation on Chinese grand strategy, and his BA from Princeton's Woodrow Wilson School with a minor in East Asian studies. He is proficient in Mandarin and Hindi.

Richard J. Ellings is President and Co-founder of the National Bureau of Asian Research (NBR). He is also Affiliate Professor of International Studies in the Henry M. Jackson School of International Studies at the University of Washington. Dr. Ellings is the author of *Embargoes and World Power: Lessons from American Foreign Policy* (1985); co-editor of and contributing author to *Axis of Authoritarians: Implications of China-Russia Cooperation* (2018); co-author of *Private Property and National Security* (1991); co-editor (with Aaron Friedberg) of *Strategic Asia 2003–04: Fragility and Crisis* (2003), *Strategic Asia 2002–03: Asian Aftershocks* (2002), and *Strategic Asia 2001–02: Power and Purpose* (2001); co-editor of *Korea's Future and the Great Powers* (with Nicholas Eberstadt, 2001) and *Southeast Asian Security in the New Millennium* (with Sheldon Simon, 1996); founding editor of the *NBR Analysis* publication series; and co-chairman of the *Asia Policy* editorial board. Previously, Dr. Ellings served as legislative assistant in the U.S. Senate, office of Senator Slade Gorton. He earned his BA in political science from the University of California–Berkley and his MA and PhD in political science from the University of Washington.

Andrew S. Erickson is Professor of Strategy in, and a core founding member of, the China Maritime Studies Institute at the U.S. Naval War College. He also serves on the editorial board of the *Naval War College Review*. Since 2008, Dr. Erickson has been an Associate in Research at Harvard University's John King Fairbank Center for Chinese Studies. In 2012, he was awarded the inaugural Ellis Joffe Prize for PLA Studies. Dr. Erickson is the author of the book *Chinese Anti-Ship Ballistic Missile (ASBM) Development* (2013) and the co-author of *Six Years at Sea...and Counting: Gulf of Aden Anti-Piracy and China's Maritime Commons Presence* (2015) and *A Low-Visibility Force Multiplier: Assessing China's Cruise Missile Ambitions* (2014). He has co-authored three additional volumes—*Charting China's International Security Activism* (2015), *Chinese Antipiracy Operations in the Gulf of Aden* (2013), and *Chinese Mine Warfare* (2009)—and co-edited numerous others. Dr. Erickson has published extensively in peer-reviewed journals such as *International Security, China Quarterly,* and *Journal of Contemporary China.* He received his PhD and MA from Princeton University and studied Mandarin at Beijing Normal University's College of Chinese Language and Culture. His research website can be found at https://www.andrewerickson.com.

François Godement is Senior Adviser, Asia, at Institut Montaigne in Paris. He has been a Professor at SciencesPo and Inalco (Paris) and a Senior Policy Fellow and Director of the Asia Program at the European Council on Foreign Relations (ECFR). Dr. Godement is also a Nonresident Senior Fellow at the Carnegie Endowment for International Peace and an external consultant at Policy Planning at the Ministry of Europe and External Affairs in Paris. His recent books include *Contemporary China: Between Mao to Market* (2015). At ECFR, he authored or edited "Xi Jinping's China" (2013), "France's Pivot to Asia" (2014), "China's Economic Downturn: The Facts Behind the Myth" (2015), "What Does India Think?" (2015), "China's Market Economy Status and the European Interest" (2016), "Expanding Ambitions, Shrinking Achievements: How China Sees the Global Order" (2017), "Preempting Defeat: In Search of North Korea's Nuclear Doctrine" (with Léonie Allard and Mathieu Duchâtel, 2017), and "China at the Gates: A New Power Audit of EU-China Relations" (with Abigaël Vasselier, 2017).

Patricia M. Kim is a Senior Policy Analyst at the United States Institute of Peace. She specializes in Chinese foreign policy, U.S.-China relations, and East Asian security issues. Previously, Dr. Kim was the Stanton Nuclear Security Fellow at the Council on Foreign Relations, a postdoctoral fellow at the Princeton-Harvard China and the World Program at Princeton University, and an International Security Program research fellow at the Belfer Center for Science and International Affairs at the Harvard Kennedy School of Government. Dr. Kim has testified before the House Permanent Select Committee on Intelligence and the House Foreign Affairs Subcommittee on Terrorism, Nonproliferation, and Trade, and her writing has been featured in *Foreign Affairs, Foreign Policy, International Security,* the *South China Morning Post,* and the *Washington Post,* among other publications. Dr. Kim received her PhD from the Department of Politics at Princeton University and her BA with highest distinction in political science and Asian studies from the University of California, Berkeley.

Alison Szalwinski is Senior Director for Political and Security Affairs at the National Bureau of Asian Research (NBR), where she manages and contributes to the Strategic Asia Program, the Pacific Trilateralism project, and the Space, Cyberspace, and Strategic Stability project. Prior to joining NBR, Ms. Szalwinski worked at the U.S. Department of State and the Center for Strategic and International Studies (CSIS). Her research interests include regional security dynamics in Northeast Asia and U.S.-China strategic relations. She is co-editor with Ashley J. Tellis and Michael Wills of *Strategic Asia 2015–16: Foundations of National Power, Strategic Asia 2016–17: Understanding Strategic Cultures in the Asia-Pacific, and Strategic Asia 2017–18: Power, Ideas, and Military Strategy in the Asia-Pacific.* Ms. Szalwinski has lived and worked as an English teacher in Shenzhen, China, where she also continued her language studies in Mandarin Chinese. She holds a BA in foreign affairs and history from the University of Virginia and an MA in Asian studies from Georgetown University's Edmund A. Walsh School of Foreign Service.

Ashley J. Tellis holds the Tata Chair for Strategic Affairs and is a Senior Fellow at the Carnegie Endowment for International Peace, specializing in international security, defense, and Asian strategic issues. He has also served as Research Director of the Strategic Asia Program at the National Bureau of Asian Research (NBR) and co-editor of the program's annual volume since 2004. While on assignment to the U.S. Department of State as Senior Adviser to the Undersecretary of State for Political Affairs, he was intimately involved in negotiating the civil nuclear agreement with India. Previously, he was commissioned into the Foreign Service and served as Senior Adviser to the Ambassador at the U.S. embassy in New Delhi. He also served on the National Security Council staff as Special Assistant to the President and Senior Director for Strategic Planning and Southwest Asia. Prior to his government service, Dr. Tellis was a Senior Policy Analyst at the RAND Corporation and Professor of Policy Analysis at the RAND Graduate School. He is the author of *India's Emerging Nuclear Posture* (2001) and co-author of *Interpreting China's Grand Strategy: Past, Present, and Future* (2000). He holds a PhD in political science from the University of Chicago.

Michael J. Tierney is the George and Mary Hylton Professor of Government and International Relations at the College of William & Mary. He directs the Global Research Institute and works with students, faculty, and staff at AidData on a variety of projects. Dr. Tierney's core research focuses on international organizations and international political economy. He has published dozens of journal articles and two books: *Greening*

Aid? Understanding the Environmental Impact of Development Assistance (2008) and *Delegation and Agency in International Organizations* (2006). Dr. Tierney is currently writing a book on Chinese development finance and editing a book that explores the relationship between international relations as a scholarly discipline and as lived by practitioners.

Michael Wills is Executive Vice President at the National Bureau of Asian Research (NBR). He coordinates all aspects of NBR's financial, business, and programmatic operations and serves as secretary to the Board of Directors. Mr. Wills also manages NBR's publications program, including the *Strategic Asia* series and the *Asia Policy* journal. His research interests include international security and the international relations of Asia, particularly China's relations with Southeast Asia. He is co-editor with Robert M. Hathaway of *New Security Challenges in Asia* (2013) and has co-edited seven previous Strategic Asia volumes with Ashley J. Tellis—including *Power, Ideas, and Military Strategy in the Asia Pacific* (2017), *Understanding Strategic Cultures in the Asia-Pacific* (2016), *Foundations of National Power in the Asia-Pacific* (2015), *Domestic Political Change and Grand Strategy* (2007), *Trade, Interdependence, and Security* (2006), *Military Modernization in an Era of Uncertainty* (2005), and *Confronting Terrorism in the Pursuit of Power* (2004). He is a contributing editor to three other *Strategic Asia* books and several other edited volumes. Before joining NBR, Mr. Wills worked at the Cambodia Development Resource Institute in Phnom Penh and with Control Risks Group, an international political and security risk management firm, in London. He holds a BA (Honors) in Chinese studies from the University of Oxford.

Elizabeth Wishnick is Professor of Political Science at Montclair State University and Senior Research Scholar in the Weatherhead East Asian Institute at Columbia University. In 2018 she received a Global Fulbright award to complete the research for her latest book project, *China's Risk: Oil, Water, Food and Regional Security* (forthcoming), which examines the security dilemmas that arise for neighboring states in China's management of transboundary resources. Professor Wishnick is the author of several articles on contemporary Sino-Russian relations and recently completed a policy study on China's interests and goals in the Arctic for the Strategic Studies Institute of the U.S. Army War College. She is the author of *Mending Fences: The Evolution of Moscow's China Policy from Brezhnev to Yeltsin* (2001 and 2015). Professor Wishnick was a public policy scholar at the Woodrow Wilson International Center for Scholars in Spring 2012 and a fellow at Columbia's Center for International Conflict Resolution from 2011 to 2013.

She was previously a Fulbright scholar in Hong Kong (2002–3) and a visiting scholar at the Academia Sinica in Taiwan, the Hoover Institution, and the Davis Center at Harvard University. She received a PhD in political science from Columbia University, an MA in Russian and East European studies from Yale University, and a BA from Barnard College. She speaks Mandarin Chinese, Russian, and French.

Joel Wuthnow is a Research Fellow in the Center for the Study of Chinese Military Affairs in the Institute for National Strategic Studies at the National Defense University (NDU). His research areas include Chinese foreign and security policy, Chinese military affairs, U.S.-China relations, and strategic developments in East Asia. He also serves as an Adjunct Professor in both the Eisenhower School at NDU and the Edmund A. Walsh School of Foreign Service at Georgetown University. Prior to joining NDU, Dr. Wuthnow was a China analyst at CNA, a postdoctoral fellow in the China and the World Program at Princeton University, and a predoctoral fellow at the Brookings Institution. His research has appeared in journals such as the *China Quarterly, Journal of Contemporary China, Asian Security, Asia Policy, Journal of Strategic Studies*, and *Joint Force Quarterly*, as well as in NDU's *China Strategic Perspectives* monograph series. He is also the author of the book *Chinese Diplomacy and the UN Security Council* (2013). Dr. Wuthnow holds an AB in public and international affairs from Princeton University, an MPhil in modern Chinese studies from Oxford University, and a PhD in political science from Columbia University. He is proficient in Mandarin.

About Strategic Asia

The **Strategic Asia Program** at the National Bureau of Asian Research (NBR) is a major ongoing research initiative that draws together top Asia studies specialists and international relations experts to assess the changing strategic environment in the Asia-Pacific. The program combines the rigor of academic analysis with the practicality of contemporary policy analyses by incorporating economic, military, political, and demographic data and by focusing on the trends, strategies, and perceptions that drive geopolitical dynamics in the region. The program's integrated set of products and activities includes:

- an annual edited volume written by leading specialists
- an executive brief tailored for public- and private-sector decision-makers and strategic planners
- briefings and presentations for government, business, and academia that are designed to foster in-depth discussions revolving around major public policy issues

Special briefings are held for key committees of Congress and the executive branch, other government agencies, and the intelligence community. The principal audiences for the program's research findings are the U.S. policymaking and research communities, the media, the business community, and academia.

To order a book, please visit the Strategic Asia website at http://www.nbr.org/strategicasia.

Previous Strategic Asia Volumes

Now in its eighteenth year, the *Strategic Asia* series has addressed how Asia functions as a zone of strategic interaction and contends with an uncertain balance of power.

Strategic Asia 2017–18: Power, Ideas, and Military Strategy in the Asia-Pacific identified how Asia's major powers have developed military strategies to address their most significant challenges.

Strategic Asia 2016–17: Understanding Strategic Cultures in the Asia-Pacific explored the strategic cultures of the region's major powers and explained how they inform decision-making about the pursuit of strategic objectives and national power.

Strategic Asia 2015–16: Foundations of National Power in the Asia-Pacific examined how the region's major powers are building their national power as geopolitical competition intensifies.

Strategic Asia 2014–15: U.S. Alliances and Partnerships at the Center of Global Power analyzed the trajectories of U.S. alliance and partner relationships in the Asia-Pacific in light of the region's shifting strategic landscape.

Strategic Asia 2013–14: Asia in the Second Nuclear Age examined the role of nuclear weapons in the grand strategies of key Asian states and assessed the impact of these capabilities—both established and latent—on regional and international stability.

Strategic Asia 2012–13: China's Military Challenge assessed China's growing military capabilities and explored their impact on the Asia-Pacific region.

Strategic Asia 2011–12: Asia Responds to Its Rising Powers—China and India explored how key Asian states have responded to the rise of China and India, drawing implications for U.S. interests and leadership in the Asia-Pacific.

Strategic Asia 2010–11: Asia's Rising Power and America's Continued Purpose provided a continent-wide net assessment of the core trends and issues affecting the region by examining Asia's performance in nine key functional areas.

Strategic Asia 2009–10: Economic Meltdown and Geopolitical Stability analyzed the impact of the global economic crisis on key Asian states and explored the strategic implications for the United States.

Strategic Asia 2008–09: Challenges and Choices examined the impact of geopolitical developments on Asia's transformation over the previous eight years and assessed the major strategic choices on Asia facing the incoming U.S. administration.

Strategic Asia 2007–08: Domestic Political Change and Grand Strategy examined internal and external drivers of grand strategy on Asian foreign policymaking.

Strategic Asia 2006–07: Trade, Interdependence, and Security addressed how changing trade relationships affect the balance of power and security in the region.

Strategic Asia 2005–06: Military Modernization in an Era of Uncertainty appraised the progress of Asian military modernization programs.

Strategic Asia 2004–05: Confronting Terrorism in the Pursuit of Power explored the effect of the U.S.-led war on terrorism on the strategic transformations underway in Asia.

Strategic Asia 2003–04: Fragility and Crisis examined the fragile balance of power in Asia, drawing out the key domestic political and economic trends in Asian states supporting or undermining this tenuous equilibrium.

Strategic Asia 2002–03: Asian Aftershocks drew on the baseline established in the 2001–02 volume to analyze changes in Asian states' grand strategies and relationships in the aftermath of the September 11 terrorist attacks.

Strategic Asia 2001–02: Power and Purpose established a baseline assessment for understanding the strategies and interactions of the major states within the region.

Research and Management Team

The Strategic Asia research team consists of leading international relations and security specialists from universities and research institutions across the United States and around the world. A new research team is selected each year. To date, more than 150 scholars have written for the program. The research team for 2018 is led by Ashley J. Tellis (Carnegie Endowment for International Peace). Aaron Friedberg (Princeton University, and Strategic Asia's founding research director) and Richard Ellings (The National Bureau of Asian Research, and Strategic Asia's founding program director) serve as senior advisers.

Attribution

Readers of *Strategic Asia* and visitors to the Strategic Asia website may use data, charts, graphs, and quotes from these sources without requesting permission from NBR on the condition that they cite NBR and the appropriate primary source in any published work. No report, chapter, separate study, extensive text, or any other substantial part of the Strategic Asia Program's products may be reproduced without the written permission of NBR. To request permission, please write to publications@nbr.org.

Index